THE BAHÁ'Í REVELATION

THE BAHÁ'Í REVELATION

BAHÁ'U'LLÁH
'ABDU'L-BAHÁ

including
Selections from the Bahá'í Holy Writings
and
Talks by 'Abdu'l–Bahá

BAHÁ'Í PUBLISHING TRUST

National Spiritual Assembly of the Bahá'ís of
the British Isles
27 Rutland Gate, London, S.W.7

First published in 1955
Revised edition 1970

Library Reference 299.15 Bahá'í

B9

Printed in Great Britain by
Fletcher & Son Ltd, Norwich, Norfolk

CONTENTS

v

Part II: 'ABDU'L-BAHÁ

Contents vii

Contents

PREFACE

PROBABLY no one will find in this compilation every piece of Bahá'í Scripture he seeks. Even the Writings of Bahá'u'lláh and 'Abdu'l-Bahá available in English are too numerous for any single volume to contain everybody's particular choice. That most people will find in this book most of the passages they value most is the apex of the compiler's aspiration.

Although intended primarily as a handy comprehensive volume for Bahá'ís, it should serve inquirers well who know something of the history and teaching of the Bahá'í Faith and wish to deepen their knowledge. For many purposes, serious students of religion will also find it adequate.

Bahá'í Scripture in a broad sense consists of the Words of all the Sacred Figures Who founded the great religions or promulgated their teachings, for Bahá'ís revere all as holy; but usually the phrase denotes the Writings of Bahá'u'lláh, the Báb and 'Abdu'l-Bahá, the Sacred Figures of this age. More strictly, the Writings of the Báb belong to the Bábí Dispensation which preceded the Dispensation of Bahá'u'lláh and they have for Bahá'ís something of the significance of an Old Testament. In this book, Works of Bahá'u'lláh and 'Abdu'l-Bahá only are included.

Bahá'u'lláh revealed His Message between 1853 and 1892. His earliest Writings, revealed in Baghdád between 1853 and 1863, include the Kitáb-i-Íqán, the Hidden Words and the Seven Valleys. In Adrianople between 1863 and 1868 most of His Tablets to kings and leaders of religion were revealed. After 1868 in 'Akká came the remainder of these and the Tablets expounding His laws. Here also was revealed the Most Holy Book of the Bahá'í Revelation, the Kitáb-i-Aqdas, of which much is included in "Gleanings from the Writings of Bahá'u'lláh", a selection of His Writings made and translated by Shoghi Effendi, the Guardian of the Bahá'í Faith. Throughout the period, Bahá'u'lláh revealed prayers and meditations, and wrote Tablets of varying weight and importance both to His followers and to others. Many of these Tablets are not yet collected and others not yet translated into English, but most of His foremost Writings have been collected and translated.

Since Bahá'ís do not recognize as scripture unauthenticated reports of the sayings of the Founders of their Faith, the authenticity of Scripture is more easily established in the Bahá'í Dispensation than formerly. Only documents in the handwriting of the Central Figures, or signed by Them, or authenticated by Them in some other way, are acceptable. The validity of translations is more difficult to determine. None except those which were made by or in consultation with the Guardian of the Bahá'í Faith, until his passing in 1957, or by the Universal House of Justice since its election in 1963, are of unexceptionable validity.

Bahá'u'lláh and 'Abdu'l-Bahá wrote in Persian and Arabic. In the early days of the Bahá'í Faith in the West, translating was done by Eastern Bahá'ís whose English was defective so that many translations of the period are faulty and few have the advantage of good literary English. Fortunately the Guardian of the Bahá'í Faith, Shoghi Effendi, has rendered into beautiful English most of the important Writings of Bahá'u'lláh and several of 'Abdu'l-Bahá's Tablets. His translation has been used wherever one exists.

'Abdu'l-Bahá's Writings are mostly Tablets to individuals and Bahá'í Assemblies, of which many are still uncollected. Until His passing in 1921, He wrote Tablets in Persian to correspondents all over the world. These Tablets were translated into English with varying competence by Eastern Bahá'ís whose native language was not English. He gave many talks, but few records have been authenticated and even those with an authentic Persian record are available in English only as unauthenticated notes of the imperfect translation accompanying the talk. Extensive compilations of 'Abdu'l-Bahá's Works have, therefore, to include either translations of authentic Works into a strange idiom, or more easily read, but unauthenticated, records of talks. Thus the quotations in this compilation from "Paris Talks", "The Promulgation of Universal Peace" and "Bahá'u'lláh and the New Era" are not authentic scripture although consistent with known teaching of Bahá'u'lláh and 'Abdu'l-Bahá.

All translations which deviate excessively from ordinary English usage, whether of the Writings of Bahá'u'lláh or 'Abdu'l-Bahá, have been excluded from the compilation. Such translations are difficult to read with true understanding and probably distort the meaning of the original.

The book comprises for the most part complete Tablets and excerpts picked out by the Guardian himself. The Tablets represent groups of teachings brought together for some reason by the One Who gave them and these have been separated only when the Guardian's authority or the context gave clear reason for doing so.

No prayers will be found here, as selections of Bahá'í Prayers are easily available, but meditations which most prayer books omit have been included.

The classification of items is the compiler's own, and no attempt will be made either to describe or to justify it. If it helps the reader to locate passages, it will have served its purpose.

FOREWORD

AN INTRODUCTION TO THE BAHÁ'Í FAITH
Extracts from the Writings of Shoghi Effendi

THE Revelation proclaimed by Bahá'u'lláh, His followers believe, is divine in origin, all-embracing in scope, broad in its outlook, scientific in its method, humanitarian in its principles and dynamic in the influence it exerts on the hearts and minds of men. The mission of the Founder of their Faith, they conceive it to be to proclaim that religious truth is not absolute but relative, that Divine Revelation is continuous and progressive, that the Founders of all past religions, though different in the non-essential aspects of their teachings, "abide in the same Tabernacle, soar in the same heaven, are seated upon the same throne, utter the same speech and proclaim the same Faith". His Cause, they have already demonstrated, stands identified with, and revolves around, the principle of the organic unity of mankind as representing the consummation of the whole process of human evolution. This final stage in this stupendous evolution, they assert, is not only necessary but inevitable, that it is gradually approaching, and that nothing short of the celestial potency with which a divinely ordained Message can claim to be endowed can succeed in establishing it.

The Bahá'í Faith recognizes the unity of God and of His Prophets, upholds the principle of an unfettered search after truth, condemns all forms of superstition and prejudice, teaches that the fundamental purpose of religion is to promote concord and harmony, that it must go hand-in-hand with science, and that it constitutes the sole and ultimate basis of a peaceful, an ordered and progressive society. It inculcates the principle of equal opportunity, rights and privileges for both sexes, advocates compulsory education, abolishes extremes of poverty and wealth, exalts work performed in the spirit of service to the rank of worship, recommends the adoption of an auxiliary international language, and provides the necessary agencies for the establishment and safe-guarding of a permanent and universal peace.

Born about the middle of the nineteenth century in darkest Persia, assailed from its infancy by the forces of religious fanaticism, the Faith has, notwithstanding the martyrdom of its Forerunner, the repeated banishments of its Founder, the almost lifelong imprisonment of its chief Promoter and the cruel death of no less than twenty thousand of its devoted followers, succeeded in diffusing quietly and steadily its spirit throughout both the East and the West, has established itself in no fewer than forty countries of the world,[1] and has recently obtained from the ecclesiastical and civil authorities in various lands written affirmations that recognize its independent religious status.

The Forerunner of the Faith was Mirza 'Ali-Muhammad of Shíráz, known as the Báb (The Gate) Who proclaimed on 23 May 1844, His twofold mission as an independent Manifestation of God and Herald of One greater than Himself, Who would inaugurate a new and unprecedented era in the religious history of mankind. On His early life, His sufferings, the heroism of His disciples, and the circumstances of His tragic martyrdom I need not dwell, as the record of His saintly life is minutely set forth in "The Dawn-Breakers: Nabil's Narrative of the Early Days of the Bahá'í Faith." Suffice it to say that at the early age of thirty-one, the Báb was publicly martyred by a military firing squad at Tabríz, Persia on 9 July 1850. On the evening of that same day His mangled body was removed from the courtyard of the barracks to the edge of the moat outside the gate of the city whence it was carried by His fervent disciples to Tihrán. There it remained concealed until such time as its transfer to the Holy Land was made possible. Faced by almost insuperable difficulties and facing the gravest dangers a band of His disciples, acting under the instructions of 'Abdu'l-Bahá succeeded in transporting overland the casket containing His remains to Haifa. In 1909, 'Abdu'l-Bahá with his own hands and in the presence of the assembled representatives of various Bahá'í communities deposited those remains within the vault of the Mausoleum he himself had erected for the Báb. Ever since that time countless followers of the

---

[1] In 1968, the Bahá'í Faith was established in more than 300 countries, dependencies and islands.

Bahá'í Faith have made the pilgrimage to this sacred spot, a spot which ever since 1921 has been further sanctified by the burial of 'Abdu'l-Bahá in an adjoining vault.

The Founder of the Faith was Bahá'u'lláh (Glory of God), Whose advent the Báb had foretold. He declared His mission in 1863 while an exile in Baghdád. He subsequently formulated the principles of that new and divine civilization which by His advent He claimed to have inaugurated. He too was bitterly opposed, was stripped of His property and rights, was exiled to 'Iráq, to Constantinople and Adrianople, and was eventually incarcerated in the penal colony of 'Akká where He passed away in 1892 in His seventy-fifth year. His remains are laid to rest in the Shrine at Bahjí, north of 'Akká.

The authorized Interpreter and Exemplar of Bahá'u'lláh's teachings was His eldest son 'Abdu'l-Bahá (Servant of Bahá) who was appointed by his Father as the Centre to whom all Bahá'ís should turn for instruction and guidance. 'Abdu'l-Bahá ever since his childhood was the closest companion of his Father, and shared all His sorrows and sufferings. He remained a prisoner until 1908, when the old regime in Turkey was overthrown and all religious and political prisoners throughout the empire were liberated. After that he continued to make his home in Palestine but undertook extensive teaching tours in Egypt, Europe and America, being ceaselessly engaged in explaining and exemplifying the principles of his Father's Faith and in inspiring and directing the activities of his friends and followers throughout the world. He passed away in 1921 in Haifa, Palestine, and, as already stated, was buried in a vault contiguous to that of the Báb on Mount Carmel.

The passing of 'Abdu'l-Bahá marked the termination of the first and Heroic Age of the Bahá'í Faith and signalized the opening of the Formative Age destined to witness the gradual emergence of its Administrative Order, whose establishement had been foretold by the Báb, whose laws were revealed by Bahá'u'lláh, whose outlines were delineated by 'Abdu'l-Bahá in His Will and Testament, and whose foundations are now being laid by the national and local councils which are elected by the professed adherents of the Faith, and which are paving the way for the constitution of the World Council, to be designated as the Universal House of

Justice, which . . . must co-ordinate and direct the affairs of the Bahá'í community, and whose seat will be permanently established in the Holy Land,[1] in close proximity to its world spiritual centre, the resting-places of its Founders.

This Administrative Order, unlike the systems evolved after the death of the Founders of the various religions, is divine in origin, rests securely on the laws, the precepts, the ordinances and institutions which the Founder of the Faith has Himself specifically laid down and unequivocally established, and functions in strict accordance with the interpretations of the authorized Interpreters of its holy scriptures. Though fiercely assailed, ever since its inception, it has, by virtue of its character, unique in the annals of the world's religious history, succeeded in maintaining the unity of the diversified and far-flung body of its supporters, and enabled them to launch, unitedly and systematically, enterprises in both Hemispheres, designed to extend its limits and consolidate its administrative institutions.

(This material was compiled from two sources, *The World Order of Bahá'u'lláh* and *The Faith of Bahá'u'lláh* (a statement prepared for the United Nations Special Palestine Committee) both written by Shoghi Effendi.)

[1] In 1963, the Universal House of Justice was established in Haifa.

Part I
BAHÁ'U'LLÁH

I. PROCLAMATION TO
THE KINGS AND LEADERS OF RELIGION

1. TO KINGS COLLECTIVELY

¶ 1. O kings of the earth! He Who is the sovereign Lord of all is come. The Kingdom is God's, the omnipotent Protector, the Self-Subsisting. Worship none but God, and, with radiant hearts, lift up your faces unto your Lord, the Lord of all names. This is a Revelation to which whatever ye possess can never be compared, could ye but know it.

We see you rejoicing in that which ye have amassed for others and shutting out yourselves from the worlds which naught except My guarded Tablet can reckon. The treasures ye have laid up have drawn you far away from your ultimate objective. This ill beseemeth you, could ye but understand it. Wash your hearts from all earthly defilements, and hasten to enter the Kingdom of your Lord, the Creator of earth and heaven, Who caused the world to tremble and all its peoples to wail, except them that have renounced all things and clung to that which the Hidden Tablet hath ordained.

This is the Day in which He Who held converse with God hath attained the light of the Ancient of Days, and quaffed the pure waters of reunion from this Cup that hath caused the seas to swell. Say: By the one true God! Sinai is circling round the Day Spring of Revelation, while from the heights of the Kingdom the Voice of the Spirit of God is heard proclaiming: "Bestir yourselves, ye proud ones of the earth, and hasten ye unto Him." Carmel hath, in this Day, hastened in longing adoration to attain His court, whilst from the heart of Zion there cometh the cry: "The promise is fulfilled. That which had been announced in the holy Writ of God, the most Exalted, the Almighty, the Best-Beloved, is made manifest."

O kings of the earth! The Most Great Law hath been revealed in this Spot, this scene of transcendent splendour. Every hidden thing hath been brought to light, by virtue of the Will of the Supreme Ordainer, He who hath ushered in the Last Hour, through Whom

3

the Moon hath been cleft, and every irrevocable decree expounded.

Ye are but vassals, O kings of the earth! He Who is the King of Kings hath appeared, arrayed in His most wondrous glory, and is summoning you unto Himself, the Help in Peril, the Self-Subsisting. Take heed lest pride deter you from recognizing the Source of Revelation, lest the things of this world shut you out as by a veil from Him Who is the Creator of heaven. Arise, and serve Him Who is the Desire of all nations, Who hath created you through a word from Him, and ordained you to be, for all time, the emblems of His sovereignty.

By the righteousness of God! It is not Our wish to lay hands on your kingdoms. Our mission is to seize and possess the hearts of men. Upon them the eyes of Bahá are fastened. To this testifieth the Kingdom of Names, could ye but comprehend it. Whoso followeth his Lord, will renounce the world and all that is therein; how much greater, then, must be the detachment of Him Who holdeth so august a station! Forsake your palaces, and haste ye to gain admittance into His Kingdom. This, indeed, will profit you both in this world and in the next. To this testifieth the Lord of the realm on high, did ye but know it.

How great the blessedness that awaiteth the king who will arise to aid My Cause in My Kingdom, who will detach himself from all else but Me! Such a king is numbered with the companions of the Crimson Ark—the Ark which God hath prepared for the people of Bahá. All must glorify his name, must reverence his station, and aid him to unlock the cities with the keys of My Name, the omnipotent Protector of all that inhabit the visible and invisible kingdoms. Such a king is the very eye of mankind, the luminous ornament on the brow of creation, the fountain-head of blessings unto the whole world. Offer up, O people of Bahá, your substance, nay your very lives, for his assistance.

¶ 2. O Kings of the earth! Give ear unto the Voice of God, calling from this sublime, this fruit-laden Tree, that hath sprung out of the Crimson Hill, upon the holy Plain, intoning the words: "There is none other God but He, the Mighty, the All-Powerful, the All-Wise." . . . Fear God, O concourse of kings, and suffer not yourselves to be deprived of this most sublime grace. Fling away, then, the things ye possess, and take fast hold on the Handle of God, the

Exalted, the Great. Set your hearts towards the Face of God, and abandon that which your desires have bidden you to follow, and be not of those who perish. Relate unto them, O servant, the story of 'Ali,[1] when He came unto them with truth, bearing His glorious and weighty Book, and holding in His hands a testimony and proof from God, and holy and blessed tokens from Him. Ye, however, O kings, have failed to heed the Remembrance of God in His days and to be guided by the lights which arose and shone forth above the horizon of a resplendent Heaven. Ye examined not His Cause when so to do would have been better for you than all that the sun shineth upon, could ye but perceive it. Ye remained careless until the divines of Persia—those cruel ones—pronounced judgment against Him, and unjustly slew Him. His spirit ascended unto God, and the eyes of the inmates of Paradise and the angels that are nigh unto Him wept sore by reason of this cruelty. Beware that ye be not careless henceforth as ye have been careless aforetime. Return, then, unto God, your Maker, and be not of the heedless . . . My face hath come forth from the veils, and shed its radiance upon all that is in heaven and on earth; and yet, ye turned not towards Him, notwithstanding that ye were created for Him, O concourse of kings! Follow, therefore, that which I speak unto you, and hearken unto it with your hearts, and be not of such as have turned aside. For your glory consisteth not in your sovereignty, but rather in your nearness unto God and your observance of His command as sent down in His holy and preserved Tablets. Should any one of you rule over the whole earth, and over all that lieth within it and upon it, its seas, its lands, its mountains, and its plains, and yet be not remembered by God, all these would profit him not, could ye but know it. . . Arise, then, and make steadfast your feet, and make ye amends for that which hath escaped you, and set then yourselves towards His holy Court, on the shore of His mighty Ocean, so that the pearls of knowledge and wisdom, which God hath stored up within the shell of His radiant heart, may be revealed unto you. . . Beware lest ye hinder the breeze of God from blowing over your hearts, the breeze through which the hearts of such as have turned unto Him can be quickened. . .

O kings of Christendom! Heard ye not the saying of Jesus, the Spirit of God, "I go away, and come again unto you"? Wherefore, then, did ye fail, when He did come again unto you in the clouds of

[1] The Báb.

heaven, to draw nigh unto Him, that ye might behold His face, and
be of them that attained His Presence? In another passage He saith:
"When He, the Spirit of Truth, is come, He will guide you into all
truth." And yet, behold how, when He did bring the truth, ye refused to turn your faces towards Him, and persisted in disporting
yourselves with your pastimes and fancies. Ye welcomed Him not,
neither did ye seek His Presence, that ye might hear the verses of
God from His own mouth, and partake of the manifold wisdom of
the Almighty, the All-Glorious, the All-Wise. Ye have, by reason
of your failure, hindered the breath of God from being wafted over
you, and have withheld from your souls the sweetness of its fragrance. Ye continue roving with delight in the valley of your corrupt desires. Ye, and all ye possess, shall pass away. Ye shall, most
certainly, return to God, and shall be called to account for your doings in the presence of Him Who shall gather together the entire
creation. . .

Twenty years have passed, O kings, during which We have,
each day, tasted the agony of a fresh tribulation. No one of them
that were before Us hath endured the things We have endured.
Would that ye could perceive it! They that rose up against Us have
put us to death, have shed our blood, have plundered our property,
and violated our honour. Though aware of most of our afflictions,
ye, nevertheless, have failed to stay the hand of the aggressor. For is
it not your clear duty to restrain the tyranny of the oppressor, and
to deal equitably with your subjects, that your high sense of justice
may be fully demonstrated to all mankind?

God hath committed into your hands the reins of the government of the people, that ye may rule with justice over them, safeguard the rights of the down-trodden, and punish the wrong-
doers. If ye neglect the duty prescribed unto you by God in His
Book, your names shall be numbered with those of the unjust in
His sight. Grievous, indeed, will be your error. Cleave ye to that
which your imaginations have devised, and cast behind your backs
the commandments of God, the Most Exalted, the Inaccessible, the
All-Compelling, the Almighty? Cast away the things ye possess,
and cling to that which God hath bidden you observe. Seek ye His
grace, for he that seeketh it treadeth His straight Path.

Consider the state in which We are, and behold ye the ills and
troubles that have tried Us. Neglect Us not, though it be for a mo-

ment, and judge ye between Us and Our enemies with equity. This will, surely, be a manifest advantage unto you. Thus do We relate to you Our tale, and recount the things that have befallen Us, that ye might take off Our ills and ease Our burden. Let him who will, relieve Us from Our trouble; and as to him that willeth not, My Lord is assuredly the best of helpers.

Warn and acquaint the people, O Servant, with the things We have sent down unto Thee, and let the fear of no one dismay Thee, and be Thou not of them that waver. The day is approaching when God will have exalted His Cause and magnified His testimony in the eyes of all who are in the heavens and all who are on the earth. Place, in all circumstances, Thy whole trust in Thy Lord, and fix Thy gaze upon Him, and turn away from all them that repudiate His truth. Let God, Thy Lord, be Thy sufficing succourer and helper. We have pledged Ourselves to secure Thy triumph upon earth and to exalt Our Cause above all men, though no king be found who would turn his face towards Thee. . .

Lay not aside the fear of God, O kings of the earth, and beware that ye transgress not the bounds which the Almighty hath fixed. Observe the injunctions laid upon you in His Book, and take good heed not to overstep their limits. Be vigilant, that ye may not do injustice to anyone, be it to the extent of a grain of mustard seed. Tread ye the path of justice, for this, verily, is the straight path.

Compose your differences, and reduce your armaments, that the burden of your expenditures may be lightened, and that your minds and hearts may be tranquillized. Heal the dissensions that divide you, and ye will no longer be in need of any armaments except what the protection of your cities and territories demandeth. Fear ye God, and take heed not to outstrip the bounds of moderation, and be numbered among the extravagant.

We have learned that you are increasing your outlay every year, and are laying the burden thereof on your subjects. This, verily, is more than they can bear, and is a grievous injustice. Decide justly between men, and be ye the emblems of justice amongst them. This if ye judge fairly, is the thing that behoveth you, and beseemeth your station.

Beware not to deal unjustly with any one that appealeth to you, and entereth beneath your shadow. Walk ye in the fear of God, and be ye of them that lead a godly life. Rest not on your power, your armies and treasures. Put your whole trust and confidence in God, Who hath created you, and seek ye His help in all your affairs. Succour cometh from Him alone. He succoureth whom He will with the hosts of the heavens and of the earth.

Know ye that the poor are the trust of God in your midst. Watch that ye betray not His trust, that ye deal not unjustly with them and that ye walk not in the ways of the treacherous. Ye will most certainly be called upon to answer for His trust on the day when the Balance of Justice shall be set, the day when unto every one shall be rendered his due, when the doings of all men, be they rich or poor, shall be weighed.

If ye pay no heed unto the counsels which, in peerless and unequivocal language, We have revealed in this Tablet, Divine chastisement shall assail you from every direction, and the sentence of His justice shall be pronounced against you. On that day ye shall have no power to resist Him, and shall recognize your own impotence. Have mercy on yourselves and on those beneath you. Judge ye between them according to the precepts prescribed by God in His most holy and exalted Tablet, a Tablet wherein He hath assigned to each and every thing its settled measure, in which He hath given, with distinctness, an explanation of all things, and which is in itself a monition unto them that believe in Him.

Examine Our Cause, inquire into the things that have befallen Us, and decide justly between Us and Our enemies, and be ye of them that act equitably towards their neighbour. If ye stay not the hand of the oppressor, if ye fail to safeguard the rights of the down-trodden, what right have ye then to vaunt yourselves among men? What is it of which ye can rightly boast? Is it on your food and your drink that ye pride yourselves, on the riches ye lay up in your treasuries, on the diversity and the cost of the ornaments with which ye deck yourselves? If true glory were to consist in the possession of such perishable things, then the earth on which ye walk must needs vaunt itself over you, because it supplieth you, and bestoweth upon you, these very things, by the decree of the Almighty. In its bowels are contained, according to what God hath ordained, all that ye possess. From it, as a sign of His mercy, ye derive your riches. Behold then your state, the thing in which ye glory! Would that ye could perceive it!

Nay! By Him Who holdeth in His grasp the kingdom of the entire creation! Nowhere doth your true and abiding glory reside except in your firm adherence unto the precepts of God, your whole-hearted observance of His laws, your resolution to see that they do not remain unenforced, and to pursue steadfastly the right course.

2. TO QUEEN VICTORIA OF BRITAIN

¶ 3. O Queen in London! Incline thine ear unto the voice of thy Lord, the Lord of all mankind, calling from the Divine Lote-Tree: Verily, no God is there but Me, the Almighty, the All-Wise! Cast away all that is on earth, and attire the head of thy kingdom with the crown of the remembrance of thy Lord, the All-Glorious. He, in truth, hath come unto the world in His most great glory, and all that hath been mentioned in the Gospel hath been fulfilled. The land of Syria hath been honoured by the footsteps of its Lord, the Lord of all men, and North and South are both inebriated with the wine of His presence. Blessed is the man that inhaled the fragrance of the Most Merciful, and turned unto the Dawning-Place of His Beauty, in this resplendent Dawn. The Mosque of Aqsá vibrateth through the breezes of its Lord, the All-Glorious whilst Baṭhá[1] trembleth at the voice of God, the Exalted, the Most High. Whereupon every single stone of them celebrateth the praise of the Lord, through this Great Name.

Lay aside thy desire, and set then thine heart towards thy Lord, the Ancient of Days. We make mention of thee for the sake of God, and desire that thy name may be exalted through thy remembrance of God, the Creator of earth and heaven. He, verily, is witness unto that which I say. We have been informed that thou hast forbidden the trading in slaves, both men and women. This, verily, is what God hath enjoined in this wondrous Revelation. God hath, truly, destined a reward for thee, because of this. He, verily, will pay the doer of good his due recompense, wert thou to follow what hath been sent unto thee by Him Who is the All-Knowing, the All-Informed. As to him who turneth aside, and swelleth with pride, after that the clear tokens have come unto him, from the Revealer of signs, his work shall God bring to naught. He, in truth, hath power over all things. Man's actions are acceptable after his having

---

[1] Mecca.

recognized.[1] He that turneth aside from the True One is indeed the most veiled amongst His creatures. Thus hath it been decreed by Him Who is the Almighty, the Most Powerful.

We have also heard that thou hast entrusted the reins of counsel into the hands of the representatives of the people. Thou, indeed, hast done well, for thereby the foundations of the edifice of thine affairs will be strengthened, and the hearts of all that are beneath thy shadow, whether high or low, will be tranquillized. It behoveth them, however, to be trustworthy among His servants, and to regard themselves as the representatives of all that dwell on earth. This is what counselleth them, in this Tablet, He Who is the Ruler, the All-Wise... Blessed is he that entereth the assembly for the sake of God, and judgeth between men with pure justice. He, indeed, is of the blissful.

O ye the elected representatives of the people in every land! Take ye counsel together, and let your concern be only for that which profiteth mankind, and bettereth the condition thereof, if ye be of them that scan heedfully. Regard the world as the human body which, though at its creation whole and perfect, hath been afflicted, through various causes, with grave disorders and maladies. Not for one day did it gain ease, nay its sickness waxed more severe, as it fell under the treatment of ignorant physicians, who gave full rein to their personal desires, and have erred grievously. And if, at one time, through the care of an able physician, a member of that body was healed, the rest remained afflicted as before. Thus informeth you the All-Knowing, the All-Wise.

We behold it, in this day, at the mercy of rulers so drunk with pride that they cannot discern clearly their own best advantage, much less recognize a Revelation so bewildering and challenging as this. And whenever any one of them hath striven to improve its condition, his motive hath been his own gain, whether confessedly so or not; and the unworthiness of this motive hath limited his power to heal or cure.

That which the Lord hath ordained as the sovereign remedy and mightiest instrument for the healing of all the world is the union of all its peoples in one universal Cause, one common Faith. This can in no wise be achieved except through the power of a skilled, an all-powerful and inspired Physician. This, verily, is the truth, and all else naught but error...

[1] The Manifestation.

O ye rulers of the earth! Wherefore have ye clouded the radiance of the Sun, and caused it to cease from shining? Hearken unto the counsel given you by the Pen of the Most High, that haply both ye and the poor may attain unto tranquillity and peace. We beseech God to assist the kings of the earth to establish peace on earth. He, verily, doth what He willeth.

O kings of the earth! We see you increasing every year your expenditures, and laying the burden thereof on your subjects. This, verily, is wholly and grossly unjust. Fear the sighs and tears of this Wronged One, and lay not excessive burdens on your peoples. Do not rob them to rear palaces for yourselves; nay rather choose for them that which ye choose for yourselves. Thus We unfold to your eyes that which profiteth you, if ye but perceive. Your people are your treasures. Beware lest your rule violate the commandments of God, and ye deliver your wards to the hands of the robber. By them ye rule, by their means ye subsist, by their aid ye conquer. Yet, how disdainfully ye look upon them! How strange, how very strange!

Now that ye have refused the Most Great Peace, hold ye fast unto this, the Lesser Peace, that haply ye may in some degree better your own condition and that of your dependents.

O rulers of the earth! Be reconciled among yourselves, that ye may need no more armaments save in a measure to safeguard your territories and dominions. Beware lest ye disregard the counsel of the All-Knowing, the Faithful.

Be united, O kings of the earth, for thereby will the tempest of discord be stilled amongst you, and your peoples find rest, if ye be of them that comprehend. Should any one among you take up arms against another, rise ye all against him, for this is naught but manifest justice. . .

Turn thou unto God and say: O my Sovereign Lord! I am but a vassal of Thine, and Thou art, in truth, the King of Kings. I have lifted my suppliant hands unto the heaven of Thy grace and Thy bounties. Send down, then, upon me from the clouds of Thy generosity that which will rid me of all save Thee, and draw me nigh unto Thyself. I beseech Thee, O my Lord, by Thy name, which Thou hast made the king of names, and the manifestation of Thyself to all who are in heaven and on earth, to rend asunder the veils that have intervened between me and my recognition of the Dawning-Place of Thy signs and the Day Spring of Thy Revelation. Thou art, verily, the Almighty, the All-Powerful, the All-Bounteous. Deprive me not, O my Lord, of the fragrances of the Robe of Thy mercy in Thy days, and write down for me that which Thou hast written down for thy handmaidens who have believed in Thee and in Thy signs, and have recognized Thee, and set their hearts towards the horizon of Thy Cause. Thou art truly the Lord of the world and of those who show mercy the Most Merciful. Assist me, then, O my God, to remember Thee amongst Thy handmaidens, and to aid Thy Cause in Thy lands. Accept, then, that which hath escaped me when the light of Thy countenance shone forth. Thou, indeed, hast power over all things. Glory be to Thee, O Thou in Whose hand is the kingdom of the heavens and of the earth.

3. TO THE EMPEROR NAPOLEON III OF FRANCE

¶ 4. O King of Paris! Tell the priest to ring the bells no longer. By God, the True One! The Most Mighty Bell hath appeared in the form of Him Who is the Most Great Name, and the fingers of the will of Thy Lord, the Most Exalted, the Most High, toll it out in the heaven of Immortality, in His name, the All-Glorious. Thus have the mighty verses of Thy Lord been again sent down unto thee, that thou mayest arise to remember God, the Creator of earth and heaven, in these days when all the tribes of the earth have mourned, and the foundations of the cities have trembled, and the dust of irreligion hath enwrapped all men, except such as God, the All-Knowing, the All-Wise, was pleased to spare. Say: He Who is the Unconditioned is come, in the clouds of light, that He may quicken all created things with the breeze of His Name, the Most Merciful, and unify the world, and gather all men around this Table which hath been sent down from heaven. Beware that ye deny not the favour of God after it hath been sent down unto you. Better is this for you than that which ye possess; for that which is yours perisheth, whilst that which is with God endureth. He, in truth, ordaineth what He pleaseth. Verily, the breezes of forgiveness have been wafted from the direction of your Lord, the God of Mercy; whoso turneth thereunto, shall be cleansed of his sins, and of all pain and sickness. Happy the man that hath turned towards them, and woe betide him that hath turned aside.

Wert thou to incline thine inner ear unto all created things, thou wouldst hear: "The Ancient of Days is come in His great glory!" Everything celebrateth the praise of its Lord. Some have known God and remember Him; others remember Him, yet know Him not. Thus have We set down Our decree in a perspicuous Tablet.

Give ear, O King, unto the Voice that calleth from the Fire which burneth in this verdant Tree, on this Sinai which hath been raised above the hallowed and snow-white Spot, beyond the Everlasting City; "Verily, there is none other God but Me, the Ever-Forgiving, the Most Merciful!" We, in truth, have sent Him Whom We aided with the Holy Spirit[1] that He may announce unto you this Light that hath shone forth from the horizon of the will of your Lord, the Most Exalted, the All-Glorious, and Whose signs have been revealed in the West. Set your faces towards Him[2] on this Day which God hath exalted above all other days, and whereon the All-Merciful hath shed the splendour of His effulgent glory upon all who are in heaven and all who are on earth. Arise thou to serve God and help His Cause. He, verily, will assist thee with the hosts of the seen and unseen, and will set thee king over all that whereon the sun riseth. Thy Lord, in truth, is the All-Powerful, the Almighty.

The breezes of the Most Merciful have passed over all created things; happy the man that hath discovered their fragrance, and set himself towards them with a sound heart. Attire thy temple with the ornament of My Name, and thy tongue with remembrance of Me, and thine heart with love for Me, the Almighty, the Most High. We have desired for thee naught except that which is better for thee than what thou dost possess and all the treasures of the earth. Thy Lord, verily, is knowing, informed of all. Arise, in My Name, amongst My servants, and say: "O ye peoples of the earth! Turn yourselves towards Him Who hath turned towards you. He, verily, is the Face of God amongst you, and His Testimony and His Guide unto you. He hath come to you with signs which none can produce." The voice of the Burning Bush is raised in the midmost heart of the world, and the Holy Spirit calleth aloud among the nations: "Lo, the Desired One is come with manifest dominion!"

O King! The stars of the heaven of knowledge have fallen, they who seek to establish the truth of My Cause through the things they possess, and who make mention of God in My Name. And yet,

---

[1] Jesus Christ.   [2] Bahá'u'lláh.

when I came unto them in My glory, they turned aside. They, indeed, are of the fallen. This is, truly, that which the Spirit of God[1] hath announced, when He came with truth unto you, He with Whom the Jewish doctors disputed, till at last they perpetrated what hath made the Holy Spirit to lament, and the tears of them that have near access to God to flow.

Say: O concourse of monks! Seclude not yourselves in your churches and cloisters. Come ye out of them by My leave, and busy, then, yourselves with what will profit you and others. Thus commandeth you He Who is the Lord of the Day of Reckoning. Seclude yourselves in the stronghold of My love. This, truly, is the seclusion that befitteth you, could ye but know it. He that secludeth himself in his house is indeed as one dead. It behooveth man to show forth that which will benefit mankind. He that bringeth forth no fruit is fit for the fire. Thus admonisheth you your Lord; He, verily, is the Mighty, the Bountiful. Enter ye into wedlock, that after you another may arise in your stead. We, verily, have forbidden you lechery, and not that which is conducive to fidelity. Have ye clung unto the promptings of your nature, and cast behind your backs the statutes of God? Fear ye God, and be not of the foolish. But for man, who on My earth, would remember Me, and how could My attributes and My names be revealed? Reflect, and be not of them that have shut themselves out as by a veil from Him, and were of those that are fast asleep. He that married not[1] could find no place wherein to abide, nor where to lay His head, by reason of what the hands of the treacherous had wrought. His holiness consisted not in the things ye have believed and imagined, but rather in the things which belong unto Us. Ask, that ye may be made aware of His station which hath been exalted above the vain imaginings of all the peoples of the earth. Blessed are they that understand.

O King! We heard the words thous didst utter in answer to the Czar of Russia, concerning the decision made regarding the war.[2] Thy Lord, verily, knoweth, is informed of all. Thou didst say: "I lay asleep upon my couch, when the cry of the oppressed, who were drowned in the Black Sea, wakened me." This is what we heard thee say, and, verily, thy Lord is witness unto what I say. We testify that that which wakened thee was not their cry but the promptings of thine own passions, for We tested thee, and

---

[1] Jesus Christ.   [2] Crimean War.

found thee wanting. Comprehend the meaning of My words, and be thou of the discerning. It is not Our wish to address thee words of condemnation, out of regard for the dignity We conferred upon thee in this mortal life. We, verily, have chosen courtesy, and made it the true mark of such as are nigh unto Him. Courtesy, is, in truth, a raiment which fitteth all men, whether young or old. Well is it with him that adorneth his temple therewith, and woe unto him who is deprived of this great bounty. Hadst thou been sincere in thy words, thou wouldst have not cast behind thy back the Book of God, when it was sent unto thee by Him Who is the Almighty, the All-Wise. We have proved thee through it, and found thee other than that which thou didst profess. Arise, and make amends for that which escaped thee. Ere long the world and all that thou possessest will perish, and the kingdom will remain unto God, thy Lord and the Lord of thy fathers of old. It behooveth thee not to conduct thine affairs according to the dictates of thy desires. Fear the sighs of this Wronged One, and shield Him from the darts of such as act unjustly.

For what thou hast done, thy kingdom shall be thrown into confusion, and thine empire shall pass from thine hands, as a punishment for that which thou hast wrought. Then wilt thou know how thou hast plainly erred. Commotions shall seize all the people in that land, unless thou arisest to help this Cause, and followest Him Who is the Spirit of God[1] in this, the Straight Path. Hath thy pomp made thee proud? By My Life! It shall not endure; nay, it shall soon pass away, unless thou holdest fast by this firm Cord. We see abasement hastening after thee, whilst thou art of the heedless. It behooveth thee when thou hearest His Voice calling from the seat of glory to cast away all that thou possessest, and cry out: "Here am I, O Lord of all that is in heaven and all that is on earth!"

O King! We were in 'Iráq, when the hour of parting arrived. At the bidding of the King of Islám.[2] We set Our steps in his direction. Upon Our arrival, there befell Us at the hands of the malicious that which the books of the world can never adequately recount. Thereupon the inmates of Paradise, and they that dwell within the retreats of holiness, lamented; and yet the people are wrapped in a thick veil! . . .

More grievous became Our plight from day to day, nay, from

---

[1] Jesus Christ.   [2] Sultán of Turkey.

hour to hour, until they took Us forth from Our prison and made Us, with glaring injustice, enter the Most Great Prison. And if any-one ask them: "For what crime were they imprisoned?" they would answer and say: "They, verily, sought to supplant the Faith with a new religion!" If that which is ancient be what ye prefer, wherefore, then, have ye discarded that which hath been set down in the Torah and the Evangel? Clear it up, O men! By My life! There is no place for you to flee to in this day. If this be My crime, then Muḥammad, the Apostle of God, committed it before Me, and before Him He Who was the Spirit of God,[1] and yet earlier He Who conversed with God.[2] And if My sin be this, that I have exalted the Word of God and revealed His Cause, then indeed am I the greatest of sinners! Such a sin I will not barter for the kingdoms of earth and heaven. . .

As My tribulations multiplied, so did My love for God and for His Cause increase, in such wise that all that befell Me from the hosts of the wayward was powerless to deter Me from My purpose. Should they hide Me away in the depths of the earth, yet would they find Me riding aloft on the clouds, and calling out unto God, the Lord of strength and of might. I have offered Myself up in the way of God, and I yearn after tribulations in My love for Him, and for the sake of His good-pleasure. Unto this bear witness the woes which now afflict Me, the like of which no other man hath suffered. Every single hair of Mine head calleth out that which the Burning Bush uttered on Sinai, and each vein of My body invoketh God and saith: "O would I had been severed in Thy path, so that the world might be quickened, and all its peoples be united!" Thus hath it been decreed by Him Who is the All-Knowing, the All-Informed.

Know of a truth that your subjects are God's trust amongst you. Watch ye, therefore, over them as ye watch over your own selves. Beware that ye allow not wolves to become the shepherds of the fold, or pride and conceit to deter you from turning unto the poor and the desolate. Arise thou, in My name, above the horizon of re-nunciation, and set, then, thy face towards the Kingdom, at the bidding of thy Lord, the Lord of strength and of might. . .

Adorn the body of Thy kingdom with the raiment of My name, and arise, then, to teach My Cause. Better is this for thee than that which thou possessest. God will, thereby, exalt thy name among all the kings. Potent is He over all things. Walk thou amongst men in

[1] Jesus Christ.   [2] Moses.

the name of God, and by the power of His might, that thou mayest show forth His signs amidst the peoples of the earth. . .

Doth it behoove you to relate yourselves to Him Who is the God of mercy, and yet commit the things which the Evil One hath committed? Nay, by the Beauty of Him Who is the All-Glorified! could ye but know it. Purge your hearts from love of the world, and your tongues from calumny, and your limbs from whatsoever may withhold you from drawing nigh unto God, the Mighty, the All-Praised. Say: By the world is meant that which turneth you aside from Him Who is the Dawning-Place of Revelation, and inclineth you unto that which is unprofitable unto you. Verily, the thing that deterreth you, in this day, from God is worldliness in its essence. Eschew it, and approach the Most Sublime Vision, this shining and resplendent Seat. Shed not the blood of anyone, O people, neither judge ye anyone unjustly. Thus have ye been commanded by Him Who knoweth, Who is informed of all. They that commit disorders in the land after it hath been well ordered, these indeed have outstepped the bounds that have been set in the Book. Wretched shall be the abode of the transgressors! . . .

Deal not treacherously with the substance of your neighbour. Be ye trustworthy on earth, and withhold not from the poor the things given unto you by God through His grace. He, verily, will bestow upon you the double of what ye possess. He, in truth, is the All-Bounteous, the Most Generous. O people of Bahá! Subdue the citadels of men's hearts with the swords of wisdom and of utterance. They that dispute, as prompted by their desires, are indeed wrapped in a palpable veil. Say: The sword of wisdom is hotter than summer heat, and sharper than blades of steel, if ye do but understand. Draw it forth in My name and through the power of My might, and conquer, then, with it the cities of the hearts of them that have secluded themselves in the stronghold of their corrupt desires. Thus biddeth you the Pen of the All-Glorious, whilst seated beneath the swords of the wayward. If ye become aware of a sin committed by another, conceal it, that God may conceal your own sin. He, verily, is the Concealer, the Lord of grace abounding. O ye rich ones on earth! If ye encounter one who is poor, treat him not disdainfully. Reflect upon that whereof ye were created. Every one of you was created of a sorry germ. . .

Regard ye the world as a man's body, which is afflicted with divers ailments, and the recovery of which dependeth upon the harmonizing of all of its component elements. Gather ye around that which We have prescribed unto you, and walk not in the ways of such as create dissension. Meditate on the world and the state of its people. He, for Whose sake the world was called into being, hath been imprisoned in the most desolate of cities,[1] by reason of that which the hands of the wayward have wrought. From the horizon of His prison-city He summoneth mankind unto the Dayspring of God, the Exalted, the Great. Exultest thou over the treasures thou dost possess, knowing they shall perish? Rejoicest thou in that thou rulest a span of earth, when the whole world, in the estimation of the people of Bahá, is worth as much as the black in the eye of a dead ant? Abandon it unto such as have set their affections upon it, and turn thou unto Him Who is the Desire of the world. Whither are gone the proud and their palaces? Gaze thou into their tombs, that thou mayest profit by this example, inasmuch as We made it a lesson unto every beholder. Were the breezes of Revelation to seize thee, thou wouldst flee the world, and turn unto the Kingdom, and wouldst expend all thou possessest, that thou mayest draw nigh unto this sublime Vision.

4. TO CZAR ALEXANDER II OF RUSSIA

¶ 5. O Czar of Russia! Incline thine ear unto the voice of God, the King, the Holy, and turn thou unto Paradise, the Spot wherein abideth He Who, among the Concourse on high, beareth the most excellent titles, and Who, in the kingdom of creation, is called by the name of God, the Effulgent, the All-Glorious. Beware lest thy desire deter thee from turning towards the face of thy Lord, the Compassionate, the Most Merciful. We, verily, have heard the thing for which thou didst supplicate thy Lord, whilst secretly communing with Him. Wherefore, the breeze of My loving-kindness wafted forth, and the sea of My mercy surged, and We answered thee in truth. Thy Lord, verily, is the All-Knowing, the All-Wise. Whilst I lay chained and fettered in the prison, one of thy ministers extended Me his aid. Wherefore hath God ordained for thee a station which the knowledge of none can comprehend except His knowledge. Beware lest thou barter away this sublime station. . .

[1] 'Akká.

Beware lest thy sovereignty withhold thee from Him Who is the Supreme Sovereign. He, verily, is come with His Kingdom, and all the atoms cry aloud: "Lo! The Lord is come in His great majesty!" He Who is the Father is come, and the Son,[1] in the holy vale, crieth out: "Here am I, here am I, O Lord, My God!" whilst Sinai circleth round the House, and the Burning Bush calleth aloud: "The All-Bounteous is come mounted upon the clouds! Blessed is he that draweth nigh unto Him, and woe betide them that are far away."

Arise thou amongst men in the name of this all-compelling Cause, and summon, then, the nations unto God, the Exalted, the Great. Be thou not of them who called upon God by one of His names, but who, when He Who is the Object of all names appeared, denied Him and turned aside from Him, and, in the end, pronounced sentence against Him with manifest injustice. Consider and call thou to mind the days whereon the Spirit of God[1] appeared, and Herod gave judgment against Him. God, however, aided Him with the hosts of the unseen, and protected Him with truth, and sent Him down unto another land, according to His promise. He, verily, ordaineth what He pleaseth. Thy Lord truly preserveth whom He willeth, be he in the midst of the seas, or in the maw of the serpent, or beneath the sword of the oppressor...

Again I say: Hearken unto My Voice that calleth from My prison that it may acquaint thee with the things that have befallen My Beauty, at the hands of them that are the manifestations of My glory, and that thou mayest perceive how great hath been My patience, notwithstanding My might, and how immense My forebearance, notwithstanding My power. By My Life! Couldst thou but know the things sent down by My Pen, and discover the treasures of My Cause, and the pearls of My mysteries which lie hid in the seas of My names and in the goblets of My words, thou wouldst, in thy love for My name, and in thy longing for My glorious and sublime Kingdom, lay down thy life in My path. Know thou that though My body be beneath the swords of My foes, and My limbs be beset with incalculable afflictions, yet My spirit is filled with a gladness with which all the joys of the earth can never compare.

Set thine heart towards Him Who is the Point of adoration for the world, and say: O peoples of the earth! Have ye denied the One

_____
[1] Jesus.

in Whose path He Who came with the truth, bearing the announcement of your Lord, the Exalted, the Great, suffered martyrdom? Say: This is an Announcement whereat the hearts of the Prophets and Messengers have rejoiced. This is the One Whom the heart of the world remembereth and is promised in the Books of God, the Mighty, the All-Wise. The hands of the Messengers were, in their desire to meet Me, upraised towards God, the Mighty, the Glorified. . . Some lamented in their separation from Me, others endured hardships in My path, and still others laid down their lives for the sake of My Beauty, could ye but know it. Say: I, verily, have not sought to extol Mine Own Self, but rather God Himself were ye to judge fairly. Naught can be seen in Me except God and His Cause, could ye but perceive it. I am the One Whom the tongue of Isaiah hath extolled, the One with Whose name both the Torah and the Evangel were adorned. . . Blessed be the king whose sovereignty hath withheld him not from his Sovereign, and who hath turned unto God with his heart. He, verily, is accounted of those that have attained unto that which God, the Mighty, the All-Wise hath willed. Ere long will such a one find himself numbered with the monarchs of the realms of the Kingdom. Thy Lord is, in truth, potent over all things. He giveth what He willeth to whomsoever He willeth, and withholdeth what He pleaseth from whomsoever He willeth. He, verily, is the All-Powerful, the Almighty.

5. TO EMPEROR WILLIAM I OF GERMANY

¶ 6. Say: O King of Berlin! Give ear unto the Voice calling from this manifest Temple: Verily, there is none other God but Me, the Everlasting, the Peerless, the Ancient of Days. Take heed lest pride debar thee from recognizing the Dayspring of Divine Revelation, lest earthly desires shut thee out, as by a veil, from the Lord of the Throne above and of the earth below. Thus counselleth thee the Pen of the Most High. He, verily, is the Most Gracious, the All-Bountiful. Do thou remember the one whose power transcended thy power,[1] and whose station excelled thy station. Where is he? Whither are gone the things he possessed? Take warning, and be not of them that are fast asleep. He it was who cast the Tablet of God behind him, when We made known unto him what

[1] Napoleon III.

the hosts of tyranny had caused Us to suffer. Wherefore, disgrace
assailed him from all sides, and he went down to dust in great loss.
Think deeply, O King, concerning him, and concerning them who,
like unto thee, have conquered cities and ruled over men. The All-
Merciful brought them down from their palaces to their graves. Be
warned, be of them who reflect. . . O banks of the Rhine! We have
seen you covered with gore, inasmuch as the swords of retribution
were drawn against you; and you shall have another turn. And We
hear the lamentations of Berlin, though she be today in conspicu-
ous glory.

6. TO EMPEROR FRANCIS JOSEPH OF AUSTRIA-HUNGARY

¶ 7. O Emperor of Austria! He who is the Dayspring of God's
Light dwelt in the prison of 'Akká, at the time when thous didst
set forth to visit the Aqsá Mosque.[1] Thou passed Him by, and
inquired not about Him, by Whom every house is exalted, and
every lofty gate unlocked. We, verily, made it[1] a place whereunto the world should turn, that they might remember Me,
and yet thou hast rejected Him Who is the Object of this remembrance, when He appeared with the Kingdom of God, thy Lord
and the Lord of the worlds. We have been with thee at all times, and
found thee clinging unto the Branch and heedless of the Root. Thy
Lord, verily, is a witness unto what I say. We grieved to see thee
circle round Our Name, whilst unaware of Us, though We were
before thy face. Open thine eyes, that thou mayest behold this
glorious Vision, and recognize Him Whom thou invokest in the
daytime and in the night-season, and gaze on the Light that shineth
above this luminous Horizon.

7. TO SULṬÁN 'ABDU'L-'AZÍZ

¶ 8. Hearken, O King to the speech of Him that speaketh the truth,
Him that doth not ask thee to recompense Him with the things God
hath chosen to bestow upon thee, Him Who unerringly treadeth
the straight Path. He it is Who summoneth thee unto God, thy
Lord, Who showeth thee the right course, the way that leadeth to

[1] Jerusalem.

true felicity, that haply thou mayest be of them with whom it shall be well.

Beware, O King, that thou gather not around thee such ministers as follow the desires of a corrupt inclination, as have cast behind their backs that which hath been committed into their hands and manifestly betrayed their trust. Be bounteous to others as God hath been bounteous to thee, and abandon not the interests of thy people to the mercy of such ministers as these. Lay not aside the fear of God, and be thou of them that act uprightly. Gather around thee those ministers from whom thou canst perceive the fragrance of faith and of justice, and take thou counsel with them, and choose whatever is best in thy sight, and be of them that act generously.

Know thou for a certainty that whoso disbelieveth in God is neither trustworthy nor truthful. This, indeed, is the truth, the undoubted truth. He that acteth treacherously towards God will, also, act treacherously towards his king. Nothing whatever can deter such a man from evil, nothing can hinder him from betraying his neighbour, nothing can induce him to walk uprightly.

Take heed that thou resign not the reins of the affairs of thy state into the hands of others, and repose not thy confidence in ministers unworthy of thy trust, and be not of them that live in heedlessness. Shun them whose hearts are turned away from thee, and place not thy confidence in them, and entrust them not with thy affairs and the affairs of such as profess thy faith. Beware that thou allow not the wolf to become the shepherd of God's flock, and surrender not the fate of His loved ones to the mercy of the malicious. Expect not that they who violate the ordinances of God will be trustworthy or sincere in the faith they profess. Avoid them, and preserve strict guard over thyself, lest their devices and mischief hurt thee. Turn away from them, and fix thy gaze upon God, thy Lord, the All-Glorious, the Most Bountiful. He that giveth up himself wholly to God, God shall, assuredly, be with him; and he that placeth his complete trust in God, God shall, verily, protect him from whatsoever may harm him, and shield him from the wickedness of every evil plotter.

Wert thou to incline thine ear unto My speech and observe My counsel, God would exalt thee to so eminent a position that the designs of no man on the whole earth could ever touch or hurt thee. Observe, O King, with thine inmost heart and with thy whole being, the precepts of God, and walk not in the paths of the oppressor. Seize thou, and hold firmly within the grasp of thy might, the reins of the affairs of thy people, and examine in person whatever pertaineth unto them. Let nothing escape thee, for therein lieth the highest good.

Render thanks unto God for having chosen thee out of the whole world, and made thee king over them that profess thy faith. It well beseemeth thee to appreciate the wondrous favours with which God hath favoured thee, and to magnify continually His name. Thou canst best praise Him if thou lovest His loved ones, and dost safeguard and protect His servants from the mischief of the treacherous, that none may any longer oppress them. Thou shouldst, moreover, arise to enforce the law of God amongst them, that thou mayest be of those who are firmly established in His law.

Shouldst thou cause rivers of justice to spread their waters amongst thy subjects, God would surely aid thee with the hosts of the unseen and of the seen and would strengthen thee in thine affairs. No God is there but Him. All creation and its empire are His. Unto Him return the works of the faithful.

Place not thy reliance on thy treasures. Put thy whole confidence in the grace of God, thy Lord. Let Him be thy trust in whatever thou doest, and be of them that have submitted themselves to His Will. Let Him be thy helper and enrich thyself with His treasures, for with Him are the treasuries of the heavens and of the earth. He bestoweth them upon whom He will, and from whom He will He withholdeth them. There is none other God but Him, the All-Possessing, the All-Praised. All are but paupers at the door of His mercy; all are helpless before the revelation of His sovereignty, and beseech His favours.

Overstep not the bounds of moderation, and deal justly with them that serve thee. Bestow upon them according to their needs and not to the extent that will enable them to lay up riches for themselves, to deck their persons, to embellish their homes, to acquire the things that are of no benefit unto them, and to be numbered with the extravagant. Deal with them with undeviating justice, so that none among them may either suffer want, or be pampered with luxuries. This is but manifest justice.

Allow not the abject to rule over and dominate them who are noble and worthy of honour, and suffer not the high-minded to be at the mercy of the contemptible and worthless, for this is what We observed upon Our arrival in the City,[1] and to it We bear witness. We found among its inhabitants some who were possessed of an affluent fortune and lived in the midst of excessive riches, whilst others were in dire want and abject poverty. This ill beseemeth thy sovereignty, and is unworthy of thy rank.

Let My counsel be acceptable to thee, and strive thou to rule with equity among men, that God may exalt thy name and spread abroad the fame of thy justice in all the world. Beware lest thou aggrandize thy ministers at the expense of thy subjects. Fear the sighs of the poor and of the upright in heart who, at every break of day, bewail their plight, and be unto them a benignant sovereign. They, verily, are thy treasures on earth. It behoveth thee, therefore, to safeguard thy treasures from the assaults of them who wish to rob thee. Inquire into their affairs, and ascertain, every year, nay every month, their condition, and be not of them that are careless of their duty.

Set before thine eyes God's unerring Balance and, as one standing in His Presence, weigh in that Balance thine actions every day, every moment of thy life. Bring thyself to account ere thou art summoned to a reckoning, on the Day when no man shall have strength to stand for fear of God, the Day when the hearts of the heedless ones shall be made to tremble.

It behoveth every king to be as bountiful as the sun, which fostereth the growth of all beings, and giveth to each its due, whose benefits are not inherent in itself, but are ordained by Him Who is the Most Powerful, the Almighty. The King should be as generous, as liberal in his mercy as the clouds, the outpourings of whose bounty are showered upon every land, by the behest of Him Who is the Supreme Ordainer, the All-Knowing.

Have a care not to entrust thine affairs of state entirely into another's hands. None can discharge thy functions better than thine own self. Thus do We make clear unto thee Our words of wisdom, and send down upon thee that which can enable thee to pass over from the left hand of oppression to the right hand of justice, and approach the resplendent ocean of His favours. Such is the path which the kings that were before thee have trodden, they that acted equitably towards their subjects, and walked in the ways of undeviating justice.

Thou art God's shadow on earth. Strive, therefore, to act in such

[1] Constantinople.

a manner as befitteth so eminent, so august a station. If thou dost depart from following the things We have caused to descend upon thee and taught thee, thou wilt, assuredly, be derogating from that great and priceless honour. Return, then, and cleave wholly unto God, and cleanse thine heart from the world and all its vanities, and suffer not the love of any stranger to enter and dwell therein. Not until thou dost purify thine heart from every trace of such love can the brightness of the light of God shed its radiance upon it, for to none hath God given more than one heart. This, verily, hath been decreed and written down in His ancient Book. And as the human heart, as fashioned by God, is one and undivided, it behoveth thee to take heed that its affections be, also, one and undivided. Cleave thou, therefore, with the whole affection of thine heart, unto His love, and withdraw it from the love of any one besides Him, that He may aid thee to immerse thyself in the ocean of His unity, and enable thee to become a true upholder of His oneness. God is My witness. My sole purpose in revealing to thee these words is to sanctify thee from the transitory things of the earth, and aid thee to enter the realm of everlasting glory, that thou mayest, by the leave of God, be of them that abide and rule therein. . .

I swear by God, O King! It is not My wish to make My plaint to thee against them that persecute Me. I only plead My grief and My sorrow to God, Who hath created Me and them, Who well knoweth Our state and Who watcheth over all things. My wish is to warn them of the consequences of their actions, if perchance they might desist from treating others as they have treated Me, and be of them that heed My warning.

The tribulations that have touched Us, the destitution from which We suffer, the various troubles with which We are encompassed, shall all pass away, as shall pass away the pleasures in which they delight and the affluence they enjoy. This is the truth which no man on earth can reject. The days in which We have been compelled to dwell in the dust will soon be ended, as will the days in which they occupied the seats of honour. God shall, assuredly, judge with truth between Us and them, and He, verily, is the best of judges.

We render thanks unto God for whatsoever hath befallen Us, and We patiently endure the things He hath ordained in the past or will ordain in the future. In Him have I placed My trust; and into

His hands have I committed My Cause. He will, certainly, repay all them that endure with patience and put their confidence in Him. His is the creation and its empire. He exalteth whom He will, and whom He will He doth abase. He shall not be asked of His doings. He, verily, is the All-Glorious, the Almighty.

Let thine ear be attentive, O King, to the words We have addressed to thee. Let the oppressor desist from his tyranny, and cut off the perpetrators of injustice from among them that profess thy faith. By the righteousness of God! The tribulations We have sustained are such that any pen that recounteth them cannot but be overwhelmed with anguish. No one of them that truly believe and uphold the unity of God can bear the burden of their recital. So great have been Our sufferings that even the eyes of Our enemies have wept over Us, and beyond them those of every discerning person. And to all these trials have We been subjected, in spite of Our action in approaching thee, and in bidding the people to enter beneath thy shadow, that thou mightest be a stronghold unto them that believe in and uphold the unity of God.

Have I, O King, ever disobeyed thee? Have I, at any time, transgressed any of thy laws? Can any of thy ministers that represented thee in 'Iráq produce any proof that can establish my disloyalty to thee? No, by Him Who is the Lord of all worlds! Not for one short moment did We rebel against thee, or against any of thy ministers. Never, God willing, shall We revolt against thee, though We be exposed to trials more severe than any We suffered in the past.

In the day time and in the night season, at even and at morn, We pray to God on thy behalf, that He may graciously aid thee to be obedient unto Him and to observe His commandment, that He may shield thee from the hosts of the evil ones. Do, therefore, as it pleaseth thee, and treat Us as befitteth thy station and beseemeth thy sovereignty. Be not forgetful of the law of God in whatever thou desirest to achieve, now or in the days to come. Say: Praise be to God, the Lord of all worlds!

8. TO NÁṢIRI'D-DÍN SHÁH OF PERSIA

¶ 9. O king! I was but a man like others, asleep upon My couch, when lo, the breezes of the All-Glorious were wafted over Me, and taught Me the knowledge of all that hath been. This thing is not from Me, but from One Who is Almighty and All-Knowing. And He bade Me lift up My voice between earth and heaven, and for this there befell Me what hath caused the tears of every man of understanding to flow. The learning current amongst men I studied not; their schools I entered not. Ask of the city wherein I dwelt, that thou mayest be well assured that I am not of them who speak falsely. This is but a leaf which the winds of the will of thy Lord, the Almighty, the All-Praised, have stirred. Can it be still when the tempestuous winds are blowing? Nay, by Him Who is the Lord of all Names and Attributes! They move it as they list. The evanescent is as nothing before Him Who is the Ever-Abiding. His all-compelling summons hath reached Me, and caused Me to speak His praise amidst all people. I was indeed as one dead when His behest was uttered. The hand of the will of thy Lord, the Compassionate, the Merciful, transformed Me. Can any one speak forth of his own accord that for which all men, both high and low, will protest against him? Nay, by Him Who taught the Pen the eternal mysteries, save him whom the grace of the Almighty, the All-Powerful, hath strengthened. The Pen of the Most High addresseth Me saying: Fear not. Relate unto His Majesty the Sháh that which befell thee. His heart, verily, is between the fingers of thy Lord, the God of Mercy, that haply the sun of justice and bounty may shine forth above the horizon of his heart. Thus hath the decree been irrevocably fixed by Him Who is the All-Wise.

Look upon this Youth, O King, with the eyes of justice; judge thou, then, with truth concerning what hath befallen Him. Of a verity, God hath made thee His shadow amongst men, and the sign of His power unto all that dwell on earth. Judge thou between Us and them that have wronged Us without proof and without an enlightening Book. They that surround thee love thee for their own sakes, whereas this Youth loveth thee for thine own sake, and hath had no desire except to draw thee nigh unto the seat of grace, and to turn thee toward the right-hand of justice. Thy Lord beareth witness unto that which I declare.

O King! Wert thou to incline thine ear unto the shrill of the Pen of Glory and the cooing of the Dove of Eternity which, on the branches of the Lote-Tree beyond which there is no passing, uttereth praises to God, the Maker of all names and Creator of earth and heaven, thou wouldst attain unto a station from which thou wouldst behold in the world of being naught save the effulgence of the Adored One, and wouldst regard thy sovereignty as the most contemptible of thy possessions, abandoning it to whosoever might desire it, and setting thy face toward the Horizon aglow with the light of His countenance. Neither wouldst thou ever be willing to bear the burden of dominion save for the purpose of helping thy Lord, the Exalted, the Most High. Then would the Concourse on high bless thee. O how excellent is this most sublime station, couldst thou ascend thereunto through the power of a sovereignty recognized as derived from the Name of God! . . .

O King of the age! The eyes of these refugees are turned towards and fixed upon the mercy of the Most Merciful. No doubt is there whatever that these tribulations will be followed by the outpourings of a supreme mercy, and these dire adversities be succeeded by an overflowing prosperity. We fain would hope, however, that His Majesty the Sháh will himself examine these matters, and bring hope to the hearts. That which We have submitted to thy Majesty is indeed for thine highest good. And God, verily, is a sufficient witness unto Me. . .

O would that thou wouldst permit Me, O Sháh, to send unto thee that which would cheer the eyes, and tranquillize the souls, and persuade every fair-minded person that with Him is the knowledge of the Book. . . But for the repudiation of the foolish and the connivance of the divines, I would have uttered a discourse that would have thrilled and carried away the hearts unto a realm from the murmur of whose winds can be heard: "No God is there but He!". . .

I have seen, O Sháh, in the path of God what eye hath not seen nor ear heard. . . How numerous the tribulations which have rained, and will soon rain, upon Me! I advance with My face set towards Him Who is the Almighty, the All-Bounteous, whilst behind Me glideth the serpent. Mine eyes have rained down tears until My bed is drenched. I sorrow not for Myself, however. By God! Mine head yearneth for the spear out of love for its Lord. I never passed a tree, but Mine heart addressed it saying: "O would that thou wert cut down in My name, and My body crucified upon thee, in the path of My Lord!". . . By God! Though weariness lay Me low, and hunger consume Me, and the bare rock be My bed, and My fellows the beasts of the field, I will not complain, but will endure patiently as those endued with constancy and firmness have endured patiently, through the power of God, the Eternal King and Creator of the nations, and will render thanks unto God under all conditions. We pray that, out of His bounty—exalted be He—He may release, through this imprisonment, the necks of men from chains and fetters, and cause them to turn, with sincere faces, towards His Face, Who is the Mighty, the Bounteous. Ready is He to answer whosoever calleth upon Him, and nigh is He unto such as commune with Him.

9. TO POPE PIUS IX

¶ 10. O Pope! Rend the veils asunder. He Who is the Lord of Lords is come overshadowed with clouds, and the decree hath been fulfilled by God, the Almighty, the Unrestrained. . . He, verily, hath again come down from Heaven even as He came down from it the first time. Beware that thou dispute not with Him even as the Pharisees disputed with Him[1] without a clear token or proof. On His right hand flow the living waters of grace, and on His left the choice Wine of justice, whilst before Him march the angels of Paradise, bearing the banners of His signs. Beware lest any name debar thee from God, the Creator of earth and heaven. Leave thou the world behind thee, and turn towards thy Lord, through Whom the whole earth hath been illumined. . . Dwellest thou in palaces whilst He Who is the King of revelation liveth in the most desolate of abodes? Leave them unto such as desire them, and set thy face with joy and delight towards the Kingdom. . . Arise in the name of thy Lord, the God of Mercy, amidst the peoples of the earth, and seize thou the Cup of Life with the hands of confidence, and first drink thou therefrom, and proffer it then to such as turn towards it amongst the peoples of all faiths. . .

Call thou to remembrance Him Who was the Spirit,[1] Who when He came, the most learned of His age pronounced judgment against Him in His own country, whilst he who was only a fisherman believed in Him. Take heed, then, ye men of understanding heart! Thou, in truth, art one of the suns of the heaven of His names. Guard thyself, lest darkness spread its veil over thee, and

[1] Jesus.

fold thee away from His light. . . Consider those who opposed the Son,[1] when He came unto them with sovereignty and power. How many the Pharisees who were waiting to behold Him, and were lamenting over their separation from Him! And yet, when the fragrance of His coming was wafted over them, and His beauty was unveiled, they turned aside from Him and disputed with Him. . . None save a very few, who were destitute of any power amongst men, turned towards His face. And yet, today, every man endowed with power and invested with sovereignty prideth himself on His Name! In like manner, consider how numerous, in these days, are the monks who, in My Name, have secluded themselves in their churches, and who, when the appointed time was fulfilled, and We unveiled Our beauty, knew Us not, though they call upon Me at eventide and at dawn. . .

The Word which the Son concealed is made manifest. It hath been sent down in the form of the human temple in this day. Blessed be the Lord Who is the Father! He, verily, is come unto the nations in His most great majesty. Turn your faces towards Him, O concourse of the righteous. . . This is the day whereon the Rock[2] crieth out and shouteth, and celebrateth the praise of its Lord, the All-Possessing, the Most High, saying: "Lo! The Father is come, and that which ye were promised in the Kingdom is fulfilled! . . ." My body longeth for the cross, and Mine head waiteth the thrust of the spear, in the path of the All-Merciful, that the world may be purged from its transgressions. . .

O Supreme Pontiff! Incline thine ear unto that which the Fashioner of mouldering bones counselleth thee, as voiced by Him Who is His Most Great Name. Sell all the embellished ornaments thou dost possess, and expend them in the path of God, Who causeth the night to return upon the day, and the day to return upon the night. Abandon thy kingdom unto the kings, and emerge from thy habitation, with thy face set towards the Kingdom, and, detached from the world, then speak forth the praises of thy Lord betwixt earth and heaven. Thus hath bidden thee He Who is the Possessor of Names, on the part of thy Lord, the Almighty, the All-Knowing. Exhort thou the kings and say: "Deal equitably with men. Beware lest ye transgress the bounds fixed in the Book." This indeed becometh thee. Beware lest thou appropriate unto thyself the things of the world and the riches thereof. Leave them unto such

[1] Jesus.   [2] Peter.

as desire them, and cleave unto that which hath been enjoined upon thee by Him Who is the Lord of creation. Should any one offer thee all the treasures of the earth, refuse to even glance upon them. Be as thy Lord hath been. Thus hath the Tongue of Revelation spoken that which God hath made the ornament of the book of creation. . . Should the inebriation of the wine of My verses seize thee, and thou determinest to present thyself before the throne of thy Lord, the Creator of earth and heaven, make My love thy vesture, and thy shield remembrance of Me, and thy provision reliance upon God, the Revealer of all power. . . Verily, the day of ingathering is come, and all things have been separated from each other. He hath stored away that which He chose in the vessels of justice, and cast into fire that which befitteth it. Thus hath it been decreed by your Lord, the Mighty, the Loving, in this promised Day. He, verily, ordaineth what He pleaseth. There is none other God save He, the Almighty, the All-Compelling.

10. TO THE LEADERS OF RELIGION COLLECTIVELY

¶ 11. Say: O leaders of religion! Weigh not the Book of God with such standards and sciences as are current amongst you, for the Book itself is the unerring balance established amongst men. In this most perfect balance whatsoever the peoples and kindreds of the earth possess must be weighed, while the measure of its weight should be tested according to its own standard, did ye but know it.

The eye of My loving-kindness weepeth sore over you, inasmuch as ye have failed to recognize the One upon Whom ye have been calling in the daytime and in the night season, at even and at morn. Advance, O people, with snow-white faces and radiant hearts, unto the blest and crimson Spot, wherein the Sadratu'l-Muntahá is calling: "Verily, there is none other God beside Me, the Omnipotent Protector, the Self-Subsisting!"

O ye leaders of religion! Who is the man amongst you that can rival Me in vision or insight? Where is he to be found that dareth to claim to be My equal in utterance or wisdom? No, by My Lord, the All-Merciful! All on the earth shall pass away; and this is the face of your Lord, the Almighty, the Well-Beloved.

We have decreed, O people, that the highest and last end of all

learning be the recognition of Him Who is the Object of all knowledge; and yet, behold how ye have allowed your learning to shut
you out, as by a veil, from Him Who is the Day Spring of this
Light, through Whom every hidden thing hath been revealed.
Could ye but discover the source whence the splendour of this utterance is diffused, ye would cast away the peoples of the world and
all that they possess, and would draw nigh unto this most blessed
Seat of glory.

Say: This, verily, is the heaven in which the Mother Book is
treasured, could ye but comprehend it. He it is Who hath caused
the Rock to shout, and the Burning Bush to lift up its voice, upon
the Mount rising above the Holy Land, and proclaim: "The Kingdom is God's, the sovereign Lord of all, the All-Powerful, the
Loving!"

We have not entered any school, nor read any of your disserta-
tions. Incline your ears to the words of this unlettered One, wherewith He summoneth you unto God, the Ever-Abiding. Better is
this for you than all the treasures of the earth, could ye but comprehend it.

¶ 12. Leaders of religion in every age have hindered their people
from attaining the shores of eternal salvation, inasmuch as they held
the reins of authority in their mighty grasp. Some for the lust of
leadership, others through want of knowledge and understanding,
have been the cause of the deprivation of the people. By their sanction and authority, every Prophet of God hath drunk from the
chalice of sacrifice, and winged His flight unto the heights of glory.
What unspeakable cruelties they that have occupied the seats of
authority and learning have inflicted upon the true Monarchs of
the world, those Gems of Divine virtue! Content with a transitory dominion, they have deprived themselves of an everlasting
sovereignty . . .

Among these "veils of glory" are the divines and doctors living
in the days of the Manifestation of God, who, because of their want
of discernment and their love and eagerness for leadership, have
failed to submit to the Cause of God, nay, have even refused to incline their ears unto the Divine Melody. "They have thrust their
fingers into their ears." And the people also, utterly ignoring God
and taking them for their masters, have placed themselves un-

reservedly under the authority of these pompous and hypocritical leaders, for they have no sight, no hearing, no heart of their own to distinguish truth from falsehood.

Notwithstanding the divinely-inspired admonitions of all the Prophets, the Saints, and Chosen Ones of God, enjoining the people to see with their own eyes and hear with their own ears, they have disdainfully rejected their counsels and have blindly followed, and will continue to follow, the leaders of their Faith. Should a poor and obscure person, destitute of the attire of the men of learning, address them saying: "Follow ye, O people, the Messengers of God," they would, greatly surprised at such a statement, reply: "What! Meanest thou that all these divines, all these exponents of learning, with all their authority, their pomp, and pageantry, have erred, and failed to distinguish truth from falsehood? Dost thou and people like thyself, pretend to have comprehended that which they have not understood?" If numbers and excellence of apparel be regarded as the criterions of learning and truth, the peoples of a bygone age, whom those of today have never surpassed in numbers, magnificence, and power, should certainly be accounted a superior and worthier people. . .

Not one Prophet of God was made manifest Who did not fall a victim to the relentless hate, to the denunciation, denial, and execration of the clerics of His day! Woe unto them for the iniquities their hands have formerly wrought! Woe unto them for that which they are now doing! What veils of glory more grievous than these embodiments of error! By the righteousness of God! to pierce such veils is the mightiest of all acts, and to rend them asunder the most meritorious of all deeds! . . .

On their tongue the mention of God hath become an empty name; in their midst His holy Word a dead letter. Such is the sway of their desires, that the lamp of conscience and reason hath been quenched in their hearts. . .

No two are found to agree on one and the same law, for they seek no God but their own desire, and tread no path but the path of error. In leadership they have recognized the ultimate object of their endeavour, and account pride and haughtiness as the highest attainments of their hearts' desire. They have placed their sordid machinations above the Divine decree, have renounced resignation unto the will of God, busied themselves with selfish calculation, and walked in the way of the hypocrite. With all their power and strength they strive to secure themselves in their petty pursuits, fearful lest the least discredit undermine their authority or blemish the display of their magnificence.

¶ 13. Those divines, who are truly adorned with the ornament of knowledge and of a goodly character are, verily, as a head to the body of the world, and as eyes to the nations. The guidance of men hath, at all times, been and is dependent upon these blessed souls.

II. SELECTIONS FROM
"GLEANINGS FROM THE WRITINGS OF
BAHÁ'U'LLÁH"

1. THE DAY OF GOD

¶ 14. The Revelation which, from time immemorial, hath been acclaimed as the Purpose and Promise of all the Prophets of God, and the most cherished Desire of His Messengers, hath now, by virtue of the pervasive Will of the Almighty and at His irresistible bidding, been revealed unto men. The advent of such a Revelation hath been heralded in all the sacred Scriptures. Behold how, notwithstanding such an announcement, mankind hath strayed from its path and shut out itself from its glory.

Say: O ye lovers of the One true God! Strive, that ye may truly recognize and know Him, and observe befittingly His precepts. This is a Revelation, under which, if a man shed for its sake one drop of blood, myriads of oceans will be his recompense. Take heed O friends, that ye forfeit not so inestimable a benefit or disregard its transcendent station. Consider the multitude of lives that have been, and are still being, sacrificed in a world deluded by a mere phantom which the vain imaginations of its people have conceived. Render thanks unto God, inasmuch as ye have attained unto your heart's Desire, and been united to Him Who is the Promise of all nations. Guard ye, with the aid of the one true God—exalted be His glory—the integrity of the station which ye have attained, and cleave to that which shall promote His Cause. He, verily, enjoineth on you what is right and conducive to the exaltation of man's station. Glorified be the All-Merciful, the Revealer of this wondrous Tablet.

¶ 15. This is the Day in which God's most excellent favours have been poured out upon men, the Day in which His most mighty grace hath been infused into all created things. It is incumbent upon all the peoples of the world to reconcile their differences, and, with perfect unity and peace, abide beneath the shadow of the Tree of His care and loving-kindness. It behoveth them to cleave to whatsoever will, in this Day, be conducive to the exaltation of their stations, and to the promotion of their best interests. Happy are those whom the all-glorious Pen was moved to remember, and blessed are those men whose names, by virtue of Our inscrutable decree, We have preferred to conceal.

Beseech ye the one true God to grant that all men may be graciously assisted to fulfil that which is acceptable in Our sight. Soon will the present-day order be rolled up, and a new one spread out in its stead. Verily, thy Lord speaketh the truth, and is the Knower of things unseen.

¶ 16. Verily I say, this is the Day in which mankind can behold the Face, and hear the Voice, of the Promised One. The Call of God hath been raised, and the light of His countenance hath been lifted up upon men. It behoveth every man to blot out the trace of every idle word from the tablet of his heart, and to gaze, with an open and unbiased mind, on the signs of His Revelation, the proofs of His Mission, and the tokens of His glory.

Great indeed is this Day! The allusions made to it in all the sacred Scriptures as the Day of God attest its greatness. The soul of every Prophet of God, of every Divine Messenger, hath thirsted for this wondrous Day. All the divers kindreds of the earth have, likewise, yearned to attain it. No sooner, however, had the Day Star of His Revelation manifested itself in the heaven of God's Will, than all, except those whom the Almighty was pleased to guide, were found dumbfounded and heedless.

O thou that hast remembered Me! The most grievous veil hath shut out the peoples of the earth from His glory, and hindered them from hearkening to His call. God grant that the light of unity may envelop the whole earth, and that the seal, "the Kingdom is God's", may be stamped upon the brow of all its peoples.

¶ 17. By the righteousness of God! These are the days in which God hath proved the hearts of the entire company of His Messengers and Prophets, and beyond them those that stand guard over His sacred and inviolable Sanctuary, the inmates of the celestial Pavilion and dwellers of the Tabernacle of Glory. How severe, therefore, the test to which they who join partners with God must needs be subjected!

¶ 18. The time fore-ordained unto the peoples and kindreds of the earth is now come. The promises of God, as recorded in the holy Scriptures, have all been fulfilled. Out of Zion hath gone forth the Law of God, and Jerusalem, and the hills and land thereof, are filled with the glory of His Revelation. Happy is the man that pondereth in his heart that which hath been revealed in the Books of God, the Help in Peril, the Self-Subsisting. Meditate upon this, O ye beloved of God, and let your ears be attentive unto His Word, so that ye may, by His grace and mercy, drink your fill from the crystal waters of constancy, and become as steadfast and immovable as the mountain in His Cause.

In the Book of Isaiah it is written: "Enter into the rock, and hide thee in the dust, for fear of the Lord, and for the glory of His majesty." No man that meditateth upon this verse can fail to recognize the greatness of this Cause, or doubt the exalted character of this Day—the Day of God Himself. This same verse is followed by these words: "And the Lord alone shall be exalted in that Day." This is the Day which the Pen of the Most High hath glorified in all the holy Scriptures. There is no verse in them that doth not declare the glory of His holy Name, and no Book that doth not testify unto the loftiness of this most exalted theme. Were We to make mention of all that hath been revealed in these heavenly Books and holy Scriptures concerning this Revelation, this Tablet would assume impossible dimensions. It is incumbent, in this Day, upon every man to place his whole trust in the manifold bounties of God, and arise to disseminate, with the utmost wisdom, the verities of His Cause. Then, and only then, will the whole earth be enveloped with the morning light of His Revelation.

¶ 19. Say: O men! This is a matchless Day. Matchless must, likewise, be the tongue that celebrateth the praise of the Desire of all nations, and matchless the deed that aspireth to be acceptable in His sight. The whole human race hath longed for this Day, that perchance it may fulfil that which well beseemeth its station, and is

worthy of its destiny. Blessed is the man whom the affairs of the
world have failed to deter from recognizing Him Who is the Lord
of all things.

So blind hath become the human heart that neither the disruption
of the city, nor the reduction of the mountain in dust, nor even the
cleaving of the earth, can shake off its torpor. The allusions made in
the Scriptures have been unfolded, and the signs recorded therein
have been revealed, and the prophetic cry is continually being
raised. And yet all, except such as God was pleased to guide, are bewildered in the drunkenness of their heedlessness!

Witness how the world is being afflicted with a fresh calamity
every day. Its tribulation is continually deepening. From the
moment the Súriy-i-Ra'ís[1] was revealed until the present day,
neither hath the world been tranquillized, nor have the hearts
of its peoples been at rest. At one time it hath been agitated by
contentions and disputes, at another it hath been convulsed by
wars, and fallen a victim to inveterate diseases. Its sickness is
approaching the stage of utter hopelessness, inasmuch as the true
Physician is debarred from administering the remedy, whilst un-
skilled practitioners are regarded with favour, and are accorded full
freedom to act... The dust of sedition hath clouded the hearts of
men, and blinded their eyes. Ere long, they will perceive the consequences of what their hands have wrought in the Day of God. Thus
warneth you He Who is the All-Informed, as bidden by One Who
is the Most Powerful, the Almighty.

¶ 20. The world's equilibrium hath been upset through the vibrat-
ing influence of this most great, this new World Order. Mankind's
ordered life hath been revolutionized through the agency of this
unique, this wondrous System—the like of which mortal eyes have
never witnessed.

Immerse yourselves in the ocean of My words, that ye may unravel its secrets, and discover all the pearls of wisdom that lie hid in
its depths. Take heed that ye do not vacillate in your determination
to embrace the truth of this Cause—a Cause through which the
potentialities of the might of God have been revealed, and His
sovereignty established. With faces beaming with joy, hasten ye
unto Him. This is the changeless Faith of God, eternal in the past,
eternal in the future. Let him that seeketh, attain it; and as to him
_____
[1] Tablet to Ra'ís.

that hath refused to seek it—verily, God is Self-Sufficient, above any need of His creatures.

Say: This is the infallible Balance which the Hand of God is holding, in which all who are in the heavens and all who are on the earth are weighed, and their fate determined, if ye be of them that believe and recognize this truth. Say: Through it the poor have been enriched, the learned enlightened, and the seekers enabled to ascend unto the presence of God. Beware, lest ye make it a cause of dissension amongst you. Be ye as firmly settled as the immovable mountain in the Cause of your Lord, the Mighty, the Loving.

¶ 21. Let not your hearts be perturbed, O people, when the glory of My Presence is withdrawn, and the ocean of My utterance is stilled. In My presence amongst you there is a wisdom, and in My absence there is yet another, inscrutable to all but God, the Incomparable, the All-Knowing. Verily, We behold you from Our realm of glory and shall aid whosoever will arise for the triumph of Our Cause with the hosts of the Concourse on high and a company of Our favoured angels.

O peoples of the earth! God, the Eternal Truth, is My witness that streams of fresh and soft-flowing waters have gushed from the rocks, through the sweetness of the words uttered by your Lord, the Unconstrained; and still ye slumber. Cast away that which ye possess, and, on the wings of detachment, soar beyond all created things. Thus biddeth you the Lord of creation, the movement of Whose Pen hath revolutionized the soul of mankind.

Know ye from what heights your Lord, the All-Glorious is calling? Think ye that ye have recognized the Pen wherewith your Lord, the Lord of all names, commandeth you? Nay, by My life! Did ye but know it, ye would renounce the world, and would hasten with your whole hearts to the presence of the Well-Beloved. Your spirits would be so transported by His Word as to throw into commotion the Greater World—how much more this small and petty one! Thus have the showers of My bounty been poured down from the heaven of My loving-kindness, as a token of My grace; that ye may be of the thankful. . .

Beware lest the desires of the flesh and of a corrupt inclination provoke divisions among you. Be ye as the fingers of one hand, the members of one body. Thus counselleth you the Pen of Revelation, if ye be of them that believe.

Consider the mercy of God and His gifts. He enjoineth upon you that which shall profit you, though He Himself can well dispense with all creatures. Your evil doings can never harm Us, neither can your good works profit Us. We summon you wholly for the sake of God. To this every man of understanding and insight will testify.

2. GOD AND HIS MANIFESTATIONS

(I) THE UNITY OF GOD

¶ 22. Praise be to God, the All-Possessing, the King of incomparable glory, a praise which is immeasurably above the understanding of all created things, and is exalted beyond the grasp of the minds of men. None else besides Him hath ever been able to sing adequately His praise, nor will any man succeed at any time in describing the full measure of His glory. Who is it that can claim to have attained the heights of His exalted Essence, and what mind can measure the depths of His unfathomable mystery? From each and every revelation emanating from the Source of His glory, holy and neverending evidences of unimaginable splendour have appeared, and out of every manifestation of His invincible power oceans of eternal light have outpoured. How immensely exalted are the wondrous testimonies of His almighty sovereignty, a glimmer of which, if it but touched them, would utterly consume all that are in the heavens and in the earth! How indescribably lofty are the tokens of His consummate power, a single sign of which, however inconsiderable, must transcend the comprehension of whatsoever hath, from the beginning that hath no beginning, been brought into being, or will be created in the future till the end that hath no end. All the Embodiments of His Names wander in the wilderness of search, athirst and eager to discover His Essence, and all the Manifestations of His Attributes implore Him, from the Sinai of Holiness, to unravel His mystery.

A drop of the billowing ocean of His endless mercy hath adorned all creation with the ornament of existence, and a breath wafted from His peerless Paradise hath invested all beings with the robe of

His sanctity and glory. A sprinkling from the unfathomed deep of His sovereign and all-pervasive Will hath, out of utter nothingness, called into being a creation which is infinite in its range and deathless in its duration. The wonders of His bounty can never cease, and the stream of His merciful grace can never be arrested. The process of His creation hath had no beginning, and can have no end.

In every age and cycle He hath, through the splendrous light shed by the Manifestations of His wondrous Essence, recreated all things, so that whatsoever reflecteth in the heavens and on the earth the signs of His glory may not be deprived of the outpourings of His mercy, nor despair of the showers of His favours. How all-encompassing are the wonders of His boundless grace! Behold how they have pervaded the whole of creation. Such is their virtue that not a single atom in the entire universe can be found which doth not declare the evidences of His might, which doth not glorify His holy Name, or is not expressive of the effulgent light of His unity. So perfect and comprehensive is His creation that no mind nor heart, however keen or pure, can ever grasp the nature of the most insignificant of His creatures; much less fathom the mystery of Him Who is the Day Star of Truth, Who is the invisible and unknowable Essence. The conceptions of the devoutest of mystics, the attainments of the most accomplished amongst men, the highest praise which human tongue or pen can render are all the product of man's finite mind and are conditioned by its limitations. Ten thousand Prophets, each a Moses, are thunderstruck upon the Sinai of their search at His forbidding voice, "Thou shalt never behold Me!" whilst a myriad Messengers, each as great as Jesus, stand dismayed upon their heavenly thrones by the interdiction, "Mine Essence thou shalt never apprehend!" From time immemorial He hath been veiled in the ineffable sanctity of His exalted Self, and will everlastingly continue to be wrapt in the impenetrable mystery of His unknowable Essence. Every attempt to attain to an understanding of His inaccessible Reality hath ended in complete bewilderment, and every effort to approach His exalted Self and envisage His Essence hath resulted in hopelessness and failure.

How bewildering to me, insignificant as I am, is the attempt to fathom the sacred depths of Thy knowledge! How futile my efforts to visualize the magnitude of the power inherent in Thine handiwork—the revelation of Thy creative power! How can mine eye, which hath no faculty to perceive itself, claim to have discerned Thine Essence, and how can mine heart, already powerless to apprehend the significance of its own potentialities, pretend to have comprehended Thy nature? How can I claim to have known Thee, when the entire creation is bewildered by Thy mystery, and how can I confess not to have known Thee, when, lo, the whole universe proclaimeth Thy Presence and testifieth to Thy truth? The portals of Thy grace have throughout eternity been open, and the means of access unto Thy Presence made available, unto all created things, and the revelations of Thy matchless Beauty have at all times been imprinted upon the realities of all beings, visible and invisible. Yet, notwithstanding this most gracious favour, this perfect and consummate bestowal, I am moved to testify that Thy court of holiness and glory is immeasurably exalted above the knowledge of all else besides Thee, and the mystery of Thy Presence is inscrutable to every mind except Thine own. No one except Thyself can unravel the secret of Thy nature, and naught else but Thy transcendental Essence can grasp the reality of Thy unsearchable being. How vast the number of those heavenly and all-glorious Beings Who, in the wilderness of their separation from Thee, have wandered all the days of their lives, and failed in the end to find Thee! How great the multitude of the sanctified and immortal Souls Who were lost and bewildered while seeking in the desert of search to behold Thy face! Myriad are Thine ardent Lovers Whom the consuming flame of remoteness from Thee hath caused to sink and perish, and numberless are the faithful Souls Who have willingly laid down their lives in the hope of gazing on the light of Thy countenance. The sighs and moans of these longing hearts that pant after Thee can never reach Thy holy court, neither can the lamentations of the Wayfarers that thirst to appear before Thy face attain Thy seat of glory.

¶ 23. Regard thou the one true God as One Who is apart from, and immeasurably exalted above, all created things. The whole universe reflecteth His glory, while He is Himself independent of, and transcendeth His creatures. This is the true meaning of Divine unity. He Who is the Eternal Truth is the one Power Who exerciseth undisputed sovereignty over the world of being, Whose image is reflected in the mirror of the entire creation. All existence is dependent upon Him, and from Him is derived the source of the sustenance of all things. This is what is meant by Divine unity; this is its fundamental principle.

Some, deluded by their idle fancies, have conceived all created things as associates and partners of God, and imagined themselves to be the exponents of His unity. By Him Who is the one true God! Such men have been, and will continue to remain, the victims of blind imitation, and are to be numbered with them that have restricted and limited the conception of God.

He is a true believer in Divine unity who, far from confusing duality with oneness, refuseth to allow any notion of multiplicity to becloud his conception of the singleness of God, who will regard the Divine Being as One Who, by His very nature, transcendeth the limitations of numbers.

The essence of belief in Divine unity consisteth in regarding Him Who is the Manifestation of God and Him Who is the invisible, the inaccessible, the unknowable Essence as one and the same. By this is meant that whatever pertaineth to the former, all His acts and doings, whatever He ordaineth or forbiddeth, should be considered in all their aspects, and under all circumstances, and without any reservation, as identical with the Will of God Himself. This is the loftiest station to which a true believer in the unity of God can ever hope to attain. Blessed is the man that reacheth this station, and is of them that are steadfast in their belief.

(II) THE MESSENGERS OF GOD

¶ 24. To every discerning and illuminated heart it is evident that God, the unknowable Essence, the Divine Being, is immensely exalted beyond every human attribute, such as corporeal existence, ascent and descent, egress and regress. Far be it from His glory that human tongue should adequately recount His praise or that human heart comprehend His fathomless mystery. He is, and hath ever been, veiled in the ancient eternity of His Essence, and will remain in His Reality everlastingly hidden from the sight of men. "No vision taketh in Him, but He taketh in all vision; He is the Subtile, the All-Perceiving." . . .

The door of the knowledge of the Ancient of Days being thus closed in the face of all beings, the Source of infinite grace, accord-

ing to His saying, "His grace hath transcended all things; My grace
hath encompassed them all," hath caused those luminous Gems of
Holiness to appear out of the realm of the spirit, in the noble form
of the human temple, and be made manifest unto all men, that they
may impart unto the world the mysteries of the unchangeable Being, and tell of the subtleties of His imperishable Essence.

These sanctified Mirrors, these Day Springs of ancient glory, are,
one and all, the Exponents on earth of Him Who is the central Orb
of the universe, its Essence and ultimate Purpose. From Him proceed their knowledge and power; from Him is derived their
sovereignty. The beauty of their countenance is but a reflection of
His image, and their revelation a sign of His deathless glory. They
are the Treasuries of Divine knowledge, and the Repositories of
celestial wisdom. Through them is transmitted a grace that is infinite, and by them is revealed the Light that can never fade. . .
These Tabernacles of Holiness, these Primal Mirrors which reflect
the light of unfading glory, are but expressions of Him Who is the
Invisible of the Invisibles. By the revelation of these Gems of
Divine virtue all the names and attributes of God, such as knowledge and power, sovereignty and dominion, mercy and wisdom,
glory, bounty, and grace, are made manifest.

These attributes of God are not, and have never been, vouchsafed specially unto certain Prophets, and withheld from others.
Nay, all the Prophets of God, His well-favoured, His holy and
chosen Messengers are, without exception, the bearers of His names
and the embodiments of His attributes. They only differ in the intensity of their revelation, and the comparative potency of their
light. Even as He hath revealed: "Some of the Apostles We have
caused to excel the others."

It hath, therefore, become manifest and evident that within the
tabernacles of these Prophets and chosen Ones of God the light of
His infinite names and exalted attributes hath been reflected, even
though the light of some of these attributes may or may not be outwardly revealed from these luminous Temples to the eyes of men.
That a certain attribute of God hath not been outwardly manifested
by these Essences of Detachment doth in no wise imply that they
who are the Day Springs of God's attributes and the Treasuries of
His holy names did not actually possess it. Therefore, these illuminated Souls, these beauteous Countenances have, each and every one

of them, been endowed with all the attributes of God, such as sovereignty, dominion, and the like, even though to outward seeming they be shorn of all earthly majesty...

¶ 25. O Salmán! The door of the knowledge of the Ancient Being hath ever been, and will continue for ever to be, closed in the face of men. No man's understanding shall ever gain access unto His holy court. As a token of His mercy, however, and as a proof of His loving-kindness, He hath manifested unto men the Day Stars of His divine guidance, the Symbols of His divine unity, and hath ordained the knowledge of these sanctified Beings to be identical with the knowledge of His own Self. Whoso recognizeth them hath recognized God. Whoso hearkeneth to their call, hath hearkened to the Voice of God, and whoso testifieth to the truth of their Revelation, hath testified to the truth of God Himself. Whoso turneth away from them, hath turned away from God, and whoso disbelieveth in them, hath disbelieved in God. Every one of them is the Way of God that connecteth this world with the realms above, and the Standard of His Truth unto everyone in the kingdoms of earth and heaven. They are the Manifestations of God amidst men, the evidences of His Truth, and the signs of His glory.

¶ 26. The Bearers of the Trust of God are made manifest unto the peoples of the earth as the Exponents of a new Cause and the Revealers of a new Message. Inasmuch as these Birds of the celestial Throne are all sent down from the heaven of the Will of God, they, therefore, are regarded as one soul and the same person. For they all drink from the one Cup of the love of God, and all partake of the fruit of the same Tree of Oneness.

These Manifestations of God have each a twofold station. One is the station of pure abstraction and essential unity. In this respect, if thou callest them all by one name, and dost ascribe to them the same attributes, thou hast not erred from the truth. Even as He hath revealed: "No distinction do We make between any of His Messengers." For they, one and all, summon the people of the earth to acknowledge the unity of God, and herald unto them the Kawthar of an infinite grace and bounty. They are all invested with the robe of prophethood, and are honoured with the mantle of glory. Thus hath Muḥammad, the Point of the Qur'án, revealed: "I am all the

Prophets." Likewise, He saith: "I am the first Adam, Noah, Moses, and Jesus." Similar statements have been made by Imám 'Alí. Sayings such as these, which indicate the essential unity of those Exponents of Oneness, have also emanated from the Channels of God's immortal utterance, and the Treasuries of the gems of Divine knowledge, and have been recorded in the Scriptures. These Countenances are the recipients of the Divine Command, and the Day Springs of His Revelation. This Revelation is exalted above the veils of plurality and the exigencies of number. Thus He saith: "Our Cause is but One." Inasmuch as the Cause is one and the same, the Exponents thereof also must needs be one and the same. Likewise, the Imáms of the Muḥammadan Faith, those lamps of certitude, have said: "Muḥammad is our first, Muḥammad is our last, Muḥammad our all."

It is clear and evident to thee that all the Prophets are the Temples of the Cause of God, Who have appeared clothed in divers attire. If thou wilt observe with discriminating eyes, thou wilt behold them all abiding in the same tabernacle, soaring in the same heaven, seated upon the same throne, uttering the same speech, and proclaiming the same Faith. Such is the unity of those Essences of Being, those Luminaries of infinite and immeasurable splendour! Wherefore, should one of these Manifestations of Holiness proclaim saying: "I am the return of all the Prophets," He, verily, speaketh the truth. In like manner, in every subsequent Revelation, the return of the former Revelation is a fact, the truth of which is firmly established. . .

The other station is the station of distinction, and pertaineth to the world of creation, and to the limitations thereof. In this respect, each Manifestation of God hath a distinct individuality, a definitely prescribed mission, a predestined revelation, and specially designated limitations. Each one of them is known by a different name, is characterized by a special attribute, fulfils a definite mission, and is entrusted with a particular Revelation. Even as He saith: "Some of the Apostles We have caused to excel the others. To some God hath spoken, some He hath raised and exalted. And to Jesus, Son of Mary, We gave manifest signs, and We strengthened Him with the Holy Spirit."

It is because of this difference in their station and mission that the words and utterances flowing from these Well Springs of Divine knowledge appear to diverge and differ. Otherwise, in the eyes of them that are initiated into the mysteries of Divine wisdom, all their utterances are, in reality, but the expressions of one Truth. As most of the people have failed to appreciate those stations to which We have referred, they, therefore, feel perplexed and dismayed at the varying utterances pronounced by Manifestations that are essentially one and the same.

It hath ever been evident that all these divergencies of utterance are attributable to differences of station. Thus, viewed from the standpoint of their oneness and sublime detachment, the attributes of Godhead, Divinity, Supreme Singleness, and Inmost Essence, have been, and are applicable to those Essences of Being, inasmuch as they all abide on the throne of Divine Revelation, and are established upon the seat of Divine Concealment. Through their appearance the Revelation of God is made manifest, and by their countenance the Beauty of God is revealed. Thus it is that the accents of God Himself have been heard uttered by these Manifestations of the Divine Being.

Viewed in the light of their second station—the station of distinction, differentiation, temporal limitations, characteristics and standards—they manifest absolute servitude, utter destitution, and complete self-effacement. Even as He saith: "I am the servant of God. I am but a man like you." . . .

Were any of the all-embracing Manifestations of God to declare: "I am God," He, verily, speaketh the truth, and no doubt attacheth thereto. For it hath been repeatedly demonstrated that through their Revelation, their attributes and names, the Revelation of God, His names and His attributes, are made manifest in the world. Thus, He hath revealed: "Those shafts were God's, not Thine." And also He saith: "In truth, they who plighted fealty unto thee, really plighted that fealty unto God." And were any of them to voice the utterance, "I am the Messenger of God," He, also, speaketh the truth, the indubitable truth. Even as He said: "Muḥammad is not the father of any man among you, but He is the Messenger of God." Viewed in this light, they are all but Messengers of that ideal King, that unchangeable Essence. And were they all to proclaim, "I am the Seal of the Prophets," they, verily, utter but the truth, beyond the faintest shadow of doubt. For they are all but one person, one soul, one spirit, one being, one revelation. They are all the manifestation of the "Beginning" and the "End", the "First" and the "Last," the "Seen" and "Hidden"—all of which pertain to Him Who is the Innermost Spirit of Spirits and Eternal Essence of Essences. And were they to say, "We are the Servants of God," this also is a manifest and indisputable fact. For they have been made manifest in the uttermost state of servitude, a servitude the like of which no man can possibly attain. Thus in moments in which these Essences of Being were deep immersed beneath the oceans of ancient and everlasting holiness, or when they soared to the loftiest summits of Divine mysteries, they claimed their utterances to be the Voice of Divinity, the Call of God Himself.

Were the eye of discernment to be opened, it would recognize that in this very state, they have considered themselves utterly effaced and non-existent in the face of Him Who is the All-Pervading, the Incorruptible. Methinks, they have regarded themselves as utter nothingness, and deemed their mention in that Court an act of blasphemy. For the slightest whisperings of self within such a Court is an evidence of self-assertion and independent existence. In the eyes of them that have attained unto that Court, such a suggestion is itself a grievous transgression. How much more grievous would it be, were aught else to be mentioned in that Presence, were man's heart, his tongue, his mind, or his soul, to be busied with any one but the Well-Beloved, were his eyes to behold any countenance other than His beauty, were his ear to be inclined to any melody but His Voice, and were his feet to tread any way but His way. . .

By virtue of this station they have claimed for themselves the Voice of Divinity and the like, whilst by virtue of their station of Messengership, they have declared themselves the Messengers of God. In every instance they have voiced an utterance that would conform to the requirements of the occasion, and have ascribed all these declarations to Themselves, declarations ranging from the realm of Divine Revelation to the realm of creation, and from the domain of Divinity even unto the domain of earthly existence. Thus it is that whatsoever be their utterance, whether it pertain to the realm of Divinity, Lordship, Prophethood, Messengership, Guardianship, Apostleship, or Servitude, all is true, beyond the shadow of a doubt. Therefore these sayings which We have quoted in support of Our argument must be attentively considered, that the divergent utterances of the Manifestations of the Unseen and Day Springs of Holiness may cease to agitate the soul and perplex the mind.

¶ 27. Beware, O believers in the Unity of God, lest ye be tempted to make any distinction between any of the Manifestations of His Cause, or to discriminate against the signs that have accompanied and proclaimed their Revelation. This indeed is the true meaning of Divine Unity, if ye be of them that apprehend and believe this truth. Be ye assured, moreover, that the works and acts of each and every one of these Manifestations of God, nay whatever pertaineth unto them, and whatsoever they may manifest in the future, are all ordained by God, and are a reflection of His Will and Purpose. Whoso maketh the slightest possible difference between their persons, their words, their messages, their acts and manners, hath indeed disbelieved in God, hath repudiated His signs, and betrayed the Cause of His Messengers.

¶ 28. It is evident that every age in which a Manifestation of God hath lived is divinely ordained, and may, in a sense, be characterized as God's appointed Day. This Day, however, is unique, and is to be distinguished from those that have preceded it. The designation "Seal of the Prophets" fully revealeth its high station. The Prophetic Cycle hath, verily, ended. The Eternal Truth is now come. He hath lifted up the Ensign of Power, and is now shedding upon the world the unclouded splendour of His Revelation.

(III) DIVINE REVELATION

¶ 29. Know of a certainty that in every Dispensation the light of Divine Revelation hath been vouchsafed unto men in direct proportion to their spiritual capacity. Consider the sun. How feeble its rays the moment it appeareth above the horizon. How gradually its warmth and potency increase as it approacheth its zenith, enabling meanwhile all created things to adapt themselves to the growing intensity of its light. How steadily it declineth until it reacheth its setting point. Were it, all of a sudden, to manifest the energies latent within it, it would, no doubt, cause injury to all created things... In like manner, if the Sun of Truth were suddenly to reveal, at the earliest stages of its manifestation, the full measure of the potencies which the providence of the Almighty hath bestowed upon it, the earth of human understanding would waste away and be consumed; for men's hearts would neither sustain the intensity of its revelation, nor be able to mirror forth the radiance of its light. Dismayed and overpowered, they would cease to exist.

¶ 30. The vitality of men's belief in God is dying out in every land; nothing short of His wholesome medicine can ever restore it. The corrosion of ungodliness is eating into the vitals of human society; what else but the Elixir of His potent Revelation can cleanse and revive it? Is it within human power, O Ḥakím, to effect in the constituent elements of any of the minute and indivisible particles of matter so complete a transformation as to transmute it into purest gold? Perplexing and difficult as this may appear, the still greater task of converting satanic strength into heavenly power is one that We have been empowered to accomplish. The Force capable of such a transformation transcendeth the potency of the Elixir itself. The Word of God, alone, can claim the distinction of being endowed with the capacity required for so great and far-reaching a change.

¶ 31. Every word that proceedeth out of the mouth of God is endowed with such potency as can instil new life into every human frame, if ye be of them that comprehend this truth. All the wondrous works ye behold in this world have been manifested through the operation of His supreme and most exalted Will, His wondrous and inflexible Purpose. Through the mere revelation of the word "Fashioner", issuing forth from His lips and proclaiming His attribute to mankind, such power is released as can generate, through successive ages, all the manifold arts which the hands of man can produce. This, verily, is a certain truth. No sooner is this resplendent word uttered, than its animating energies, stirring within all created things, give birth to the means and instruments whereby such arts can be produced and perfected. All the wondrous achievements ye now witness are the direct consequences of the Revelation of this Name. In the days to come, ye will, verily, behold things of which ye have never heard before. Thus hath it been decreed in the Tablets of God, and none can comprehend it except they whose sight is sharp. In like manner, the moment the word expressing My attribute "The Omniscient" issueth forth from My mouth, every created thing will, according to its capacity and limitations, be invested with the power to unfold the knowledge of the most marvellous sciences, and will be empowered to manifest them in the course of time at the bidding of Him Who is the Almighty, the All-Knowing. Know thou of a certainty that the Revelation of every other Name is accompanied by a similar manifestation of Divine power. Every single letter proceeding out of the mouth of God is indeed a mother letter, and every word uttered by Him Who is the Well Spring of Divine Revelation is a mother word, and His Tablet a Mother Tablet. Well is it with them that apprehend this truth.

¶ 32. Know assuredly that just as thou firmly believest that the Word of God, exalted be His glory, endureth for ever, thou must, likewise, believe with undoubting faith that its meaning can never be exhausted. They who are its appointed interpreters, they whose hearts are the repositories of its secrets, are, however, the only ones who can comprehend its manifold wisdom. Whoso, while reading the Sacred Scriptures, is tempted to choose therefrom whatever may suit him with which to challenge the authority of the Representative of God among men, is, indeed, as one dead, though to outward seeming, he may walk and converse with his neighbours, and share with them their food and their drink.

O, would that the world could believe Me! Were all the things that lie enshrined within the heart of Bahá, and which the Lord, His God, the Lord of all names, hath taught Him, to be unveiled to mankind, every man on earth would be dumbfounded.

How great the multitude of truths which the garment of words can never contain! How vast the number of such verities as no expression can adequately describe, whose significance can never be unfolded, and to which not even the remotest allusions can be made! How manifold are the truths which must remain unuttered until the appointed time is come! Even as it hath been said: "Not everything that a man knoweth can be disclosed, nor can everything that he can disclose be regarded as timely, nor can every timely utterance be considered as suited to the capacity of those who hear it."

Of these truths some can be disclosed only to the extent of the capacity of the repositories of the light of Our knowledge, and the recipients of Our hidden grace. We beseech God to strengthen thee with His power and enable thee to recognize Him Who is the Source of all knowledge, that thou mayest detach thyself from all human learning, for, "what would it profit any man to strive after learning when he hath already found and recognized Him Who is the Object of all knowledge?" Cleave to the Root of Knowledge, and to Him Who is the Fountain thereof, that thou mayest find thyself independent of all who claim to be well versed in human learning, and whose claim no clear proof, nor the testimony of any enlightening book, can support.

(IV) THE SEQUENCE OF THE PROPHETS

¶ 33. Consider the past. How many, both high and low, have, at all times, yearningly awaited the advent of the Manifestations of God in the sanctified persons of His chosen Ones. How often have they expected His coming, how frequently have they prayed that the breeze of Divine mercy might blow, and the promised Beauty step forth from behind the veil of concealment, and be made manifest to all the world. And whensoever the portals of grace did open, and the clouds of divine bounty did rain upon mankind, and the light of the Unseen did shine above the horizon of celestial might, they all denied Him, and turned away from His face—the face of God Himself. . .

Reflect, what could have been the motive for such deeds? What could have prompted such behaviour towards the Revealers of the beauty of the All-Glorious? Whatever in days gone by hath been the cause of the denial and opposition of those people hath now led to the perversity of the people of this age. To maintain that the testimony of Providence was incomplete, that it hath therefore been the cause of the denial of the people, is but open blasphemy. How far from the grace of the All-Bountiful and from His loving providence and tender mercies it is to single out a soul from amongst all men for the guidance of His creatures, and, on one hand, to withhold from Him the full measure of His divine testimony, and, on the other, inflict severe retribution on His people for having turned away from His chosen One! Nay, the manifold bounties of the

Lord of all beings have, at all times, through the Manifestations of His Divine Essence, encompassed the earth and all that dwell therein. Not for a moment hath His grace been withheld, nor have the showers of His loving-kindness ceased to rain upon mankind. Consequently, such behaviour can be attributed to naught save the petty-mindedness of such souls as tread the valley of arrogance and pride, are lost in the wilds of remoteness, walk in the ways of their idle fancy, and follow the dictates of the leaders of their faith. Their chief concern is mere opposition; their sole desire is to ignore the truth. Unto every discerning observer it is evident and manifest that had these people in the days of each of the Manifestations of the Sun of Truth sanctified their eyes, their ears, and their hearts from whatever they had seen, heard, and felt, they surely would not have been deprived of beholding the beauty of God, nor strayed far from the habitations of glory. But having weighed the testimony of God by the standard of their own knowledge, gleaned from the teachings of the leaders of their faith, and found it at variance with their limited understanding, they arose to perpetrate such unseemly acts. . .

Consider Moses! Armed with the rod of celestial dominion, adorned with the white hand of Divine knowledge, and proceeding from the Párán of the love of God, and wielding the serpent of power and everlasting majesty, He shone forth from the Sinai of light upon the world. He summoned all the peoples and kindreds of the earth to the kingdom of eternity, and invited them to partake of the fruit of the tree of faithfulness. Surely you are aware of the fierce opposition of Pharaoh and his people, and of the stones of idle fancy which the hands of infidels cast upon that blessed Tree. So much so that Pharaoh and his people finally arose and exerted their utmost endeavour to extinguish with the waters of falsehood and denial the fire of that sacred Tree, oblivious of the truth that no earthly water can quench the flames of Divine wisdom, nor mortal blasts extinguish the lamp of everlasting dominion. Nay, rather, such water cannot but intensify the burning of the flame, and such blasts cannot but ensure the preservation of the lamp, were ye to observe with the eye of discernment, and walk in the way of God's holy will and pleasure. . .

And when the days of Moses were ended, and the light of Jesus, shining forth from the Day Spring of the Spirit, encompassed the world, all the people of Israel arose in protest against Him. They clamoured that He Whose advent the Bible had foretold must needs promulgate and fulfil the laws of Moses, whereas this youthful Nazarene, who laid claim to the station of the divine Messiah, had annulled the law of divorce and of the sabbath day—the most weighty of all the laws of Moses. Moreover, what of the signs of the Manifestation yet to come? These people of Israel are even unto the present day still expecting that Manifestation which the Bible hath foretold! How many Manifestations of Holiness, how many Revealers of the light everlasting, have appeared since the time of Moses, and yet Israel, wrapt in the densest veils of satanic fancy and false imaginings, is still expectant that the idol of her own handiwork will appear with such signs as she herself hath conceived! Thus hath God laid hold of them for their sins, hath extinguished in them the spirit of faith, and tormented them with the flames of the nethermost fire. And this for no other reason except that Israel refused to apprehend the meaning of such words as have been revealed in the Bible concerning the signs of the coming Revelation. As she never grasped their true significance, and, to outward seeming, such events never came to pass, she, therefore, remained deprived of recognizing the beauty of Jesus and of beholding the Face of God. And they still await His coming! From time immemorial even unto this day, all the kindreds and peoples of the earth have clung to such fanciful and unseemly thoughts, and thus have deprived themselves of the clear waters streaming from the springs of purity and holiness. . .

To them that are endowed with understanding, it is clear and manifest that, when the fire of the love of Jesus consumed the veils of Jewish limitations, and His authority was made apparent and partially enforced, He, the Revealer of the unseen Beauty, addressing one day His disciples, referred unto His passing, and, kindling in their hearts the fire of bereavement, said unto them: "I go away and come again unto you." And in another place He said: "I go and another will come, Who will tell you all that I have not told you, and will fulfil all that I have said." Both these sayings have but one meaning, were ye to ponder upon the Manifestations of the Unity of God with Divine insight.

Every discerning observer will recognize that in the Dispensation of the Qur'án both the Book and the Cause of Jesus were confirmed.

As to the matter of names, Muḥammad, Himself, declared: "I am Jesus." He recognized the truth of the signs, prophecies, and words of Jesus, and testified that they were all of God. In this sense, neither the person of Jesus nor His writings hath differed from that of Muḥammad and of His holy Book, inasmuch as both have championed the Cause of God, uttered His praise, and revealed His commandments. Thus it is that Jesus, Himself, declared: "I go away and come again unto you." Consider the sun. Were it to say now, "I am the sun of yesterday," it would speak the truth. And should it, bearing the sequence of time in mind, claim to be other than that sun, it still would speak the truth. In like manner, if it be said that all the days are but one and the same, it is correct and true. And if it be said, with respect to their particular names and designations, that they differ, that again is true. For though they are the same, yet one doth recognize in each a separate designation, a specific attribute, a particular character. Conceive accordingly the distinction, variation, and unity characteristic of the various Manifestations of holiness, that thou mayest comprehend the allusions made by the Creator of all names and attributes to the mysteries of distinction and unity, and discover the answer to thy question as to why that everlasting Beauty should have, at sundry times, called Himself by different names and titles. . .

When the Unseen, the Eternal, the Divine Essence, caused the Day Star of Muḥammad to rise above the horizon of knowledge, among the cavils which the Jewish divines raised against Him was that after Moses no Prophet should be sent of God. Yea, mention hath been made in the scriptures of a Soul Who must needs be made manifest and Who will advance the Faith, and promote the interests of the people of Moses, so that the Law of the Mosaic Dispensation may encompass the whole earth. Thus hath the King of eternal glory referred in His Book to the words uttered by those wanderers in the vale of remoteness and error: " 'The hand of God,' say the Jews, 'is chained up.' Chained up be their own hands! And for that which they have said, they were accursed. Nay, outstretched are both His hands!" "The hand of God is above their hands." Although the commentators of the Qur'án have related in divers manners the circumstances attending the revelation of this verse, yet thou shouldst endeavour to apprehend the purpose thereof. He saith: How false is that which the Jews have imagined! How can the hand of Him Who is the King in truth, Who caused the countenance of Moses to be made manifest, and conferred upon Him the robe of Prophethood—how can the hand of such a One be chained and fettered? How can He be conceived as powerless to raise up yet another Messenger after Moses? Behold the absurdity of their saying; how far it hath strayed from the path of knowledge and understanding! Observe how in this Day also, all these people have occupied themselves with such foolish absurdities. For over a thousand years they have been reciting this verse, and unwittingly pronouncing their censure against the Jews, utterly unaware that they themselves, openly and privily, are voicing the sentiments and belief of the Jewish people Thou art surely aware of their idle contention, that all Revelation is ended, that the portals of Divine mercy are closed, that from the day springs of eternal holiness no Sun shall rise again, that the Ocean of everlasting bounty is forever stilled, and that out of the Tabernacle of ancient glory the Messengers of God have ceased to be made manifest. Such is the measure of the understanding of these small-minded, contemptible people. These people have imagined that the flow of God's all-encompassing grace and plenteous mercies, the cessation of which no mind can contemplate, has been halted. From every side they have risen and girded up the loins of tyranny, and exerted the utmost endeavour to quench with the bitter waters of their vain fancy the flame of God's Burning Bush, oblivious that the globe of power shall, within its own mighty stronghold, protect the Lamp of God. . .

Behold how the sovereignty of Muḥammad, the Messenger of God, is today apparent and manifest amongst the people. You are well aware of what befell His Faith in the early days of His Dispensation. What woeful sufferings did the hand of the infidel and erring, the divines of that age and their associates, inflict upon that spiritual Essence, that most pure and holy Being! How abundant the thorns and briars which they have strewn over His path! It is evident that that wretched generation, in their wicked and satanic fancy, regarded every injury to that immortal Being as a means to the attainment of an abiding felicity; inasmuch as the recognized divines of that age, such as 'Abdu'lláh-i-Ubayy, Abú 'Ámir, the hermit, Ka'b-Ibn-i-Ashraf, and Naḍr-Ibn-i-Ḥárith, all treated Him as an impostor, and pronounced Him a lunatic and a calumniator. Such sore accusations they brought against Him that in recounting them God forbiddeth the ink to flow, Our pen to move, or the page to bear them. These malicious imputations provoked the people to arise and torment Him. And how fierce that torment, if the divines of the age be its chief instigators, if they denounce Him to their followers, cast Him out from their midst, and declare Him a miscreant! Hath not the same befallen this Servant, and been witnessed by all?

For this reason did Muḥammad cry out: "No Prophet of God hath suffered such harm as I have suffered." And in the Qur'án are recorded all the calumnies and reproaches uttered against Him, as well as all the afflictions which He suffered. Refer ye thereunto, that haply ye may be informed of that which hath befallen His Revelation. So grievous was His plight, that for a time all ceased to hold intercourse with Him and His companions. Whoever associated with Him fell a victim to the relentless cruelty of His enemies. . .

Consider, how great is the change today! Behold, how many are the Sovereigns who bow the knee before His name! How numerous the nations and kingdoms who have sought the shelter of His shadow, who bear allegiance to His Faith, and pride themselves therein! From the pulpit-top there ascendeth today the words of praise which, in utter lowliness, glorify His blessed name; and from the heights of minarets there resoundeth the call that summoneth the concourse of His people to adore Him. Even those Kings of the earth who have refused to embrace His Faith and to put off the garment of unbelief, none-the-less confess and acknowledge the greatness and overpowering majesty of that Day Star of loving-kindness. Such is His earthly sovereignty, the evidences of which thou dost on every side behold. This sovereignty must needs be revealed and established either in the lifetime of every Manifestation of God or after His ascension unto His true habitation in the realms above. . .

It is evident that the changes brought about in every Dispensation constitute the dark clouds that intervene between the eye of man's understanding and the Divine Luminary which shineth forth from the day spring of the Divine Essence. Consider how men for generations have been blindly imitating their fathers, and have been trained according to such ways and manners as have been laid down by the dictates of their Faith. Were these men, therefore, to discover suddenly that a Man, Who hath been living in their midst,

Who, with respect to every human limitation, hath been their equal, had risen to abolish every established principle imposed by their Faith—principles by which for centuries they have been disciplined, and every opposer and denier of which they have come to regard as infidel, profligate and wicked—they would of a certainty be veiled and hindered from acknowledging His truth. Such things are as "clouds" that veil the eyes of those whose inner being hath not tasted the Salsabíl of detachment, nor drunk from the Kawthar of the knowledge of God. Such men, when acquainted with those circumstances, become so veiled that, without the least question, they pronounce the Manifestation of God as infidel, and sentence Him to death. You must have heard of such things taking place all down the ages, and are now observing them in these days.

It behoveth us, therefore, to make the utmost endeavour, that, by God's invisible assistance, these dark veils, these clouds of Heaven-sent trials, may not hinder us from beholding the beauty of His shining Countenance, and that we may recognize Him only by His own Self.

¶ 34. Know thou that when the Son of Man yielded up His breath to God, the whole creation wept with a great weeping. By sacrificing Himself, however, a fresh capacity was infused into all created things. Its evidences, as witnessed in all the peoples of the earth, are now manifest before thee. The deepest wisdom which the sages have uttered, the profoundest learning which any mind hath unfolded, the arts which the ablest hands have produced, the influence exerted by the most potent of rulers, are but manifestations of the quickening power released by His transcendent, His all-pervasive, and resplendent Spirit.

We testify that when He came into the world, He shed the splendour of His glory upon all created things. Through Him the leper recovered from the leprosy of perversity and ignorance. Through Him, the unchaste and wayward were healed. Through His power, born of Almighty God, the eyes of the blind were opened, and the soul of the sinner sanctified.

Leprosy may be interpreted as any veil that interveneth between man and the recognition of the Lord, his God. Whoso alloweth himself to be shut out from Him is indeed a leper, who shall not be remembered in the Kingdom of God, the Mighty, the All-Praised.

We bear witness that through the power of the Word of God every leper was cleansed, every sickness was healed, every human infirmity was banished. He it is Who purified the world. Blessed is the man who, with a face beaming with light, hath turned towards Him.

(v) THE GLORY OF GOD

¶ 35. O Jews! If ye be intent on crucifying once again Jesus, the Spirit of God, put Me to death, for He hath once more, in My person, been made manifest unto you. Deal with Me as ye wish, for I have vowed to lay down My life in the path of God. I will fear no one, though the powers of earth and heaven be leagued against Me. Followers of the Gospel! If ye cherish the desire to slay Muḥammad, the Apostle of God, seize Me and put an end to My life, for I am He, and My Self is His Self. Do unto Me as you like, for the deepest longing of Mine heart is to attain the presence of My Best-Beloved in His Kingdom of Glory. Such is the Divine decree, if ye know it. Followers of Muḥammad! If it be your wish to riddle with your shafts the breast of Him Who hath caused His Book the Bayán to be sent down unto you, lay hands on Me and persecute Me, for I am His Well-Beloved, the revelation of His own Self, though My name be not His name. I have come in the shadows of the clouds of glory, and am invested by God with invincible sovereignty. He, verily, is the Truth, the Knower of things unseen. I, verily, anticipate from you the treatment ye have accorded unto Him that came before Me. To this all things, verily, witness, if ye be of those who hearken. O people of the Bayán! If ye have resolved to shed the blood of Him Whose coming the Báb hath proclaimed, Whose advent Muḥammad hath prophesied, and Whose Revelation Jesus Christ Himself hath announced, behold Me standing, ready and defenceless, before you. Deal with Me after your own desires.

¶ 36. The Ancient Beauty hath consented to be bound with chains that mankind may be released from its bondage, and hath accepted to be made a prisoner within this most mighty Stronghold that the whole world may attain unto true liberty. He hath drained to its dregs the cup of sorrow, that all the peoples of the earth may attain unto abiding joy, and be filled with gladness. This is of the mercy of your Lord, the Compassionate, the Most Merciful. We have accepted to be abased, O believers in the Unity of God, that ye may be exalted, and have suffered manifold afflictions, that ye might prosper and flourish. He Who hath come to build anew the whole world, behold, how they that have joined partners with God have forced Him to dwell within the most desolate of cities!

¶ 37. I sorrow not for the burden of My imprisonment. Neither do I grieve over My abasement, or the tribulation I suffer at the hands of Mine enemies. By My life! They are My glory, a glory wherewith God hath adorned His own Self. Would that ye knew it!

The shame I was made to bear hath uncovered the glory with which the whole of creation had been invested, and through the cruelties I have endured, the Day Star of Justice hath manifested itself, and shed its splendour upon men.

My sorrows are for those who have involved themselves in their corrupt passions, and claim to be associated with the Faith of God, the Gracious, the All-Praised.

It behoveth the people of Bahá to die to the world and all that is therein, to be so detached from all earthly things that the inmates of Paradise may inhale from their garment the sweet-smelling savour of sanctity, that all the peoples of the earth may recognize in their faces the brightness of the All-Merciful, and that through them may be spread abroad the signs and tokens of God, the Almighty, the All-Wise. They that have tarnished the fair name of the Cause of God, by following the things of the flesh—these are in palpable error!

¶ 38. Know verily that whenever this Youth turneth His eyes towards His own self, he findeth it the most insignificant of all creation. When He contemplates, however, the bright effulgences He hath been empowered to manifest, lo, that self is transfigured before Him into a sovereign Potency permeating the essence of all things visible and invisible. Glory be to Him Who, through the power of truth, hath sent down the Manifestation of His own Self and entrusted Him with His message unto all mankind.

3. MAN

(I) THE SOUL OF MAN

¶ 39. Whatever is in the heavens and whatever is on the earth is a direct evidence of the revelation within it of the attributes and names of God, inasmuch as within every atom are enshrined the signs that bear eloquent testimony to the revelation of that Most Great Light. Methinks, but for the potency of that revelation, no being could ever exist. How resplendent the luminaries of knowledge that shine in an atom, and how vast the oceans of wisdom that surge within a drop! To a supreme degree is this true of man, who, among all created things, hath been invested with the robe of such gifts, and hath been singled out for the glory of such distinction. For in him are potentially revealed all the attributes and names of God to a degree that no other created being hath excelled or surpassed. All these names and attributes are applicable to him. Even as He hath said: "Man is My mystery, and I am his mystery." Manifold are the verses that have been repeatedly revealed in all the Heavenly Books and the Holy Scriptures, expressive of this most subtle and lofty theme. Even as He hath revealed: "We will surely show them Our signs in the world and within themselves." Again He saith: "And also in your own selves: will ye not, then, behold the signs of God?" And yet again He revealeth: "And be ye not like those who forget God, and whom He hath therefore caused to forget their own selves." In this connection, He Who is the eternal King—may the souls of all that dwell within the mystic Tabernacle be a sacrifice unto Him—hath spoken: "He hath known God who hath known himself."

. . . From that which hath been said it becometh evident that all things, in their inmost reality, testify to the revelation of the names and attributes of God within them. Each according to its capacity, indicateth, and is expressive of, the knowledge of God. So potent and universal is this revelation, that it hath encompassed all things visible and invisible. Thus hath He revealed: "Hath aught else save Thee a power of revelation which is not possessed by Thee, that it could have manifested Thee? Blind is the eye which doth not perceive Thee." Likewise hath the eternal King spoken: "No thing have I perceived, except that I perceived God within it, God before it, or God after it." Also in the tradition of Kumayl it is written:

"Behold, a light hath shone forth out of the morn of eternity, and lo, its waves have penetrated the inmost reality of all men." Man, the noblest and most perfect of all created things, excelleth them all in the intensity of this revelation, and is a fuller expression of its glory. And of all men, the most accomplished, the most distinguished, and the most excellent are the Manifestations of the Sun of Truth. Nay, all else besides these Manifestations, live by the operation of their Will, and move and have their being through the outpourings of their grace.

¶ 40. As to thy question concerning the origin of creation. Know assuredly that God's creation hath existed from eternity, and will continue to exist forever. Its beginning hath had no beginning, and its end knoweth no end. His name, the Creator, presupposeth a creation, even as His title, the Lord of Men, must involve the existence of a servant.

As to those sayings, attributed to the Prophets of old, such as "In the beginning was God; there was no creature to know Him," and "The Lord was alone; with no one to adore Him," the meaning of these and similar sayings is clear and evident, and should at no time be misapprehended. To this same truth bear witness these words which He hath revealed: "God was alone; there was none else besides Him. He will always remain what He hath ever been." Every discerning eye will readily perceive that the Lord is now manifest, yet there is none to recognize His glory. By this is meant that the habitation wherein the Divine Being dwelleth is far above the reach and ken of any one besides Him. Whatsoever in the contingent world can either be expressed or apprehended can never transgress the limits which by its inherent nature have been imposed upon it. God, alone, transcendeth such limitations. He, verily is from everlasting. No peer or partner has been, or can ever be, joined with Him. No name can be compared with His Name. No pen can portray His nature, neither can any tongue depict His glory. He will, for ever, remain immeasurably exalted above any one except Himself.

Consider the hour at which the supreme Manifestation of God revealeth Himself unto men. Ere that hour cometh, the Ancient Being, Who is still unknown of men and hath not as yet given utterance to the Word of God, is Himself the All-Knower in a world devoid of any man that hath known Him. He is indeed the Creator without a creation. For at the very moment preceding His Revelation, each and every created thing shall be made to yield up its soul to God. This is indeed the Day of which it hath been written: "Whose shall be the Kingdom this Day?" And none can be found ready to answer!

¶ 41. Thou hast asked Me concerning the nature of the soul. Know, verily, that the soul is a sign of God, a heavenly gem whose reality the most learned of men hath failed to grasp, and whose mystery no mind, however acute, can ever hope to unravel. It is the first among all created things to declare the excellence of its Creator, the first to recognize His glory, to cleave to His truth, and to bow down in adoration before Him. If it be faithful to God, it will reflect His light, and will, eventually, return unto Him. If it fail, however, in its allegiance to its Creator, it will become a victim to self and passion, and will, in the end, sink in their depths.

Whoso hath, in this Day, refused to allow the doubts and fancies of men to turn him away from Him Who is the Eternal Truth, and hath not suffered the tumult provoked by the ecclesiastical and secular authorities to deter him from recognizing His Message, such a man will be regarded by God, the Lord of all men, as one of His mighty signs, and will be numbered among them whose names have been inscribed by the Pen of the Most High in His Book. Blessed is he that hath recognized the true stature of such a soul, that hath acknowledged its station, and discovered its virtues.

Much hath been written in the books of old concerning the various stages in the development of the soul, such as concupiscence, irascibility, inspiration, benevolence, contentment, Divine good-pleasure, and the like; the Pen of the Most High, however, is disinclined to dwell upon them. Every soul that walketh humbly with its God, in this Day, and cleaveth unto Him, shall find itself invested with the honour and glory of all goodly names and stations.

When man is asleep, his soul can, in no wise, be said to have been inherently affected by any external object. It is not susceptible of any change in its original state or character. Any variation in its functions is to be ascribed to external causes. It is to these external influences that any variations in its environment, its understanding, and perception should be attributed.

Consider the human eye. Though it hath the faculty of perceiving all created things, yet the slightest impediment may so obstruct its vision as to deprive it of the power of discerning any object whatsoever. Magnified be the name of Him Who hath created, and is the Cause of, these causes, Who hath ordained that every change and variation in the world of being be made dependent upon them. Every created thing in the whole universe is but a door leading into His knowledge, a sign of His sovereignty, a revelation of His names, a symbol of His majesty, a token of His power, a means of admittance into His straight Path. . .

Verily I say, the human soul is, in its essence, one of the signs of God, a mystery among His mysteries. It is one of the mighty signs of the Almighty, the harbinger that proclaimeth the reality of all the worlds of God. Within it lieth concealed that which the world is now utterly incapable of apprehending. Ponder in thine heart the revelation of the Soul of God that pervadeth all His Laws, and contrast it with that base and appetitive nature that hath rebelled against Him, that forbiddeth men to turn unto the Lord of Names, and impelleth them to walk after their lusts and wickedness. Such a soul hath, in truth, wandered far in the path of error. . .

Thou hadst, moreover, asked Me concerning the state of the soul after its separation from the body. Know thou, of a truth, that if the soul of man hath walked in the ways of God, it will, assuredly, return and be gathered to the glory of the Beloved. By the righteousness of God! It shall attain a station such as no pen can depict, or tongue describe. The soul that hath remained faithful to the Cause of God, and stood unwaveringly firm in His Path shall, after his ascension, be possessed of such power that all the worlds which the Almighty hath created can benefit through him. Such a soul provideth, at the bidding of the Ideal King and Divine Educator, the pure leaven that leaveneth the world of being, and furnisheth the power through which the arts and wonders of the world are made manifest. Consider how meal needeth leaven to be leavened with. Those souls that are the symbols of detachment are the leaven of the world. Meditate on this, and be of the thankful.

In several of Our Tablets We have referred to this theme, and have set forth the various stages in the development of the soul. Verily I say, the human soul is exalted above all egress and regress. It is still, and yet it soareth; it moveth, and yet it is still. It is, in itself, a testimony that beareth witness to the existence of a world that is contingent, as well as to the reality of a world that hath neither beginning nor end. Behold how the dream thou hast dreamed is, after the lapse of many years, re-enacted before thine eyes. Consider how strange is the mystery of the world that appeareth to thee in thy dream. Ponder in thine heart upon the unsearchable wisdom of God, and meditate on its manifold revelations. . .

Witness the wondrous evidences of God's handiwork, and reflect upon its range and character. He Who is the Seal of the Prophets hath said: "Increase my wonder and amazement at Thee, O God!"

As to thy question whether the physical world is subject to any limitations, know thou that the comprehension of this matter dependeth upon the observer himself. In one sense, it is limited: in another, it is exalted beyond all limitations. The one true God hath everlastingly existed, and will everlastingly continue to exist. His creation, likewise, hath had no beginning, and will have no end. All that is created, however, is preceded by a cause. This fact, in itself establisheth, beyond the shadow of a doubt, the unity of the Creator.

Thou hadst, moreover, asked Me concerning the nature of the celestial spheres. To comprehend their nature, it would be necessary to inquire into the meaning of the allusions that have been made in the Books of old to the celestial spheres and the heavens, and to discover the character of their relationship to this physical world, and the influence which they exert upon it. Every heart is filled with wonder at so bewildering a theme, and every mind is perplexed by its mystery. God, alone, can fathom its import. The learned men, that have fixed at several thousand years the life of this earth, have failed, throughout the long period of their observation, to consider either the number or the age of the other planets. Consider, moreover, the manifold divergencies that have resulted from the theories propounded by these men. Know thou that every fixed star hath its own planets, and every planet its own creatures, whose number no man can compute.

O thou that hast fixed thine eyes upon My countenance! The Day Spring of Glory hath, in this Day, manifested its radiance, and the Voice of the Most High is calling. We have formerly uttered these words: "This is not the day for any man to question his Lord. It behoveth whosoever hath hearkened to the Call of God, as voiced by Him Who is the Day Spring of Glory, to arise and cry out: 'Here am I, here am I, O Lord of all Names; here am I, here am I, O Maker of the heavens! I testify that, through Thy Revelation, the things hidden in the Books of God have been revealed, and that whatsoever hath been recorded by Thy Messengers in the sacred Scriptures hath been fulfilled.' "

¶ 42. Know thou that, according to what thy Lord, the Lord of all men, hath decreed in His Book, the favours vouchsafed by Him unto mankind have been, and will ever remain, limitless in their range. First and foremost among these favours, which the Almighty hath conferred upon man, is the gift of understanding. His purpose in conferring such a gift is none other except to enable His creature to know and recognize the one true God—exalted be His glory. This gift giveth man the power to discern the truth in all things, leadeth him to that which is right, and helpeth him to discover the secrets of creation. Next in rank, is the power of vision, the chief instrument whereby his understanding can function. The senses of hearing, of the heart, and the like, are similarly to be reckoned among the gifts with which the human body is endowed. Immeasurably exalted is the Almighty Who hath created these powers, and revealed them in the body of man.

Every one of these gifts is an undoubted evidence of the majesty, the power, the ascendancy, the all-embracing knowledge of the one true God—exalted be His glory. Consider the sense of touch. Witness how its power hath spread itself over the entire human body. Whereas the faculties of sight and of hearing are each localized in a particular centre, the sense of touch embraceth the whole human frame. Glorified be His power, magnified be His sovereignty!

These gifts are inherent in man himself. That which is preeminent above all other gifts is incorruptible in nature, and pertaineth to God Himself, is the gift of Divine Revelation. Every bounty conferred by the Creator upon man, be it material or spiritual, is subservient unto this. It is, in its essence, and will ever so remain, the Bread which cometh down from Heaven. It is God's supreme testimony, the clearest evidence of His truth, the sign of His consummate bounty, the token of His all-encompassing mercy, the proof of His most loving providence, the symbol of His most perfect grace. He hath, indeed, partaken of this highest gift of God who hath recognized His Manifestation in this Day.

Render thanks unto thy Lord for having vouchsafed unto thee so great a bounty. Lift up thy voice and say: All praise be to Thee, O Thou, the Desire of every understanding heart!

¶ 43. Consider the rational faculty with which God hath endowed the essence of man. Examine thine own self, and behold how thy motion and stillness, thy will and purpose, thy sight and hearing, thy sense of smell and power of speech, and whatever else is related to, or transcendeth, thy physical senses or spiritual perceptions all proceed from, and owe their existence to, this same faculty. So closely are they related unto it, that if in less than the twinkling of an eye its relationship to the human body be severed, each and every one of these senses will cease immediately to exercise its function, and will be deprived of the power to manifest the evidences of its activity. It is indubitably clear and evident that each of these aforementioned instruments has depended, and will ever continue to depend, for its proper functioning on this rational faculty, which should be regarded as a Sign of the revelation of Him Who is the sovereign Lord of all. Through its manifestation all these names and attributes have been revealed, and by the suspension of its action they are all destroyed and perish.

It would be wholly untrue to maintain that this faculty is the same as the power of vision, inasmuch as the power of vision is derived from it and acteth in dependence upon it. It would, likewise, be idle to contend that this faculty can be identified with the sense of hearing, as the sense of hearing receiveth from the rational faculty the requisite energy for performing its functions.

This same relationship bindeth this faculty with whatsoever hath been the recipient of these names and attributes within the human temple. These diverse names and revealed attributes have been generated through the agency of this Sign of God. Immeasurably exalted is this Sign, in its essence and reality, above all such names and attributes. Nay, all else besides it will, when compared with its glory, fade into utter nothingness and become a thing forgotten.

Wert thou to ponder in thine heart, from now until the end that hath no end, and with all the concentrated intelligence and understanding which the greatest minds have attained in the past or will attain in the future, this divinely ordained and subtle Reality, this Sign of the revelation of the All-Abiding, All-Glorious God, thou wilt fail to comprehend its mystery or to appraise its virtue. Having recognized thy powerlessness to attain to an adequate understanding of that Reality which abideth within thee, thou wilt readily admit the futility of such efforts as may be attempted by thee, or by any of the created things, to fathom the mystery of the Living God, the Day Star of unfading glory, the Ancient of everlasting days. This confession of helplessness which mature contemplation must eventually impel every mind to make is in itself the acme of human understanding, and marketh the culmination of man's development.

¶ 44. As to thy question concerning the worlds of God. Know thou of a truth that the worlds of God are countless in their number, and infinite in their range. None can reckon or comprehend them except God, the All-Knowing, the All-Wise. Consider thy state when asleep. Verily, I say, this phenomenon is the most mysterious of the signs of God amongst men, were they to ponder it in their hearts. Behold how the thing which thou hast seen in thy dream is, after a considerable lapse of time, fully realized. Had the world in which thou didst find thyself in thy dream been identical with the world in which thou livest, it would have been necessary for the event occurring in that dream to have transpired in this world at the very moment of its occurrence. Were it so, you yourself would have borne witness unto it. This being not the case, however, it must necessarily follow that the world in which thou livest is different and apart from that which thou hast experienced in thy dream. This latter world hath neither beginning nor end. It would be true if thou wert to contend that this same world is, as decreed by the All-Glorious and Almighty God, within thy proper self and is wrapped up within thee. It would equally be true to maintain that thy spirit, having transcended the limitations of sleep and having stripped itself of all earthly attachment, hath, by the act of God, been made to traverse a realm which lieth hidden in the innermost reality of this world. Verily I say, the creation of God embraceth worlds besides this world, and creatures apart from these creatures. In each of these worlds He hath ordained things which none can search except Himself, the All-Searching, the All-Wise. Do thou meditate on that which We have revealed unto thee, that thou mayest discover the purpose of God, thy Lord, and the Lord of all worlds. In these words the mysteries of Divine Wisdom have been treasured. We have refrained from dwelling upon this theme owing to the sorrow that hath encompassed Us from the actions of them that have been created through Our words, if ye be of them that will hearken unto Our Voice.

(II) LIFE AFTER DEATH

❡ 45. Thou has asked Me whether man, as apart from the Prophets of God and His chosen ones, will retain, after his physical death, the self-same individuality, personality, consciousness, and understanding that characterize his life in this world. If this should be the case, how is it, thou hast observed, that whereas such slight injuries to his mental faculties as fainting and severe illness deprive him of his understanding and consciousness, his death, which must involve the decomposition of his body and the dissolution of its elements, is powerless to destroy that understanding and extinguish that consciousness? How can any one imagine that man's consciousness and personality will be maintained, when the very instruments necessary to their existence and function will have completely disintegrated?

Know thou that the soul of man is exalted above, and is independent of all infirmities of body or mind. That a sick person showeth signs of weakness is due to the hindrances that interpose themselves between his soul and his body, for the soul itself remaineth unaffected by any bodily ailments. Consider the light of the lamp. Though an external object may interfere with its radiance, the light itself continueth to shine with undiminished power. In like manner, every malady afflicting the body of man is an impediment that preventeth the soul from manifesting its inherent might and power. When it leaveth the body, however, it will evince such ascendency, and reveal such influence as no force on earth can equal. Every pure, every refined and sanctified soul will be endowed with tremendous power, and shall rejoice with exceeding gladness.

Consider the lamp which is hidden under a bushel. Though its light be shining, yet its radiance is concealed from men. Likewise, consider the sun which hath been obscured by the clouds. Observe how its splendour appeareth to have diminished, when in reality the source of that light hath remained unchanged. The soul of man should be likened unto this sun, and all things on earth should be regarded as his body. So long as no external impediment interveneth between them, the body will, in its entirety, continue to reflect the light of the soul, and to be sustained by its power. As soon as, however, a veil interposeth itself between them, the brightness of that light seemeth to lessen.

Consider again the sun when it is completely hidden behind the clouds. Though the earth is still illumined with its light, yet the measure of light which it receiveth is considerably reduced. Not until the clouds have dispersed, can the sun shine again in the plenitude of its glory. Neither the presence of the cloud nor its absence can, in any way, affect the inherent splendour of the sun. The soul of man is the sun by which his body is illumined, and from which it draweth its sustenance, and should be so regarded.

Consider, moreover, how the fruit, ere it is formed, lieth potentially within the tree. Were the tree to be cut into pieces, no sign nor any part of the fruit, however small, could be detected. When it appeareth, however, it manifesteth itself, as thou hast observed, in its wondrous beauty and glorious perfection. Certain fruits, indeed, attain their fullest development only after being severed from the tree.

¶ 46. And now concerning thy question regarding the soul of man and its survival after death. Know thou of a truth that the soul, after its separation from the body, will continue to progress until it attaineth the presence of God, in a state and condition which neither the revolution of ages and centuries, nor the changes and chances of this world, can alter. It will endure as long as the Kingdom of God, His sovereignty, His dominion and power will endure. It will manifest the signs of God and His attributes, and will reveal His loving kindness and bounty. The movement of My Pen is stilled when it attempteth to befittingly describe the loftiness and glory of so exalted a station. The honour with which the Hand of Mercy will invest the soul is such as no tongue can adequately reveal, nor any other earthly agency describe. Blessed is the soul which, at the hour of its separation from the body, is sanctified from the vain imaginings of the peoples of the world. Such a soul liveth and moveth in accordance with the Will of its Creator, and entereth the all-highest

Paradise. The Maids of Heaven, inmates of the loftiest mansions, will circle around it, and the Prophets of God and His chosen ones will seek its companionship. With them that soul will freely converse, and will recount unto them that which it had been made to endure in the path of God, the Lord of all worlds. If any man be told that which hath been ordained for such a soul in the worlds of God, the Lord of the throne on high and of earth below, his whole being will instantly blaze out in his great longing to attain that most exalted, that sanctified and resplendent station. . . The nature of the soul after death can never be described, nor is it meet and permissible to reveal its whole character to the eyes of men. The Prophets and Messengers of God have been sent down for the sole purpose of guiding mankind to the straight Path of Truth. The purpose underlying their revelation hath been to educate all men, that they may, at the hour of death, ascend, in the utmost purity and sanctity and with absolute detachment, to the throne of the Most High. The light which these souls radiate is responsible for the progress of the world and the advancement of its peoples. They are like unto leaven which leaveneth the world of being, and constitute the animating force through which the arts and wonders of the world are made manifest. Through them the clouds rain their bounty upon men, and the earth bringeth forth its fruits. All things must needs have a cause, a motive power, an animating principle. These souls and symbols of detachment have provided, and will continue to provide, the supreme moving impulse in the world of being. The world beyond is as different from this world as this world is different from that of the child while still in the womb of its mother. When the soul attaineth the Presence of God, it will assume the form that best befitteth its immortality and is worthy of its celestial habitation. Such an existence is a contingent and not an absolute existence, inasmuch as the former is preceded by a cause, whilst the latter is independent thereof. Absolute existence is strictly confined to God, exalted be His glory. Well is it with them that apprehend this truth. Wert thou to ponder in thine heart the behaviour of the Prophets of God thou wouldst assuredly and readily testify that there must needs be other worlds besides this world. The majority of the truly wise and learned have, throughout the ages, as it hath been recorded by the Pen of Glory in the Tablet of Wisdom, borne witness to the truth of that which the holy Writ of God hath revealed. Even the

materialists have testified in their writings to the wisdom of these
divinely-appointed Messengers, and have regarded the references
made by the Prophets to Paradise, to hell fire, to future reward and
punishment, to have been actuated by a desire to educate and uplift
the souls of men. Consider, therefore, how the generality of mankind, whatever their beliefs or theories, have recognized the excellence, and admitted the superiority, of these Prophets of God.
These Gems of Detachment are acclaimed by some as the embodiments of wisdom, while others believe them to be the mouthpiece
of God Himself. How could such Souls have consented to surrender
themselves unto their enemies if they believed all the worlds of God
to have been reduced to this earthly life? Would they have willingly
suffered such afflictions and torments as no man hath ever experienced or witnessed?

¶ 47. And now concerning thy question whether human souls
continue to be conscious one of another after their separation from
the body. Know thou that the souls of the people of Bahá, who
have entered and been established within the Crimson Ark, shall
associate and commune intimately one with another, and shall be so
closely associated in their lives, their aspirations, their aims and
strivings as to be even as one soul. They are indeed the ones who are
well-informed, who are keen-sighted, and who are endued with
understanding. Thus hath it been decreed by Him Who is the All-
Knowing, the All-Wise.

The people of Bahá, who are the inmates of the Ark of God, are
one and all, well aware of one another's state and condition, and are
united in the bonds of intimacy and fellowship. Such a state, however, must depend upon their faith and their conduct. They that are
of the same grade and station are fully aware of one another's capacity, character, accomplishments and merits. They that are of a
lower grade, however, are incapable of comprehending adequately
the station, or of estimating the merits, of those that rank above
them. Each shall receive his share from thy Lord. Blessed is the man
that hath turned his face towards God, and walked steadfastly in
His love, until his soul hath winged its flight unto God, the Sovereign Lord of all, the Most Powerful, the Ever-Forgiving, the All-
Merciful.

The souls of the infidels, however, shall—and to this I bear witness—when breathing their last be made aware of the good things that have escaped them, and shall bemoan their plight, and shall humble themselves before God. They shall continue doing so after the separation of their souls from their bodies.

It is clear and evident that all men shall, after their physical death, estimate the worth of their deeds, and realize all that their hands have wrought. I swear by the Day Star that shineth above the horizon of Divine power! They that are the followers of the one true God shall, the moment they depart out of this life, experience such joy and gladness as would be impossible to describe, while they that live in error shall be seized with such fear and trembling, and shall be filled with such consternation, as nothing can exceed. Well is it with him that hath quaffed the choice and incorruptible wine of faith through the gracious favour and the manifold bounties of Him Who is the Lord of all Faiths. . .

This is the Day when the loved ones of God should keep their eyes directed towards His Manifestation, and fasten them upon whatsoever that Manifestation may be pleased to reveal. Certain traditions of bygone ages rest on no foundations whatever, while the notions entertained by past generations, and which they have recorded in their books, have, for the most part, been influenced by the desires of a corrupt inclination. Thou dost witness how most of the commentaries and interpretations of the words of God, now current amongst men, are devoid of truth. Their falsity hath, in some cases, been exposed when the intervening veils were rent asunder. They themselves have acknowledged their failure in apprehending the meaning of any of the words of God.

Our purpose is to show that should the loved ones of God sanctify their hearts and their ears from the vain sayings that were uttered aforetime, and turn with their inmost souls to Him Who is the Day Spring of His Revelation, and to whatsoever things He hath manifested, such behaviour would be regarded as highly meritorious in the sight of God. . .

Magnify His Name, and be thou of the thankful. Convey My greetings to My loved ones, whom God hath singled out for His love, and caused them to achieve their objects. All glory be to God, the Lord of all worlds.

4. TOWARDS WORLD UNITY

(I) THE WORLD'S SICKNESS

¶ 48. The world is in travail, and its agitation waxeth day by day. Its face is turned towards waywardness and unbelief. Such shall be its plight, that to disclose it now would not be meet and seemly. Its perversity will long continue. And when the appointed hour is come, there shall suddenly appear that which shall cause the limbs of mankind to quake. Then, and only then, will the Divine Standard be unfurled, and the Nightingale of Paradise warble its melody.

¶ 49. The All-Knowing Physician hath His finger on the pulse of mankind. He perceiveth the disease, and prescribeth, in His unerring wisdom, the remedy. Every age hath its own problem, and every soul its particular aspiration. The remedy the world needeth in its present-day afflictions can never be the same as that which a subsequent age may require. Be anxiously concerned with the needs of the age ye live in, and centre your deliberations in its exigencies and requirements.

We can well perceive how the whole human race is encompassed with great, with incalculable afflictions. We see it languishing on its bed of sickness, sore-tried and disillusioned. They that are intoxicated by self-conceit have interposed themselves between it and the Divine and infallible Physician. Witness how they have entangled all men, themselves included, in the mesh of their devices. They can neither discover the cause of the disease, nor have they any knowledge of the remedy. They have conceived the straight to be crooked, and have imagined their friend an enemy.

Incline your ears to the sweet melody of this Prisoner. Arise, and lift up your voices, that haply they that are fast asleep may be awakened. Say: O ye who are as dead! The Hand of Divine bounty proffereth unto you the Water of Life. Hasten and drink your fill. Whoso hath been re-born in this Day, shall never die; whoso remaineth dead, shall never live.

(II) THE DIVINE PHYSICIAN'S REMEDY

¶ 50. O contending peoples and kindreds of the earth! Set your faces towards unity, and let the radiance of its light shine upon you.

Gather ye together, and for the sake of God resolve to root out whatever is the source of contention amongst you. Then will the effulgence of the world's great Luminary envelop the whole earth, and its inhabitants become the citizens of one city, and the occupants of one and the same throne. This wronged One hath, ever since the early days of His life, cherished none other desire but this, and will continue to entertain no wish except this wish. There can be no doubt whatever that the peoples of the world, of whatever race or religion, derive their inspiration from one heavenly Source, and are the subjects of one God. The difference between the ordinances under which they abide should be attributed to the varying requirements and exigencies of the age in which they were revealed. All of them, except a few which are the outcome of human perversity, were ordained of God, and are a reflection of His Will and Purpose. Arise and, armed with the power of faith, shatter to pieces the gods of your vain imaginings, the sowers of dissension amongst you. Cleave unto that which draweth you together and uniteth you. This, verily, is the most exalted Word which the Mother Book hath sent down and revealed unto you. To this beareth witness the Tongue of Grandeur from His habitation of glory.

¶ 51. Behold the disturbances which, for many a long year, have afflicted the earth, and the perturbation that hath seized its peoples. It hath either been ravaged by war, or tormented by sudden and unforeseen calamities. Though the world is encompassed with misery and distress, yet no man hath paused to reflect what the cause or source of that may be. Whenever the True Counsellor uttered a word in admonishment, lo, they all denounced Him as a mover of mischief and rejected His claim. How bewildering, how confusing is such behaviour! No two men can be found who may be said to be outwardly and inwardly united. The evidences of discord and malice are apparent everywhere, though all were made for harmony and union. The Great Being saith: O well-beloved ones! The tabernacle of unity hath been raised; regard ye not one another as strangers. Ye are the fruits of one tree, and the leaves of one branch. We cherish the hope that the light of justice may shine upon the world and sanctify it from tyranny. If the rulers and kings of the earth, the symbols of the power of God, exalted be His glory, arise and resolve to dedicate themselves to whatever will promote the highest interests of the whole of humanity, the reign of justice will assuredly be established amongst the children of men, and the effulgence of its light will envelop the whole earth. The Great Being saith: The structure of world stability and order hath been reared upon, and will continue to be sustained by, the twin pillars of reward and punishment. . . In another passage He hath written: Take heed, O concourse of the rulers of the world! There is no force on earth that can equal in its conquering power the force of justice and wisdom. . . Blessed is the king who marcheth with the ensign of wisdom unfurled before him, and the battalions of justice massed in his rear. He verily is the ornament that adorneth the brow of peace and the countenance of security. There can be no doubt whatever that if the Day Star of justice, which the clouds of tyranny have obscured, were to shed its light upon men, the face of the earth would be completely transformed.

¶ 52. The Great Being, wishing to reveal the prerequisites of the peace and tranquillity of the world and the advancement of its peoples, hath written: The time must come when the imperative necessity for the holding of a vast, an all-embracing assemblage of men will be universally realized. The rulers and kings of the earth must needs attend it, and, participating in its deliberations, must consider such ways and means as will lay the foundations of the world's Great Peace amongst men. Such a peace demandeth that the Great Powers should resolve, for the sake of the tranquillity of the peoples of the earth, to be fully reconciled among themselves. Should any king take up arms against another, all should unitedly arise and prevent him. If this be done, the nations of the world will no longer require any armaments, except for the purpose of preserving the security of their realms and of maintaining internal order within their territories. This will ensure the peace and composure of every people, government and nation. We fain would hope that the kings and rulers of the earth, the mirrors of the gracious and almighty name of God, may attain unto this station, and shield mankind from the onslaught of tyranny. . . The day is approaching when all the peoples of the world will have adopted one universal language and one common script. When this is achieved, to whatsoever city a man may journey, it shall be as if he were entering his own home. These things are obligatory and absolutely

essential. It is incumbent upon every man of insight and understanding to strive to translate that which hath been written into
reality and action. . . That one indeed is a man who, today, dedicat-
eth himself to the service of the entire human race. The Great Being
saith: Blessed and happy is he that ariseth to promote the best interests of the peoples and kindreds of the earth. In another passage He
hath proclaimed: It is not for him to pride himself who loveth his
own country, but rather for him who loveth the whole world. The
earth is but one country, and mankind its citizens.

¶ 53. The Great Being saith: O ye children of men! The fundamental purpose animating the Faith of God and His Religion is to
safeguard the interests and promote the unity of the human race,
and to foster the spirit of love and fellowship amongst men. Suffer
it not to become a source of dissension and discord, of hate and enmity. This is the straight Path, the fixed and immovable foundation.
Whatsoever is raised on this foundation, the changes and chances of
the world can never impair its strength, nor will the revolution of
countless centuries undermine its structure. Our hope is that the
world's religious leaders and the rulers thereof will unitedly arise
for the reformation of this age and the rehabilitation of its fortunes.
Let them, after meditating on its needs, take counsel together and,
through anxious and full deliberation, administer to a diseased and
sorely-afflicted world the remedy it requires. . . It is incumbent
upon them who are in authority to exercise moderation in all
things. Whatsoever passeth beyond the limits of moderation will
cease to exert a beneficial influence. Consider for instance such
things as liberty, civilization and the like. However much men of
understanding may favourably regard them, they will, if carried to
excess, exercise a pernicious influence upon men. . . Please God, the
peoples of the world may be led, as the result of the high endeavours
exerted by their rulers and the wise and learned amongst men, to
recognize their best interests. How long will humanity persist in
its waywardness? How long will injustice continue? How long is
chaos and confusion to reign amongst men? How long will discord agitate the face of society? The winds of despair are, alas, blowing from every direction, and the strife that divideth and afflicteth
the human race is daily increasing. The signs of impending con-
vulsions and chaos can now be discerned, inasmuch as the prevailing

order appeareth to be lamentably defective. I beseech God, exalted be His glory, that He may graciously awaken the peoples of the earth, may grant that the end of their conduct may be profitable unto them, and aid them to accomplish that which beseemeth their station.

¶ 54. O Kamál! The heights which, through the most gracious favour of God, mortal man can attain, in this Day, are as yet unrevealed to his sight. The world of being hath never had, nor doth it yet possess the capacity for such a revelation. The day, however, is approaching when the potentialities of so great a favour will, by virtue of His behest, be manifested unto men. Though the forces of the nations be arrayed against Him, though the kings of the earth be leagued to undermine His Cause, the power of His might shall stand unshaken. He, verily, speaketh the truth, and summoneth all mankind to the way of Him Who is the Incomparable, the All-Knowing.

All men have been created to carry forward an ever-advancing civilization. The Almighty beareth Me witness: To act like the beasts of the field is unworthy of man. Those virtues that befit his dignity are forbearance, mercy, compassion and loving-kindness towards all the peoples and kindreds of the earth. Say: O friends! Drink your fill from this crystal stream that floweth through the heavenly grace of Him Who is the Lord of Names. Let others partake of its waters in My name, that the leaders of men in every land may fully recognize the purpose for which the Eternal Truth hath been revealed, and the reason for which they themselves have been created.

(III) CONTRIBUTION OF THE INDIVIDUAL

¶ 55. The Pen of the Ancient King hath never ceased to remember the loved ones of God. At one time, rivers of mercy have streamed from His Pen, at another, through its movement, God's perspicuous Book hath been revealed. He is the One to Whom none can compare, Whose utterance mortal man can never rival. He it is Who from everlasting hath been established upon the seat of ascendancy and might, He from Whose lips have gone out counsels that can satisfy the needs of the whole of mankind, and admonitions that can profit them.

The One true God beareth Me witness, and His creatures will testify, that not for a moment did I allow Myself to be hidden from the eyes of men, nor did I consent to shield My person from their injury. Before the face of all men I have arisen, and bidden them fulfil My pleasure. My object is none other than the betterment of the world and the tranquillity of its peoples. The well-being of mankind, its peace and security, are unattainable unless and until its unity is firmly established. This unity can never be achieved so long as the counsels which the Pen of the Most High hath revealed are suffered to pass unheeded.

Through the power of the words He hath uttered the whole of the human race can be illumined with the light of unity, and the remembrance of His Name is able to set on fire the hearts of all men, and burn away the veils that intervene between them and His glory. One righteous act is endowed with a potency that can so elevate the dust as to cause it to pass beyond the heaven of heavens. It can tear every bond asunder, and hath the power to restore the force that hath spent itself and vanished. . . .

Be pure, O people of God, be pure; be righteous, be righteous. . . Say: O people of God! That which can ensure the victory of Him Who is the Eternal Truth, His hosts and helpers on earth, have been set down in the sacred Books and Scriptures, and are as clear and manifest as the sun. These hosts are such righteous deeds, such conduct and character, as are acceptable in His sight. Whoso ariseth, in this Day, to aid Our Cause, and summoneth to his assistance the hosts of a praiseworthy character and upright conduct, the influence flowing from such an action will, most certainly, be diffused throughout the whole world.

¶ 56. He Who is the Eternal Truth hath, from the Day Spring of Glory, directed His eyes towards the people of Bahá, and is addressing them in these words: "Address yourselves to the promotion of the well-being and tranquillity of the children of men. Bend your minds and wills to the education of the peoples and kindreds of the earth, that haply the dissensions that divide it may, through the power of the Most Great Name, be blotted out from its face, and all mankind become the upholders of one Order, and the inhabitants of one City. Illumine and hallow your hearts; let them not be profaned by the thorns of hate or the thistles of malice. Ye dwell in one world, and have been created through the operation of one Will. Blessed is he who mingleth with all men in a spirit of utmost kindliness and love."

¶ 57. O Afnán, O thou that hast branched from Mine ancient Stock! My glory and My loving-kindness rest upon thee. How vast is the tabernacle of the Cause of God! It hath overshadowed all the peoples and kindreds of the earth, and will, ere long, gather together the whole of mankind beneath its shelter. Thy day of service is now come. Countless Tablets bear the testimony of the bounties vouchsafed unto thee. Arise for the triumph of My Cause, and, through the power of thine utterance, subdue the hearts of men. Thou must show forth that which will ensure the peace and the well-being of the miserable and the down-trodden. Gird up the loins of thine endeavour, that perchance thou mayest release the captive from his chains, and enable him to attain unto true liberty.

Justice is, in this day, bewailing its plight, and Equity groaneth beneath the yoke of oppression. The thick clouds of tyranny have darkened the face of the earth, and enveloped its peoples. Through the movement of Our Pen of glory We have, at the bidding of the omnipotent Ordainer, breathed a new life into every human frame, and instilled into every word a fresh potency. All created things proclaim the evidences of this world-wide regeneration. This is the most great, the most joyful tidings imparted by the pen of this wronged One to mankind. Wherefore, fear ye, O My well-beloved ones! Who is it that can dismay you? A touch of moisture sufficeth to dissolve the hardened clay out of which this perverse generation is moulded. The mere act of your gathering together is enough to scatter the forces of these vain and worthless people . . .

Every man of insight will, in this day, readily admit that the counsels which the Pen of this wronged One hath revealed constitute the supreme animating power for the advancement of the world and the exaltation of its peoples. Arise, O people, and, by the power of God's might, resolve to gain the victory over your own selves, that haply the whole earth may be freed and sanctified from its servitude to the gods of its idle fancies—gods that have inflicted such loss upon, and are responsible for the misery of, their wretched worshippers. These idols form the obstacle that impeded man in his efforts to advance in the path of perfection. We cherish the hope that the Hand of Divine power may lend its assistance to mankind, and deliver it from its state of grievous abasement.

In one of the Tablets these words have been revealed: O people of God! Do not busy yourselves in your own concerns; let your thoughts be fixed upon that which will rehabilitate the fortunes of mankind and sanctify the hearts and souls of men. This can best be achieved through pure and holy deeds, through a virtuous life and a goodly behaviour. Valiant acts will ensure the triumph of this Cause, and a saintly character will reinforce its power. Cleave unto righteousness, O people of Bahá! This, verily, is the commandment which this wronged One hath given unto you, and the first choice of His unrestrained Will for every one of you.

O friends! It behoveth you to refresh and revive your souls through the gracious favours which in this Divine, this soul-stirring Springtime are being showered upon you. The Day Star of His great glory hath shed its radiance upon you, and the clouds of His limitless grace have overshadowed you. How high the reward of him that hath not deprived himself of so great a bounty, nor failed to recognize the beauty of his Best-Beloved in this, His new attire. Watch over yourselves, for the Evil One is lying in wait, ready to entrap you. Gird yourselves against his wicked devices, and, led by the light of the name of the All-Seeing God, make your escape from the darkness that surroundeth you. Let your vision be world-embracing, rather than confined to your own self. The Evil One is he that hindereth the rise and obstructeth the spiritual progress of the children of men.

It is incumbent upon every man, in this Day, to hold fast unto whatsoever will promote the interests, and exalt the station, of all nations and just governments. Through each and every one of the verses which the Pen of the Most High hath revealed, the doors of love and unity have been unlocked and flung open to the face of men. We have erewhile declared—and Our Word is the truth—: "Consort with the followers of all religions in a spirit of friendliness and fellowship." Whatsoever hath led the children of men to shun one another, and hath caused dissensions and divisions amongst them, hath, through the revelation of these words, been nullified and abolished. From the heaven of God's Will, and for the purpose of ennobling the world of being and of elevating the mind and souls of men, hath been sent down that which is the most effective instrument for the education of the whole human race. The highest essence and most perfect expression of whatsoever the peoples of old have either said or written hath, through this most potent Revelation, been sent down from the heaven of the Will of the All-Possessing, the Ever-Abiding God. Of old it hath been revealed: "Love of one's country is an element of the Faith of God." The Tongue of Grandeur hath, however, in the day of His manifestation proclaimed: "It is not his to boast who loveth his country, but it is his who loveth the world." Through the power released by these exalted words He hath lent a fresh impulse, and set a new direction, to the birds of men's hearts, and hath obliterated every trace of restriction and limitation from God's holy Book.

O people of Justice! Be as brilliant as the light, and as splendid as the fire that blazed in the Burning Bush. The brightness of the fire of your love will no doubt fuse and unify the contending peoples and kindreds of the earth, whilst the fierceness of the flame of enmity and hatred cannot but result in strife and ruin. We beseech God that He may shield His creatures from the evil designs of His enemies. He verily hath power over all things.

All-praise be to the one true God—exalted be His glory—inasmuch as He hath, through the Pen of the Most High, unlocked the doors of men's hearts. Every verse which this Pen hath revealed is a bright and shining portal that discloseth the glories of a saintly and pious life, of pure and stainless deeds. The summons and the message which We gave were never intended to reach or to benefit one land or one people only. Mankind in its entirety must firmly adhere to whatsoever hath been revealed and vouchsafed unto it. Then and only then will it attain unto true liberty. The whole earth is illuminated with the resplendent glory of God's Revelation. In the year sixty He Who heralded the light of Divine Guidance—may all creation be a sacrifice unto Him—arose to announce a fresh revelation of the Divine Spirit, and was followed, twenty years later, by Him through Whose coming the world was made the recipient of this promised glory, this wondrous favour. Behold how the generality of mankind hath been endued with the capacity to hearken unto God's most exalted Word—the Word upon which must depend the gathering together and spiritual resurrection of all men. . .

Incline your hearts, O people of God, unto the counsels of your true, your incomparable Friend. The Word of God may be likened unto a sapling, whose roots have been implanted in the hearts of men. It is incumbent upon you to foster its growth through the living waters of wisdom, of sanctified and holy words, so that its root may become firmly fixed and its branches may spread out as high as the heavens and beyond.

O ye that dwell on earth! The distinguishing feature that marketh the pre-eminent character of this Supreme Revelation consisteth in that We have, on the one hand, blotted out from the pages of God's holy Book whatsoever hath been the cause of strife, of malice and mischief amongst the children of men, and have, on the other, laid down the essential prerequisites of concord, of understanding, of complete and enduring unity. Well is it with them that keep My statutes.

Time and again have We admonished Our beloved ones to avoid, nay to flee from, anything whatsoever from which the odour of mischief can be detected. The world is in great turmoil, and the minds of its people are in a state of utter confusion. We entreat the Almighty that He may graciously illuminate them with the glory of His justice, and enable them to discover that which will be profitable unto them at all times and under all conditions. He, verily is the All-Possessing, the Most High.

(IV) THE LAWS OF BAHÁ'U'LLÁH

¶ 58. The first duty prescribed by God for His servants is the recognition of Him Who is the Day Spring of His Revelation and the Fountain of His laws, Who representeth the Godhead in both the Kingdom of His Cause and the world of creation. Whoso achieveth this duty hath attained unto all good; and whoso is deprived thereof, hath gone astray, though he be the author of every righteous deed. It behoveth every one who reacheth this most sublime station, this summit of transcendent glory, to observe every ordinance of Him Who is the Desire of the world. These twin duties are inseparable. Neither is acceptable without the other. Thus hath it been decreed by Him Who is the Source of Divine inspiration.

They whom God hath endued with insight will readily recognize that the precepts laid down by God constitute the highest means for the maintenance of order in the world and the security of its peoples. He that turneth away from them, is accounted among the abject and foolish. We verily, have commanded you to refuse the dictates of your evil passions and corrupt desires, and not to transgress the bounds which the Pen of the Most High hath fixed, for these are the breath of life unto all created things. The seas of Divine wisdom and divine utterance have risen under the breath of the breeze of the All-Merciful. Hasten to drink your fill, O men of understanding! They that have violated the Covenant of God by breaking His commandments, and have turned back on their heels, these have erred grievously in the sight of God, the All-Possessing, the Most High.

O ye peoples of the world! Know assuredly that My commandments are the lamps of My loving providence among My servants, and the keys of My mercy for My creatures. Thus hath it been sent down from the heaven of the Will of your Lord, the Lord of Revelation. Were any man to taste the sweetness of the words which the lips of the All-Merciful have willed to utter, he would, though the treasures of the earth be in his possession, renounce them one and all, that he might vindicate the truth of even one of His commandments shining above the day spring of His bountiful care and loving-kindness.

Say: From My laws the sweet smelling savour of My garment can be smelled, and by their aid the standards of Victory will be planted upon the highest peaks. The Tongue of My power hath, from the heaven of My omnipotent glory, addressed to My creation these words: "Observe My commandments, for the love of My beauty." Happy is the lover that hath inhaled the divine fragrance of his Best-Beloved from these words, laden with the perfume of a grace which no tongue can describe. By My life! He who hath drunk the choice wine of fairness from the hands of My bountiful favour, will circle around My commandments that shine above the Day Spring of My creation.

Think not that We have revealed unto you a mere code of laws. Nay, rather, We have unsealed the choice Wine with the fingers of might and power. To this beareth witness that which the Pen of Revelation hath revealed. Meditate upon this, O men of insight! . . .

Whenever My laws appear like the sun in the heaven of Mine utterance, they must be faithfully obeyed by all, though My decree be such as to cause the heaven of every religion to be cleft asunder. He doth what He pleaseth. He chooseth; and none may question His choice. Whatsoever He, the Well-Beloved, ordaineth, the same is, verily, beloved. To this He Who is the Lord of all creation beareth Me witness. Whoso hath inhaled the sweet fragrance of the All-Merciful, and recognized the Source of this utterance, will welcome with his own eyes the shafts of the enemy, that he may establish the truth of the laws of God amongst men. Well is it with him that hath turned thereunto, and apprehended the meaning of His decisive decree.

¶ 59. Consider the pettiness of men's minds. They ask for that which injureth them, and cast away the thing that profiteth them. They are, indeed, of those that are far astray. We find some men desiring liberty, and priding themselves therein. Such men are in the depths of ignorance.

Liberty must, in the end, lead to sedition, whose flames none can quench. Thus warneth you He Who is the Reckoner, the All-Knowing. Know ye that the embodiment of liberty and its symbol is the animal. That which beseemeth man is submission unto such restraints as will protect him from his own ignorance, and guard him against the harm of the mischief-maker. Liberty causeth man to overstep the bounds of propriety, and to infringe on the dignity of his station. It debaseth him to the level of extreme depravity and wickedness.

Regard men as a flock of sheep that need a shepherd for their protection. This, verily, is the truth, the certain truth. We approve of liberty in certain circumstances, and refuse to sanction it in others. We, verily, are the All-Knowing.

Say: True liberty consisteth in man's submission unto My commandments, little as ye know it. Were men to observe that which We have sent down unto them from the Heaven of Revelation, they would, of a certainty, attain unto perfect liberty. Happy is the man that hath apprehended the Purpose of God in whatever He hath revealed from the Heaven of His Will, that pervadeth all created things. Say: The liberty that profiteth you is to be found nowhere except in complete servitude unto God, the Eternal Truth. Whoso hath tasted of its sweetness will refuse to barter it for all the dominion of earth and heaven.

¶ 60. Know verily that the essence of justice and the source thereof are both embodied in the ordinances prescribed by Him who is the Manifestation of the Self of God amongst men, if ye be of them that recognize this truth. He doth verily incarnate the highest, the infallible standard of justice unto all creation. Were His law to be such as to strike terror into the hearts of all that are in heaven and on earth, that law is naught but manifest justice. The fears and agitation which the revelation of this law provokes in men's hearts should indeed be likened to the cries of the suckling babe weaned from his mother's milk, if ye be of them that perceive. Were men to discover the motivating purpose of God's Revelation, they would assuredly cast away their fears, and, with hearts filled with gratitude, rejoice with exceeding gladness.

¶ 61. Give a hearing ear, O people, to that which I, in truth, say unto you. The one true God, exalted be His glory, hath ever regarded, and will continue to regard, the hearts of men as His own, His exclusive possession. All else, whether pertaining to land or sea, whether riches or glory, He hath bequeathed unto the Kings and rulers of the earth. From the beginning that hath no beginning the ensign proclaiming the words "He doeth whatsoever He willeth" hath been unfurled in all its splendour before His Manifestation. What mankind needeth in this day is obedience unto them that are in authority, and a faithful adherence to the cord of wisdom. The instruments which are essential to the immediate protection, the security and assurance of the human race have been entrusted to the hands, and lie in the grasp, of the governors of human society. This is the wish of God and His decree... We cherish the hope that one of the kings of the earth will, for the sake of God, arise for the triumph of this wronged, this oppressed people. Such a king will be eternally extolled and glorified. God hath prescribed unto this people the duty of aiding whosoever will aid them, of serving his best interests, and of demonstrating to him their abiding loyalty. They who follow Me must strive, under all circumstances, to promote the welfare of whosoever will arise for the triumph of My Cause, and must at all times prove their devotion and fidelity unto him. Happy is the man that hearkeneth and observeth My counsel. Woe unto him that faileth to fulfil My wish.

(V) WHEN THE VICTORY ARRIVETH

¶ 62. When the victory arriveth, every man shall profess himself as believer and shall hasten to the shelter of God's Faith. Happy are they who in the days of world-encompassing trials have stood fast in the Cause and refused to swerve from its truth.

5. INDIVIDUAL CONDUCT AND THE PATH OF GOD

(I) GENERAL ETHICAL TEACHINGS

¶ 63. The beginning of all things is the knowledge of God, and the end of all things is strict observance of whatsoever hath been sent down from the empyrean of the Divine Will that pervadeth all that is in the heavens and all that is on the earth.

¶ 64. Be generous in prosperity, and thankful in adversity. Be worthy of the trust of thy neighbour, and look upon him with a bright and friendly face. Be a treasure to the poor, an admonisher to the rich, an answerer of the cry of the needy, a preserver of the sanctity of thy pledge. Be fair in thy judgment, and guarded in thy speech. Be unjust to no man, and show all meekness to all men. Be as a lamp unto them that walk in darkness, a joy to the sorrowful, a sea for the thirsty, a haven for the distressed, an upholder and defender of the victim of oppression. Let integrity and uprightness distinguish all thine acts. Be a home for the stranger, a balm to the suffering, a tower of strength for the fugitive. Be eyes to the blind, and a guiding light unto the feet of the erring. Be an ornament to the countenance of truth, a crown to the brow of fidelity, a pillar of the temple of righteousness, a breath of life to the body of mankind, an ensign of the hosts of justice, a luminary above the horizon of virtue, a dew to the soil of the human heart, an ark on the ocean of knowledge, a sun in the heaven of bounty, a gem on the diadem of wisdom, a shining light in the firmament of thy generation, a fruit upon the tree of humility.

¶ 65. Say: Deliver your souls, O people, from the bondage of self, and purify them from all attachment to anything besides Me. Remembrance of Me cleanseth all things from defilement, could ye but perceive it. Say: Were all created things to be entirely divested of the veil of worldly vanity and desire, the Hand of God would in this Day clothe them, one and all, with the robe "He doeth whatsoever He willeth in the kingdom of creation," that thereby the sign of His sovereignty might be manifested in all things. Exalted then be He, the Sovereign Lord of all, the Almighty, the Supreme Protector, the All-Glorious, the Most Powerful.

Intone, O My servant, the verses of God that have been received by thee, as intoned by them who have drawn nigh unto Him, that the sweetness of thy melody may kindle thine own soul, and attract the hearts of all men. Whoso reciteth, in the privacy of his chamber, the verses revealed by God, the scattering angels of the Almighty shall scatter abroad the fragrance of the words uttered by his mouth, and shall cause the heart of every righteous man to throb. Though he may, at first, remain unaware of its effect yet the virtue of the grace vouchsafed unto him must needs sooner or later exercise its influence upon his soul. Thus have the mysteries of the Revelation of God been decreed by virtue of the Will of Him Who is the Source of power and wisdom.

O Khalíl! God beareth Me witness. Though My Pen be still moving on My Tablet, yet, in its very heart, it weepeth and is sore distressed. The lamp burning before the Throne, likewise, weepeth and groaneth by reason of the things which the Ancient Beauty hath suffered at the hands of them who are but a creation of His Will. God, Himself, knoweth and testifieth to the truth of My words. No man that hath purged his ear from the loud clamour of the infidels, and inclined it to all created things, can fail to hear the voice of their lamentation and weeping over the trouble that hath befallen Us at the hands of those of Our servants that have disbelieved in, and rebelled against, Us. Thus have We disclosed to thee a glimmer of the woes that have come upon us, that thou mayest be made aware of Our sufferings, and patiently endure thy sorrows.

Arise to aid thy Lord at all times and in all circumstances, and be thou one of His helpers. Admonish, then, the people to lend a hearing ear to the words which the Spirit of God hath uttered in this irradiant and resplendent Tablet. Say: Sow not, O people, the seeds of dissension amongst men, and contend not with your neighbour. Be patient under all conditions, and place your whole trust and confidence in God. Aid ye your Lord with the sword of wisdom and of utterance. This indeed well becometh the station of man. To depart from it would be unworthy of God, the Sovereign Lord of all, the Glorified. The people, however, have been led astray, and are truly of the heedless.

Unlock, O people, the gates of the hearts of men with the keys of the remembrance of Him Who is the Remembrance of God and the Source of wisdom amongst you. He hath chosen out of the whole world the hearts of His servants, and made them each a seat for the revelation of His glory. Wherefore, sanctify them from every defilement, that the things for which they were created may be engraven upon them. This indeed is a token of God's bountiful favour.

Beautify your tongues, O people, with truthfulness, and adorn your souls with the ornament of honesty. Beware, O people, that ye deal not treacherously with any one. Be ye the trustees of God amongst His creatures, and the emblems of His generosity amidst His people. They that follow their lusts and corrupt inclinations, have erred and dissipated their efforts. They, indeed, are of the lost. Strive, O people, that your eyes may be directed towards the mercy of God, that your hearts may be attuned to His wondrous remembrance, that your souls may rest confidently upon His grace and bounty, that your feet may tread the path of His good-pleasure. Such are the counsels which I bequeath unto you. Would that ye might follow My counsels!

⁋ 66. To whatever place We may be banished, however great the tribulation We may suffer, they who are the people of God must, with fixed resolve and perfect confidence, keep their eyes directed towards the Day Spring of Glory, and be busied in whatever may be conducive to the betterment of the world and the education of its peoples. All that hath befallen Us in the past hath advanced the interests of Our Revelation and blazoned its fame; and all that may befall Us in the future will have a like result. Cling ye, with your inmost hearts, to the Cause of God, a Cause that hath been sent down by Him Who is the Ordainer, the All-Wise. We have, with the utmost kindliness and mercy, summoned and directed all peoples and nations to that which shall truly profit them.

The Day Star of Truth that shineth in its meridian splendour beareth Us witness! They who are the people of God have no ambition except to revive the world, to ennoble its life, and regenerate its peoples. Truthfulness and goodwill have, at all times, marked their relations with all men. Their outward conduct is but a reflection of their inward life, and their inward life a mirror of their outward conduct. No veil hideth or obscureth the verities on which their Faith is established. Before the eyes of all men these verities have been laid bare, and can be unmistakably recognized. Their very acts attest the truth of these words.

Every discerning eye can, in this Day, perceive the dawning light of God's Revelation, and every attentive ear can recognize the Voice that was heard from the Burning Bush. Such is the rushing of the waters of Divine mercy, that He Who is the Day Spring of the signs of God and the Revealer of the evidences of His glory is without veil or concealment associating and conversing with the peoples of the earth and its kindreds. How numerous are those who, with hearts intent upon malice, have sought Our Presence, and departed from its loyal and loving friends! The portals of grace are wide open before the face of all men. In Our outward dealings with them We have treated alike the righteous and the sinner, that perchance the evil-doer may attain the limitless ocean of Divine forgiveness. Our name "the Concealer" hath shed such a light upon men that the froward hath imagined himself to be numbered with the pious. No man that seeketh Us will We ever disappoint, neither shall he that hath set his face towards Us be denied access unto Our court...

O friends! Help ye the one true God, exalted be His glory, by your goodly deeds, by such conduct and character as shall be acceptable in His sight. He that seeketh to be a helper of God in this Day, let him close his eyes to whatever he may possess, and open them to the things of God. Let him cease to occupy himself with that which profiteth him, and concern himself with that which shall exalt the all-compelling name of the Almighty. He should cleanse his heart from all evil passions and corrupt desires, for the fear of God is the weapon that can render him victorious, the primary instrument whereby he can achieve his purpose. The fear of God is the shield that defendeth His Cause, the buckler that enableth His people to attain to victory. It is a standard that no man can abase, a force that no power can rival. By its aid, and by the leave of Him Who is the Lord of Hosts, they that have drawn nigh unto God have been able to subdue and conquer the citadels of the hearts of men.

¶ 67. The first and foremost duty prescribed unto men, next to the recognition of Him Who is the Eternal Truth, is the duty of steadfastness in His Cause. Cleave thou unto it, and be of them whose minds are firmly fixed and grounded in God. No act, however meritorious, did or can ever compare unto it. It is the king of all acts, and to this thy Lord, the All-Highest, the Most Powerful, will testify. . .

The virtues and attributes pertaining unto God are all evident and manifest, and have been mentioned and described in all the heavenly Books. Among them are trustworthiness, truthfulness, purity of heart while communing with God, forbearance, resignation to whatever the Almighty hath decreed, contentment with the things His Will hath provided, patience, nay, thankfulness in the midst of tribulation, and complete reliance, in all circumstances, upon Him. These rank, according to the estimate of God, among the highest and most laudable of all acts. All other acts are, and will ever remain, secondary and subordinate unto them. . .

The spirit that animateth the human heart is the knowledge of God and its truest adorning is the recognition of the truth that "He doeth whatsoever He willeth, and ordaineth that which He pleaseth." Its raiment is the fear of God, and its perfection steadfastness in His Faith. Thus God instructeth whosoever seeketh Him. He, verily, loveth the one that turneth towards Him. There is none other God but Him, the Forgiving, the Most Bountiful. All praise be to God, the Lord of all worlds.

¶ 68. The Most Great Name beareth Me witness! How sad if any man were, in this Day, to rest his heart on the transitory things of this world! Arise, and cling firmly to the Cause of God. Be most loving one to another. Burn away, wholly for the sake of the Well-Beloved, the veil of self with the flame of the undying Fire, and with faces, joyous and beaming with light, associate with your neighbour. Ye have well observed, in all its aspects, the behaviour of Him Who is the Word of Truth amidst you. Ye know full well how hard it is for this Youth to allow, though it be for one night, the heart of any one of the beloved of God to be saddened by Him.

The Word of God hath set the heart of the world afire; how regrettable if ye fail to be enkindled with its flame! Please God, ye will regard this blessed night as the night of unity, will knit your

souls together, and resolve to adorn yourselves with the ornament
of a goodly and praiseworthy character. Let your principal concern
be to rescue the fallen from the slough of impending extinction,
and to help him embrace the ancient Faith of God. Your behaviour
towards your neighbour should be such as to manifest clearly the
signs of the one true God, for ye are the first among men to be recreated by His Spirit, the first to adore and bow the knee before
Him, the first to circle round His throne of glory. I swear by Him
Who hath caused Me to reveal whatever hath pleased Him! Ye
are better known to the inmates of the Kingdom on high than ye
are known to your own selves. Think ye these words to be vain
and empty? Would that ye had the power to perceive the things
your Lord, the All-Merciful, doth see—things that attest the excellence of your rank, that bear witness to the greatness of your
worth, that proclaim the sublimity of your station! God grant
that your desires and unmortified passions may not hinder you
from that which hath been ordained for you.

¶ 69. It is Our wish and desire that every one of you may become
a source of all goodness unto men, and an example of uprightness
to mankind. Beware lest ye prefer yourselves above your neighbours. Fix your gaze upon Him Who is the Temple of God
amongst men. He, in truth, hath offered up His life as a ransom for
the redemption of the world. He, verily, is the All-Bountiful, the
Gracious, the Most High. If any differences arise amongst you, behold Me standing before your face, and overlook the faults of one
another for My name's sake and as a token of your love for My
manifest and resplendent Cause. We love to see you at all times
consorting in amity and concord within the paradise of My good-
pleasure, and to inhale from your acts the fragrance of friendliness
and unity, of loving-kindness and fellowship. Thus counselleth you
the All-Knowing, the Faithful. We shall always be with you; if
We inhale the perfume of your fellowship, Our heart will assuredly
rejoice, for naught else can satisfy Us. To this beareth witness every
man of true understanding.

¶ 70. If ye meet the abased or the down-trodden, turn not away
disdainfully from them, for the King of Glory ever watcheth over
them and surroundeth them with such tenderness as none can fath-

om except them that have suffered their wishes and desires to be merged in the Will of your Lord, the Gracious, the All-Wise. O ye rich ones of the earth! Flee not from the face of the poor that lieth in the dust, nay rather befriend him and suffer him to recount the tale of the woes with which God's inscrutable Decree hath caused him to be afflicted. By the righteousness of God! Whilst ye consort with him, the Concourse on high will be looking upon you, will be interceding for you, will be extolling your names and glorifying your action. Blessed are the learned that pride not themselves on their attainments; and well is it with the righteous that mock not the sinful, but rather conceal their misdeeds, so that their own shortcomings may remain veiled to men's eyes.

(II) THE CAUSE OF GOD

¶ 71. The Book of God is wide open, and His Word is summoning mankind unto Him. No more than a mere handful, however, hath been found willing to cleave to His Cause, or to become the instruments for its promotion. These few have been endued with the Divine Elixir that can, alone, transmute into purest gold the dross of the world, and have been empowered to administer the infallible remedy for all the ills that afflict the children of men. No man can obtain everlasting life, unless he embraceth the truth of this inestimable, this wondrous, and sublime Revelation.

Incline your ears, O friends of God, to the voice of Him Whom the world hath wronged, and hold fast unto whatsoever will exalt His Cause. He, verily, guideth whomsoever He pleaseth unto His straight Path. This is a Revelation that infuseth strength into the feeble, and crowneth with wealth the destitute.

With the utmost friendliness and in a spirit of perfect fellowship take ye counsel together, and dedicate the precious days of your lives to the betterment of the world and the promotion of the Cause of Him Who is the Ancient and Sovereign Lord of all. He, verily, enjoineth upon all men what is right, and forbiddeth whatsoever degradeth their station.

¶ 72. The Pen of the Most High hath decreed and imposed upon everyone the obligation to teach this Cause... God will, no doubt, inspire whosoever detacheth himself from all else but Him, and will cause the pure waters of wisdom and utterance to gush out and flow copiously from his heart. Verily, thy Lord, the All-Merciful, is powerful to do as He willeth, and ordaineth whatsoever He pleaseth.

Wert thou to consider this world, and realize how fleeting are the things that pertain unto it, thou wouldst choose to tread no path except the path of service to the Cause of thy Lord. None would have the power to deter thee from celebrating His praise, though all men should arise to oppose thee.

Go thou straight on and persevere in His service. Say: O people! The Day, promised unto you in all the Scriptures, is now come. Fear ye God, and withhold not yourselves from recognizing the One Who is the Object of your creation. Hasten ye unto Him. Better is this for you than the world and all that is therein. Would that ye could perceive it!

¶ 73. They that have forsaken their country for the purpose of teaching Our Cause—these shall the Faithful Spirit strengthen through its power. A company of Our chosen angels shall go forth with them, as bidden by Him Who is the Almighty, the All-Wise. How great the blessedness that awaiteth him that hath attained the honour of serving the Almighty! By My life! No act, however great, can compare with it, except such deeds as have been ordained by God, the All-Powerful, the Most Mighty. Such a service is, indeed the prince of all goodly deeds, and the ornament of every goodly act. Thus hath it been ordained by Him Who is the Sovereign Revealer, the Ancient of Days.

Whoso ariseth to teach Our Cause must needs detach himself from all earthly things, and regard, at all times, the triumph of Our Faith as his supreme objective. This hath, verily, been decreed in the Guarded Tablet. And when he determineth to leave his home, for the sake of the Cause of his Lord, let him put his whole trust in God, as the best provision for his journey, and array himself with the robe of virtue. Thus hath it been decreed by God, the Almighty, the All-Praised.

If he be kindled with the fire of His love, if he foregoeth all created things, the words he uttereth shall set on fire them that hear him. Verily, thy Lord is the Omniscient, the All-Informed. Happy is the man that hath heard Our voice, and answered Our call. He, in truth, is of them that shall be brought nigh unto Us.

¶ 74. Should any man, in this Day, arise and, with absolute detachment from all that is in the heavens and all that is on the earth, set his affections on Him Who is the Day Spring of God's holy Revelation, he will, verily, be empowered to subdue all created things, through the potency of one of the Names of the Lord, his God, the All-Knowing, the All-Wise. Know thou of a certainty that the Day Star of Truth hath, in this Day, shed upon the world a radiance, the like of which bygone ages have never witnessed. Let the light of His glory, O people, shine upon you, and be not of the negligent.

¶ 75. Gird up the loins of thine endeavour, that haply thou mayest guide thy neighbour to the law of God, the Most Merciful. Such an act, verily, excelleth all other acts in the sight of God, the All-Possessing, the Most High. Such must be thy steadfastness in the Cause of God, that no earthly thing whatsoever will have the power to deter thee from thy duty. Though the powers of earth be leagued against thee, though all men dispute with thee, thou must remain unshaken.

Be unrestrained as the wind, while carrying the Message of Him Who hath caused the Dawn of Divine Guidance to break. Consider how the wind, faithful to that which God hath ordained, bloweth upon all the regions of the earth, be they inhabited or desolate. Neither the sight of desolation, nor the evidences of prosperity, can either pain or please it. It bloweth in every direction, as bidden by its Creator. So should be every one that claimeth to be a lover of the one true God. It behoveth him to fix his gaze upon the fundamentals of His Faith, and to labour diligently for its propagation. Wholly for the sake of God he should proclaim His Message, and with that same spirit accept whatever response his words may evoke in his hearer. He who shall accept and believe, shall receive his reward; and he who shall turn away, shall receive none other than his own punishment.

On the eve of Our departure from 'Iráq, We have warned the faithful to anticipate the appearance of the Birds of Darkness. There can be no doubt whatever that the croaking of the Raven shall be raised in certain lands, as it hath been heard in recent years. Whatever may betide, seek refuge in the one true God, that He may shield you from the wiles of the impostor.

Verily I say, in this most mighty Revelation, all the Dispensations of the past have attained their highest, their final consummation. Thus counselleth you your Lord, the All-Knowing, the All-Wise. Praise be to God, the Lord of all worlds.

The All-Merciful hath conferred upon man the faculty of vision, and endowed him with the power of hearing. Some have described him as the "lesser world", when, in reality, he should be regarded as the "greater world". The potentialities inherent in the station of man, the full measure of his destiny on earth, the innate excellence of his reality, must all be manifested in this promised Day of God.

The Pen of the Most High hath, at all times and under all conditions, remembered, with joy and tenderness, His loved ones, and hath counselled them to follow in His way. Well is it with him whom the changes and chances of this world have failed to deter from recognizing the Day Spring of the Unity of God, who hath quaffed, with unswerving resolve, and in the name of the Self-Subsisting, the sealed wine of His Revelation. Such a man shall be numbered with the inmates of Paradise, in the Book of God, the Lord of all worlds.

¶ 76. The Pen of the Most High is unceasingly calling; and yet, how few are those that have inclined their ear to its voice! The dwellers of the kingdom of names have busied themselves with the gay livery of the world, forgetful that every man that hath eyes to perceive and ears to hear cannot but readily recognize how evanescent are its colours.

A new life is, in this age, stirring within all the peoples of the earth; and yet none hath discovered its cause or perceived its motive. Consider the peoples of the West. Witness how, in their pursuit of that which is vain and trivial, they have sacrificed, and are still sacrificing, countless lives for the sake of its establishment and promotion. The peoples of Persia, on the other hand, though the repository of a perspicuous and luminous Revelation, the glory of whose loftiness and renown hath encompassed the whole earth, are dispirited and sunk in deep lethargy.

O friends! Be not careless of the virtues with which ye have been endowed, neither be neglectful of your high destiny. Suffer not your labours to be wasted through the vain imaginations which certain hearts have devised. Ye are the stars of the heaven of understanding, the breeze that stirreth at the break of day, the soft-flowing waters upon which must depend the very life of all men, the letters inscribed upon His sacred scroll. With the utmost unity, and in a spirit of perfect fellowship, exert yourselves, that ye may be enabled to achieve that which beseemeth this Day of God. Verily I say, strife and dissension, and whatsoever the mind of man abhorreth are entirely unworthy of his station. Centre your energies in the propagation of the Faith of God. Whoso is worthy of so high a calling, let him arise and promote it. Whoso is unable, it is his duty to appoint him who will, in his stead, proclaim this Revelation, whose power hath caused the foundations of the mightiest structures to quake, every mountain to be crushed into dust, and every soul to be dumbfounded. Should the greatness of this Day be revealed in its fullness, every man would forsake a myriad lives in his longing to partake, though it be for one moment, of its great glory —how much more this world and its corruptible treasures!

Be ye guided by wisdom in all your doings, and cleave ye tenaciously unto it. Please God ye may all be strengthened to carry out that which is the Will of God, and may be graciously assisted to appreciate the rank conferred upon such of His loved ones as have arisen to serve Him and magnify His name. Upon them be the glory of God, the glory of all that is in the heavens and all that is on the earth, and the glory of the inmates of the most exalted Paradise, the heaven of heavens.

(III) THE PATH OF GOD

¶ 77. O My brother! When a true seeker determineth to take the step of search in the path leading unto the knowledge of the Ancient of Days, he must, before all else, cleanse his heart, which is the seat of the revelation of the inner mysteries of God, from the obscuring dust of all acquired knowledge, and the allusions of the embodiments of satanic fancy. He must purge his breast, which is the sanctuary of the abiding love of the Beloved, of every defilement, and sanctify his soul from all that pertaineth to water and clay, from all shadowy and ephemeral attachments. He must so cleanse his heart that no remnant of either love or hate may linger therein, lest that love blindly incline him to error, or that hate repel him away from the truth. Even as thou dost witness in this Day how most of the people, because of such love and hate, are bereft of the immortal

Face, have strayed far from the Embodiments of the Divine mysteries, and, shepherdless, are roaming through the wilderness of oblivion and error.

That seeker must, at all times, put his trust in God, must renounce the peoples of the earth, must detach himself from the world of dust, and cleave unto Him Who is the Lord of Lords. He must never seek to exalt himself above any one, must 'wash away from the tablet of his heart every trace of pride and vain-glory, must cling unto patience and resignation, observe silence and refrain from idle talk. For the tongue is a smouldering fire, and excess of speech a deadly poison. Material fire consumeth the body, whereas the fire of the tongue devoureth both heart and soul. The force of the former lasteth but for a time, whilst the effects of the latter endureth a century.

That seeker should, also, regard backbiting as grievous error, and keep himself aloof from its dominion, inasmuch as backbiting quencheth the light of the heart, and extinguisheth the life of the soul. He should be content with little, and be freed from all inordinate desire. He should treasure the companionship of them that have renounced the world, and regard avoidance of boastful and worldly people a precious benefit. At the dawn of every day he should commune with God, and, with all his soul, persevere in the quest of his Beloved. He should consume every wayward thought with the flame of His loving mention, and, with the swiftness of lightning, pass by all else save Him. He should succour the dispossessed, and never withhold his favour from the destitute. He should show kindness to animals, how much more unto his fellow-man, to him who is endowed with the power of utterance. He should not hesitate to offer up his life for his Beloved, nor allow the censure of the people to turn him away from the Truth. He should not wish for others that which he doth not wish for himself, nor promise that which he doth not fulfil. With all his heart he should avoid fellowship with evil-doers, and pray for the remission of their sins. He should forgive the sinful, and never despise his low estate, for none knoweth what his own end shall be. How often hath a sinner attained, at the hour of death, to the essence of faith, and, quaffing the immortal draught, hath taken his flight unto the Concourse on high! And how often hath a devout believer, at the hour of his soul's ascension, been so changed as to fall into the nethermost fire!

Our purpose in revealing these convincing and weighty utterances is to impress upon the seeker that he should regard all else beside God as transient, and count all things save Him, Who is the Object of all adoration, as utter nothingness.

These are among the attributes of the exalted, and constitute the hallmark of the spiritually-minded. They have already been mentioned in connection with the requirements of the wayfarers that tread the path of Positive Knowledge. When the detached wayfarer and sincere seeker hath fulfilled these essential conditions, then and only then can he be called a true seeker. Whensoever he hath fulfilled the conditions implied in the verse: "Whoso maketh efforts for Us," he shall enjoy the blessings conferred by the words: "In Our Ways shall We assuredly guide him."

Only when the lamp of search, of earnest striving, of longing desire, of passionate devotion, of fervid love, of rapture, and ecstasy, is kindled within the seeker's heart, and the breeze of His loving-kindness is wafted upon his soul, will the darkness of error be dispelled, the mists of doubts and misgivings be dissipated, and the lights of knowledge and certitude envelop his being. At that hour will the Mystic Herald, bearing the joyful tidings of the Spirit, shine forth from the City of God resplendent as the morn, and through the trumpet-blast of knowledge, will awaken the heart, the soul, and the spirit from the slumber of heedlessness. Then will the manifold favours and outpouring grace of the holy and everlasting Spirit confer such new life upon the seeker that he will find himself endowed with a new eye, a new ear, a new heart, and a new mind. He will contemplate the manifest signs of the universe, and will penetrate the hidden mysteries of the soul. Gazing with the eye of God, he will perceive within every atom a door that leadeth him to the stations of absolute certitude. He will discover in all things the mysteries of Divine Revelation, and the evidences of an everlasting Manifestation.

I swear by God! Were he that treadeth the path of guidance and seeketh to scale the heights of righteousness to attain unto this glorious and exalted station, he would inhale, at a distance of a thousand leagues, the fragrance of God, and would perceive the resplendent morn of a Divine guidance rising above the Day Spring of all things. Each and every thing, however small, would be to him a revelation, leading him to his Beloved, the Object of his quest. So great shall be the discernment of this seeker that he will discriminate between truth and falsehood, even as he doth distinguish the sun from shadow. If in the uttermost corners of the East the sweet savours of God be wafted, he will assuredly recognize and inhale their fragrance, even though he be dwelling in the uttermost ends of the West. He will, likewise, clearly distinguish all the signs of God—His wondrous utterances, His great works, and mighty deeds—from the doings, the words and ways of men, even as the jeweller who knoweth the gem from the stone, or the man who distinguisheth the spring from autumn, and heat from cold. When the channel of the human soul is cleansed of all worldly and impeding attachments, it will unfailingly perceive the breath of the Beloved across immeasurable distances, and will, led by its perfume, attain and enter the City of Certitude.

Therein he will discern the wonders of His ancient Wisdom, and will perceive all the hidden teachings from the rustling leaves of the Tree that flourisheth in that City. With both his inner and outer ear, he will hear from its dust the hymns of glory and praise ascending unto the Lord of Lords, and with his inner eye will he discover the mysteries of "return" and "revival".

How unspeakably glorious are the signs, the tokens, the revelations, and splendours which He, Who is the King of Names and Attributes, hath destined for that City! The attainment unto this City quencheth thirst without water, and kindleth the love of God without fire. Within every blade of grass are enshrined the mysteries of an inscrutable Wisdom, and upon every rose-bush a myriad nightingales pour out, in blissful rapture, their melody. Its wondrous tulips unfold the mystery of the undying Fire in the Burning Bush, and its sweet savours of holiness breathe the perfume of the Messianic Spirit. It bestoweth wealth without gold, and conferreth immortality without death. In each one of its leaves ineffable delights are treasured, and within every chamber unnumbered mysteries lie hidden.

They that valiantly labour in quest of God, will, when once they have renounced all else but Him, be so attached and wedded unto that City, that a moment's separation from it would to them be unthinkable. They will hearken unto infallible proofs from the Hyacinth of that assembly, and will receive the surest testimonies from the beauty of its Rose, and the melody of its Nightingale. Once in about a thousand years shall this City be renewed and readorned...

That City is none other than the Word of God revealed in every age and dispensation. In the days of Moses it was the Pentateuch; in the days of Jesus, the Gospel; in the days of Muḥammad, the Messenger of God, the Qur'án; in this day, the Bayán; and in the Dispensation of Him Whom God will make manifest, His own Book—the Book unto which all the Books of former Dispensations must needs be referred, the Book that standeth amongst them all transcendent and supreme.

¶ 78. O banished and faithful friend! Quench the thirst of heedlessness with the sanctified waters of My grace, and chase the gloom of remoteness through the morning-light of My Divine presence. Suffer not the habitation wherein dwelleth My undying love for thee to be destroyed through the tyranny of covetous desires, and overcloud not the beauty of the heavenly Youth with the dust of self and passion. Clothe thyself with the essence of righteousness, and let thine heart be afraid of none except God. Obstruct not the luminous spring of thy soul with the thorns and brambles of vain and inordinate affections, and impede not the flow of the living waters that stream from the fountain of thine heart. Set all thy hope in God, and cleave tenaciously to His unfailing mercy. Who else but Him can enrich the destitute, and deliver the fallen from his abasement?

O My servants! Were ye to discover the hidden, the shoreless oceans of My incorruptible wealth, ye would, of a certainty, esteem as nothing the world, nay the entire creation. Let the flame of search burn with such fierceness within your hearts as to enable you to attain your supreme and most exalted goal—the station at which ye can draw nigh unto, and be united with, your Best-Beloved...

O My servants! Let not your vain hopes and idle fancies sap the foundations of your belief in the All-Glorious God, inasmuch as such imaginings have been wholly unprofitable unto men, and failed to direct their steps unto the straight Path. Think ye, O My servants, that the Hand of My all-encompassing, My overshadowing, and transcendent sovereignty is chained up, that the flow of Mine ancient, My ceaseless, and all-pervasive mercy is checked, or that the clouds of My sublime and unsurpassed favours have ceased to rain their gifts upon men? Can ye imagine that the wondrous works that have proclaimed My divine and resistless power are withdrawn, or that the potency of My will and purpose hath been deterred from directing the destinies of mankind? If it be not so, wherefore, then, have ye striven to prevent the deathless Beauty of My sacred and gracious Countenance from being unveiled to men's eyes? Why have ye struggled to hinder the Manifestation of the Almighty and All-Glorious Being from shedding the radiance of His Revelation upon the earth? Were ye to be fair in your judgment, ye would readily recognize how the realities of all created things are inebriated with the joy of this new and wondrous Revelation, how all the atoms of the earth have been illuminated through the brightness of its glory. Vain and wretched is that which ye have imagined and still imagine!

Retrace your steps, O My servants, and incline your hearts to Him Who is the Source of your creation. Deliver yourselves from your evil and corrupt affections, and hasten to embrace the light of the undying Fire that gloweth on the Sinai of this mysterious and transcendent Revelation. Corrupt not the holy, the all-embracing, and primal Word of God, and seek not to profane its sanctity or to debase its exalted character. O heedless ones! Though the wonders of My mercy have encompassed all created things, both visible and invisible, and though the revelations of My grace and bounty have permeated every atom of the universe, yet the rod with which I can chastise the wicked is grievous, and the fierceness of Mine anger against them terrible. With ears that are sanctified from vain-glory and worldly desires hearken unto the counsels which I, in My merciful kindness, have revealed unto you, and with your inner and outer eyes contemplate the evidences of My marvellous Revelation. . .

O My servants! Deprive not yourselves of the unfading and resplendent Light that shineth within the Lamp of Divine glory. Let the flame of the love of God burn brightly within your radiant hearts. Feed it with the oil of Divine guidance, and protect it within the shelter of your constancy. Guard it within the globe of trust and detachment from all else but God, so that the evil whisperings of the ungodly may not extinguish its light. O My servants! My holy, My divinely ordained Revelation may be likened unto an ocean in whose depths are concealed innumerable pearls of great price, of surpassing lustre. It is the duty of every seeker to bestir himself and strive to attain the shores of this ocean, so that he may, in proportion to the eagerness of his search and the efforts he hath exerted, partake of such benefits as have been pre-ordained in God's irrevocable and hidden Tablets. If no one be willing to direct his steps towards its shores, if everyone should fail to arise and find Him, can such a failure be said to have robbed this ocean of its power or to have lessened, to any degree, its treasures? How vain, how contemptible, are the imaginations which your hearts have devised, and are still devising! O My servants! The one true God is My witness! This most great, this fathomless and surging Ocean is near, astonishingly near, unto you. Behold it is closer to you than your life-vein! Swift as the twinkling of an eye ye can, if ye but wish it, reach and partake of this imperishable favour, this God-given grace, this incorruptible gift, this most potent and unspeakably glorious bounty.

O My servants! Could ye apprehend with what wonders of My munificence and bounty I have willed to entrust your souls, ye would, of a truth, rid yourselves of attachment to all created things, and would gain a true knowledge of your own selves—a knowledge which is the same as the comprehension of Mine own Being. Ye would find yourselves independent of all else but Me, and would perceive, with your inner and outer eye, and as manifest as the revelation of My effulgent name, the seas of My loving-kindness and bounty moving within you. Suffer not your idle fancies, your evil passions, your insincerity and blindness of heart to dim the lustre, or stain the sanctity, of so lofty a station. Ye are even as the bird which soareth, with the full force of its mighty wings and with complete and joyous confidence, through the immensity of the heavens, until, impelled to satisfy its hunger, it turneth longingly to the water and clay of the earth below it, and, having been entrapped in the mesh of its desire, findeth itself impotent to resume its flight to the realms whence it came. Powerless to shake off the burden weighing on its sullied wings, that bird, hitherto an inmate of the heavens, is now forced to seek a dwelling-place upon the dust. Wherefore, O My servants, defile not your wings with the clay of waywardness and vain desires, and suffer them not to be stained with the dust of envy and hate, that ye may not be hindered from soaring in the heavens of My divine knowledge.

O My servants! Through the might of God and His power, and out of the treasury of His knowledge and wisdom, I have brought forth and revealed unto you the pearls that lay concealed in the depths of His everlasting ocean. I have summoned the Maids of Heaven to emerge from behind the veil of concealment, and have clothed them with these words of Mine—words of consummate power and wisdom. I have, moreover, with the hand of divine power, unsealed the choice wine of My Revelation, and have wafted its holy, its hidden, and musk-laden fragrance upon all created things. Who else but yourselves is to be blamed if ye choose to remain unendowed with so great an outpouring of God's transcendent and all-encompassing grace, with so bright a revelation of His resplendent mercy? . . .

O My servants! There shineth nothing else in Mine heart except the unfading light of the Morn of Divine guidance, and out of My mouth proceedeth naught but the essence of truth, which the Lord your God hath revealed. Follow not, therefore, your earthly desires, and violate not the Covenant of God, nor break your pledge to Him. With firm determination, with the whole affection of your heart, and with the full force of your words, turn ye unto Him, and walk not in the ways of the foolish. The world is but a show, vain and empty, a mere nothing, bearing the semblance of reality. Set not your affections upon it. Break not the bond that uniteth you with your Creator, and be not of those that have erred and strayed from His ways. Verily I say, the world is like the vapour in a desert, which the thirsty dreameth to be water and striveth after it with all his might, until when he cometh unto it, he findeth it to be mere illusion. It may, moreover, be likened unto the lifeless image of the beloved whom the lover hath sought and found, in the end, after long search and to his utmost regret, to be such as cannot "fatten nor appease his hunger".

O My servants! Sorrow not if, in these days and on this earthly plane, things contrary to your wishes have been ordained and manifested by God, for days of blissful joy, of heavenly delight, are assuredly in store for you. Worlds, holy and spiritually glorious, will be unveiled to your eyes. You are destined by Him, in this world and hereafter, to partake of their benefits, to share in their joys, and to obtain a portion of their sustaining grace. To each and every one of them you will, no doubt, attain.

¶ 79. O Salmán! All that the sages and mystics have said or written have never exceeded, nor can they ever hope to exceed, the limitations to which man's finite mind hath been strictly subjected. To whatever heights the mind of the most exalted of men may soar, however great the depths which the detached and understanding heart can penetrate, such mind and heart can never transcend that which is the creature of their own conceptions and the product of their own thoughts. The meditations of the profoundest thinker, the devotions of the holiest of saints, the highest expressions of praise from either human pen or tongue, are but a reflection of that which hath been created within themselves, through the revelation of the Lord, their God. Whoever pondereth this truth in his heart will readily admit that there are certain limits which no human being can possibly transgress. Every attempt which, from the beginning that hath no beginning, hath been made to visualize and know God is limited by the exigencies of His own creation—a creation which He, through the operation of His own Will and for the purposes of none other but His own Self, hath called into being. Immeasurably exalted is He above the strivings of human mind to grasp His Essence, or of human tongue to describe His mystery. No tie of direct intercourse can ever bind Him to the things He hath created, nor can the most abstruse and most remote allusions of His creatures do justice to His being. Through His world-pervading Will He hath brought into being all created things. He is and hath ever been veiled in the ancient eternity of His own exalted and indivisible Essence, and will everlastingly continue to remain concealed in His inaccessible majesty and glory. All that is in heaven and all that is in the earth have come to exist at His bidding, and by His Will all have stepped out of utter nothingness into the realm of being. How can, therefore, the creature which the Word of God hath fashioned comprehend the nature of Him Who is the Ancient of Days?

¶ 80. O wayfarer in the path of God! Take thou thy portion of the ocean of His grace, and deprive not thyself of the things that lie hidden in its depths. Be thou of them that have partaken of its treasures. A dewdrop out of this ocean would, if shed upon all that are in the heavens and on the earth, suffice to enrich them with the bounty of God, the Almighty, the All-Knowing, the All-Wise. With the hands of renunciation draw forth from its life-giving waters, and sprinkle therewith all created things, that they may be cleansed from all man-made limitations and may approach the mighty seat of God, this hallowed and resplendent Spot.

Be not grieved if thou performest it thyself alone. Let God be all-sufficient for thee. Commune intimately with His Spirit, and be thou of the thankful. Proclaim the Cause of thy Lord unto all who are in the heavens and on the earth. Should any man respond to thy call, lay bare before him the pearls of the wisdom of the Lord, thy God, which His Spirit hath sent down unto thee, and be thou of them that truly believe. And should any one reject thy offer, turn thou away from him, and put thy trust and confidence in the Lord, thy God, the Lord of all worlds.

By the righteousness of God! Whoso openeth his lips in this Day and maketh mention of the name of his Lord, the hosts of Divine inspiration shall descend upon him from the heaven of My name, the All-Knowing, the All-Wise. On him shall also descend the Concourse on High, each bearing aloft a chalice of pure light. Thus hath it been foreordained in the realm of God's Revelation, by the behest of Him Who is the All-Glorious, the Most Powerful.

There lay concealed within the Holy Veil, and prepared for the service of God, a company of His chosen ones who shall be manifested unto men, who shall aid His Cause, who shall be afraid of no one, though the entire human race rise up and war against them. These are the ones who, before the gaze of the dwellers on earth and the denizens of heaven, shall arise and, shouting aloud, acclaim the name of the Almighty, and summon the children of men to the path of God, the All-Glorious, the All-praised. Walk thou in their way, and let no one dismay thee. Be of them whom the tumult of the world, however much it may agitate them in the path of their Creator, can never sadden, whose purpose the blame of the blamer will never defeat.

Go forth with the Tablet of God and His signs, and rejoin them that have believed in Me, and announce unto them tidings of Our most holy Paradise. Warn, then, those that have joined partners with Him. Say: I am come to you, O people, from the Throne of glory, and bear you an announcement from God, the Most Powerful, the Most Exalted, the Most Great. In mine hand I carry the testimony of God, your Lord and the Lord of your sires of old. Weigh it with the just Balance that ye possess, the Balance of the testimony of the Prophets and Messengers of God. If ye find it to be established in truth, if ye believe it to be of God, beware, then, lest ye cavil at it, and render your works vain, and be numbered with the infidels. It is indeed the sign of God that hath been sent down through the power of truth, through which the validity of His Cause hath been demonstrated unto His creatures, and the ensigns of purity lifted up betwixt earth and heaven.

Say: This is the sealed and mystic Scroll, the repository of God's irrevocable Decree, bearing the words which the Finger of Holiness hath traced, that lay wrapt within the veil of impenetrable mystery, and hath now been sent down as a token of the grace of Him Who is the Almighty, the Ancient of Days. In it have We decreed the destinies of all the dwellers of the earth and the denizens of heaven, and written down the knowledge of all things from first to last. Nothing whatsoever can escape or frustrate Him, whether created in the past or to be created in the future, could ye but perceive it.

Say: The Revelation sent down by God hath most surely been repeated, and the outstretched Hand of Our power hath overshadowed all that are in the heavens and all that are on the earth. We have, through the power of truth, the very truth, manifested an infinitesimal glimmer of Our impenetrable Mystery, and lo, they that have recognized the radiance of the Sinaic splendour expired, as they caught a lightning glimpse of this Crimson Light enveloping the Sinai of Our Revelation. Thus hath He Who is the Beauty of the All-Merciful come down in the clouds of His testimony, and the decree accomplished by virtue of the Will of God, the All-Glorious, the All-Wise.

Say: Step out of Thy holy chamber, O Maid of Heaven, inmate of the Exalted Paradise! Drape thyself in whatever manner pleaseth Thee in the silken Vesture of Immortality, and put on, in the name of the All-Glorious, the broidered Robe of Light. Hear, then, the sweet, the wondrous accent of the Voice that cometh from the Throne of Thy Lord, the Inaccessible, the Most High. Unveil Thy face, and manifest the beauty of the black-eyed Damsel, and suffer not the servants of God to be deprived of the light of Thy shining countenance. Grieve not if Thou hearest the sighs of the dwellers of the earth, or the voice of the lamentation of the denizens of heaven. Leave them to perish on the dust of extinction. Let them be reduced to nothingness, inasmuch as the flame of hatred hath been

kindled within their breasts. Intone, then, before the face of the
peoples of earth and heaven, and in a most melodious voice, the
anthem of praise, for a remembrance of Him Who is the King of
the names and attributes of God. Thus have We decreed Thy
destiny. Well able are We to achieve Our purpose.

Beware that Thou divest not Thyself, Thou Who art the Essence
of Purity, of Thy robe of effulgent glory. Nay, enrich Thyself in-
creasingly, in the kingdom of creation, with the incorruptible ves-
tures of Thy God, that the beauteous image of the Almighty may
be reflected through Thee in all created things and the grace of Thy
Lord be infused in the plenitude of its power into the entire creation.

If Thou smellest from any one the smell of the love of Thy Lord,
offer up Thyself for him, for We have created Thee to this end, and
have covenanted with Thee, from time immemorial, and in the
presence of the congregation of Our well-favoured ones, for this
very purpose. Be not impatient if the blind in heart hurl down the
shafts of their idle fancies upon Thee. Leave them to themselves, for
they follow the promptings of the evil ones.

Cry out before the gaze of the dwellers of heaven and of earth: I
am the Maid of Heaven, the Offspring begotten by the Spirit of
Bahá. My habitation is the Mansion of His Name, the All-Glorious.
Before the Concourse on high I was adorned with the ornament of
His names. I was wrapt within the veil of an inviolable security, and
lay hidden from the eyes of men. Methinks that I heard a Voice of
divine and incomparable sweetness, proceeding from the right
hand of the God of Mercy, and lo, the whole Paradise stirred and
trembled before Me, in its longing to hear its accents, and gaze on
the beauty of Him that uttered them. Thus have We revealed in
this luminous Tablet, in the sweetest of languages, the verses which
the Tongue of Eternity was moved to utter in the Qayyúmu'l-
Asmá.

Say: He ordaineth as He pleaseth, by virtue of His sovereignty,
and doeth whatsoever He willeth at His own behest. He shall not
be asked of the things it pleaseth Him to ordain. He, in truth, is the
Unrestrained, the All-Powerful, the All-Wise.

They that have disbelieved in God and rebelled against His
sovereignty are the helpless victims of their corrupt inclinations
and desires. These shall return to their abode in the fire of hell:
wretched is the abode of the deniers!

III. SELECTION FROM "THE HIDDEN WORDS"

1. FROM THE ARABIC

¶ 81. This is that which hath descended from the realm of glory, uttered by the tongue of power and might, and revealed unto the Prophets of old. We have taken the inner essence thereof and clothed it in the garment of brevity, as a token of grace unto the righteous, that they may stand faithful unto the covenant of God, may fulfil in their lives His trust, and in the realm of spirit obtain the gem of Divine virtue.

¶ 82. O Son of Spirit! My first counsel is this: Possess a pure, kindly and radiant heart, that thine may be a sovereignty ancient, imperishable and everlasting.

¶ 83. O Son of Spirit! The best beloved of all things in My sight is Justice; turn not away therefrom if thou desirest Me, and neglect it not that I may confide in thee. By its aid thou shalt see with thine own eyes and not through the eyes of others, and shalt know of thine own knowledge and not through the knowledge of thy neighbour. Ponder this in thy heart; how it behoveth thee to be. Verily justice is My gift to thee and the sign of My loving-kindness. Set it then before thine eyes.

¶ 84. O Son of Man! Veiled in My immemorial being and in the ancient eternity of My essence, I knew My love for thee; therefore I created thee, have engraved on thee Mine image and revealed to thee My beauty.

¶ 85. O Son of Man! I loved thy creation, hence I created thee. Wherefore, do thou love Me, that I may name thy name and fill thy soul with the spirit of life.

¶ 86. O Son of Being! Love Me, that I may love thee. If thou lovest Me not, My love can in no wise reach thee. Know this, O servant.

¶ 87. O Son of Man! If thou lovest Me, turn away from thyself; and if thou seekest My pleasure, regard not thine own; that thou mayest die in Me and I may eternally live in thee.

¶ 88. O Son of Being! My love is My stronghold; he that entereth therein is safe and secure, and he that turneth away shall surely stray and perish.

¶ 89. O Son of Being! Thou art My lamp and My light is in thee. Get thou from it thy radiance and seek none other than Me. For I have created thee rich and have bountifully shed My favour upon thee.

¶ 90. O Son of Light! Forget all save Me and commune with My spirit. This is of the essence of My command, therefore turn unto it.

¶ 91. O Son of Spirit! Ask not of Me that which We desire not for thee, then be content with what We have ordained for thy sake, for this is that which profiteth thee, if therewith thou dost content thyself.

¶ 92. O Son of Man! Breathe not the sins of others so long as thou art thyself a sinner. Shouldst thou transgress this command, accursed wouldst thou be, and to this I bear witness.

¶ 93. O Son of Man! Deny not My servant should he ask anything from thee, for his face is My face; be then abashed before Me.

¶ 94. O Son of Being! Bring thyself to account each day ere thou art summoned to a reckoning; for death, unheralded, shall come upon thee and thou shalt be called to give account for thy deeds.

¶ 95. O Son of the Supreme! I have made death a messenger of joy to thee. Wherefore dost thou grieve? I made the light to shed on thee its splendour. Why dost thou veil thyself therefrom?

¶ 96. O Son of Spirit! With the joyful tidings of light I hail thee:

rejoice! To the court of holiness I summon thee; abide therein that thou mayest live in peace for evermore.

¶ 97. O Son of Man! Rejoice in the gladness of thine heart, that thou mayest be worthy to meet Me and to mirror forth My beauty.

¶ 98. O Son of Man! Wert thou to speed through the immensity of space and traverse the expanse of heaven, yet thou shouldst find no rest save in submission to Our Command and humbleness before Our Face.

¶ 99. O Son of Man! Humble thyself before Me, that I may graciously visit thee. Arise for the triumph of My cause, that while yet on earth thou mayest obtain the victory.

¶ 100. O Son of the Throne! Thy hearing is My hearing, hear thou therewith. Thy sight is My sight, do thou see therewith, that in thine inmost soul thou mayest testify unto My exalted sanctity, and I within Myself may bear witness unto an exalted station for thee.

¶ 101. O Son of Man! For everything there is a sign. The sign of love is fortitude under My decree and patience under My trials.

¶ 102. O Son of Man! The true lover yearneth for tribulation even as doth the rebel for forgiveness and the sinful for mercy.

¶ 103. O Son of Man! If adversity befall thee not in My path, how canst thou walk in the ways of them that are content with My pleasure? If trials afflict thee not in thy longing to meet Me, how wilt thou attain the light in thy love for My beauty?

¶ 104. O Son of Being! If thine heart be set upon this eternal, imperishable dominion, and this ancient, everlasting life, forsake this mortal and fleeting sovereignty.

¶ 105. O Son of Being! Busy not thyself with this world, for with fire We test the gold, and with gold We test Our servants.

¶ 106. O Son of Being! Thy heart is My home; sanctify it for My descent. Thy spirit is My place of revelation; cleanse it for My manifestation.

¶ 107. O Son of Man! Ascend unto My heaven, that thou mayest obtain the joy of reunion, and from the chalice of imperishable glory quaff the peerless wine.

¶ 108. O Son of Beauty! By My spirit and by My favour! By My mercy and by My beauty! All that I have revealed unto thee, with the tongue of power, and have written for thee with the pen of might, hath been in accordance with thy capacity and understanding, not with My state and the melody of My voice.

¶ 109. O Children of Men! Know ye not why We created you all from the same dust? That no one should exalt himself over the other. Ponder at all times in your hearts how ye were created. Since We have created you all from one same substance it is incumbent on you to be even as one soul, to walk with the same feet, eat with the same mouth and dwell in the same land, that from your inmost being, by your deeds and actions, the signs of oneness and the essence of detachment may be made manifest. Such is My counsel to you, O concourse of light! Heed ye this counsel that ye may obtain the fruit of holiness from the tree of wondrous glory.

2. FROM THE PERSIAN

¶ 110. O Ye People that have Minds to Know and Ears to Hear! The first call of the Beloved is this: O mystic nightingale! Abide not but in the rose-garden of the spirit. O messenger of the Solomon of love! Seek thou no shelter except in the Sheba of the well-beloved, and O immortal phoenix! dwell not save on the mount of faithfulness. Therein is thy habitation, if on the wings of thy soul thou soarest to the realm of the infinite and seekest to attain thy goal.

¶ 111. O Friend! In the garden of thy heart plant naught but the rose of love, and from the nightingale of affection and desire loosen not thy hold. Treasure the companionship of the righteous and eschew all fellowship with the ungodly.

¶ 112. O Son of Justice! Whither can a lover go but to the land of his beloved? and what seeker findeth rest away from his heart's desire? To the true lover reunion is life, and separation is death. His breast is void of patience and his heart hath no peace. A myriad lives he would forsake to hasten to the abode of his beloved.

¶ 113. O Son of Dust! Verily I say unto thee of all men the most negligent is he that disputeth idly and seeketh to advance himself over his brother. Say, O brethren! Let deeds, not words, be your adorning.

¶ 114. O Son of Earth! Know, verily, the heart wherein the least remnant of envy yet lingers, shall never attain My everlasting dominion, nor inhale the sweet savours of holiness breathing from My kingdom of sanctity.

¶ 115. O Son of Glory! Be swift in the path of holiness, and enter the heaven of communion with Me. Cleanse thy heart with the burnish of the spirit, and hasten to the court of the Most High.

¶ 116. O Man of Two Visions! Close one eye and open the other. Close one to the world and all that is therein, and open the other to the hallowed beauty of the Beloved.

¶ 117. O Friends! Abandon not the everlasting beauty for a beauty that must die, and set not your affections on this mortal world of dust.

¶ 118. O Essence of Negligence! Myriads of mystic tongues find utterance in one speech, and myriads of hidden mysteries are revealed in a single melody; yet, alas! there is no ear to hear, nor heart to understand.

¶ 119. O Ye Dwellers in the Highest Paradise! Proclaim unto the children of assurance that within the realms of holiness, nigh unto the celestial paradise, a new garden hath appeared, round which circle the denizens of the realm on high and the immortal dwellers of the exalted paradise. Strive, then, that ye may attain that station, that ye may unravel the mysteries of love from its wind-flowers and learn the secret of divine and consummate wisdom from its eternal fruits. Solaced are the eyes of them that enter and abide therein!

¶ 120. O My Friends! Quench ye the lamp of error, and kindle within your hearts the everlasting torch of divine guidance. For ere long the assayers of mankind shall, in the holy presence of the Adored, accept naught but purest virtue and deeds of stainless holiness.

¶ 121. O Son of Spirit! Burst thy cage asunder, and even as the phoenix of love soar into the firmament of holiness. Renounce thyself and, filled with the spirit of mercy, abide in the realm of celestial sanctity.

¶ 122. O My Servant! Free thyself from the fetters of this world, and loose thy Soul from the prison of self. Seize thy chance, for it will come to thee no more.

¶ 123. O Son of My Handmaid! Didst thou behold immortal sovereignty, thou wouldst strive to pass from this fleeting world. But to conceal the one from thee and to reveal the other is a mystery which none but the pure in heart can comprehend.

¶ 124. O Companion of My Throne! Hear no evil, and see no evil, abase not thyself, neither sigh and weep. Speak no evil, that thou mayest not hear it spoken unto thee, and magnify not the faults of others that thine own faults may not appear great; and wish not the abasement of anyone, that thine own abasement be not exposed. Live then the days of thy life, that are less than a fleeting moment, with thy mind stainless, thy heart unsullied, thy thoughts pure, and thy nature sanctified, so that, free and content, thou mayest put away this mortal frame and repair unto the mystic paradise, and abide in the eternal kingdom for evermore.

¶ 125. O Quintessence of Passion! Put away all covetousness and seek contentment; for the covetous hath ever been deprived, and the contented hath ever been loved and praised.

¶ 126. O Ye that Pride Yourselves on Mortal Riches! Know ye in truth that wealth is a mighty barrier between the seeker and his desire, the lover and his beloved. The rich, but for a few, shall in no wise attain the court of His presence nor enter the city of content and resignation. Well is it then with him, who being rich, is not hindered by his riches from the eternal kingdom, nor deprived by them of imperishable dominion. By the most great name! The splendour of such a wealthy man shall illuminate the dwellers of heaven, even as the sun enlightens the people of the earth!

¶ 127. O My Son! The company of the ungodly increaseth sorrow, whilst fellowship with the righteous cleaneth the rust from off the heart. He that seeketh to commune with God, let him betake himself to the companionship of His loved ones; and he that desireth to hearken unto the word of God, let him give ear to the words of His chosen ones.

¶ 128. O Heedless Ones! Think not the secrets of hearts are hidden, nay, know ye of a certainty that in clear characters they are engraved and are openly manifest in the holy Presence.

¶ 129. O Emigrants! The tongue I have designed for the mention of Me, defile it not with detraction. If the fire of self overcome you, remember your own faults and not the faults of My creatures, inasmuch as everyone of you knoweth his own self better than he knoweth others.

¶ 130. O Son of Worldliness! Pleasant is the realm of being, wert thou to attain thereto: glorious is the domain of eternity, shouldst thou pass beyond the world of mortality; sweet is the holy ecstasy if thou drinkest of the mystic chalice from the hands of the celestial Youth. Shouldst thou attain this station, thou wouldst be freed from destruction and death, from toil and sin.

¶ 131. O Son of My Handmaid! Guidance hath ever been given by words, and now it is given by deeds. Everyone must show forth deeds that are pure and holy, for words are the property of all alike, whereas such deeds as these belong only to Our loved ones. Strive then with heart and soul to distinguish yourselves by your deeds. In this wise We counsel you in this holy and resplendent tablet.

¶ 132. O Son of My Handmaid! Quaff from the tongue of the merciful the stream of divine mystery, and behold from the day-spring of divine utterance the unveiled splendour of the day-star of wisdom. Sow the seeds of My divine wisdom in the pure soil of the heart, and water them with the waters of certitude, that the hyacinths of knowledge and wisdom may spring up fresh and green from the holy city of the heart.

¶ 133. O My Servants! Ye are the trees of My garden; ye must give forth goodly and wondrous fruits, that ye yourselves and others may profit therefrom. Thus it is incumbent on everyone to engage in crafts and professions, for therein lies the secret of wealth, O men of understanding! For results depend upon means, and the grace of God shall be all sufficient unto you. Trees that yield no fruit have been and will ever be for the fire.

IV. THE SEVEN VALLEYS

In the Name of God, the Clement, the Merciful

¶ 134. Praise be to God Who hath made being to come forth from nothingness; graven upon the tablet of man the mysteries of pre-existence; taught him from the Bayán that which he knew not; made him a Luminous Book unto those who believed and surrendered themselves; caused him to witness the creation of all things (Kullu Shay') in this black and ruinous age, and to speak forth from the apex of eternity with a wondrous voice in the Excellent Temple:[1] to the end that every man may testify, in himself, by himself, in the station of the Manifestation of his Lord, that verily there is no God save Him, and that every man may thereby win his way to the summit of realities, until none shall contemplate anything whatsoever but that he shall see God therein.

And I praise and glorify the first sea which hath branched from the ocean of the Divine Essence, and the first morn which hath glowed from the Horizon of Oneness, and the first sun which hath risen in the Heaven of Eternity, and the first fire which was lit from the Lamp of Pre-existence in the lantern of singleness: He who was Aḥmad in the kingdom of the exalted ones, and Muḥammad amongst the concourse of the near ones, and Maḥmúd[2] in the realm of the sincere ones. ". . . by whichsoever (name) ye will, invoke Him: He hath most excellent names"[3] in the hearts of those who know. And upon His household and companions be abundant and abiding and eternal peace!

Further, we have hearkened to what the nightingale of knowledge sang on the boughs of the tree of thy being, and learned what the dove of certitude cried on the branches of the bower of thy heart. Methinks I verily inhaled the pure fragrances of the garment

[1] The Manifestation.
[2] Muḥammad, Aḥmad and Maḥmúd are names and titles of the Prophet, derived from the verb "to praise", "to exalt".
[3] Qur'án 17:110.

of thy love, and attained thy very meeting from perusing thy letter. And since I noted thy mention of thy death in God, and thy life through Him, and thy love for the beloved of God and the Manifestations of His Names and the Dawning-Points of His Attributes —I therefore reveal unto thee sacred and resplendent tokens from the planes of glory, to attract thee into the court of holiness and nearness and beauty, and draw thee to a station wherein thou shalt see nothing in creation save the Face of thy Beloved One, the Honoured, and behold all created things only as in the day wherein none hath a mention.

Of this hath the nightingale of oneness sung in the garden of Ghawthíyyih.[1] He saith: "And there shall appear upon the tablet of thine heart a writing of the subtle mysteries of 'Fear God and God will give you knowledge'[2]; and the bird of thy soul shall recall the holy sanctuaries of pre-existence and soar on the wings of longing in the heaven of 'walk the beaten paths of thy Lord',[3] and gather the fruits of communion in the gardens of 'Then feed on every kind of fruit'."[3]

By My life, O friend, wert thou to taste of these fruits, from the green garden of these blossoms which grow in the lands of knowledge, beside the orient lights of the Essence in the mirrors of names and attributes—yearning would seize the reins of patience and reserve from out thy hand, and make thy soul to shake with the flashing light, and draw thee from the earthy homeland to the first, heavenly abode in the Centre of Realities, and lift thee to a plane wherein thou wouldst soar in the air even as thou walkest upon the earth, and move over the water as thou runnest on the land. Wherefore, may it rejoice Me, and thee, and whosoever mounteth into the heaven of knowledge, and whose heart is refreshed by this, that the wind of certitude hath blown over the garden of his being, from the Sheba of the All-Merciful.

Peace be upon him who followeth the Right Path!

And further: The stages that mark the wayfarer's journey from the abode of dust to the heavenly homeland are said to be seven. Some have called these Seven Valleys, and others, Seven Cities. And they say that until the wayfarer taketh leave of self, and traverseth these stages, he shall never reach to the ocean of nearness and union, nor drink of the peerless wine. The first is:

[1] Sermon by 'Alí.   [2] Qur'án 2:282.   [3] Qur'án 16:71.

THE VALLEY OF SEARCH

The steed of this Valley is patience; without patience the way-farer on this journey will reach nowhere and attain no goal. Nor should he ever be downhearted; if he strive for a hundred thousand years and yet fail to behold the beauty of the Friend, he should not falter. For those who seek the Ka'bih[1] of "for Us" rejoice in the tidings: "In Our ways will We guide them."[2] In their search, they have stoutly girded up the loins of service, and seek at every moment to journey from the plane of heedlessness into the realm of being. No bond shall hold them back, and no counsel shall deter them.

It is incumbent on these servants that they cleanse the heart—which is the well-spring of divine treasures—from every marking, and that they turn away from imitation, which is following the traces of their forefathers and sires, and shut the door of friendliness and enmity upon all the people of the earth.

In this journey the seeker reacheth a stage wherein he seeth all created things wandering distracted in search of the Friend. How many a Jacob will he see, hunting after his Joseph; he will behold many a lover, hasting to seek the Beloved, he will witness a world of desiring ones searching after the One Desired. At every moment he findeth a weighty matter, in every hour he becometh aware of a mystery; for he hath taken his heart away from both worlds, and set out for the Ka'bih[1] of the Beloved. At every step, aid from the Invisible Realm will attend him and the heat of his search will grow.

One must judge of search by the standard of the Majnún of Love.[3] It is related that one day they came upon Majnún sifting the dust, and his tears flowing down. They said, "What doest thou?" He said, "I seek for Laylí." They cried, "Alas for thee! Laylí is of pure spirit, and thou seekest her in the dust!" He said, "I seek her everywhere; haply somewhere I shall find her."

---

[1] The holy Sanctuary at Mecca. Here the word means "goal".

[2] Qur'án 29:69: "And whoso maketh efforts for Us, in Our ways will We guide them."

[3] Literally, Majnún means "insane". This is the title of the celebrated lover of ancient Persian and Arabian lore, whose beloved was Laylí, daughter of an Arabian prince. Symbolizing true human love bordering on the divine, the story has been made the theme of many a Persian romantic poem, particularly that of Niẓámí, written in A.D. 1188–9.

Yea, although to the wise it be shameful to seek the Lord of Lords in the dust, yet this betokeneth intense ardour in searching. "Whoso seeketh out a thing with zeal shall find it."[1]

The true seeker hunteth naught but the object of his quest, and the lover hath no desire save union with his beloved. Nor shall the seeker reach his goal unless he sacrifice all things. That is, whatever he hath seen, and heard, and understood, all must he set at naught that he may enter the realm of the spirit, which is the City of God. Labour is needed, if we are to seek Him; ardour is needed, if we are to drink of the honey of reunion with Him; and if we taste of this cup, we shall cast away the world.

On this journey the traveller abideth in every land and dwelleth in every region. In every face, he seeketh the beauty of the Friend; in every country he looketh for the Beloved. He joineth every company, and seeketh fellowship with every soul, that haply in some mind he may uncover the secret of the Friend, or in some face he may behold the beauty of the Loved One.

And if, by the help of God, he findeth on this journey a trace of the traceless Friend, and inhaleth the fragrance of the long-lost Joseph from the heavenly messenger,[2] he shall straightway step into

THE VALLEY OF LOVE

and be dissolved in the fire of love. In this city the heaven of ecstasy is upraised and the world-illuming sun of yearning shineth, and the fire of love is ablaze; and when the fire of love is ablaze, it burneth to ashes the harvest of reason.

Now is the traveller unaware of himself, and of aught besides himself. He seeth neither ignorance nor knowledge, neither doubt nor certitude: he knoweth not the morn of guidance from the night of error. He fleeth both from unbelief and faith, and deadly poison is a balm to him. Wherefore 'Attár[3] saith:

> "For the infidel, error—for the faithful, faith;
> For 'Attár's heart, an atom of Thy pain."

The steed of this Valley is pain; and if there be no pain this journey

[1] Arabian proverb.
[2] Refer to the story of Joseph in the Qur'án and the Old Testament.
[3] Farídu'd-Dín 'Attár (c. A.D. 1150–1230), the great Persian Ṣúfí poet.

will never end. In this station the lover hath no thought save the Beloved, and seeketh no refuge save the Friend. At every moment he offereth a hundred lives in the path of the Loved One, at every step he throweth a thousand heads at the feet of the Beloved.

O My Brother! Until thou enter the Egypt of love, thou shalt never come to the Joseph of the Beauty of the Friend; and until, like Jacob, thou forsake thine outward eyes, thou shalt never open the eye of thine inward being; and until thou burn with the fire of love, thou shalt never commune with the Lover of Longing.

A lover feareth nothing and no harm can come nigh him: Thou seest him chill in the fire and dry in the sea.

"A lover is he who is chill in hell fire;
    A knower is he who is dry in the sea."[1]

Love accepteth no existence and wisheth no life: He seeth life in death, and in shame seeketh glory. To merit the madness of love, man must abound in sanity; to merit the bonds of the Friend, he must be full of spirit. Blessed the neck that is caught in His noose, happy the head that falleth on the dust in the pathway of His love. Wherefore, O friend, give up thy self that thou mayest find the Peerless One, pass by this mortal earth that thou mayest seek a home in the nest of heaven. Be as naught, if thou wouldst kindle the fire of being and be fit for the pathway of love.

"Love seizeth not upon a living soul,
    The falcon preyeth not on a dead mouse."[1]

Love setteth a world aflame at every turn, and he wasteth every land where he carrieth his banner. Being hath no existence in his kingdom; the wise wield no command within his realm. The leviathan of love swalloweth the master of reason and destroyeth the lord of knowledge. He drinketh the seven seas, but his heart's thirst is still unquenched, and he saith, "Is there yet any more?"[2] He shunneth himself and draweth away from all on earth.

"Love's a stranger to earth and heaven too;
    In him are lunacies seventy-and-two."[3]

He hath bound a myriad victims in his fetters, wounded a myriad

[1] Persian mystic poem.   [2] Qur'án 50:29.
[3] Jalálu'd-Dín Rúmí (A.D. 1207–3); The *Mathnaví*. Jalálu'd-Dín, called Mawláná ("our Master"), is the greatest of all Persian Ṣúfí poets, and founder of the Mawlaví "whirling" dervish order.

wise men with his arrow. Know that every redness in the world is from his anger, and every paleness in men's cheeks is from his poison. He yieldeth no remedy but death, he walketh not save in the valley of the shadow; yet sweeter than honey is his venom on the lover's lips, and fairer his destruction in the seeker's eyes than a hundred thousand lives.

Wherefore must the veils of the satanic self be burned away at the fire of love, that the spirit may be purified and cleansed and thus may know the station of the Lord of the Worlds.

> "Kindle the fire of love and burn away all things,
> Then set thy foot into the land of the lovers."[1]

And if, confirmed by the Creator, the lover escapes from the claws of the eagle of love, he will enter

THE VALLEY OF KNOWLEDGE

and come out of doubt into certitude, and turn from the darkness of illusion to the guiding light of the fear of God. His inner eyes will open and he will privily converse with his Beloved; he will set ajar the gate of truth and piety, and shut the doors of vain imaginings. He in this station is content with the decree of God, and seeth war as peace, and findeth in death the secrets of everlasting life. With inward and outward eyes he witnesseth the mysteries of resurrection in the realms of creation and the souls of men, and with a pure heart apprehendeth the divine wisdom in the endless Manifestations of God. In the ocean he findeth a drop, in a drop he beholdeth the secrets of the sea.

> "Split the atom's heart, and lo!
> Within it thou wilt find a sun."[2]

The wayfarer in this Valley seeth in the fashionings of the True One nothing save clear providence, and at every moment saith: "No defect canst thou see in the creation of the God of Mercy: Repeat the gaze: Seest thou a single flaw?"[3] He beholdeth justice in injustice, and in justice, grace. In ignorance he findeth many a knowledge hidden, and in knowledge a myriad wisdoms manifest. He breaketh the cage of the body and the passions, and consorteth with the people of the immortal realm. He mounteth on the ladders of inner truth and hasteneth to the heaven of inner significance. He rideth in the ark of "We shall show them our signs in the regions

[1] From an ode by Bahá'u'lláh. [2] Persian mystic poem. [3] Qur'án 67:3.

and in themselves,"[1] and journeyeth over the sea of "until it become plain to them that (this Book) is the truth."[1] And if he meeteth with injustice he shall have patience, and if he cometh upon wrath he shall manifest love.

There was once a lover who had sighed for long years in separation from his beloved, and wasted in the fire of remoteness. From the rule of love, his heart was empty of patience, and his body weary of his spirit; he reckoned life without her as a mockery, and time consumed him away. How many a day he found no rest in longing for her; how many a night the pain of her kept him from sleep: his body was worn to a sigh, his heart's wound had turned him to a cry of sorrow. He had given a thousand lives for one taste of the cup of her presence, but it availed him not. The doctors knew no cure for him, and companions avoided his company: yea, physicians have no medicine for one sick of love, unless the favour of the beloved one deliver him.

At last, the tree of his longing yielded the fruit of despair, and the fire of his hope fell to ashes. Then one night he could live no more, and he went out of his house and made for the market-place. On a sudden, a watchman followed after him. He broke into a run, with the watchman following; then other watchmen came together, and barred every passage to the weary one. And the wretched one cried from his heart, and ran here and there, and moaned to himself: "Surely this watchman is 'Izrá'íl, my angel of death, following so fast upon me; or he is a tyrant of men, seeking to harm me." His feet carried him on, the one bleeding with the arrow of love, and his heart lamented. Then he came to a garden wall, and with untold pain he scaled it, for it proved very high; and forgetting his life, he threw himself down to the garden.

And there he beheld his beloved with a lamp in her hand, searching for a ring she had lost. When the heart-surrendered lover looked on his ravishing love, he drew a great breath and raised up his hands in prayer, crying: "O God! Give Thou glory to the watchman, and riches and long life. For the watchman was Gabriel, guiding this poor one; or he was Isráfíl, bringing life to this wretched one!"

Indeed, his words were true, for he had found many a secret justice in this seeming tyranny of the watchman, and seen how many a

[1] Qur'án 41:53.

mercy lay hid behind the veil. Out of wrath, the guard had led him who was athirst in love's desert to the sea of his loved one, and lit up the dark night of absence with the light of reunion. He had driven one who was afar, into the garden of nearness, had guided an ailing soul to the heart's physician.

Now if the lover could have looked ahead, he would have blessed the watchman at the start, and prayed on his behalf, and he would have seen that tyranny as justice; but since the end was veiled to him, he moaned and made his plaint in the beginning. Yet those who journey in the garden-land of knowledge, because they see the end in the beginning, see peace in war and friendliness in anger.

Such is the state of the wayfarers in this Valley; but the people of the Valleys above this see the end and the beginning as one; nay, they see neither beginning nor end, and witness neither "first" nor "last."[1] Nay rather, the denizens of the undying city, who dwell in the green garden-land, see not even "neither first nor last"; they fly from all that is first, and repulse all that is last. For these have passed over the worlds of names, and fled beyond the worlds of attributes as swift as lightning. Thus is it said: "Absolute Unity excludeth all attributes."[2] And they have made their dwelling-place in the shadow of the Essence.

Wherefore, relevant to this, <u>Kh</u>ájih 'Abdu'lláh[3]—may God the Most High sanctify his beloved spirit—hath made a subtle point and spoken an eloquent word as to the meaning of "Guide Thou us on the straight path,"[4] which is: "Show us the right way, that is, honour us with the love of Thine Essence, that we may be freed from turning toward ourselves and toward all else save Thee, and may become wholly Thine, and know only Thee, and see only Thee, and think of none save Thee."

Nay, these even mount above this station, wherefore it is said:
"Love is a veil betwixt the lover and the loved one;
More than this I am not permitted to tell."[5]

---

[1] Qur'án 57:3. [2] Saying attributed to 'Alí.

[3] <u>Shaykh</u> Abú Ismá'íl 'Abdu'lláh Anṣárí of Hirát (A.D. 1006–88) Ṣúfí leader, descended from the Prophet's companion Abú Ayyúb. Chiefly known for his *Munáját* (Supplications) and *Rubá'í'yyát* (Quatrains). "Anṣár" means the "Helpers" or companions of Muḥammad in Medina.

[4] Qur'án 1:5. [5] See n. 3, p. 121.

At this hour the morn of knowledge hath arisen and the lamps of wayfaring and wandering are quenched.[1]

> "Veiled from this was Moses
> Though all strength and light;
> Then thou who hast no wings at all,
> Attempt not flight."[2]

If thou be a man of communion and prayer, soar up on the wings of assistance from Holy Souls, that thou mayest behold the mysteries of the Friend and attain to the lights of the Beloved. "Verily, we are from God and to Him shall we return."[3]

After passing through the Valley of Knowledge, which is the last plane of limitation, the wayfarer cometh to

THE VALLEY OF UNITY

and drinketh from the cup of the Absolute, and gazeth on the Manifestations of Oneness. In this station he pierceth the veils of plurality, fleeth from the worlds of the flesh, and ascendeth into the heaven of singleness. With the ear of God he heareth, with the eye of God he beholdeth the mysteries of divine creation. He steppeth into the sanctuary of the Friend, and shareth as an intimate the pavilion of the Loved One. He stretcheth out the hand of truth from the sleeve of the Absolute; he revealeth the secrets of power. He seeth in himself neither name nor fame nor rank, but findeth his own praise in praising God. He beholdeth in his own name the name of God; to him, "all songs are from the King,"[2] and every melody from Him. He sitteth on the throne of "Say, all is from God,"[4] and taketh his rest on the carpet of "There is no power or might but in God."[5] He looketh on all things with the eye of oneness, and seeth the brilliant rays of the divine sun shining from the dawning-point of Essence alike on all created things, and the lights of singleness reflected over all creation.

It is clear to thy Eminence that all the variations which the wayfarer in the stages of his journey beholdeth in the realms of being,

[1] This refers to the mystic wandering and search for truth guided by "Lights" or Ṣúfí leaders. Bahá'u'lláh here warns the mystics that the coming of the Divine Manifestation in His Day makes further search unnecessary, as it was said by 'Alí: "Quench the lamp when the sun hath risen"—the sun referring to the Manifestation of God in the New Day.

[2] See n. 3, p. 121.   [3] Qur'án 2:151.   [4] Qur'án 4:80.
[5] Qur'án 18:37.

proceed from his own vision. We shall give an example of this, that its meaning may become fully clear: Consider the visible sun; although it shineth with one radiance upon all things, and at the behest of the King of Manifestation bestoweth light on all creation, yet in each place it becometh manifest and sheddeth its bounty according to the potentialities of that place. For instance, in a mirror it reflecteth its own disk and shape and this is due to the sensitivity of the mirror; in a crystal it maketh fire to appear, and in other things it showeth only the effect of its shining, but not its full disk. And yet, through that effect, by the command of the Creator, it traineth each thing according to the quality of that thing, as thou observest.

In like manner, colours become visible in every object according to the nature of that object. For instance, in a yellow globe, the rays shine yellow; in a white the rays are white; and in a red, the red rays are manifest. Then these variations are from the object, not from the shining light. And if a place be shut away from the light, as by walls or a roof, it will be entirely bereft of the splendour of the light, nor will the sun shine thereon.

Thus it is that certain invalid souls have confined the lands of knowledge within the wall of self and passion, and clouded them with ignorance and blindness, and have been veiled from the light of the mystic sun and the mysteries of the Eternal Beloved; they have strayed afar from the jewelled wisdom of the lucid Faith of the Lord of Messengers, have been shut out of the sanctuary of the All-Beauteous One, and banished from the Ka'bih[1] of splendour. Such is the worth of the people of this age!

And if a nightingale[2] soar upward from the clay of self and dwell in the rose-bower of the heart, and in Arabian melodies and sweet Íránian songs recount the mysteries of God—a single word of which quickeneth to fresh, new life the bodies of the dead, and bestoweth the Holy Spirit upon the mouldering bones of this existence— thou wilt behold a thousand claws of envy, a myriad beaks of rancour hunting after Him and with all their power intent upon His death.

Yea, to the beetle a sweet fragrance seemeth foul, and to the man sick of a rheum a pleasant perfume is as naught. Wherefore, it hath been said for the guidance of the ignorant:

[1] See n. 1, p. 119. [2] This refers to Bahá'u'lláh's own Manifestation.

"Cleanse thou the rheum from out thine head
And breathe the breath of God instead."[1]

In sum, the differences in objects hath now been made plain. Thus when the wayfarer gazeth only upon the place of appearance —that is, when he seeth only the man-coloured globes—he beholdeth yellow and red and white; hence it is that conflict hath prevailed among the creatures, and a darksome dust from limited souls hath hid the world. And some do gaze upon the effulgence of the light; and some have drunk of the wine of oneness and these see nothing but the sun itself.

Thus, for that they move on these three differing planes, the understanding and the words of the wayfarers have differed; and hence the sign of conflict doth continually appear on earth. For some there are who dwell upon the plane of oneness and speak of that world, and some inhabit the realms of limitation, and some the grades of self, while others are completely veiled. Thus do the ignorant people of the day, who have no portion of the radiance of Divine Beauty, make certain claims, and in every age and cycle inflict on the people of the sea of oneness what they themselves deserve. "Should God punish men for their perverse doings, He would not leave on earth a moving thing! But to an appointed term doth He respite them. . ."[2]

O My Brother! A pure heart is as a mirror; cleanse it with the burnish of love and severance from all save God, that the true sun may shine within it and the eternal morning dawn. Then wilt thou clearly see the meaning of "Neither doth My earth nor My heaven contain Me, but the heart of My faithful servant containeth Me."[3] And thou wilt take up thy life in thine hand, and with infinite longing cast it before the new Beloved One.

Whensoever the light of Manifestation of the King of Oneness settleth upon the throne of the heart and soul, His shining becometh visible in every limb and member. At that time the mystery of the famed tradition gleameth out of the darkness: "A servant is drawn unto Me in prayer until I answer him; and when I have answered him, I become the ear wherewith he heareth. . ." For thus the Master of the house hath appeared within His home, and all the

---

[1] See n. 3, p. 121.   [2] Qur'án 16:63.
[3] Hadíth, i.e. action or utterance traditionally attributed to the Prophet Muḥammad or to one of the holy Imáms.

pillars of the dwelling are ashine with His light. And the action and effect of the light are from the Light-Giver; so it is that all move through Him and arise by His will. And this is that spring whereof the near ones drink, as it is said. "A fount whereof the near unto God shall drink. . ."[1]

However, let none construe these utterances to be anthropomorphism, nor see in them the descent of the worlds of God into the grades of the creatures; nor should they lead thy Eminence to such assumptions. For God is, in His Essence, holy above ascent and descent, entrance and exit; He hath through all eternity been free of the attributes of human creatures, and ever will remain so. No man hath ever known Him; no soul hath ever found the pathway to His Being. Every mystic knower hath wandered far astray in the valley of the knowledge of Him; every saint hath lost his way in seeking to comprehend His Essence. Sanctified is He above the understanding of the wise; exalted is He above the knowledge of the knowing! The way is barred and to seek it is impiety; His proof is His signs; His being is His evidence.[2]

Wherefore, the lovers of the face of the Beloved have said: "O Thou, the One Whose Essence alone showeth the way to His Essence, and Who is sanctified above any likeness to His creatures."[3] How can utter nothingness gallop its steed in the field of pre-existence, or a fleeting shadow reach to the everlasting sun? The Friend[4] hath said, "But for Thee, we had not known Thee," and the Beloved[4] hath said, "nor attained Thy presence."

Yea, these mentionings that have been made of the grades of knowledge relate to the knowledge of the Manifestations of that Sun of Reality, which casteth Its light upon the Mirrors. And the splendour of that light is in the hearts, yet it is hidden under the veilings of sense and the conditions of this earth, even as a candle within a lantern of iron, and only when the lantern is removed doth the light of the candle shine out.

In like manner, when thou strippest the wrappings of illusion from off thy heart, the lights of oneness will be made manifest.

Then it is clear that even for the rays there is neither entrance nor exit—how much less for that Essence of Being and that longed-for Mystery. O My Brother, journey upon these planes in the spirit of

---

[1] Qur'án 83:28.   [2] Sermon by 'Alí.   [3] See n. 3, p. 127.
[4] The Prophet Muḥammad.

search, not in blind imitation. A true wayfarer will not be kept back by the warning of allusions.

"How shall a curtain part the lover and the loved one?
Not Alexander's wall can separate them!"[1]

Secrets are many, but strangers are myriad. Volumes will not suffice to hold the mystery of the Beloved One, nor can it be exhausted in these pages, although it be no more than a word, no more than a sign. "Knowledge is a single point, but the ignorant have multiplied it."[2]

On this same basis, ponder likewise the differences among the worlds. Although the divine worlds be never-ending, yet some refer to them as four: The world of time (*zamán*), which is the one that hath both a beginning and an end; the world of duration (*dahr*), which hath a beginning, but whose end is not revealed; the world of perpetuity (*sarmad*), whose beginning is not to be seen but which is known to have an end; and the world of eternity (*azal*), neither a beginning nor an end of which is visible. Although there are many differing statements as to these points, to recount them in detail would result in weariness. Thus, some have said that the world of perpetuity hath neither beginning nor end, and have named the world of eternity as the invisible, impregnable Empyrean. Others have called these the worlds of the Heavenly Court (Láhút), of the Empryean Heaven (Jabarút), of the Kingdom of the Angels (Malakút), and of the mortal world (Násút).

The journeys in the pathway of love are reckoned as four: From the creatures to the True One; from the True One to the creatures; from the creatures to the creatures; from the True One to the True One.

There is many an utterance of the mystic seers and doctors of former times which I have not mentioned here, since I mislike the copious citation from sayings of the past; for quotation from the words of others proveth acquired learning, not the divine bestowal. Even so much as We have quoted here is out of deference to the wont of men and after the manner of the friends. Further, such matters are beyond the scope of this epistle. Our unwillingness to recount their sayings is not from pride, rather is it a manifestation of wisdom and a demonstration of grace.

[1] Háfiz: Shamsu'd-Dín Muhammad, of Shíráz, died c. A.D. 1389 One of the greatest of Persian poets.   [2] See n. 3, p. 127.

>   "If K͟hiḍr did wreck the vessel on the sea,
>   Yet in this wrong there are a thousand rights."[1]

Otherwise, this Servant regardeth Himself as utterly lost and as nothing, even beside one of the beloved of God, how much less in the presence of His holy ones. Exalted be My Lord, the Supreme! Moreover, our aim is to recount the stages of the wayfarer's journey, not to set forth the conflicting utterances of the mystics.

Although a brief example hath been given concerning the beginning and ending of the relative world, the world of attributes, yet a second illustration is now added, that the full meaning may be manifest. For instance, let thy Eminence consider his own self; thou art first in relation to thy son, last in relation to thy father. In thine outward appearance, thou tellest of the appearance of power in the realms of divine creation; in thine inward being thou revealest the hidden mysteries which are the divine trust deposited within thee. And thus firstness and lastness, outwardness and inwardness are, in the sense referred to, true of thyself, that in these four states conferred upon thee thou shouldst comprehend the four divine states, and that the nightingale of thy heart on all the branches of the rosetree of existence, whether visible or concealed, should cry out: "He is the first and the last, the Seen and the Hidden..."[2]

These statements are made in the sphere of that which is relative, because of the limitations of men. Otherwise, those personages who in a single step have passed over the world of the relative and the limited, and dwelt on the fair plane of the Absolute, and pitched their tent in the worlds of authority and command—have burned away these relativities with a single spark, and blotted out these words with a drop of dew. And they swim in the sea of the spirit, and soar in the holy air of light. Then what life have words, on such a plane, that "first" and "last" or other than these be seen or mentioned! In this realm, the first is the last itself, and the last is but the first.

>   "In thy souls of love build thou a fire
>   And burn all thoughts and words entire."[1]

O my friend, look upon thyself: Hadst thou not become a father nor begotten a son, neither wouldst thou have heard these sayings. Now forget them all, that thou mayest learn from the Master of

---

[1] See n. 3, p. 121.   [2] Qur'án 57:3.

Love in the schoolhouse of oneness, and return unto God, and forsake the inner land of unreality[1] for thy true station, and dwell within the shadow of the tree of knowledge.

O thou dear one! Impoverish thyself, that thou mayest enter the high court of riches; and humble thy body, that thou mayest drink from the river of glory, and attain to the full meaning of the poems whereof thou hadst asked.

Thus it hath been made clear that these stages depend on the vision of the wayfarer. In every city he will behold a world, in every Valley reach a spring, in every meadow hear a song. But the falcon of the mystic heaven hath many a wondrous carol of the spirit in His breast, and the Persian bird keepeth in His soul many a sweet Arab melody; yet these are hidden, and hidden shall remain.

"If I speak forth, many a mind will shatter,
And if I write, many a pen will break."[2]

Peace be upon him who concludeth this exalted journey and followeth the True One by the lights of guidance.

And the wayfarer, after traversing the high planes of this supernal journey, entereth

THE VALLEY OF CONTENTMENT

In this Valley he feeleth the winds of divine contentment blowing from the plane of the spirit. He burneth away the veils of want, and with inward and outward eye, perceiveth within and without all things the day of: "God will compensate each one out of His abundance."[3] From sorrow he turneth to bliss, from anguish to joy. His grief and mourning yield to delight and rapture.

Although to outward view, the wayfarers in this Valley may dwell upon the dust, yet inwardly they are throned in the heights of mystic meaning; they eat of the endless bounties of inner significances, and drink of the delicate wines of the spirit.

The tongue faileth in describing these three Valleys, and speech falleth short. The pen steppeth not into this region, the ink leaveth only a blot. In these planes, the nightingale of the heart hath other songs and secrets, which make the heart to stir and the soul to

---

[1] This refers to the Ṣúfí idea of the inner plane, which compared to Revealed Truth is but unreal.

[2] This refers to Bahá'u'lláh Himself, Who had not yet declared His mission. See also n. 3, p. 121.   [3] Qur'án 4:129.

clamour, but this mystery of inner meaning may be whispered only
from heart to heart, confided only from breast to breast.

> "Only heart to heart can speak the bliss of mystic
>   knowers:
> No messenger can tell it and no missive bear it."[1]

> "I am silent from weakness on many a matter,
>   For my words could not reckon them and my speech
>   would fall short."[2]

O friend, till thou enter the garden of such mysteries, thou shalt
never set lip to the undying wine of this Valley. And shouldst thou
taste of it, thou wilt shield thine eyes from all things else, and drink
of the wine of contentment; and thou wilt loose thyself from all
things else, and bind thyself to Him, and throw thy life down in His
path, and cast thy soul away. However, there is no other in this region that thou need forget: "There was God and there was naught
beside Him."[3] For on this plane the traveller witnesseth the beauty
of the Friend in everything. Even in fire, he seeth the face of the Beloved. He beholdeth in illusion the secret of reality, and readeth from
the attributes the riddle of the Essence. For he hath burnt away the
veils with his sighing, and unwrapped the shroudings with a single
glance; with piercing sight he gazeth on the new creation; with
lucid heart he graspeth subtle verities. This is sufficiently attested by:
"And we have made thy sight sharp this day."[4]

After journeying through the planes of pure contentment, the
traveller cometh to

THE VALLEY OF WONDERMENT

and is tossed in the oceans of grandeur, and at every moment his
wonder groweth. Now he seeth the shape of wealth as poverty itself, and the essence of freedom as sheer impotence. Now is he
struck dumb with the beauty of the All-Glorious; again is he wearied out with his own life. How many a mystic tree hath this whirl-
wind of wonderment snatched by the roots, how many a soul hath
it exhausted. For in this Valley the traveller is flung into confusion,
albeit, in the eye of him who hath attained, such marvels are esteemed and well-beloved. At every moment he beholdeth a

---

[1] See n. 1, p. 129.   [2] Arabian poem.   [3] See n. 3, p. 127.
[4] From Qur'án 50:21.

wondrous world, a new creation, and goeth from astonishment to astonishment, and is lost in awe at the works of the Lord of Oneness.

Indeed, O Brother, if we ponder each created thing, we shall witness a myriad perfect wisdoms and learn a myriad new and wondrous truths. One of the created phenomena is the dream. Behold how many secrets are deposited therein, how many wisdoms treasured up, how many worlds concealed. Observe, how thou art asleep in a dwelling, and its doors are barred; on a sudden thou findest thyself in a far-off city, which thou enterest without moving thy feet or wearying thy body; without using thine eyes, thou seest; without taxing thine ears, thou hearest; without a tongue, thou speakest. And perchance when ten years are gone, thou wilt witness in the outer world the very things thou hast dreamed tonight.

Now there are many wisdoms to ponder in the dream, which none but the people of this Valley can comprehend in their true elements. First, what is this world, where, without eye and ear and hand and tongue, a man puts all of these to use? Second, how is it that in the outer world thou seest today the effect of a dream, when thou didst vision it in the world of sleep some ten years past? Consider the difference between these two worlds and the mysteries which they conceal, that thou mayest attain to divine confirmations and heavenly discoveries and enter the regions of holiness.

God, the Exalted, hath placed these signs in men, to the end that philosophers may not deny the mysteries of the life beyond nor belittle that which hath been promised them. For some hold to reason and deny whatever the reason comprehendeth not, and yet weak minds can never grasp the matters which we have related, but only the Supreme, Divine Intelligence can comprehend them:

"How can feeble reason encompass the Qur'án,
   Or the spider snare a phoenix in his web?"[1]

All these states are to be witnessed in the Valley of Wonderment, and the traveller at every moment seeketh for more, and is not wearied. Thus the Lord of the First and the Last in setting forth the grades of contemplation, and expressing wonderment hath said: "O Lord, increase my astonishment at Thee!"

Likewise, reflect upon the perfection of man's creation, and that

[1] Persian mystic poem.

all these planes and states are folded up and hidden away within him.

> "Dost thou reckon thyself only a puny form
> When within thee the universe is folded?"[1]

Then we must labour to destroy the animal condition, till the meaning of humanity shall come to light.

Thus, too, Luqmán, who had drunk from the wellspring of wisdom and tasted of the waters of mercy, in proving to his son Nathan the planes of resurrection and death, advanced the dream as an evidence and an example. We relate it here, that through this evanescent Servant a memory may endure of that youth of the school of Divine Unity, that elder of the art of instruction and the Absolute. He said: "O Son, if thou art able not to sleep, then thou art able not to die. And if thou art able not to waken after sleep, then thou shalt be able not to rise after death."

O friend, the heart is the dwelling of eternal mysteries, make it not the home of fleeting fancies; waste not the treasure of thy precious life in employment with this swiftly-passing world. Thou comest from the world of holiness—bind not thine heart to the earth; thou art a dweller in the court of nearness—choose not the homeland of the dust.

In sum, there is no end to the description of these stages, but because of the wrongs inflicted by the peoples of the earth, this Servant is in no mood to continue:

> "The tale is still unfinished and I have no heart for it—
> Then pray forgive me."[2]

The pen groaneth and the ink sheddeth tears, and the river[3] of the heart moveth in waves of blood. "Nothing can befall us but what God hath destined for us."[4] Peace be upon him who followeth the Right Path!

After scaling the high summits of wonderment the wayfarer cometh to

THE VALLEY OF TRUE POVERTY AND ABSOLUTE NOTHINGNESS

This station is the dying from self and the living in God, the being poor in self and rich in the Desired One. Poverty as here referred to signifieth being poor in the things of the created world, rich in the

---

[1] 'Alí.   [2] See n. 3, p. 121.   [3] Literally "Jayḥún", a river in Turkistán.
[4] Qur'án 9:51.

things of God's world. For when the true lover and devoted friend reacheth to the presence of the Beloved, the sparkling beauty of the Loved One and the fire of the lover's heart will kindle a blaze and burn away all veils and wrappings. Yea, all he hath, from heart to skin, will be set aflame, so that nothing will remain save the Friend.

"When the qualities of the Ancient of Days stood revealed,
Then the qualities of earthly things did Moses burn away."[1]
He who hath attained this station is sanctified from all that pertaineth to the world. Wherefore, if those who have come to the sea of His presence are found to possess none of the limited things of this perishable world, whether it be outer wealth or personal opinions, it mattereth not. For whatever the creatures have is limited by their own limits, and whatever the True One hath is sanctified therefrom; this utterance must be deeply pondered that its purport may be clear. "Verily the righteous shall drink of a winecup tempered at the camphor fountain."[2] If the interpretation of "camphor" become known, the true intention will be evident. This state is that poverty of which it is said, "Poverty is My glory."[3] And of inward and outward poverty there is many a stage and many a meaning which I have not thought pertinent to mention here; hence I have reserved these for another time, dependent on what God may desire and fate may seal.

This is the plane whereon the vestiges of all things (Kullu S͟hay') are destroyed in the traveller, and on the horizon of eternity the Divine Face riseth out of the darkness, and the meaning of "All on the earth shall pass away, but the face of thy Lord. . ."[4] is made manifest.

O My friend, listen with heart and soul to the songs of the spirit, and treasure them as thine own eyes. For the heavenly wisdoms, like the clouds of spring, will not rain down on the earth of men's hearts forever; and though the grace of the All-Bounteous One is never stilled and never ceasing, yet to each time and era a portion is allotted and a bounty set apart, this in a given measure. "And no one thing is there, but with Us are its storehouses; and We send it not down but in settled measure."[5] The cloud of the Loved One's mercy raineth only on the garden of the spirit, and bestoweth this

---

[1] See n. 3. p. 121. [2] Qur'án 76:5. [3] Muḥammad.
[4] Qur'án 55:26, 27. [5] Qur'án 15:21.

bounty only in the season of spring. The other seasons have no share in this greatest grace, and barren lands no portion of this favour.

O Brother! Not every sea hath pearls; not every branch will flower, nor will the nightingale sing thereon. Then, ere the nightingale of the mystic paradise repair to the garden of God, and the rays of the heavenly morning return to the Sun of Truth—make thou an effort, that haply in this dust-heap of the mortal world thou mayest catch a fragrance from the everlasting garden, and live forever in the shadow of the peoples of this city. And when thou hast attained this highest station and come to this mightiest plane, then shalt thou gaze on the Beloved, and forget all else.

> "The Beloved shineth on gate and wall
> Without a veil, O men of vision."[1]

Now hast thou abandoned the drop of life and come to the sea of the Life-Bestower. This is the goal thou didst ask for; if it be God's will, thou wilt gain it.

In this city, even the veils of light are split asunder and vanish away. "His beauty hath no veiling save light, His face no covering save revelation."[2] How strange that while the Beloved is visible as the sun, yet the heedless still hunt after tinsel and base metal. Yea, the intensity of His revelation hath covered Him, and the fullness of His shining forth hath hidden Him.

> "Even as the sun, bright hath He shined,
> But alas, He hath come to the town of the blind!"[3]

In this Valley, the wayfarer leaveth behind him the stages of the "oneness of Being and Manifestation"[4] and reacheth a oneness that is sanctified above those two stations. Ecstasy alone can encompass this theme, not utterance nor argument; and whosoever hath dwelt at this stage of the journey, or caught a breath from this garden-land, knoweth whereof We speak.

In all these journeys the traveller must stray not the breadth of a hair from the "Law", for this is indeed the secret of the "Path" and the fruit of the Tree of "Truth"; and in all these stages he must cling to the robe of obedience to the commandments, and hold fast to the cord of shunning all forbidden things, that he may be nourished

---

[1] See n. 3. p. 120.   [2] See n. 3. p. 127.   [3] See n. 3. p. 121.
[4] Pantheism, a Ṣúfí doctrine derived from the formula: "Only God exists; He is in all things, and all things are in Him."

from the cup of the Law and informed of the mysteries of Truth.[1]

If any of the utterances of this Servant may not be comprehended or may lead to perturbation, the same must be inquired of again, that no doubt may linger, and the meaning be clear as the Face of the Beloved One shining from the "Glorious Station."[2]

These journeys have no visible ending in the world of time, but the severed wayfarer—if invisible confirmation descend upon him and the Guardian of the Cause assist him—may cross these seven stages in seven steps, nay rather in seven breaths, nay rather in a single breath, if God will and desire it. And this is of "His grace on such of His servants as He pleaseth."[3]

They who soar in the heaven of singleness and reach to the sea of the Absolute, reckon this city—which is the station of life in God—as the furthermost state of mystic knowers, and the farthest homeland of the lovers. But to this evanescent One of the mystic ocean, this station is the first gate of the heart's citadel, that is, man's first entrance to the city of the heart; and the heart is endowed with four stages, which would be recounted should a kindred soul be found.

> "When the pen set to picturing this station,
> It broke in pieces and the page was torn."[4]

Salám![5]

---

[1] This refers to the three stages of Ṣúfí life: 1. Sharí'at, or Religious Laws; 2. Ṭaríqat, or the Path on which the mystic wayfarer journeys in search of the True One; this stage also includes anchoretism. 3. Ḥaqíqat, or the Truth which, to the Ṣúfí, is the goal of the journey through all three stages. Here Bahá'u'lláh teaches that, contrary to the belief of certain Súfís who in their search for the Truth consider themselves above all law, obedience to the Laws of Religion is essential.

[2] *Maqám-i-Maḥmúd*. Qur'án 17-81.   [3] Qur'án 2:84.

[4] Persian mystic poem.

[5] "Peace". This word is used in concluding a thesis.

V. SOME IMPORTANT TABLETS

1. WORDS OF WISDOM

¶ 135. The source of all good is trust in God, submission unto His command, and contentment in His holy will and pleasure.

The essence of wisdom is the fear of God, the dread of His scourge and the apprehension of His justice and decree.

The essence of religion is to testify unto that which the Lord hath revealed, and follow that which He hath ordained in His mighty Book.

The source of all glory is acceptance of whatsoever the Lord hath bestowed, and contentment with that which God hath ordained.

The essence of love is for man to turn his heart to the Beloved One, and sever himself from all else but God, and desire naught save that which is the desire of His Lord.

True remembrance is to make mention of the Lord, the All-Praised, and forget all else beside Him.

True reliance is for the servant to pursue his profession and calling in this world, to hold fast unto the Lord, to seek naught but His grace, inasmuch as in His hands is the destiny of all His servants.

The essence of detachment is for man to turn his face toward the courts of the Lord, to enter His presence, behold His countenance, and stand as witness before Him.

The essence of understanding is to testify to one's poverty, and submit to the will of the Lord, the Sovereign, the Gracious, the All-Powerful.

The source of courage and power is the promotion of the Word of God, and steadfastness in His Love.

The essence of charity is for the servant to recount the blessings of his Lord, and to render thanks unto Him at all times, and under all conditions.

The essence of wealth is love for Me. Whoso loveth Me is the possessor of all things, and he that loveth Me not is, indeed, of the poor and needy. This is that which the Finger of Glory and Splendour hath revealed. . .

The essence of faith is fewness of words and abundance of deeds; he whose words exceed his deeds, know verily his death is better than his life. . .

The source of all evil is for man to turn away from his Lord and set his heart on things ungodly.

The most burning fire is to question the signs of God, to dispute idly that which He hath revealed, to deny Him and carry one's self proudly before Him.

The source of all learning is the knowledge of God, exalted be His Glory, and this cannot be attained save through the knowledge of His Divine Manifestation.

The essence of abasement is to pass from under the shadow of the Merciful, and seek the shelter of the Evil One.

The source of error is to disbelieve in the one true God, rely upon aught else but Him, and flee from His Decree.

True loss is for him whose days have been spent in utter ignorance of his true self.

The essence of all that We have revealed for thee is Justice, is for man to free himself from idle fancies and imitation, discern with the eye of oneness His glorious handiwork, and look into all things with a searching eye.

Thus have We instructed thee, manifested unto thee words of wisdom, that thou mayest be thankful unto the Lord, thy God, and glory therein amidst all peoples.

2. THE TABLET OF CARMEL

¶ 136. All glory be to this Day, the Day in which the fragrances of mercy have been wafted over all created things, a Day so blest that past ages and centuries can never hope to rival it, a Day in which the countenance of the Ancient of Days hath turned towards His holy seat. Thereupon the voices of all created things, and beyond them those of the Concourse on high, were heard calling aloud: "Haste thee, O Carmel, for lo, the light of the countenance of God, the Ruler of the Kingdom of Names and Fashioner of the heavens, hath been lifted upon thee."

Seized with transports of joy, and raising high her voice, she thus exclaimed: "May my life be a sacrifice to Thee, inasmuch as Thou hast fixed Thy gaze upon me, hast bestowed upon me Thy bounty, and hast directed towards me Thy steps. Separation from Thee, O Thou Source of everlasting life, hath well nigh consumed me, and my remoteness from Thy presence hath burned away my soul. All praise be to Thee for having enabled me to hearken to Thy call, for having honoured me with Thy footsteps, and for having quickened my soul through the vitalizing fragrance of Thy Day and the thrilling voice of Thy Pen, a voice Thou didst ordain as Thy trumpet-call amidst Thy people. And when the hour at which Thy resistless Faith was to be made manifest did strike, Thou didst breathe a breath of Thy spirit into Thy Pen, and lo, the entire creation shook to its very foundations, unveiling to mankind such mysteries as lay hidden within the treasuries of Him Who is the Possessor of all created things."

No sooner had her voice reached that most exalted Spot than We made reply: "Render thanks unto Thy Lord, O Carmel. The fire of thy separation from Me was fast consuming thee, when the ocean of My presence surged before thy face, cheering thine eyes and those of all creation, and filling with delight all things visible and invisible. Rejoice, for God hath in this Day established upon thee His throne, hath made thee the dawning-place of His signs and the day spring of the evidences of His Revelation. Well is it with him that circleth around thee, that proclaimeth the revelation of thy glory, and recounteth that which the bounty of the Lord thy God hath showered upon thee. Seize thou the Chalice of Immortality in the name of thy Lord, the All-Glorious, and give thanks unto Him, inasmuch as He, in token of His mercy unto thee, hath turned thy sorrow into gladness, and transmuted thy grief into blissful joy. He, verily, loveth the spot which hath been made the seat of His throne, which His footsteps have trodden, which hath been honoured by His presence, from which He raised His call, and upon which He shed His tears.

"Call out to Zion, O Carmel, and announce the joyful tidings: He that was hidden from mortal eyes is come! His all-conquering sovereignty is manifest; His all-encompassing splendour is revealed. Beware lest thou hesitate or halt. Hasten forth and circumambulate the City of God that hath descended from heaven, the celestial Kaaba round which have circled in adoration the favoured of God, the pure in heart, and the company of the most exalted angels. Oh, how I long to announce, unto every spot on the surface of the earth, and to carry to each one of its cities, the glad-tidings of this Revelation—a Revelation to which the heart of Sinai hath been attracted, and in whose name the Burning Bush is calling: 'Unto God, the Lord of Lords, belong the kingdoms of earth and heaven.' Verily this is the Day in which both land and sea rejoice at this announcement, the Day for which have been laid up those things which God, through a bounty beyond the ken of mortal mind or heart, hath destined for revelation. Ere long will God sail His Ark upon thee, and will manifest the people of Bahá who have been mentioned in the Book of Names.'

Sanctified be the Lord of all mankind, at the mention of Whose name all the atoms of the earth have been made to vibrate, and the Tongue of Grandeur hath been moved to disclose that which had been wrapt in His knowledge and lay concealed within the treasury of His might. He, verily, through the potency of His name, the Mighty, the All-Powerful, the Most High, is the ruler of all that is in the heavens and all that is on earth.

3. THE RIḌVÁN TABLET

❡ 137. The Divine Springtime is come, O Most Exalted Pen, for the Festival of the All-Merciful is fast approaching. Bestir thyself, and magnify, before the entire creation, the name of God, and celebrate His praise, in such wise that all created things may be regenerated and made new. Speak, and hold not thy peace. The day star of blissfulness shineth above the horizon of Our name, the Blissful, inasmuch as the kingdom of the name of God hath been adorned with the ornament of the name of thy Lord, the Creator of the heavens. Arise before the nations of the earth, and arm thyself with the power of this Most Great Name, and be not of those who tarry.

Methinks that thou hast halted and movest not upon My Tablet. Could the brightness of the Divine Countenance have bewildered thee, or the idle talk of the froward filled thee with grief and paralysed thy movement? Take heed lest anything deter thee from extolling the greatness of this Day—the Day whereon the Finger of majesty and power hath opened the seal of the Wine of Reunion, and called all who are in the heavens and all who are on the earth. Preferrest thou to tarry when the breeze announcing the Day of God hath already breathed over thee, or art thou of them that are shut out as by a veil from Him?

No veil whatever have I allowed, O Lord of all names and Creator of the heavens, to shut me from the recognition of the glories of Thy Day—the Day which is the lamp of guidance unto the whole world, and the sign of the Ancient of Days unto all them that dwell therein. My silence is by reason of the veils that have blinded Thy creatures' eyes to Thee, and my muteness is because of the impediments that have hindered Thy people from recognizing Thy truth. Thou knowest what is in me, but I know not what is in Thee. Thou art the All-Knowing, the All-Informed. By Thy name that excelleth all other names! If Thy overruling and all-compelling behest should ever reach me, it would empower me to revive the souls of all men, through Thy most exalted Word, which I have heard uttered by Thy Tongue of power in Thy Kingdom of glory. It would enable me to announce the revelation of Thy effulgent countenance wherethrough that which lay hidden from the eyes of men hath been manifested in Thy name, the Perspicuous, the sovereign Protector, the Self-Subsisting.

Canst thou discover any one but Me, O Pen, in this Day? What hath become of the creation and the manifestations thereof? What of the names and their kingdom? Whither are gone all created things, whether seen or unseen? What of the hidden secrets of the universe and its revelations? Lo, the entire creation hath passed away! Nothing remaineth except My Face, the Ever-Abiding, the Resplendent, the All-Glorious.

This is the Day whereon naught can be seen except the splendours of the Light that shineth from the face of Thy Lord, the Gracious, the Most Bountiful. Verily, We have caused every soul to expire by virtue of Our irresistible and all-subduing sovereignty. We have, then, called into being a new creation, as a token of Our grace unto men. I am, verily, the All-Bountiful, the Ancient of Days.

This is the Day whereon the unseen world crieth out: "Great is thy blessedness, O earth, for thou hast been made the foot-stool of thy God, and been chosen as the seat of His mighty throne." The realm of glory exclaimeth: "Would that my life could be sacrificed for thee, for He Who is the Beloved of the All-Merciful hath established His sovereignty upon thee, through the power of His Name that hath been promised unto all things, whether of the past or of the future." This is the Day whereon every sweet smelling thing hath derived its fragrance from the smell of My Garment—a garment that hath shed its perfume upon the whole of creation. This is the Day whereon the rushing waters of everlasting life have gushed out of the Will of the All-Merciful. Haste ye, with your hearts and souls, and quaff your fill, O Concourse of the realms above!

Say: He it is Who is the Manifestation of Him Who is the Unknowable, the Invisible of the Invisibles, could ye but perceive it. He it is Who hath laid bare before you the hidden and treasured Gem, were ye to seek it. He it is Who is the one Beloved of all things, whether of the past or of the future. Would that ye might set your hearts and hopes upon Him!

We have heard the voice of thy pleading, O Pen, and excuse thy silence. What is it that hath so sorely bewildered thee?

The inebriation of Thy presence, O Well-Beloved of all worlds, hath seized and possessed me.

Arise, and proclaim unto the entire creation the tidings that He who is the All-Merciful hath directed His steps towards the Riḍván and entered it. Guide, then, the people unto the garden of delight which God hath made the Throne of His Paradise. We have chosen thee to be our most mighty Trumpet, whose blast is to signalize the resurrection of all mankind.

Say: This is the Paradise on whose foliage the wine of utterance hath imprinted the testimony: "He that was hidden from the eyes of men is revealed, girded with sovereignty and power!" This is the Paradise, the rustling of whose leaves proclaims: "O ye that inhabit the heavens and the earth! There hath appeared what hath never previously appeared. He Who, from everlasting, had concealed His Face from the sight of creation is now come." From the whispering breeze that wafteth amidst its branches there cometh the cry: "He Who is the sovereign Lord of all is made manifest. The Kingdom is God's," while from its streaming waters can be heard the murmur: "All eyes are gladdened, for He Whom none hath beheld, Whose secret no one hath discovered, hath lifted the veil of glory, and uncovered the countenance of Beauty."

Within this Paradise, and from the heights of its loftiest chambers the Maids of Heaven have cried out and shouted: "Rejoice, ye dwellers of the realms above, for the fingers of Him Who is the Ancient of Days are ringing, in the name of the All-Glorious, the Most Great Bell, in the midmost heart of the heavens. The hands of bounty have borne round the cup of everlasting life. Approach, and quaff your fill. Drink with healthy relish, O ye that are the very incarnations of longing, ye who are the embodiments of vehement desire!"

This is the Day whereon He Who is the Revealer of the names of God hath stepped out of the Tabernacle of glory, and proclaimed unto all who are in the heavens and all who are on the earth: "Put away the cups of Paradise and all the life-giving waters they contain, for lo, the people of Bahá have entered the blissful abode of the Divine Presence, and quaffed the wine of reunion, from the chalice of the beauty of their Lord, the All-Possessing, the Most High."

Forget the world of creation, O Pen, and turn thou towards the face of thy Lord, the Lord of all names. Adorn, then, the world with the ornament of the favours of thy Lord, the King of everlasting days. For We perceive the fragrance of the Day whereon He Who is the Desire of all nations hath shed upon the kingdoms of the unseen and of the seen the splendour of the light of His most excellent names, and enveloped them with the radiance of the luminaries of His most gracious favours—favours which none can reckon except Him, Who is the omnipotent Protector of the entire creation.

Look not upon the creatures of God except with the eye of kindliness and of mercy, for Our loving providence hath pervaded all created things, and Our grace encompassed the earth and the heavens. This is the Day whereon the true servants of God partake of the life-giving waters of reunion, the Day whereon those that are nigh unto Him are able to drink of the soft-flowing river of immortality, and they who believe in His unity, the wine of His Presence, through their recognition of Him Who is the Highest and Last End of all, in Whom the Tongue of Majesty and Glory voiceth the call: "The Kingdom is Mine. I, Myself, am, of Mine own right, its Ruler."

Attract the hearts of men, through the call of Him the one alone Beloved. Say: This is the Voice of God, if ye do but hearken. This is the Day Spring of the Revelation of God, did ye but know it. This is the Dawning-Place of the Cause of God, were ye to recognize it. This is the Source of the commandment of God, did ye but judge it fairly. This is the manifest and hidden Secret; would that ye might perceive it. O peoples of the world! Cast away, in My name that transcendeth all other names, the things ye possess, and immerse yourselves in this Ocean in whose depths lay hidden the pearls of wisdom and of utterance, an ocean that surgeth in My name, the All-Merciful. Thus instructeth you He with Whom is the Mother Book.

The Best-Beloved is come. In His right hand is the sealed Wine of His name. Happy is the man that turneth unto Him, and drinketh his fill, and exclaimeth: "Praise be to Thee, O Revealer of the signs of God!" By the righteousness of the Almighty! Every hidden thing hath been manifested through the power of truth. All the favours of God have been sent down, as a token of His grace. The waters of everlasting life have, in their fullness, been proffered unto men. Every single cup hath been borne round by the hand of the Well-Beloved. Draw near, and tarry not, though it be for one short moment.

Blessed are they that have soared on the wings of detachment and attained the station which, as ordained by God, overshadoweth the entire creation, whom neither the vain imaginations of the learned, nor the multitude of the hosts of the earth have succeeded in deflecting from His Cause. Who is there among you, O people, who will renounce the world, and draw nigh unto God, the Lord of all names? Where is he to be found who, through the power of My name that transcendeth all created things, will cast away the things that men possess, and cling, with all his might, to the things which God, the Knower of the unseen and of the seen, hath bidden him observe? Thus hath His bounty been sent down unto men, His testimony fulfilled, and His proof shone forth above the Horizon of mercy. Rich is the prize that shall be won by him who hath believed and exclaimed: "Lauded art Thou, O Beloved of all worlds! Magnified be Thy name, O Thou the Desire of every understanding heart!"

Rejoice with exceeding gladness, O people of Bahá, as ye call to remembrance the Day of supreme felicity, the Day whereon the Tongue of the Ancient of Days,hath spoken, as He departed from His House, proceeding to the Spot from which He shed upon the whole of creation the splendours of His name, the All-Merciful. God is Our witness. Were We to reveal the hidden secrets of that Day, all they that dwell on earth and in the heavens would swoon away and die, except such as will be preserved by God, the Almighty, the All-Knowing, the All-Wise.

Such is the inebriating effect of the words of God upon Him Who is the Revealer of His undoubted proofs, that His Pen can move no longer. With these words He concludeth His Tablet: "No God is there but Me, the Most Exalted, the Most powerful, the Most Excellent, the All-Knowing."

4. THE TABLET OF ṬARÁZÁT

In My Name, the Protector over all Names!

¶ 138. Praise and glory belong unto the King of Names and the Creator of heavens, the waves of the sea of Whose appearances are manifest and evident before the faces of all in the world. The sun of His command is submitted to no covering, and His word of affirmation is beyond the reach of negation. Neither the restriction of tyrants nor the oppression wrought by Pharaohs could withhold Him from His Will. Glorified is His Power and great is His Grandeur!

Praise be unto God! Although Signs have encompassed the world, and proofs and arguments are shining forth and manifest from all directions like unto the light, yet ignorant servants are found heedless, nay, even contradictory. O that they were content with mere contradicting! Nay, but they are all the time plotting to cut down the Blessed Tree. From the beginning of this Dispensation the manifestors of selfishness have exerted themselves with all tyranny and injustice to extinguish the light of God; but, verily, God prevented them therefrom, and through His power caused the light to appear and protected it through His might, until the heaven and earth were illuminated with its radiance and brightness! Praise be unto Him under all circumstances!

All praise be to Thee, O Thou Lord of the worlds and the Desire of the kingdoms. Thou hast become manifest in the Greatest Name whereby the pearls of jewelled utterance have appeared from the shells of the ocean of Thy knowledge, and the heavens of all the religions have been adorned, penetrated with light by the appearance of the glory of Thy Countenance.

We beg of Thee, by that Word whereby Thy proof was made perfect among Thy creatures, and Thine argument among Thy servants, to strengthen Thy people that the face of Thy Cause will radiate in Thy dominion, and that the standards of Thy power and the banners of Thy guidance will be planted in all lands and among all people. O my God! Behold Thy servants clinging to the robe of Thy grace and grasping the hem of the mantle of Thy beneficence. Ordain for us that which will draw us nearer to Thee, and withhold us from all save Thee.

We beg of Thee, O Thou King of existence and Protector of the seen and the unseen, to make whosoever arises to serve Thy Cause as a sea moving by Thy desire, ignited by the fire of Thy verses, shining from the horizon of the heaven of Thy will.

Verily, Thou art the Mighty One, Whom neither the power of all the worlds, nor the strength of all created beings can alter.

There is no God but Thee, the One, the Single, the Protector, the Self-Subsistent.

O thou who hast drunk the choice wine of My utterance from the cup of My knowledge!

In this day, the following words were heard from the rustling of the Sadratu'l-Muntahá, which is planted by the hand of power of the King of Names, in the exalted paradise:

THE FIRST ṬARÁZ

and the First Tajallí, which has risen from the horizon of the Mother-Book, is that man should know his own self, and know those things which lead to loftiness or to baseness, to shame or to honour, to affluence or to poverty. After man has realized his own being and become mature, then for him wealth is needed. If this wealth is acquired through a craft and profession, it is approvable and worthy of praise to men of wisdom, especially to those servants who arise to train the world and beautify the souls of nations. These are the cup-bearers of the kawthar of knowledge and the guides to the ideal path. They direct the people of the whole world unto the right path, and instruct them in that which is conducive to the elevation and progress of being.

The right path is a path which leads man to the day spring of perception and dawning-place of knowledge and directs him to that which is the cause of honour and glory and greatness. We hope that, by the providence of the wise Physician, the dust will be removed from his eyes and the clearness of his sight will increase; so that he may discover that for which he has been created. In this day that which will decrease blindness and increase sight is worthy of attention. To the possessors of wisdom this spiritual sight is the minister and guide of knowledge. The apprehension of knowledge is due to the power of insight. The people of Bahá must, in all cases, act and advise people in that which is worthy.

THE SECOND ṬARÁZ

is to consort with the people of religions with joy and fragrance; to show forth that which is declared by the Speaker of the Mount; and to render justice in affairs. The followers of sincerity and faithfulness must consort with all the people of the world with joy and fragrance; for association is always conducive to union and harmony, and union and harmony are the cause of the order of the world and the life of nations. Blessed are they who hold fast to the rope of compassion and kindness and are detached from animosity and hatred!

This oppressed One exhorts the people of the world to forbearance and benevolence. These are as two lights for the darkness of the world and as two teachers to lead nations to knowledge. Blessed are those who attain thereto, and woe unto those who are heedless!

THE THIRD ṬARÁZ

is concerning good character. A good character is, verily, the best mantle for men from God. With it He adorneth the temples of His loved ones. By My Life! The light of good character surpasseth the light of the sun and the radiance thereof. He who attains thereto is accounted as the essence of men. Upon this the honour and glory of the world are based and are dependent. Good character is the means of guiding men to the right path and the great message. Blessed is he who is adorned with the attributes and virtue of the Supreme Concourse!

Gaze toward justice and equity under all circumstances. This exalted Utterance has been revealed, from the Pen of Abhá, in the *Hidden Words*:

"O Son of Spirit! The best beloved of all things in My sight is Justice; turn not away therefrom if thou desirest Me, and neglect it not that I may confide in thee. By its aid thou shalt see with thine own eyes and not through the eyes of others, and shalt know of thine own knowledge and not through the knowledge of thy neighbour. Ponder this in thy heart; how it behoveth thee to be. Verily justice is My gift to thee and the sign of My loving-kindness. Set it then before thine eyes."

The possessors of justice and equity occupy the highest station and loftiest rank: the lights of righteousness and piety radiate and shine from such souls. It is hoped that nations and countries may not be deprived of the lights of these two orbs.

THE FOURTH ṬARÁZ

is on trustworthiness. Verily, this is the door of tranquillity to all in the world, and the sign of glory from the presence of the merciful One. Whosoever attains thereto has attained to treasuries of wealth and affluence. Trustworthiness is the greatest door to the security and tranquillity of mankind. The stability of every affair always depends on it, and the worlds of honour, glory and affluence are illuminated by its light.

Sometime since, this sweet Utterance was revealed from the Supreme Pen:

"We will now mention unto thee Trustworthiness and the station thereof in the estimation of God, thy Lord, the Lord of the Mighty Throne, One day of days We repaired unto Our Green Island. Upon Our arrival, We beheld it's streams flowing, and it's trees luxuriant, and the sunlight playing in their midst. Turning Our face to the right, We beheld what the pen is powerless to describe; nor can it set forth that which the eye of the Lord of Mankind witnessed in that most sanctified, that most sublime, that blest, and most exalted Spot. Turning, then, to the left We gazed on one of the Beauties of the Most Sublime Paradise, standing on a pillar of light, and calling aloud saying: 'O inmates of earth and heaven! Behold ye My beauty, and My radiance, and My revelation, and My effulgence. By God, the True One! I am Trustworthiness and the revelation thereof, and the beauty thereof. I will recompense whosoever will cleave unto Me, and recognize My rank and station, and hold fast unto My hem. I am the most great ornament of the people of Bahá, and the vesture of glory unto all who are in the kingdom of creation. I am the supreme instrument for the prosperity of the world, and the horizon of assurance unto all beings.' Thus have We sent down for thee that which will draw men nigh unto the Lord of creation."

"O people of Bahá! Trustworthiness is the best garment for your temples and the most splendid crown for your heads. Adhere thereto by the command of the Omnipotent Commander!"

THE FIFTH ṬARÁZ

regards the preservation and protection of the stations of the servants of God. They must not make light of any matter, but speak in truthfulness and sincerity. The people of Bahá must not refuse to discharge the due reward of any one, and must respect possessors of talent; and they must not stain their tongues with slander like unto the former community. In this day the sun of arts and crafts is manifest from the horizon of the heaven of the Occident, and the river of skill is flowing from the sea of that part. One must speak with justice and recognize the worth of benefits. By the life of God, the word Justice is shining and luminous like unto the sun: We beg of God to illuminate all with its lights. Verily, He is powerful in all things and is worthy to grant!

In these days, truthfulness and sincerity are captive in the claws of falsehood, and justice is oppressed by the scourges of injustice. The smoke of corruption has so enveloped the world that naught is seen from any direction save armies and naught is heard from any region except the clashing of swords. We beg of God to assist the appearances of His power in that which is conducive to the reformation of the world and the welfare of nations.

THE SIXTH ṬARÁZ

Knowledge is one of the greatest benefits of God. To acquire knowledge is incumbent on all. These visible arts and present implements are from the results of His knowledge and wisdom, which have been revealed from the Supreme Pen. The Supreme Pen is that pen from the treasury of which the gems of wisdom and utterance, and the arts of all the world have appeared and become manifest. In this day the mysteries of this earth are unfolded and visible before the eyes, and the pages of swiftly appearing newspapers are indeed the mirror of the world; they display the doings and actions of the different nations; they both illustrate them and cause them to be heard. Newspapers are as a mirror which is endowed with hearing, sight and speech; they are a wonderful phenomenon and a great matter. But it behoveth the writers thereof to be sanctified from the prejudice of egotism and desire and to be adorned with the ornament of equity and justice; they must inquire into matters as much as possible, in order that they may be informed of the real facts, and commit the same to writing.

Concerning this oppressed One, whatever the newspapers have mentioned is mostly devoid of truth. Good speech and truthfulness are, in loftiness of position and rank, like unto the sun which hath risen from the horizon of the heaven of knowledge. The waves of this sea are visible before the faces of all in the world, and the traces of the Pen of wisdom and utterance are manifest.

They have written in newspapers that this servant hath fled from Írán and gone to 'Iráq 'Arabí! Praise be to God, this servant hath not concealed Himself even for an instant and hath been always standing and present before all faces. Verily, We have not fled, nor do We flee; nay, rather, the ignorant servants have fled from Us! We left our native land, and horsemen, commissioned by the Íránian and Russian governments, escorted us until We arrived at 'Iráq with glory and power. Praise be to God, the matter of this Oppressed One is exalted like unto heaven and is shining and luminous as the sun. Concealment hath no access to this Station, and dread and silence have no place therein! . . .

5. THE TABLET OF TAJALLÍYÁT

¶ 139. He is the Hearer from His Supreme Horizon!

I testify that verily there is no God save He! and He who hath come is verily the hidden mystery, the concealed secret, the most great Book for the nations, and the heaven of beneficence to the world: He is the mighty sign among mankind, and the dawning-place of highest attributes in the world of emanation. Through

Him hath appeared that which was concealed from all eternity and was hidden from men of discernment. Verily, He is the One whose Manifestation was announced by the Books of God in former and in latter times.

Whoever acknowledges Him, His signs, and His evidences hath verily acknowledged that which the Tongue of Grandeur hath uttered before the creation of heaven and earth, and before the appearance of the kingdom of Names. Through Him the sea of knowledge hath moved among mankind, and the running water of wisdom hath flowed from the presence of God, the King of Days. Blessed is the discerning one who witnessed and perceived, the hearing one who heard His sweet voice, and the hand that took hold of the Book through the power of its Lord, the king of this world and of the world to come! Blessed is the hastener who hastened toward His Supreme horizon, and the strong one whom neither the influence of princes nor the clamour of religious doctors did weaken! But woe unto him who disbelieved the grace of God and His bounty, His mercy and His power! Verily, such an one is of those who reject the proof of God and His argument throughout all eternity.

Joy unto him who, in this Day, casts away that which is possessed by the people, and holds fast to that which is commanded on the part of God, the King of Names and the Creator of things, viz.: The one who hath come from the heaven of pre-existence with the Greatest Name, and with a power that the hosts of the earth fail to withstand—whereunto testifies the "Mother-Book" in the Highest Station.

O 'Alí Qabl-i-Akbar! We have heard thy voice repeatedly, and We have responded to thee in that which the sayings of the world cannot equal, and from which the sincere ones find the perfume of the utterance of the clement One, the lovers the fragrances of union, and the thirsty ones the murmur of the kawthar of life. Blessed is he who attains thereto, and discovers that sweet fragrance which is now being diffused from the Pen of God, the Protector, the Mighty, the Bestower!

We testify that verily thou hast advanced, hast journeyed until thou arrived and presented thyself here, and hast hearkened unto the voice of the oppressed One who is imprisoned because of that which was wrought by the hands of those who denied the Verses of

God and His commands and rejected this grace by which the regions of the world are illuminated.

Blessed is thy face, for it turned unto Our direction; thine ears, for they heard; and thy tongue, for it uttered the praise of God, the Lord of Lords! We beg of God to make thee a banner for assistance of His Cause, and to draw thee nearer unto Him under all circumstances. We make mention of the friends of God and His beloved ones in that place, and we gladden them through that which is revealed unto them from the kingdom of the utterance of their Lord, the King of the Day of Judgment.

Remember them on My part, and illumine them with the lights of the orb of My utterance. Verily thy Lord is the mighty, the gracious.

O thou who art speaking My praise! Hearken to that which the oppressors say in My days. Some say, "Verily he hath claimed divinity!" others say, "He hath calumniated God," and still others say, "He hath appeared for corruption." Woe unto them! Grief unto them! Are they not the worshippers of imaginations?

Verily, We now desire to leave the "Eloquent Language." Verily thy Lord is the powerful, the independent! It is our desire to speak in the Íránian language, so that perchance the people of Persia may all hear the Utterance of the Clement One, and may come forth and find the truth.

THE FIRST TAJALLÍ

which hath shone forth from the Sun of Truth is the knowledge of God—exalted in His Glory—and the knowledge of the King of Pre-existence cannot be attained except by knowing the Greatest Name. He is the speaker of the Mount who is established and seated upon the throne of Manifestation, and He is the hidden, invisible One, the concealed Mystery.

All the former and later Books of God are adorned with His commemoration and speak His praise. Through Him the standard of knowledge is planted in the world, and the banner of unity is hoisted among nations. The meeting of God cannot be obtained except through meeting Him. Through Him appeared all that was hidden and invisible from all eternity.

Verily, He hath appeared in Truth, and hath uttered a Word whereby "all in the heavens and earth—except those whom God wished—are stunned." Faith in God, and the knowledge of Him cannot be fully realized except through believing in all that hath proceeded from Him, and by practising all that He hath command-ed and all that is revealed in the Book from the Supreme Pen. Those submerged in the sea of Divine utterance must at all times observe the commands and prohibitions of God. His command-ments are the greatest fortress for the protection of the world and for the preservation of mankind. Light is upon those who confess and acknowledge them, and fire is on those who reject and oppose them.

THE SECOND TAJALLÍ

is steadfastness in the Cause of God and in His love—exalted is His glory! This cannot be attained except through knowledge of Him, and a perfect knowledge of Him cannot be obtained except by confessing the blessed Word: "God doeth that which He willeth." He who adheres to this exalted Word, and drinks from the kawthar of divine utterance which is deposited therein, will find himself so steadfast that all the books of the world shall not withhold him from the "Mother-Book". Oh! Great is this lofty station, exalted position, and furthermost end!

O 'Alí Qabl-i-Akbar! Think how low is the station of the deniers. All of them speak the blessed Words: "Verily, He is to be praised in His deeds, and to be obeyed in His Command;" never-theless, if something may appear, in the least degree against their lust and desire, they will reject it. Say: No one is informed of the expediencies of the consummate wisdom of God. Verily, were He to declare the earth to be heaven, no one hath the right to contra-dict Him. This is that whereunto the Point of El-Bayán[1] hath testified in all that was revealed unto Him on the part of God, the cleaver of dawns.

THE THIRD TAJALLÍ

is concerning sciences, crafts and arts. Knowledge is as wings to man's life, and a ladder for his ascent. It's acquisition is incumbent upon everyone. The knowledge of such sciences, however, should be aquired as can profit the peoples of the earth, and not those which begin with words and end with words. Great indeed is the claim of scientists and craftsmen on the peoples of the world.

[1] The Báb.

Whereunto testifies the mother of divine utterance in the day of return. Joy unto those who hear!

Indeed, the real treasury of man is his knowledge. Knowledge is the means of honour, prosperity, joy, gladness, happiness and exultation. Thus hath the Tongue of Grandeur spoken in this Great Prison!

THE FOURTH TAJALLÍ

concerns the declaration of divinity, lordship, and similar statements. Were one endowed with perception to gaze upon this evident, blessed Tree, and upon its fruits, he would verily become independent of all else save It, and would acknowledge that which the speaker of the mount hath uttered on the throne of Manifestation.

O 'Alí Qabl-i-Akbar! Speak unto people concerning the signs of thy Lord, and make known unto them His right path and His great Message. Say: O servants! If ye are the people of justice and equity, ye will confess all that has flowed from the Supreme Pen. If ye are of the people of Bayán, the Persian Bayán will guide you and suffice you, and, if ye are of the people of El-Furqán, reflect upon the "Splendour" and the "Voice" revealed in the Sinaitic Tree for the Son of Imrán.

Praise be to God! It was supposed that at the manifestation of God knowledge had waxed perfect and mature, and had reached the furthermost end. Now it has become evident that knowledge has decreased among the deniers, and has remained immature.

O 'Alí! They refuse to accept from the Tree of being that which they accepted from the Tree of Sinai! Say: O people of Bayán! Speak not after the self and desire! Most of the peoples of the world confess the blessed Word which has proceeded from the Tree. By the life of God, were it not for the mention of "Divinity" made by the Precursor,[1] this oppressed One would not have spoken in that which is the cause of distraction and destruction of the ignorant.

In the beginning of the Bayán, He says in description of "He whom God shall manifest": "He, verily, is the One Who, under all conditions, proclaimeth: 'I, in very truth, am God! There is no God but Me, the Lord of all things, and all besides Me is created by Me! O ye, My creatures! Ye are to worship Me.'" Likewise, in another place, in speaking of "He whom God shall

---

[1] The Báb.

manifest," He says: "Verily, I am the first one of those who worship Him."

Now, man must reflect upon the "Worshipper," and the "Worshipped One": perchance the people of the earth may attain to a drop of the sea of knowledge, and comprehend the station of this manifestation. Verily, He hath appeared, and hath spoken in truth. Blessed is he who confesses and acknowledges, and woe unto every remote denier!

O ye concourse of the earth! Hearken to the voice of the Sadrat, the shade of which hath encompassed the loftiest positions of the world; and be not of the tyrants of the earth who denied the manifestation of God and His power, and renounced His bounty. Are they not of the contemptible, in the Book of God, the Lord of the creatures?

Glory, shining from the heaven of My Providence, be upon thee, and upon him who is with thee and hearkens to thy saying in the Cause of God, the Mighty, the Praiseworthy!

6. THE TABLET OF ISHRÁQÁT

¶ 140. . . . O Jalíl! The oppressed One of the world says: The orb of justice is concealed; the sun of equity is behind the clouds; thieves occupy the position of guardians and protectors, and traitors are seated in the place of trustworthy ones. In the preceding year, a tyrant occupied the seat of the governorship of this city. At every instance We suffered a harm from him. By the life of God, he wrought that which caused the greatest dread. But the tyranny of the whole world can never withhold the Supreme Pen. Out of especial grace and mercy to the princes and counsellors of the earth We wrote that which is conducive to protection, security, tranquillity and composure—perchance the servants may be protected from the wickedness of tyrants. Verily He is the guardian, the helper, the confirmer!

The men of the House of Justice of God must, night and day, gaze toward that which hath been revealed from the horizon of the heaven of the Supreme Pen for the training of the servants, for the upbuilding of countries, for the protection of men and for the preservation of human honour.

THE FIRST ISHRÁQ

When the Day-star of Wisdom rose above the horizon of God's Holy Dispensation it voiced this all-glorious utterance: They that are possessed of wealth and invested with authority and power must show the profoundest regard for religion. In truth, religion is a radiant light and an impregnable stronghold for the protection and welfare of the peoples of the world, for the fear of God impelleth man to hold fast to that which is good and shun all evil. Should the lamp of religion be obscured, chaos and confusion will ensue, and the lights of fairness and justice, of tranquility and peace cease to shine. Unto this will bear witness every man of true understanding.

THE SECOND ISHRÁQ

We have enjoined upon all mankind the Most Great Peace—the surest of all means for the protection of humanity. The sovereigns of the world should with one accord hold fast thereunto, for this is the supreme instrument that can insure the security and welfare of all peoples and nations. They verily are the manifestations of the power of God and the day-springs of His authority. We beseech the Almighty that He may graciously assist them in that which leadeth to the well-being of their subjects. The account of this subject has been previously revealed from the Supreme Pen. Blessed are those who act accordingly.

THE THIRD ISHRÁQ

It is incumbent upon everyone to observe God's holy commandments inasmuch as they are the well-spring of life unto the world. The firmament of Divine Wisdom is illumined with the twin orbs of Counsel and Compassion, and the canopy of world order is upraised upon the two pillars of Reward and Punishment.

THE FOURTH ISHRÁQ

The triumphant hosts of this Divine Dispensation are laudable deeds and praiseworthy character, and the leader and marshal thereof is the fear of God. Verily this comprehendeth and ruleth all things.

THE FIFTH IS͟HRÁQ

Governments should fully acquaint themselves with the condition of those they govern, and confer upon them positions according to desert and merit. It is enjoined upon every ruler and sovereign to consider this matter with the utmost care that the traitor may not usurp the position of the faithful nor the despoiler rule in the place of the trustworthy.

In this Most Great Prison, among the officials formerly and recently appointed, some have been—praise be to God!—adorned with the ornament of Justice; but some others of them ——. We take refuge in God! We beg of God that He may guide them all, perchance they may not be deprived of the fruits of the tree of trustworthiness and integrity, nor withheld from the lights of the sun of equity and justice.

THE SIXTH IS͟HRÁQ

is concerning union and harmony among mankind. From the beginning of time the light of unity hath shed its Divine Radiance upon the world, and the greatest means for the promotion of that unity is for the peoples of the world to understand one another's writing and speech. In former Epistles we have enjoined upon the Trustees of the House of Justice either to choose one language from among those now existing or to adopt a new one, and in like manner to select a common script, both of which should be taught in all the schools of the world. Thus will the earth be regarded as one country and one home. The most glorious fruit of the Tree of Knowledge is this exalted word: "Of one tree ye are all the fruit, and of one bough the leaves." "Let not man glory in this that he loves his country, let him rather glory in this that he loves his kind."

In this connection We have formerly revealed that which is the means for the prosperity of the world and the unification of nations. Blessed are those who attain! Blessed are those who practise!

THE SEVENTH IS͟HRÁQ

The Pen of Glory counseleth every one regarding the instruction and education of children. Upon Our arrival in the Prison, the following verses have in this connection been revealed in the

Book of Aqdas, from the heaven of the Divine Will: "It is enjoined upon every father to provide for the instruction of his sons and daughters in the art of learning and writing and in that which hath been prescribed in My Epistles. He that neglecteth that whereunto he is bidden, if he be wealthy, the Trustees are to take from him that which is required for their education, and if he be poor, the matter shall devolve upon the House of Justice— verily, have We made it a shelter for the poor and a refuge for the needy. He that bringeth up his own son or the son of another, it is as though he had brought up a child of Mine own; upon him rest My glory, My loving-kindness and My mercy that encompasseth all mankind.

THE EIGHTH ISHRÁQ

This passage is written, at this time, by the Supreme Pen and is accounted of the book of Aqdas. The affairs of the people are in charge of the men of the House of Justice of God. They are the trustees of God among His servants and the sources of command in His countries.

O people of God! That which traineth the world is Justice, for it is upheld by two pillars, reward and punishment. These two pillars are the sources of life to the world.

Inasmuch as for each day and time a particular decree or order is expedient, affairs are therefore entrusted to the House of Justice, so that it may execute that which it deems advisable at the time. Those souls who arise to serve the Cause sincerely, to please God, shall be inspired by the invisible inspiration of God. It is incumbent upon all to obey them.

Administrative affairs are all in charge of the House of Justice, and devotional acts must be observed according as they are revealed in the Book.

O people of Bahá! Ye are dawning-places of the love and day-springs of the favour of God. Defile not the tongues with cursing and execrating anyone and guard your eyes from that which is not worthy. Show forth that which ye possess. If it is accepted, the aim is attained; if not, interference with those who reject it is not allowable. Leave him to himself, and advance toward God, the protector, the self-subsistent. Be not the cause of sorrow, how much less of

sedition and strife! It is hoped ye may be trained under the shadow
of the tree of divine favour and act in that which God desireth. Ye
are all leaves of one tree and drops of one sea.

THE NINTH ISHRÁQ

The religion of God and the creed of God hath been revealed and
made manifest from the heaven of the will of the king of pre-
existence for the sake of union and harmony among the people of
the world; make it not a means for disagreement and discord!

The religion of God and His law is the greatest cause and mightiest means for the appearance and effulgence of the orb of unity. The
development of the world, the training of nations, the tranquillity
of the servants and the security of the people of all lands have been
due to the divine precepts and ordinances. Religion is the greatest
cause for the appearance of this great gift. It bestows the cup of
vitality, confers immortal life and imparts eternal benefit to the
people. The rulers of the earth, especially the trustees of the House
of Justice, must make abundant effort to preserve this station and
guard and promote it. Likewise it is necessary that they should inquire into the conditions of the subjects and be acquainted with the
deeds and affairs of every one in the communities.

We ask the manifestors of the divine power, that is, kings and
leaders, to endeavour, perchance discord may vanish and the world
be illumined with the light of accord. All must adhere to and practise that which hath been revealed from the Supreme Pen. The true
One testifies and the atoms of the universe bear witness that We
have spoken and revealed in Tablets and Epistles from the Supreme
Pen that which is conducive to the exaltation, elevation, training,
protection, and progress of the people of the earth. We beg of
God to strengthen the servants. What this oppressed One requires
of all is justice and equity. Let them not satisfy themselves with
mere hearing, but reflect upon that which hath proceeded from
this oppressed One. I swear by the sun of divine utterance which
hath arisen from the horizon of the kingdom of the clement One,
that were there an exponent or speaker to be found We would
not have made ourself an object of censure, derision, and calumnies
on the part of the people. . .

VI. THE COVENANT

¶ 141. Although the Most High Horizon is devoid of trivial possessions of the earth, we have nevertheless bequeathed unto our heirs a noble and peerless heritage within the treasure-house of trust and resignation.

We have left no treasure nor have we added to man's pains.

By the Life of God! In earthly riches fear is hidden and peril is concealed. Consider, then take warning by what the God of Mercy hath revealed in the Qur'án: "Woe unto those who malign and speak evil of their fellows; who hoard earthly goods and count their riches."

Earthly possessions are unstable; wherefore whatsoever passeth or suffereth vicissitudes is unworthy of regard except to a limited measure.

In bearing hardships and tribulations and in revealing verses and expounding proofs, it has been the purpose of this oppressed One to extinguish the fire of hate and animosity, that, haply, the horizons of the hearts of mankind be illumined with the light of concord and attain real tranquillity.

The light of the following utterance shineth from the horizon of the Divine Tablet, which should be observed by all: O people of the world! I counsel you to act in a manner which shall tend to elevate your stations. Cling to divine virtue and obey the divine law. Truly I say, the tongue is for mentioning that which is good; do not defile it by evil speech. "God hath forgiven your past ways." You must henceforth speak that which is worthy. Shun reviling, maligning, and whatsoever will offend your fellowmen.

Man's station is great. Ere this, the following exalted words have flowed forth from the Pen of Abhá: "This is a Day great and blessed. Whatsoever was hidden in man is today being revealed." The station of man is great, were he to cling to truth and righteousness and be firm and steadfast in the Cause. Before the God of Mercy, a true man appears like unto heaven. The sun and the moon of that heaven are his sight and hearing and its stars are his shining attributes. His station is the highest and his signs are the educator of the world.

In this Day, every believer who discovered the fragrance of the garment and turned with a pure heart unto the most high horizon is indeed recorded in the Crimson Tablet as of the people of Bahá.

Hold the chalice of My grace in My name. Then drain it in My mention, the mighty, the wonderful!

O people of the world! The religion of God is to create love and unity; do not make it the cause of enmity and discord. All that is regarded by men of insight and the people of the most lofty outlook as the means for safeguarding and effecting the peace and tranquillity of man has flowed from the Supreme Pen. But the ignorant ones who are the victim of self and desire are heedless of the consummate wisdom of the truly wise One, and their words and deeds are prompted by fancy and superstition.

O ye chosen of God and His trusted ones! Kings are the manifestors of God's power and the source of His majesty and affluence. Pray ye in their behalf. The government of the earth has been vouchsafed unto them. But the hearts of men He decreed unto Himself. He forbade conflict and strife—a rigid prohibition in the Book. This is the Decree of God in this most great Manifestation; and God hath preserved it from annulment and clothed it with the broidered garment of confirmation. Verily, He is the All-Knowing, the All-Wise.

It is incumbent upon all to support those rulers and chiefs of state who are adorned with the raiment of justice and equity. Blessed are the rulers and the learned in el-Bahá! They verily are My trustees amongst My servants, and the sources of My Decrees amongst My people. Upon them rest My Bahá, My mercy, and My grace which hath encircled the world!

Anent this matter, we have revealed in the Book of Aqdas the following words which radiate the light of divine mercy: "O my Branches! A mighty power and supreme potency is hidden and concealed in the world of being. Focus your gaze upon it and upon the direction of its unity, not upon the differences which are apparent therein."

God's Will and Testament enjoins upon the Aghsán, the Afnán, and My kindred, one and all, their faces towards the Most Mighty Branch. Consider that which We have revealed in Our

Most Mighty Book: "When the ocean of My presence hath ebbed and the Book of My Revelation is ended, turn your faces toward Him Whom God hath purposed, Who hath branched from this Ancient Root." The object of this sacred verse is none other except the Most Mighty Branch.[1] Thus have We graciously revealed unto you Our potent Will, and I am the Gracious, the All-Powerful.

God hath, verily, decreed the station of the Great Branch next to that of the Most Great Branch. Verily He is the Wise Ordainer. We have chosen el-Akbar after the el-A'zam, as a command on the part of God, the All-Knowing, the Omniscient.

All must regard the other Branches with affection, but God hath not decreed unto them any right to the people's property.

O My Branches, My Twigs, and My Kinsfolk! I counsel you to manifest divine virtue, and to act in accord with the Law, and with whatsoever is befitting and will elevate your stations.

Truly I say, virtue is the greatest commander which leads the Cause of God to victory, and the legions which deserve this commander are pure, sanctified, and praiseworthy deeds and attributes.

Say: O servants! Do not make the cause of order a cause for disorder, nor the means of unity a means for disunity. It is hoped that the people of Bahá will observe the sacred verse: "Say: All are created by God." This lofty utterance is like unto water for quenching the fire of hate and hostility which is hidden and stored in men's hearts and minds. This single utterance will cause the various sects and creeds to attain the true light of unity. Verily He speaketh truth and guideth to the right path; and He is the mighty, the glorious, the omnipotent.

For the honour of the Cause and the promotion of the Word—it is necessary that all shall respect and have regard for the Branches. This command has been recorded once and again in the divine Book. Blessed is he who obeys whatsoever hath been ordained on the part of God, the ancient ruler. All shall also have respect for the women-members of Our household and for the Afnán and kinsfolk. We likewise counsel you to serve mankind and bring peace to the world.

All that leads to the quickening of the peoples and the salvation of the world hath been revealed from the kingdom of utterance by the Lord of mankind. Hearken to the exhortations of the Supreme

[1] 'Abdu'l-Bahá.

Pen with ideal ears. These are preferable unto you above all that is on the earth. Whereunto beareth witness my Book, the blessed, the glorious!

¶ 142. Whoso layeth claim to a Revelation direct from God, ere the expiration of a full thousand years, such a man is assuredly a lying impostor. We pray God that He may graciously assist him to retract and repudiate such claim. Should he repent, God will, no doubt, forgive him. If, however, he persists in his error, God will, assuredly, send down one who will deal mercilessly with him. Terrible, indeed, is God in punishing! Whosoever interpreteth this verse otherwise than its obvious meaning is deprived of the Spirit of God and of His mercy which encompasseth all created things. Fear God, and follow not your idle fancies. Nay, rather follow the bidding of your Lord, the Almighty, the All-Wise.

VII. MEDITATIONS

¶ 143. Lauded and glorified art Thou, O Lord, my God! How can I make mention of Thee, assured as I am that no tongue, however deep its wisdom, can befittingly magnify Thy name, nor can the bird of the human heart, however great its longing, ever hope to ascend into the heaven of Thy majesty and knowledge.

If I describe Thee, O my God, as Him Who is the All-Perceiving, I find myself compelled to admit that They Who are the highest Embodiments of perception have been created by virtue of Thy behest. And if I extol Thee as Him Who is the All-Wise, I, likewise, am forced to recognize that the Well Springs of wisdom have themselves been generated through the operation of Thy Will. And if I proclaim Thee as the Incomparable One, I soon discover that they Who are the inmost essence of oneness have been sent down by Thee and are but the evidences of Thine handiwork. And if I acclaim Thee as the Knower of all things, I must confess that they Who are the Quintessence of knowledge are but the creation and instruments of Thy Purpose.

Exalted, immeasurably exalted, art Thou above the strivings of mortal man to unravel Thy mystery, to describe Thy glory, or even to hint at the nature of Thine Essence. For whatever such strivings may accomplish, they never can hope to transcend the limitations imposed upon Thy creatures, inasmuch as these efforts are actuated by Thy decree, and are begotten of Thine invention. The loftiest sentiments which the holiest of saints can express in praise of Thee, and the deepest wisdom which the most learned of men can utter in their attempts to comprehend Thy nature, all revolve around that Centre Which is wholly subjected to Thy sovereignty, Which adoreth Thy Beauty, and is propelled through the movement of Thy Pen.

Nay, forbid it, O my God, that I should have uttered such words as must of necessity imply the existence of any direct relationship between the Pen of Thy Revelation and the essence of all created things. Far, far are They Who are related to Thee above the conception of such relationship! All comparisons and likenesses fail to do justice to the Tree of Thy Revelation, and every way is barred to the comprehension of the Manifestation of Thy Self and the Day Spring of Thy Beauty.

Far, far from Thy glory be what mortal man can affirm of Thee, or attribute unto Thee, or the praise with which he can glorify Thee! Whatever duty Thou hast prescribed unto Thy servants of extolling to the utmost Thy majesty and glory is but a token of Thy grace unto them, that they may be enabled to ascend unto the station conferred upon their own inmost being, the station of the knowledge of their own selves.

No one else besides Thee hath, at any time, been able to fathom Thy mystery, or befittingly to extol Thy greatness. Unsearchable and high above the praise of men wilt Thou remain for ever. There is none other God but Thee, the Inaccessible, the Omnipotent, the Omniscient, the Holy of Holies.

¶ 144. Glorified art Thou, O Lord my God! Every man of insight confesseth Thy Sovereignty and Thy dominion, and every discerning eye perceiveth the greatness of Thy majesty and the compelling power of Thy might. The winds of tests are powerless to hold back them that enjoy near access to Thee from setting their faces towards the horizon of Thy glory, and the tempests of trials must fail to draw away and hinder such as are wholly devoted to Thy will from approaching Thy court.

Methinks, the lamp of Thy love is burning in their hearts, and the light of Thy tenderness is lit within their breasts. Adversities are incapable of estranging them from Thy Cause, and the vicissitudes of fortune can never cause them to stray from Thy pleasure.

I beseech Thee, O my God, by them and by the sighs which their hearts utter in their separation from Thee, to keep them safe from the mischief of Thine adversaries, and to nourish their souls with what Thou hast ordained for Thy loved ones on whom shall come no fear and who shall not be put to grief.

¶ 145. Magnified be Thy name, O Lord my God! I know not what the water is with which Thou hast created me, or what the fire Thou hast kindled within me, or the clay wherewith Thou hast kneaded me. The restlessness of every sea hath been stilled, but not the restlessness of this Ocean which moveth at the bidding of the winds of Thy will. The flame of every fire hath been extinguished except the Flame which the hands of Thine omnipotence have kindled, and whose radiance Thou hast, by the power of Thy name, shed abroad before all that are in Thy heaven and all that are on Thy earth. As the tribulations deepen, it waxeth hotter and hotter.

Behold, then, O my God, how Thy Light hath been compassed with the onrushing winds of Thy decree, how the tempests that blow and beat upon it from every side have added to its brightness and increased its splendour. For all this let Thee be praised.

I implore Thee, by Thy Most Great Name, and Thy most ancient sovereignty, to look upon Thy loved ones whose hearts have been sorely shaken by reason of the troubles that have touched Him Who is the Manifestation of Thine own Self. Powerful art Thou to do what pleaseth Thee. Thou art, verily, the All-Knowing, the All-Wise.

¶ 146. Praised be Thou, O my God! How can I thank Thee for having singled me out and chosen me above all Thy servants to reveal Thee, at a time when all had turned away from Thy beauty! I testify, O my God, that if I were given a thousand lives by Thee, and offered them up all in Thy path, I would still have failed to repay the least of the gifts which, by Thy grace, Thou hast bestowed upon me.

I lay asleep on the bed of self when lo, Thou didst waken me with the divine accents of Thy voice, and didst unveil to me Thy beauty, and didst enable me to listen to Thine utterances, and to recognize Thy Self, and to speak forth Thy praise, and to extol Thy virtues, and to be steadfast in Thy love. Finally I fell a captive into the hands of the wayward among Thy servants.

Thou beholdest, therefore, the exile which I suffer in Thy days, and art aware of my vehement longing to look upon Thy face, and of mine irrepressible yearnings to enter the court of Thy glory, and of the stirrings of my heart under the influences of the winds of Thy mercy.

I entreat Thee, O Thou Who art the Ruler of the kingdoms of creation and the Author of all names, to write down my name with the names of them who, from eternity, have circled round the

Tabernacle of Thy majesty, and clung to the hem of Thy loving-kindness, and held fast the cord of Thy tender mercy.

Thou art, in truth, the Help in Peril, the Self-Subsisting.

¶ 147. Lauded be Thy name, O Lord my God! Thou seest me in this day shut up in my prison, and fallen into the hands of Thine adversaries, and beholdest my son[1] lying on the dust before Thy face. He is Thy servant, O my Lord, whom Thou hast caused to be related to Him Who is the Manifestation of Thyself and the Day-Spring of Thy Cause.

At his birth he was afflicted through his separation from Thee, according to what had been ordained for him through Thine irrevocable decree. And when he had quaffed the cup of reunion with Thee, he was cast into prison for having believed in Thee and in Thy signs. He continued to serve Thy Beauty until he entered into this Most Great Prison. Thereupon I offered him up, O my God, as a sacrifice in Thy path. Thou well knowest what they who love Thee have endured through this trial that hath caused the kindreds of the earth to wail, and beyond them the Concourse on high to lament.

I beseech Thee, O my Lord, by him and by his exile and his imprisonment, to send down upon such as loved him what will quiet their hearts and bless their works. Potent art Thou to do as Thou willest. No God is there but Thee, the Almighty, the Most Powerful.

¶ 148. Glorified art Thou, O my God! Thou knowest that my sole aim in revealing Thy Cause hath been to reveal Thee and not my self, and to manifest Thy glory rather than my glory. In Thy path, and to attain Thy pleasure, I have scorned rest, joy, delight. At all times and under all conditions my gaze hath been fixed on Thy precepts, and mine eyes bent upon the things Thou hast bidden me observe in Thy Tablets. I have wakened every morning to the light of Thy praise and Thy remembrance, and reached every evening inhaling the fragrances of Thy mercy.

And when the entire creation was stirred up, and the whole earth was convulsed, and the sweet savours of Thy name, the All-Praised, had almost ceased to breathe over Thy realms, and the winds of Thy mercy had well-nigh been stilled throughout Thy

---

[1] The Purest Branch.

dominions, Thou didst, through the power of Thy might, raise me up among Thy servants, and bid me to show forth Thy sovereignty amidst Thy people. Thereupon I arose before all Thy creatures, strengthened by Thy help and Thy power, and summoned all the multitudes unto Thee, and announced unto all Thy servants Thy favours and Thy gifts, and invited them to turn towards this Ocean, every drop of the waters of which crieth out, proclaiming unto all that are in heaven and on earth that He is, in truth, the Fountain of all life, and the Quickener of the entire creation, and the Object of the adoration of all worlds, and the Best-Beloved of every understanding heart, and the Desire of all them that are nigh unto Thee.

Though the fierce winds of the hatred of the wicked doers blew and beat on this Lamp, He was, at no time, in His love for Thy beauty, hindered from shedding the fragrance of His light. As the transgressions committed against Thee waxed greater and greater, my eagerness to reveal Thy Cause correspondingly increased, and as the tribulations deepened—and to this Thy glory beareth me witness—a fuller measure of Thy sovereignty and of Thy power was vouchsafed by me unto Thy creatures.

And finally, I was cast by the transgressors into the prison-city of 'Akká, and my kindred were made captives in Baghdád. The power of Thy might beareth me witness, O my God! Every trouble that hath touched me in Thy path hath added to my joy and increased my gladness. I swear by Thee, O Thou Who art the King of Kings! None of the kings of the earth hath power to hinder me from remembering Thee or from extolling Thy virtues. Were they to be leagued—as they have been leagued—against me, and to brandish their sharpest swords and most afflictive spears against me, I would not hesitate to magnify Thy name before all them that are in Thy heaven and on Thy earth. Nay rather, I would cry out and say: "This, O my Beloved, is my face which I have offered up for Thy face, and this is my spirit which I have sacrificed for Thy spirit, and this is my blood that seetheth in my veins, in its longing to be shed for love of Thee and in Thy path."

Though—as Thou beholdest me, O my God—I be dwelling in a place within whose walls no voice can be heard except the sound of the echo, though all the gates of ease and comfort be shut against us, and thick darkness appear to have compassed us on every side, yet my soul hath been so inflamed by its love for Thee, that nothing whatsoever can either quench the fire of its love or abate the consuming flame of its desire. Lifting up its voice, it crieth aloud amidst Thy servants, and calleth them, at all times and under all conditions, unto Thee.

I beseech Thee, by Thy Most Great Name, to open the eyes of Thy servants, that they may behold Thee shining above the horizon of Thy majesty and glory, and that they may not be hindered by the croaking of the raven from hearkening to the voice of the Dove of Thy sublime oneness, nor be prevented by the corrupt waters from partaking of the pure wine of Thy bounty and the everlasting streams of Thy gifts.

Gather them, then, together around this Divine Law, the covenant of which Thou hast established with all Thy Prophets and Thy Messengers, and Whose ordinances Thou hast written down in Thy Tablets and Thy Scriptures. Raise them up, moreover, to such heights as will enable them to perceive Thy Call.

Potent art Thou to do what pleaseth Thee. Thou art, verily, the Inaccessible, the All-Glorious.

¶ 149. The hearts that yearn after Thee, O my God, are burnt up with the fire of their longing for Thee, and the eyes of them that love Thee weep sore by reason of their crushing separation from Thy court, and the voice of the lamentation of such as have set their hopes on Thee hath gone forth throughout Thy dominions.

Thou hast Thyself, O my God, protected them, by Thy sovereign might, from both extremities. But for the burning of their souls and the sighing of their hearts, they would be drowned in the midst of their tears, and but for the flood of their tears they would be burnt up by the fire of their hearts and the heat of their souls. Methinks, they are like the angels which Thou hast created of snow and of fire. Wilt Thou, despite such vehement longing, O my God, debar them from Thy presence, or drive them away, notwithstanding such fervour, from the door of Thy mercy? All hope is ready to be extinguished in the hearts of Thy chosen ones, O my God! Where are the breezes of Thy grace? They are hemmed in on all sides by their enemies; where are the ensigns of Thy triumph which Thou didst promise in Thy Tablets?

Thy glory is my witness! At each daybreak they who love Thee wake to find the cup of woe set before their faces, because they have believed in Thee and acknowledged Thy signs. Though I firmly believe that Thou hast a greater compassion on them than they have on their own selves, though I recognize that Thou hast afflicted them for no other purpose except to proclaim Thy Cause, and to enable them to ascend into the heaven of Thine eternity and the precincts of Thy court, yet Thou knowest full well the frailty of some of them, and art aware of their impatience in their sufferings.

Help them through Thy strengthening grace, I beseech Thee, O my God, to suffer patiently in their love for Thee, and unveil to their eyes what Thou hast decreed for them behind the Tabernacle of Thine unfailing protection, so that they may rush forward to meet what is preordained for them in Thy path, and may vie in hasting after tribulation in their love towards Thee. And if not, do Thou, then, reveal the standards of Thine ascendancy, and make them to be victorious over Thine adversaries, that Thy sovereignty may be manifested unto all the dwellers of Thy realm, and the power of Thy might demonstrated amidst Thy creatures. Powerful art Thou to do what Thou willest. No God is there but Thee, the Omniscient, the All-Wise.

Make steadfast Thou, O my God, Thy servant who hath believed in Thee to help Thy Cause, and keep him safe from all dangers in the stronghold of Thy care and Thy protection, both in this life and in the life which is to come. Thou, verily, rulest as Thou pleasest. No God is there save Thee, the Ever-Forgiving, the Most Generous.

¶ 150. Praise be to Thee, O Lord my God! Thou beholdest what the tongue of no one except Thee can utter, and bearest witness unto things which no mouth can recount. The floods of afflictions are let loose, and the winds of Thy judgment have blown, and from the clouds rain down the darts of tests, and the heavens of Thy decree pour forth the arrows of trial.

Thou seest, O my Lord, how Thy servants, who have believed on Thee and acknowledged Thy signs, have fallen into the clutches of Thine enemies, how the doors of ease and comfort have been shut against them, how they languish in the Fortress wherein neither pleasantness nor hope can be found. They have suffered in Thy path what no man before them hath suffered. To this bear witness they who abide around Thy throne, and the dwellers of the earth, and the Concourse on high.

These, O my God, are Thy servants who, for love of Thy beauty, have forsaken their homes, and been so stirred up by the gentle winds of their desire for Thee that they have sundered every tie in Thy path. Such of Thy servants as dwell in Thy land and have transgressed against Thee have assailed them, and banished them from Thy cities, and made them captives, and delivered them into the hands of workers of iniquity among Thy people and the perverse amidst the wicked doers in Thy realm. And finally, they were made to abide in this place with which no other place, however loathsome, in all Thy dominion, can compare. They were seized with such trials that the clouds weep over them and the thunder groaneth by reason of the manifold tribulations that have afflicted them in their love for Thee and for the sake of Thy pleasure.

Thou knowest full well, O my God, that there is no one on Thine earth who can claim to be related to Thee except these, some of whom have suffered martyrdom for Thy sake, while the rest have been permitted to survive. Though for such as are like unto us, O my God, it beseemeth not to claim to be related to Thee, inasmuch as our misdeeds and our waywardness have hindered us from reaching the depths of the ocean of Thy oneness, and from immersing ourselves beneath the waters of Thy transcendent mercy, yet our tongues, O my God, bear witness, and our hearts testify, and our limbs confess that Thy mercy hath enveloped all created things and Thy compassion surpassed all that are in heaven and all that are on earth.

I beseech Thee, by Thy Most Great Name, through which all created things were rent asunder and the whole creation was shaken, to send down from the clouds of Thy mercy that which will purge them from every ordeal and from whatever is hateful to Thee. Raise them up, then, to such heights that no amount of tribulation will keep them back from Thy wondrous remembrance, nor any trouble hinder them from turning toward the court of Thy transcendent oneness.

By Thy might, O Well-Beloved of Bahá and his heart's Desire! I myself cry out, under all conditions, unto Thee saying: "Would I had, ere this day, drawn nigh unto Thee!" When I hear, however, the sighs of such of Thy people as are wholly devoted to Thee, and

those of Thy servants as enjoy near access to Thy court, who have
taken no other friend than Thee, and sought no refuge except Thee,
and have chosen for themselves, in Thy path, what no man hath
chosen in the days of the Manifestations of Thy transcendent unity
and the Day-Springs of Thy most holy sovereignty, then my heart
is saddened and my soul is vexed, and I cry to Thee, imploring
Thee to protect them, by Thy power that hath encompassed the
entire creation both visible and invisible, from whatsoever may be
abhorrent to Thee. This is not for their own sakes, but that Thy
name may, through them, abide amongst Thy servants, and Thy
remembrance may continue to endure in Thy dominions.

Thou knowest, O my God, that all Thy servants have turned
back from Thee and risen up against Thee. Thou knowest that
Thou hast no one to obey Thee except them and such as have believed in Thy Revelation, through which the foundations of the
entire universe have been shaken, and the souls of all men have
trembled, and all that lay asleep were quickened. Thou art, O my
God, the God of bounty, Whose grace is immense.

Send down, then, upon them that which will assure their hearts,
and quiet their souls, and renew their spirits, and refresh their
bodies. Thou art, verily, their Lord and the Lord of the worlds.

Praised be God, the Lord of all creation!

¶ 151. Glory to Thee, O Thou Who art the Lord of all worlds, and
the Beloved of all such as have recognized Thee! Thou seest me sitting under a sword hanging on a thread and art well aware that in
such a state I have not fallen short of my duty towards Thy Cause,
nor failed to shed abroad Thy praise, and declare Thy virtues, and
deliver all Thou hadst prescribed unto me in Thy Tablets. Though
the sword be ready to fall on my head, I call Thy loved ones with
such a calling that the hearts are carried away towards the horizon
of Thy majesty and grandeur.

Purge out thoroughly their ears, O my Lord, that they may
hearken unto the sweet melodies that have ascended from the right
hand of the throne of Thy glory. I swear by Thy might! Were any
one to attune his ears to their harmony he would soar up to the
kingdom of Thy revelation, wherein every created thing proclaimeth that Thou art God, and that there is none other God save Thee,
the Omnipotent, the Help in Peril, the Self-Subsisting. Cleanse

Thou, O my God, the eyes of Thy servants, and so transport them by the sweetness of Thine utterances that calamities will be powerless to hinder them from turning unto Thee, and from directing their eyes towards the horizon of Thy Revelation.

Darkness hath encompassed every land, O my God, and caused most of Thy servants to tremble. I beseech Thee, by Thy Most Great Name, to raise in every city a new creation that shall turn towards Thee, and shall remember Thee amidst Thy servants, and shall unfurl by virtue of their utterances and wisdom the ensigns of Thy victory, and shall detach themselves from all created things.

Potent art Thou to do Thy pleasure. No God is there but Thee, the Most Powerful, He Whose help is implored by all men.

¶ 152. Praised be Thou, O my God! Thou beholdest both the helplessness of Thy dear ones and the ascendancy of Thy foes, both the wretchedness of Thy chosen ones and the glory of them who gainsaid Thy Cause and repudiated Thy signs. The latter deny Thy tokens, and fail to repay Thee for the temporal benefits Thou didst bestow upon them, while the former yield Thee thanks for what hath befallen them in their eagerness to partake of the everlasting gifts Thou dost possess.

How sweet is the thought of Thee in times of adversity and trial, and how delightful to glorify Thee when compassed about with the fierce winds of Thy decree! Thou knowest full well, O my God, that I endure patiently whatsoever toucheth me in Thy path. Nay, I perceive that all the members and limbs of my body long for tribulation, that I may manifest Thy Cause, O Thou Who art the Lord of all names! The waters of Thy love have preserved me in the kingdom of Thy creation, and the fire of my remembrance of Thee hath set me ablaze before all that are in heaven and on earth. Great is my blessedness, and great the blessedness of this fire whose flame crieth out: "No God is there save Thee, Who art the Object of my heart's adoration, and the Source and Centre of my soul!"

Thy glory beareth me witness! Were all that are in the heavens and all that are on earth to unite and seek to hinder me from remembering Thee and from celebrating Thy praise, they would assuredly have no power over me, and would fail in their purpose. And were the infidels to slay me, my blood would, at Thy command, lift up its voice and proclaim: "There is no God but Thee, O

Thou Who art all my heart's Desire!" And were my flesh to be boiled in the cauldron of hate, the smell which it would send forth would rise towards Thee and cry out: "Where art Thou, O Lord of the worlds, Thou One Desire of them that have known Thee!" And were I to be cast into fire, my ashes would—I swear by Thy glory—declare: "The Youth hath, verily, attained that for which he had besought his Lord, the All-Glorious, the Omniscient."

How, then, can such a man be fearful of the combination of the kings to injure him in Thy Cause? No, no, I swear by Thyself, O Thou Who art the King of kings! Such is my love for Thee that I can fear no one, though the powers of all the worlds be arrayed against me. Alone and unaided I have, by the power of Thy might, arisen to proclaim Thy Cause, unafraid of the host of my oppressors.

To all that dwell on earth I cry aloud and say: "Fear ye God, O ye servants of God, and suffer not yourselves to be kept back from this pure Wine that hath flowed from the right hand of the throne of the mercy of your Lord, the Most Merciful. I swear by God! Better for you is what He possesseth than the things ye yourselves possess and the things ye have sought and are now seeking in this vain and empty life. Forsake the world, and set your faces towards the all-glorious Horizon. Whoso hath partaken of the wine of His remembrance will forget every other remembrance, and whoso hath recognized Him will rid himself of all attachment to this life and to all that pertaineth unto it."

I implore Thee, O my God and my Master, by The word through which they who have believed in Thy unity have soared up into the atmosphere of Thy knowledge, and they who are devoted to Thee have ascended into the heaven of Thy oneness, to inspire Thy loved ones with that which will assure their hearts in Thy Cause. Endue them with such steadfastness that nothing whatsoever will hinder them from turning towards Thee.

Thou art, verily, the Bountiful, the Munificent, the Forgiving, the Compassionate.

¶ 153. Thou seest, O my God, how Thy servants have been cleaving fast to Thy names, and have been calling on them in the daytime and in the night season. No sooner, however, had He been made manifest through Whose word the kingdom of names and the heaven of eternity were created, than they broke away from Him and disbelieved in the greatest of Thy signs. They finally banished Him from the land of His birth, and caused Him to dwell within the most desolate of Thy cities, though all the world had been built up by Thee for His sake. Within this, the Most Great Prison, He hath established His seat. Though sore tried by trials, the like of which the eye of creation hath not seen, He summoneth the people unto Thee, O Thou Who art the Fashioner of the universe!

I beseech Thee, O Thou the Shaper of all the nations and the Quickener of every mouldering bone, to graciously enable Thy servants to recognize Him Who is the Manifestation of Thy Self and the Revealer of Thy transcendent might, that they may cut down, by Thy power, all the idols of their corrupt inclinations, and enter beneath the shadow of Thine all-encompassing mercy, which, by virtue of Thy name, the Most Exalted, the All-Glorious, hath surpassed the entire creation.

I know not, O my God, how long will Thy creatures continue to slumber on the bed of forgetfulness and evil desires, and remain far removed from Thee and shut out from Thy presence. Draw them nearer, O my God, unto the scene of Thine effulgent glory, and enrapture their hearts with the sweet savours of Thine inspiration, through which they who adore Thy unity have soared on the wings of desire towards Thee, and they who are devoted to Thee have reached unto Him Who is the Dawning-Place of the Day-Star of Thy creation.

Cleave asunder, O my Lord, the veils that shut them out from Thee, that they may behold Thee shining above the horizon of Thy oneness and shedding Thy radiance from the dawning-place of Thy sovereignty. By Thy glory! Were they to discover the sweetness of Thy remembrance and apprehend the excellence of the things that are sent down upon them from the right hand of the throne of Thy majesty, they would cast away all that they possess, and would rush forth into the wilderness of their longing after Thee, that the glance of Thy loving-kindness may be directed towards them and the radiance of the Day-Star of Thy beauty may be shed upon them.

Let their hearts, O my Lord, be carried away by Thy remembrance, and their souls enriched by Thy riches, and their wills strengthened to proclaim Thy Cause amidst Thy creatures. Thou art, verily, the Great Giver, the Ever-Forgiving, the Most Compassionate.

¶ 154. Lauded be Thy name, O my God! Thou seest how I have been sorely vexed among Thy servants, and beholdest the things that have befallen me in Thy path. Thou knowest full well that I have not spoken a word but by Thy leave, that my lips have never been opened except at Thy bidding and in accordance with Thy pleasure, that every breath I have breathed hath been animated with Thy praise and Thy remembrance, that I have summoned all men to naught else except that whereunto Thy chosen ones have through all eternity been summoned, and that I have bidden them observe only the things that would draw them nearer unto the Day-Spring of Thy loving-kindness, and the Dawning-Place of Thy favours, and the Horizon of Thy riches, and the Manifestation of Thine inspiration and Thy revelation.

Thou art well aware, O my God, that I have not failed in my duty towards Thy Cause. At all times and under all conditions I have wafted, in every direction, the breezes of Thine inspiration, and shed abroad the sweet smell of the raiment of Thy mercy, that haply Thy servants may discover its fragrance, and through it be enabled to turn towards Thee.

I implore Thee, O my God, by the Lights of Thy unity and the Repositories of Thy revelation, to send down from the clouds of Thy mercy that which will cleanse the hearts of all such as have turned towards Thee. Blot out, then, from their hearts all that may induce Thy servants to cavil at Thy Cause.

Thy will hath overruled my will, O my God, and I have shown forth what hath grievously vexed me. Have mercy, then, upon me, O Thou Who of all those who show mercy art the Most Merciful!

Assist Thou Thy servants, O my God, to help Thy Cause, and give them to drink what will quicken their hearts in Thy realm, lest anything hinder them from remembering Thee and from extolling Thy virtues, that they may quit their homes in Thy name, and summon all the multitudes unto Thee. Guard their faces, O my God, from turning to any one save Thee, and their ears from hearkening unto the sayings of all such as have turned away from Thy beauty and repudiated Thy signs.

Supreme art Thou over all things. There is none other God save Thee, the All-Knowing, the All-Wise.

¶ 155. Praise be to Thee, O Lord my God! Thou seest and knowest that I have called upon Thy servants to turn nowhere except in the direction of Thy bestowals, and have bidden them observe naught save the things Thou didst prescribe in Thy Perspicuous Book, the Book which hath been sent down according to Thine inscrutable decree and irrevocable purpose.

I can utter no word, O my God, unless I be permitted by Thee, and can move in no direction until I obtain Thy sanction. It is Thou, O my God, Who hast called me into being through the power of Thy might, and hast endued me with Thy grace to manifest Thy Cause. Wherefore I have been subjected to such adversities that my tongue hath been hindered from extolling Thee and from magnifying Thy glory.

All praise be to Thee, O my God, for the things Thou didst ordain for me through Thy decree and by the power of Thy sovereignty. I beseech Thee that Thou wilt fortify both myself and them that love me in our love for Thee, and wilt keep us firm in Thy Cause. I swear by Thy might, O my God! Thy servant's shame is to be shut out as by a veil from Thee, and his glory is to know Thee. Armed with the power of Thy name nothing can ever hurt me, and with Thy love in my heart all the world's afflictions can in no wise alarm me.

Send down, therefore, O my Lord, upon me and upon my loved ones that which will protect us from the mischief of those that have repudiated Thy truth and disbelieved in Thy signs.

Thou art, verily, the All-Glorious, the Most Bountiful.

¶ 156. I give Thee thanks, O my God, for that Thou hast made me to be a target for the darts of Thine adversaries in Thy path. I offer Thee most high praise, O Thou Who art the Knower of the seen and unseen and the Lord of all being, that Thou hast suffered me to be cast into prison for love of Thee, and caused me to quaff the cup of woe, that I may reveal Thy Cause and glorify Thy word.

Which of my tribulations am I to recount before Thy face, O my Lord? Am I to recite before Thee what in days of old befell me at the hands of the workers of iniquity among Thy creatures, or to describe the vexations which have compassed me about in these days for the sake of Thy good pleasure?

Thanks be to Thee, O Thou the Lord of all names; and glory be to Thee, O Maker of the heavens, for all that I have sustained in these days at the hands of such of Thy servants as have transgressed against Thee, and of Thy people that have dealt frowardly towards Thee.

Number us, we implore Thee, with them who have stood fast in Thy Cause until their souls finally winged their flight unto the heaven of Thy grace and the atmosphere of Thy loving-kindness. Thou art, verily, the Ever-Forgiving, the Most Merciful.

¶ 157. Glorified art Thou, O my God! I give praise to Thee, that Thou hast made me able so to reveal Thine utterances, and manifest Thy proofs and Thy testimonies, that every proof hath been made to circle round my will, and every testimony to compass my pleasure. Thou seest me, O my Lord, lying at the mercy of Thine adversaries, who have repudiated Thy signs, and refuted Thy testimony, and turned back from Thy beauty, and resolved to shed Thy blood. I beseech Thee, O Thou Who are the Lord of all names, by Thy name through which Thou hast subdued all created things, to graciously aid Thy servants and Thy loved ones to cleave steadfastly to Thy Cause. Give them, then, to drink what will quicken their hearts in Thy days. Enable them, moreover, O my Lord, to fix their gaze at all times upon Thy pleasure, and to yield Thee thanks for the evidences of Thine irrevocable decree. For Thou art, verily, praiseworthy in all that Thou hast done in the past, or wilt do in the future, and art to be obeyed in whatsoever Thou hast wished or wilt wish, and to be loved in all that Thou hast desired or wilt desire. Thou lookest upon them that are dear to Thee with the eyes of Thy loving-kindness, and sendest down for them only that which will profit them through Thy grace and Thy gifts.

We entreat Thee, O Thou Who art the Cloud of Bounty and the Succourer of the distressed, that Thou wilt aid us to remember Thee, and to make known Thy Cause, and to arise to help Thee. Though all weakness, we yet have clung to Thy Name, the Most Powerful, the Almighty.

Bless Thou, O my God, them that have stood fast in Thy Cause, and whom the evil suggestions of the workers of iniquity have failed to deter from turning towards Thy face, and who have hastened with their whole hearts toward Thy grace, until they finally quaffed the water that is life indeed from the hands of Thy bounty.

Potent art Thou to do Thy pleasure. No God is there save Thee, the Mighty, the Most Generous.

Part II
'ABDU'L-BAHÁ

VIII. THE COVENANT

1. THE CENTRE OF THE COVENANT

¶ 158. His Holiness Abraham, on Him be peace, made a covenant concerning His Holiness Moses and gave the glad-tidings of His coming. His Holiness Moses made a covenant concerning the Promised One, i.e. His Holiness Christ, and announced the good news of His Manifestation to the world. His Holiness Christ made a covenant concerning the Paraclete and gave the tidings of His coming. His Holiness the Prophet Muḥammad made a covenant concerning His Holiness the Báb and the Báb was the One promised by Muḥammad, for Muḥammad gave the tidings of His coming. The Báb made a covenant concerning the Blessed Beauty of Bahá'u'lláh and gave the glad-tidings of His coming for the Blessed Beauty was the One promised by His Holiness the Báb. Bahá'u'lláh made a covenant concerning a promised One who will become manifest after one thousand or thousands of years. He likewise, with His Supreme Pen, entered into a great Covenant and Testament with all the Bahá'ís whereby they were all commanded to follow the Centre of the Covenant after His departure, and turn not away even to a hair's breadth from obeying Him.

In the Book of Aqdas, He has given positive command in two clear instances and has explicitly appointed the Interpreter of the Book. Also in all the Divine Tablets, especially in the Chapter of the Branch—all the meanings of which mean the Servitude of 'Abdu'l-Bahá, that is 'Abdu'l-Bahá—all that was needed to explain the Centre of the Covenant and the Interpreter of the Book has been revealed from the Supreme Pen. Now as 'Abdu'l-Bahá is the Interpreter of the Book He says that the "Chapter of the Branch" means 'Abdu'l-Bahá, that is the Servitude of 'Abdu'l-Bahá, and none other.

¶ 159. In former cycles no distinct Covenant was made in writing by the Supreme Pen; no distinct personage was appointed to be the

Standard differentiating falsehood from truth, so that whatsoever he said was to stand as truth and that which he repudiated was to be known as falsehood. At most His Holiness Jesus Christ gave only an intimation, a symbol, and that was but an indication of the solidity of Peter's faith. When He mentioned his faith, His Holiness said, "Thou art Peter," which means rock, "and upon this rock will I build My church." This was a sanction of Peter's faith; it was not indicative of his[1] being the Expounder of the Book—but was a confirmation of Peter's faith.

But in this Dispensation of the Blessed Beauty[2] among its distinctions is that He did not leave people in perplexity. He entered into a Covenant and Testament with the people. He appointed a Centre of the Covenant. He wrote with His own Pen and revealed it in the Kitáb-i-Aqdas, the Book of Laws, and Kitáb-i-'Ahd, the Book of the Covenant, appointing Him[3] the Expounder of the Book. You must ask Him[3] regarding the meanings of the texts of the verses. Whatever He says is correct. Outside of this, in numerous Tablets He[2] has explicitly recorded it, with clear, sufficient, valid and forceful statements. In the Tablet of the Branch He explicitly states: "Whatsoever the Branch says is right, or correct; and every person must obey The Branch with his life, with his heart, with his tongue. Without his will, not a word shall anyone utter." This is an explicit text of the Blessed Beauty. So there is no excuse left for anybody. No soul shall, of himself, speak anything. Whatsoever His[3] tongue utters, whatsoever His pen records, that is correct; according to the explicit text of Bahá'u'lláh in the Tablet of the Branch.

¶ 160. The Blessed Beauty is the Sun of Truth, and His light the light of truth. The Báb is likewise the Sun of Truth, and His light the light of truth... My station is the station of servitude—a servitude which is complete, pure and real, firmly established, enduring, obvious, explicitly revealed and subject to no interpretation whatever... I am the Interpreter of the Word of God; such is my interpretation.

[1] Peter.   [2] Bahá'u'lláh.   [3] 'Abdu'l-Bahá.

2. THE POWER OF THE COVENANT

¶ 161. There is a power in this Cause—a mysterious power—far, far, far away from the ken of men and angels; that invisible power is the cause of all these outward activities. It moves the hearts. It rends the mountains. It administers the complicated affairs of the Cause. It inspires the friends. It dashes into a thousand pieces all the forces of opposition. It creates new spiritual worlds. This is the mystery of the Kingdom of Abhá!

¶ 162. So firm and mighty is this Covenant that from the beginning of time until the present day no religious Dispensation hath produced its like.

¶ 163. The spirit of this age is the Covenant and the Testament of God. It is like the pulsating artery in the body of the world.

¶ 164. Turn thy face unto the Kingdom of the Covenant, thy heart beating with the love of God, thy soul attracted to the fragrances of God, thy tongue speaking of the appearances of the Kingdom of God, thy insight rending veils asunder and disclosing the realities of things—and with a power which may move the heart of all in the world.

This is a confirmation from the Lord of the effulgence, while all else save this shall never profit thee! This is that by reason of which thy face shall gleam, thy heart shall be dilated with joy, thy soul become pure, thy back strengthened, thy spirit rejoiced and thy identity quickened. Leave the people of suspicion behind thy back and adhere to the manifest signs.

¶ 165. The world of the Covenant is like unto the Blessed Tree which is growing beside the river of the Water of Life in the utmost delicacy and beauty, and day by day it is developing and adding to its verdancy.

¶ 166. Today the stirring power that exhibits itself throughout all regions is the power of the Covenant, which, like unto the artery, beats and pulsates in the body of the world. He who is firmer in the Covenant is more assisted, just as ye are manifestly witnessing how firm souls are enkindled, attracted and confirmed.

¶ 167. The Covenant of God is like a vast and fathomless ocean. A billow shall rise and surge therefrom and shall cast ashore all accumulated foam.

Today, every wise, vigilant and foresighted person is awakened, and to him are unveiled the mysteries of the future, that nothing save the power of the Covenant is able to stir and move the hearts of humanity.

¶ 168. Know thou, verily, the Covenant is an Orb which shines and gleams forth unto the universe. Verily, its light will dispel darkness, its sea will cast out the thick foam of suspicions upon the shore of perdition. Verily, naught in the world can ever resist the power of the kingdom. Should all mankind assemble, could they prevent the sun from its light, the winds from their blowing, the clouds from their showers, the mountains from their firmness or the stars from their beaming? No! By thy Lord, the Clement! Everything is subject to corruption; but the Covenant of thy Lord shall continue to pervade all regions.

¶ 169. This Covenant is the Ancient Covenant, the Illuminator of the horizons. . . It is the Testament and the Covenant and it is mentioned in all the early Books and in later tablets. . . It is the holy fragrance of His Holiness, the Creator, and the Breaths of Life of the Garden of the Creator. It is the strong fortress; therefore it is a sure shelter for all created beings, and in brief, it is the sum of all sacred writings, ancient and modern!

¶ 170. Now in the world of being the Hand of divine power hath firmly laid the foundations of this all-highest bounty and this wondrous gift. Whatsoever is latent in the innermost of this holy cycle shall gradually appear and be made manifest, for now is but the beginning of its growth and the day-spring of the revelation of its signs. Ere the close of this century and of this age, it shall be made clear and evident how wondrous was that springtide and how heavenly was that gift!

3. FIRMNESS IN THE COVENANT

¶ 171. That which has come out of the centre of the Covenant you must take fast hold of. That which issues from my lips and that which is written with my pen is the reality. With this you can irrigate the vineyard of God. With this you can make the tree of the Cause of God become verdant. Through this the name of the Kingdom of God will be spread over the world. Through this the sun of reality will shine. Through this the clouds of mercy will pour down.

¶ 172. Today the most important affair is firmness in the Covenant, because firmness in the Covenant wards off differences.

¶ 173. Whosoever is firm in the Covenant and Testament is today endowed with a seeing eye, and a responsive ear, and daily advances in the divine realm until he becomes a heavenly angel.

¶ 174. O ye beloved of God, know that steadfastness and firmness in this new and wonderful Covenant is indeed the spirit that quickeneth the hearts which are overflowing with the love of the Glorious Lord; verily, it is the power which penetrates into the hearts of the people of the world! Your Lord hath assuredly promised His servants who are firm and steadfast to render them victorious at all times, to exalt their word, propagate their power, diffuse their lights, strengthen their hearts, elevate their banners, assist their hosts, brighten their stars, increase the abundance of the showers of mercy upon them, and enable the brave lions to conquer.

¶ 175. Hasten, hasten, O ye firm believers! Hasten, hasten, O ye steadfast! Abandon the heedless, set aside every ignorant, take hold of the strong rope, be firm in this Great Cause, draw light from this Evident Light, be patient and be steadfast in this wise Religion! Ye shall see the hosts of inspiration descending successively from the Supreme World, the procession of attraction falling incessantly from the heights of heaven, the abundance of the Kingdom of El Abhá outpouring continually and the teachings of God penetrating with the utmost power, while the heedless are indeed in evident loss.

¶ 176. Be ye assured with the greatest assurance that, verily, God will help those who are firm in His Covenant in every matter, through His confirmation and favour, the lights of which will shine forth unto the east of the earth, as well as the west thereof. He will make them the signs of guidance among the creation and as shining and glittering stars from all horizons.

¶ 177. O ye who are firm in the Covenant! 'Abdu'l-Bahá is constantly engaged in ideal communication with any Spiritual Assembly which is instituted through the divine bounty, and the members of which are in the utmost devotion turning to the divine kingdom and are firm in the Covenant. To them He is heartily attached and with them He is linked by everlasting ties. Thus correspondence with them is sincere, constant and uninterrupted.

¶ 178. O ye Cohorts of God! If you observe that a soul has turned his face completely toward the Cause of God, his intention is centralized upon the penetration of the Word of God, he is serving the Cause day and night with the utmost fidelity, no scent of selfishness is inhaled from his manners and deeds, and no trace of egotism or prejudice is seen in his personality—nay rather is he a wanderer in the wilderness of the love of God, and one intoxicated with the wine of the knowledge of God, occupied wholly with the diffusion of the fragrances of God, and attracted to the signs of the Kingdom of God; know ye of a certainty that he is confirmed with the powers of the Kingdom, assisted by the heaven of Might; and he will shine, gleam and sparkle like unto the morning star with the utmost brilliancy and splendour from the horizon of the everlasting gift. If he is alloyed with the slightest trace of passion, desire, ostentation or self-interest, it is certain that the results of all efforts will prove fruitless, and he will become deprived and hopeless.

¶ 179. Today, those who are firm in the Covenant are soaring by the bounties of the Holy Spirit in lofty regions, while the wavering ones are depressed, dejected and afflicted with a thousand pains and calamities. This is because the confirmations of the Abhá Kingdom have been cut off from them. They have been deprived of the Light of the Sun of Truth and have no share from the breezes of the Holy Spirit. They resemble these souls who arose to agitate the minds of men after the time of Christ. Each one, by every subtle means, gathered around himself a group of souls, but all were eventually led to face disappointment, loss and failure. This was because the result of their principles was like unto a tree destitute of roots, or like the ocean foam. A rootless tree, no matter how tall and hardy it may seem, will ultimately wither away; and the ocean foam, however formidable it may appear, shall at last vanish and disappear.

In brief—the Covenant is like unto the ocean which preserves Bahá'í unity, and these souls are like unto the foam upon it. They manifest a temporary activity, but soon, like unto Judas Iscariot and his associates and those who approved of his conduct, they shall be completely forgotten. The ocean of the Covenant, on the other hand, is eternally surging, for it preserves Bahá'í unity.

Today, the Lord of Hosts is the defender of the Covenant, the forces of the Kingdom protect it, heavenly souls tender their services, and heavenly angels promulgate and spread it broadcast. If it is considered with insight, it will be seen that all the forces of the universe, in the last analysis, serve the Covenant. In the future it shall be made evident and manifest. In view of this fact, what can these weak and feeble souls achieve?

¶ 180. Be sure therefore that if the believers are not united in the will of God, they will not be assisted. This is especially necessary because all of them are under the Tent of the Covenant in this Revelation. There is strength only in unity. Under one tent there is union and harmony. The Covenant of God in this day of Manifestation is a lifeboat and Ark of Salvation. All true followers of the Blessed Perfection are sheltered and protected in this Ark. Whoever leaves it trusting in his own will and strength will drown and be destroyed. For the Blessed Perfection left no possibility for discord, disagreement and dissension. The Covenant is like the sea and the believers are as the fishes in the sea. If a fish leaves the water it cannot live. There is nothing to equal, nothing so effective as the Covenant of God to bring about and continue unity.

¶ 181. All previous Books are subordinate to this Book of the Covenant, for it has been revealed subsequent to all the previous ones. He has named it the "Book of the Covenant", therefore consider that if the friends remain firm in the Covenant will there be any misunderstandings among them? No, by God! Except those souls who have an evil intention and are thinking of leadership and of forming a party; those souls, although they have written epistles with their own pen and have execrated the violators, denouncing them as having destroyed the foundation of the monument erected by His Holiness Bahá'u'lláh, and have written that He has written this Covenant with His own pen and that whoever deviated the least from the Centre of the Covenant is of the people of treachery and well deserves the wrath of God—these souls are themselves at present among the pioneers of violation. This is because of their personal motives, for they had thought of securing leadership and wealth, but when they considered that in remaining firm in the Covenant their purpose would not be realized, they deviated from it. . . Their lie is now manifest. Notwithstanding this, some souls who are not aware of this fact waver when these people cast the seeds of suspicion. . . The Covenant of God is like unto a vast and fathomless ocean. A billow shall rise and surge therefrom, and all accumulated foam it shall cast ashore.

IX. THE MASTER'S LAST TABLET TO AMERICA

¶ 182. O ye friends of God! 'Abdu'l-Bahá is day and night thinking of you and mentioning you, for the friends of God are dear to Him. Every morning at dawn I supplicate the Kingdom of God and ask that you may be filled with the breath of the Holy Spirit, so that you may become brilliant candles, shine with the light of guidance and dispel the darkness of error. Rest assured that the confirmations of the Abhá Kingdom will continuously reach you.

Through the power of the divine springtime, the downpour of the celestial clouds and the heat of the Sun of Reality, the tree of life is just beginning to grow. Before long, it will produce buds, bring forth leaves and fruits, and cast its shade over the East and the West. This Tree of Life is the Book of the Covenant.

In America, in these days, severe winds have surrounded the Lamp of the Covenant, hoping that this brilliant Light may be extinguished, and this Tree of Life may be uprooted. Certain weak, capricious, malicious and ignorant souls have been shaken by the earthquake of hatred, of animosity, have striven to efface the Divine Covenant and Testament, and render the clear water muddy so that in it they might fish. They have arisen against the Centre of the Covenant like the people of the Bayán who attacked the Blessed Beauty and every moment uttered a calumny. Every day they seek a pretext and secretly arouse doubts, so that the Covenant of Bahá'u'lláh may be completely annihilated in America.

O friends of God! Be awake, be awake; be vigilant, be vigilant! His Holiness, the Báb, made a Covenant for Bahá'u'lláh with all the people of the Bayán, so that on the day of appearance of "Him Whom God shall manifest"—and of the radiation of the Light of Bahá'u'lláh, they might believe and be assured, arise in service and promulgate the Word of God. Later the people of the Bayán, like Mírzá Yaḥyá and many others, arose against the Blessed Beauty, invented every sort of calumny, aroused doubt in the minds of the people, and from the Books of His Holiness the Báb—that were full of references to "Him Whom God shall manifest"—tried to prove Bahá'u'lláh false. Every day they wrote and spread a pamphlet opposing Bahá'u'lláh, caused trouble and perplexity among the people; they inflicted the greatest injury and cruelty, yet counted themselves firm in the Covenant of His Holiness, the Báb. However, when the light of the Covenant of His Holiness, the Báb, lighted the universe, then all the faithful and sincere souls were freed from the darkness of the violation of the people of the Bayán and shone like brilliant candles.

Bahá'u'lláh, in all the Tablets and Epistles, forbade the true and firm friends from associating and meeting the violators of the Covenant of His Holiness the Báb, saying that no one should go near them because their breath is like the poison of the snake that kills instantly.

In the Hidden Words, He says: "Treasure the companionship of the righteous and eschew all fellowship with the ungodly."

Addressing one of the friends, He says: "It is clear to your honour that before long Satan, in the garb of man, will reach that land and will try to mislead the friends of the Divine Beauty through temptations which arouse the desires of self, and will cause them to follow the footsteps of Satan away from the right and glorious path, and prevent them from attaining the Blessed Shore of the King of Oneness. This is a hidden information of which we have informed the chosen ones lest they may be deprived of their praiseworthy station by associating with the embodiments of hatred. Therefore, it is incumbent upon all the friends of God to shun any person in whom they perceive the emanation of hatred for the Glorious Beauty of Abhá, though he may quote all the Heavenly Utterances and cling to all the Books." He continues—Glorious be His Name! "Protect yourselves with utmost vigilance, lest you be entrapped in the snare of deception and fraud." This is the advice of the Pen of Destiny.

In another address, He says: "Therefore, to avoid these people will be the nearest path by which to attain the divine good pleasure; because their breath is infectious, like unto poison."

In another Tablet, He says: "O Kázim, close thine eye to the people of the world; drink the water of knowledge from the heavenly cup bearers, and listen not to the nonsensical utterances of the manifestations of Satan, because the manifestations of Satan are occupying today the observation posts of the glorious path of God, and preventing the people by every means of deception and ruse. Before long you will witness the turning away of the people of Bayán from the Manifestation of the Merciful."

In another Tablet, He says: "Endeavour to your utmost to protect yourselves, because Satan appears in different robes and appeals to everyone according to each person's own way, until he becomes like unto him—then he will leave him alone."

In another Tablet, He says: "Shun any man in whom you perceive enmity for this Servant, though he may appear in the garb of piety of the former and latter people, or may arise to the worship of the two worlds."

In another Tablet, He says: "O Mihdí! Be informed by these utterances and shun the manifestations of the people of hell, the rising place of Nimrods, the rising place of Pharees, the fountain of Tagut, and the soothsayers."

Again He says: "Say O my friend and my pure ones! Listen to the Voice of this Beloved Prisoner in this Great Prison. If you detect in any man the least perceptible breath of violation, shun him and keep away from him." Then He says: "Verily, they are manifestations of Satan."

In another Tablet, He says: "And turn your faces to the Great Countenance for before long the foul odours of the wicked persons will pass over these regions. God willing, you may remain protected during these days."

In the 18th chapter of the Gospel of Matthew, 6th to 9th verses, His Holiness Christ says: "But whoso shall offend one of these little ones which believe in Me, it were better for him that a millstone were hanged about his neck, and that he were drowned in the depth of the sea. Woe unto the world because of offences! for it must needs be that offences come; but woe to that man by whom the offence cometh! Wherefore if thy hand or thy foot offend thee, cut them off, and cast them from thee: it is better for thee to enter into life halt or maimed, rather than having two hands or two feet to be cast into everlasting fire. And if thine eye offend thee, pluck it out, and cast it from thee."

And in the 21st chapter and the 38th verse of the Gospel of

Matthew, He says: "But when the husbandmen saw the son, they said among themselves, this is the heir, come let us kill him and let us seize on his inheritance. And they caught him and cast him out of the vineyard, and slew him."

Also in the 22nd chapter and the 14th verse of the gospel of Matthew, He says: "For many are called, but few are chosen."

In the Holy Writings of His Holiness, Bahá'u'lláh, in a thousand places at least, the violators of the Covenant are execrated and condemned. Some of the heavenly passages will be mentioned.

In short, all the friends in America know that the founders of this sedition—namely, the violators of the Covenant—are people whose aims are known to all the friends. Yet, O glorious God, they are deceived by them!

Praise be to God, you know with perfect clearness that His Holiness Christ was extremely kind and loving, yet there were people like Judas Iscariot who—by their own deeds—separated themselves from Christ. Therefore, what fault of Christ's could that be? Now, the Náqizín say that 'Abdu'l-Bahá is despotic, drives some people out and excommunicates like the Pope. This is not so at all! Any person who has left (the Cause), did so because of his own actions, intrigues and evil plots. If this objection be raised against 'Abdu'l-Bahá, they must also object to the Blessed Beauty who, with distinct and conclusive command, forbids the friends from companionship and familiarity with the violators of the people of Bayán.

Supplication! O Lord of the Covenant! O luminous Star of the world! The persecuted 'Abdu'l-Bahá has fallen into the hands of persons who appear as sheep and in reality are ferocious wolves; they exercise every sort of oppression, endeavour to destroy the foundation of the Covenant—and claim to be Bahá'ís. They strike at the root of the Tree of the Covenant—and count themselves persecuted—just as did the people of Bayán who broke the Covenant of His Holiness, the Báb, and from six directions shot arrows of reproach and calumny at Thy Blessed Body. Notwithstanding this great oppression, they call themselves oppressed. Now this Servant of Thy Threshold has also fallen into the hands of the oppressors. Every hour they contrive new intrigues and fraud, and bring forth new calumny.

Yá-Bahá'u'l-Abhá! Protect the Stronghold of Thy Cause from

these thieves, and safeguard the lamps of the Kingdom from these malevolent winds!

Yá-Bahá'u'l-Abhá! 'Abdu'l-Bahá did not rest a moment until he had raised Thy Cause and the Standard of the Kingdom of Abhá waved over the world. Now some people have arisen with intrigues and evil aspirations to trample this flag in America, but My hope is in Thy confirmations. Leave Me not single, alone and oppressed! As thou didst promise, verbally and in writing, that Thou wouldst protect this deer of the pasture of Thy love from the attacks of the hounds of hatred and animosity, and that Thou wouldst safeguard this persecuted sheep from the claws and teeth of the ferocious wolves—now do I await the appearance of Thy bounties and the realization of Thy definite promise. Thou art the true Protector, and Thou art the Lord of the Covenant! Therefore, protect this Lamp which Thou hast lighted, from the severe winds.

Yá-Bahá'u'l-Abhá! I have forsaken the world and its people, am heartbroken because of the unfaithful, and am weary. In the cage of this world I flutter like a frightened bird and long for the flight to Thy Kingdom.

Yá-Bahá'u'l-Abhá! Make Me to drink the cup of sacrifice and free Me! Relieve Me from these difficulties, hardships, afflictions, and troubles! Thou art the Assister, the Helper, the Protector and the Supporter!

Now some of the writings, prayers, and verses of the Blessed Beauty will be mentioned in which association with the violators is forbidden. In the Íránian Commune He says:

"Protect this Servant from the doubts of the persons who have turned away from Thee and are deprived of the sea of Thy knowledge. O God! O God! Protect this Servant through Thy bounty and generosity from the evil of Thine enemies who have broken Thy Covenant and Testament."

In another place He says: "O My God and the Aim of My Life! Protect this weak one with Thy Mighty hand from the voice of the Náiq."

Also He says: "Ye have taken one whom I hate to be thy beloved, and My enemy to be thy friend."

Also He says: "The company of the ungodly increaseth sorrow, whilst fellowship with the righteous cleanseth the rust from off the heart. He that seeketh to commune with God, let him betake himself to the companionship of His loved ones; and he that desireth to hearken unto the word of God, let him give ear to the words of His chosen ones."

Also He says: "Do not associate with the wicked, because the company of the wicked changeth the light of life into the fire of remorse. If thou asketh for the bounties of the Holy Spirit, associate with the pure ones, because they have quaffed the eternal chalice from the hands of the Cupbearer of eternity."

Also He says: "The essence of abasement is to pass from under the shadow of the Merciful, and seek the shelter of the Evil One."

Also He says: "O ye servants! There is nothing in this heart save the effulgences of the splendour of the Morn of Meeting, and it does not speak but the absolute truth from your Lord. Therefore, do not follow self; break not God's Covenant and violate not His Testament. Proceed with perfect steadfastness, and with heart, soul and tongue, turn unto Him, and be not of the thoughtless."

And still He says: "You have forgotten God's Covenant and violated His Testament."

And again He says; "If anyone comes to you with the book of the wicked, put him behind you."

"Among the people are those who have broken the Covenant and among them are those who have followed what was ordained by the All-Knower, the All-Wise. My affliction is not from My imprisonment and persecution, or from what comes to Me from My rebellious servants, but from the actions of those who attribute themselves to this persecuted One and commit among the people that which is degrading to the honour of God. Verily, they are of the seditious."

Likewise speaking for the violators, He says: "Thou hast made the pulpits for Thy mention, the proclamation of Thy Word and the manifestation of Thy Cause, and we have ascended them to proclaim the breaking of Thy Covenant and Testament."

Likewise, He says: "Take what has been ordained for you and follow not those who have broken God's Covenant and Testament, for lo! they are the people of error."

Again He says: "Those who have broken the Covenant of God, notwithstanding His Commands, and have turned away, they are the people of error before the most Opulent, the Exalted."

And He says: "Those who have been faithful to God's Covenant are of the highest ones in the sight of the exalted Lord. Those who have become negligent are of the people of fire in the sight of Thy Lord, the Beloved, the Independent."

Likewise He says: "Blessed is the servant or maidservant who believes, and woe to the polytheists who have violated the Covenant of God and His Testament, and deviated from My Right Path."

Likewise He says: "I implore of Thee not to deprive me of what Thou possessest or what Thou hast ordained for Thy chosen ones who have not broken Thy Covenant and Testament. Say! Die with your hatred! Verily, He is come by Whom the pillars of the world have been shaken and because of Whom the feet have stumbled—save those who have not broken the Covenant, but have followed what God revealed in His Book."

Likewise He says: "The Supreme Concourse will pray for the one who is adorned with the garment of faithfulness between heaven and earth; but he who breaks the Covenant is cursed by heaven and earth."

Likewise He says: "Take hold of what has been revealed unto you, with a power superior to that of the hands of the unbelievers who have violated the Covenant of God and His Testament, and have turned from the Face."

Also He says: "O Yaḥyá! Verily the Book has come! Take it with a power from Us and do not follow those who have broken the Covenant of God and His Testament, and have denied what has been revealed from the Powerful, the All-Knower."

Likewise He says: "I awoke this morning, O My God, under the shadow of Thy great bounty and have taken, with Thy power, the pen to mention Thee with such mention as shall be a light unto the pure, and fire unto the wicked who have violated Thy Covenant, denied Thy Verses and put aside the Kawthar of life which appeared by Thy command and was revealed by the finger of Thy Will."

Here, in a Tablet to 'Abdu'l-Bahá, He says also: "O God! This is a Branch which has sprung forth from the Tree of Oneness, the sadrat of Thy Unity. O God! Thou seest Him looking to Thee and clinging to the rope of Thy Bounties. Protect Him in the shelter of Thy Mercy! Thou knowest, O my God, that I desire for Him naught except that which Thou didst desire, and have chosen Him for no purpose save that which Thou hadst intended for Him. Render Him victorious, therefore, through Thy hosts of earth and heaven. Assist, O God, those who assist Him, and choose those who choose Him. Confirm those who draw nigh unto

Him, and debase those who deny Him and do not want Him. O God, Thou seest that at this moment of Revelation My Pen shakes and My Being trembles. Ordain, I beseech Thee, by the ardour of My love for Thee and My yearning to manifest Thy Cause, for Him, as well as for them that love Him, that which Thou hast destined for Thy Messengers and the Trustees of Thy Revelation. Verily, Thou art the Almighty, the All-Powerful. By God, O people! Mine eye weepeth, and the eye of 'Alí[1] weepeth amongst the Concourse on high, and Mine heart crieth out, and the heart of Muhammad crieth out within the Most Glorious Tabernacle, and My soul shouteth and the souls of the Prophets shout before them that are endued with understanding. . . . My sorrow is not for Myself, but for Him Who shall come after Me, in the shadow of My Cause, with manifest and undoubted sovereignty, inasmuch as they will not welcome His appearance, will repudiate His signs, will dispute His sovereignty, will contend with Him and will betray His Cause—as they did to His Person in those days —and ye were witnesses."

Again in a Tablet to 'Abdu'l-Bahá, He says: "O Greatest Branch! Verily, Thy illness caused Me sorrow, but God will cure Thee, and He is the most generous and best helper. The glory of God rest upon Thee, and upon whosoever serveth Thee and circleth around Thee. Woe, great woe, betide him that opposeth and injureth Thee. Well is it with him that sweareth fealty to Thee; the fire of hell torment him who is Thine enemy."

Likewise He says: "Can it be possible, that after the dawning of the day-star of Thy Testament above the horizon of Thy Most Great Tablet, the feet of anyone shall slip in Thy Straight Path? Unto this We answered: 'O My most exalted Pen! It behoveth Thee to occupy Thyself with that whereunto Thou hast been bidden by God, the Exalted, the Great. Ask not of that which will consume Thine heart and the hearts of the denizens of Paradise, who have circled round My wondrous Cause. It behoveth Thee not to be acquainted with that which we have veiled from Thee. Thy Lord is, verily, the Concealer, the All-Knowing! Turn Thy most luminous face to the greatest aspect and say: O My Merciful God! Decorate the Heaven of Bayán with the stars of steadfastness, trust and truth. Verily, Thou art the Powerful over what Thou willest. There is no God save Thee, the Wise and the Generous."

In short, from these Holy Utterances and those of His Holiness

[1] The Báb.

Christ, it becomes clear, evident and proved, that man should associate with people who are firm in the Covenant and Testament, and befriend the pure ones; because bad associates bring about infection of bad qualities. It is like leprosy; it is impossible for a man to associate and befriend a leper and not be infected. This command is for the sake of protection and to safeguard.

Consider this text of the New Testament; the brothers of His Holiness Christ, came to Him and they said: "These are your brothers." He answered that His brothers were those who believed in God, and refused to associate with His own brothers.

Likewise Qurratu'l-'Ayn, who is celebrated in all the world, when she believed in God and was attracted to the Divine Breaths, she forsook her two eldest sons, although they were her two oldest children, because they did not become believers, and thereafter did not meet them. She said: "All the friends of God are my children, but these two are not. I will have nothing to do with them."

Consider! The Divine Gardener cuts off the dry or weak branch from the good tree and grafts to it, a branch from another tree. He both separates and unites. This is that which His Holiness Christ says: that from all the world they come and enter the Kingdom, and the children of the Kingdom shall be cast out. Noah's grandson, Canaan, was detested in the sight of Noah and others were accepted. The brothers of the Blessed Beauty detached themselves from Him, and the Blessed Beauty never met them. He said: "This is an eternal separation between you and Me." All this was not because the Blessed Beauty was despotic; but because these persons, through their own actions and words, deprived themselves from the bounties and bestowals of the Blessed Beauty. His Holiness Christ did not exercise despotism in the case of Judas Iscariot and His own brothers—but they separated themselves.

In short, the point is this: 'Abdu'l-Bahá is extremely kind, but when the disease is leprosy, what am I to do? Just as in bodily diseases we must prevent intermingling and infection and put into effect sanitary laws—because the infectious physical diseases uproot the foundation of humanity; likewise one must protect and safeguard the blessed souls from the breaths and fatal spiritual diseases; otherwise violation, like the plague, will become a contagion and all will perish. In the early days, after the Ascension of the Blessed Beauty, the centre of violation was alone; little by little the infection spread; and this was due to companionship and association.

X. FROM THE TABLETS OF
THE DIVINE PLAN

1. THE NEED FOR DETACHMENT

¶ 183. You have observed that while 'Abdu'l-Bahá was in the utmost bodily weakness and feebleness, while He was indisposed, and had not the power to move—notwithstanding this physical state He travelled through many countries, in Europe and America, and in churches, meetings and conventions was occupied with the promotion of the divine principles and summoned the people to the manifestation of the Kingdom of Abhá. You have also observed how the confirmations of the Blessed Perfection encompassed all. What result is forthcoming from material rest, tranquillity, luxury and attachment to this corporeal world! It is evident that the man who pursues these things will in the end become afflicted with regret and loss.

Consequently, one must close his eyes wholly to these thoughts, long for eternal life, the sublimity of the world of humanity, the celestial developments, the Holy Spirit, the promotion of the Word of God, the guidance of the inhabitants of the globe, the promulgation of Universal Peace and the proclamation of the oneness of the world of humanity! *This is the work!* Otherwise like unto other animals and birds one must occupy himself with the requirements of this physical life, the satisfaction of which is the highest aspiration of the animal kingdom, and one must stalk across the earth like unto the quadrupeds.

Consider ye! No matter how much man gains wealth, riches and opulence in this world, he will not become as independent as a cow. For these fattened cows roam freely over the vast tableland. All the prairies and meadows are theirs for grazing, and all the springs and rivers are theirs for drinking! No matter how much they graze, the fields will not be exhausted! It is evident that they have earned these material bounties with the utmost facility.

Still more ideal than this life is the life of the bird. A bird, on the summit of a mountain, on the high, waving branches, has built for itself a nest more beautiful than the palaces of the kings! The air is in the utmost purity, the water cool and clear as crystal, the panorama charming and enchanting. In such glorious surroundings, he expends his numbered days. All the harvests of the plain are his possessions, having earned all this wealth without the least labour. Hence, no matter how much man may advance in this world, he shall not attain to the station of this bird! Thus it becomes evident that in the matters of this world, however much man may strive and work to the point of death, he will be unable to earn the abundance, the freedom and the independent life of a small bird. This proves and establishes the fact that man is not created for the life of this ephemeral world—nay, rather, is he created for the acquirement of infinite perfections, for the attainment to the sublimity of the world of humanity, to be drawn nigh unto the divine threshold, and to sit on the throne of everlasting sovereignty!

Upon you be Bahá'u'l-Abhá!

2. MEANS FOR UNITY

¶ 184. God says in the Qur'án, "Take ye hold of the Cord of God, all of you, and become ye not disunited."

In the contingent world there are many collective centres which are conducive to association and unity between the children of men. For example, patriotism is a collective centre; nationalism is a collective centre; identity of interests is a collective centre; political alliance is a collective centre; the union of ideals is a collective centre; and the prosperity of the world of humanity is dependent upon the organization and promotion of the collective centres. Nevertheless, all the above institutions are, in reality, the matter and not the substance, accidental and not eternal—temporary and not everlasting. With the appearance of great revolutions and upheavals, all these collective centres are swept away. But the Collective Centre of the Kingdom, embodying the Institutes and Divine Teachings, is the eternal Collective Centre. It establishes relationship between the East and the West, organizes the oneness of the world of humanity, and destroys the foundation of differences. It overcomes and includes all the other collective centres.

Like unto the ray of the sun, it dispels entirely the darkness encompassing all the regions, bestows ideal life, and causes the effulgence of divine illumination. Through the breaths of the Holy Spirit it performs miracles; the Orient and the Occident embrace each other, the North and South become intimates and associates, conflicting and contending opinions disappear, antagonistic aims are brushed aside, the law of the struggle for existence is abrogated, and the canopy of the oneness of the world of humanity is raised on the apex of the globe, casting its shade over all the races of men. Consequently, the real Collective Centre is the body of the divine teachings, which include all the degrees and embrace all the universal relations and necessary laws of humanity.

Consider! The people of the East and the West were in the utmost strangeness. Now to what a high degree they are acquainted with each other and united together! How far are the inhabitants of Persia from the remotest countries of America! And now observe how great has been the influence of the heavenly power, for the distance of thousands of miles has become identical with one step! How various nations that have had no relations or similarity with each other are now united and agreed through this divine potency! Indeed to God belongs power in the past and in the future! And verily God is powerful over all things!

Consider! When the rain, the heat, the sun and the gentle zephyrs co-operate with each other, what beautiful gardens are produced! How the various kinds of hyacinths, flowers, trees and plants associate with each other and are conducive to the adornment and charm of one another. Hence the oneness of the bounty of the sun, the oneness of rain and the oneness of the breeze have so overcome all other considerations that the variety of hues, fragrances and tastes have increased the adornment, the attraction and sweetness of the whole. In a similar manner, when the divine Collective Centre and the outpouring of the Sun of Reality and the breaths of the Holy Spirit are brought together, the variety of races and the differences existing between countries will become the cause of the embellishment, decoration, and elegance of the world of humanity. . .

Consider how the religions of God served the world of humanity! How the religion of Torah became conducive to the glory and honour and progress of the Israelitish nation! How the breaths of the Holy Spirit of His Holiness Christ created affinity and unity between divergent communities and quarrelling families! How the sacred power of His Holiness Muḥammad became the means of uniting and harmonizing the contentious tribes and the different clans of Peninsular Arabia—to such an extent that one thousand tribes were welded into one tribe; strife and discord were done away with; all of them unitedly and with one accord strove in advancing the cause of culture and civilization, and thus were freed from the lowest degree of degradation, soaring towards the height of everlasting glory! Is it possible to find a greater Collective Centre in the phenomenal world than this? In comparison to this Divine Collective Centre, the national collective centre, the patriotic collective centre, the political collective centre and the cultural and intellectual collective centre are like child's play!

Now strive ye that the Collective Centre of the sacred religions—for the inculcation of which all the Prophets were manifested and which is no other than the spirit of the Divine Teachings—be spread in all parts of America, so that each one of you may shine forth from the horizon of Reality like unto the morning star, divine illumination may overcome the darkness of nature, and the world of humanity may become enlightened. This is the most great work! Should you become confirmed therein, this world will become another world, the surface of the earth will become the delectable Paradise, and eternal Institutions be founded.

3. CONDITIONS FOR SUCCESS

¶ 185. The blessed Person of the Promised One is interpreted in the Holy Book as the Lord of Hosts—the heavenly armies. By heavenly armies those souls are intended who are entirely freed from the human world, transformed into celestial spirits and have become divine angels. Such souls are the rays of the Sun of Reality who will illumine all the continents. Each one is holding in his hand a trumpet, blowing the breath of life over all the regions. They are delivered from human qualities and the defects of the world of nature, are characterized with the characteristics of God, and are attracted with the fragrances of the Merciful. Like unto the apostles of Christ, who were filled with Him, these souls also have become filled with His Holiness Bahá'u'lláh; that is, the love of Bahá'u'lláh has so mastered every organ, part and limb of their bodies, as to leave no effect from the promptings of the human world.

These souls are the armies of God and the conquerors of the East and the West. Should one of them turn his face toward some direction and summon the people to the Kingdom of God, all the ideal forces and lordly confirmations will rush to his support and reinforcement. He will behold all the doors open and all the strong fortifications and impregnable castles razed to the ground. Singly and alone he will attack the armies of the world, defeat the right and left wings of the hosts of all the countries, break through the lines of the legions of all the nations and carry his attack to the very centre of the powers of the earth. This is the meaning of the Hosts of God.

Any soul from among the believers of Bahá'u'lláh who attains to this station, will become known as the Apostle of Bahá'u'lláh. Therefore strive ye with heart and soul so that ye may reach this lofty and exalted position, be established on the throne of everlasting glory, and crown your heads with the shining diadem of the Kingdom, whose brilliant jewels may irradiate upon centuries and cycles.

O ye kind friends! Uplift your magnanimity and soar high toward the apex of heaven so that your blessed hearts may become illumined more and more, day by day, through the Rays of the Sun of Reality, that is, His Holiness Bahá'u'lláh; at every moment the spirits may obtain a new life, and the darkness of the world of nature may be entirely dispelled; thus you may become incarnate light and personified spirit, become entirely unaware of the sordid matters of this world and in touch with the affairs of the divine world.

Behold the portals which Bahá'u'lláh hath opened before you! Consider how exalted and lofty is the station you are destined to attain; how unique the favours with which you have been endowed. Should we become intoxicated with this cup, the sovereignty of this globe of earth will become lower in our estimation that the children's plays. Should they place in the arena the crown of the government of the whole world, and invite each one of us to accept it, undoubtedly we shall not condescend, and shall refuse to accept it.

To attain to this supreme station is, however, dependent on the realization of certain conditions:

The first condition is firmness in the Covenant of God. For the power of the Covenant will protect the Cause of Bahá'u'lláh from the doubts of the people of error. It is the fortified fortress of the Cause of God and the firm pillar of the religion of God. Today no power can conserve the oneness of the Bahá'í world save the Covenant of God; otherwise differences like unto a most great tempest will encompass the Bahá'í world. It is indubitably clear that the pivot of the oneness of mankind is nothing else but the power of the Covenant. Had the Covenant not come to pass, had it not been revealed from the Supreme Pen and had not the Book of the Covenant, like unto the ray of the Sun of Reality, illuminated the world, the forces of the Cause of God would have been utterly scattered and certain souls who were the prisoners of their own passions and lusts would have taken into their hands an axe, cutting the root of this Blessed Tree. Every person would have pushed forward his own desire and every individual aired his own opinion! Notwithstanding this great Covenant, a few negligent souls galloped with their chargers into the battlefield, thinking perchance they might be able to weaken the foundation of the Cause of God: but praise be to God all of them were afflicted with regret and loss, and ere long they shall see themselves in poignant despair. Therefore, in the beginning one must make his steps firm in the Covenant so that the confirmations of Bahá'u'lláh may encircle from all sides, the cohorts of the Supreme Concourse may become the supporters and the helpers, and the exhortations and advices of 'Abdu'l-Bahá, like unto the pictures engraved on stone, may remain permanent and ineffaceable in the tablets of the hearts.

The second condition: Fellowship and love amongst the believers. The divine friends must be attracted to and enamoured of each other and ever be ready and willing to sacrifice their own lives for each other. Should one soul from amongst the believers meet another, it must be as though a thirsty one with parched lips has reached to the fountain of the water of life, or a lover has met his true beloved. For one of the greatest divine wisdoms regarding the appearance of the Holy Manifestations is this: The souls may come to know each other and become intimate with each other; the power of the love of God may make all of them the waves of one sea, the flowers of one rose garden, and the stars of one heaven. This is the wisdom for the appearance of the Holy Manifestations! When the most great bestowal reveals itself in the hearts of the believers, the world of nature will be transformed, the darkness of the contingent being will vanish, and heavenly illumination will be obtained. Then the whole world will become the Paradise of Abhá, every one of the believers of God will become a blessed tree, producing wonderful fruits.

O ye friends! Fellowship, fellowship! Love, love! Unity, unity! So that the power of the Bahá'í Cause may appear and become manifest in the world of existence. My thoughts are turned towards you, and my heart leaps within me at your mention. Could ye know how my soul gloweth with your love, so great a happiness would flood your hearts as to cause you to become enamoured with each other.

The third condition: Teachers must continually travel to all parts of the continent, nay, rather, to all parts of the world, but they must travel like 'Abdu'l-Bahá, who journeyed throughout the cities of America. He was sanctified and free from every attachment and in the utmost severance. Just as His Holiness Christ says, "Shake off the very dust from your feet."

You have observed that while in America many souls in the utmost of supplication and entreaty desired to offer some gifts, but this servant, in accord with the exhortations and behests of the Blessed Perfection, never accepted a thing, although on certain occasions we were in most straitened circumstances. But on the other hand, if a soul for the sake of God, voluntarily and out of his pure desire, wishes to offer a contribution (toward the expenses of a teacher) in order to make the contributor happy, the teacher may accept a small sum, but must live with the utmost contentment.

The aim is this: The intention of the teacher must be pure, his heart independent, his spirit attracted, his thought at peace, his resolution firm, his magnanimity exalted, and in the love of God a shining torch. Should he become as such, his sanctified breath will even affect the rock; otherwise there will be no result whatsoever. As long as a soul is not perfected, how can he efface the defects of others. Unless he is detached from aught else save God, how can he teach severance to others!

In short, O ye believers of God! Endeavour ye, so that you may take hold of every means in the promulgation of the religion of God and the diffusion of the fragrances of God. . .

In brief, O ye believers of God! The text of the Divine Book is this: If two souls quarrel and contend about a question of the Divine questions, differing and disputing, *both are wrong*. The wisdom of this incontrovertible law of God is this: That between two souls from amongst the believers of God, no contention and dispute may arise; that they may speak with each other with infinite amity and love. Should there appear the least trace of controversy, they must remain silent, and both parties must continue their discussions no longer, but ask the reality of the question from the Interpreter. This is the irrefutable command!

Upon you be Bahá'u'l-Abhá!

XI. TABLET TO THE HAGUE

*A letter written by 'Abdu'l-Bahá to the Central Organization for a
Durable Peace, The Hague, 17 December 1919*

¶ 186. O ye esteemed ones who are pioneers among the well-wishers of the world of humanity!

The letters which ye sent during the war were not received, but a letter dated 11 February 1916, has just come to hand, and immediately an answer is being written. Your intention deserves a thousand praises, because you are serving the world of humanity, and this is conducive to the happiness and welfare of all. This recent war has proved to the world and the people that war is destruction while Universal Peace is construction; war is death while peace is life; war is rapacity and bloodthirstiness while peace is beneficence and humaneness; war is an appurtenance of the world of nature while peace is of the foundation of the religion of God; war is darkness upon darkness while peace is heavenly light; war is the destroyer of the edifice of mankind while peace is the everlasting life of the world of humanity; war is like a devouring wolf while peace is like the angels of heaven; war is the struggle for existence while peace is mutual aid and co-operation among the peoples of the world and the cause of the good-pleasure of the True One is the heavenly realm.

There is not one soul whose conscience does not testify that in this day there is no more important matter in the world than that of Universal Peace. Every just one bears witness to this and adores that esteemed Assembly because its aim is that this darkness may be changed into light, this bloodthirstiness into kindness, this torment into bliss, this hardship into ease and this enmity and hatred into fellowship and love. Therefore, the effort of those esteemed souls is worthy of praise and commendation.

But the wise souls who are aware of the essential relationships emanating from the realities of things consider that one single matter cannot, by itself, influence the human reality as it ought and should, for until the minds of men become united, no important matter can be accomplished. At present Universal Peace is a matter of great importance, but unity of conscience is essential, so that the foundation of this matter may become secure, its establishment firm and its edifice strong.

Therefore His Holiness Bahá'u'lláh, fifty years ago, expounded this question of Universal Peace at a time when he was confined in the fortress of 'Akká and was wronged and imprisoned. He wrote about this important matter of Universal Peace to all the great sovereigns of the world, and established it among his friends in the Orient. The horizon of the East was in utter darkness, nations displayed the utmost hatred and enmity towards each other, religions thirsted for each other's blood, and it was darkness upon darkness. At such a time His Holiness Bahá'u'lláh shone forth like the sun from the horizon of the East and illumined Persia with the lights of these teachings.

Among his teachings was the declaration of Universal Peace. People of different nations, religions and sects who followed him came together to such an extent that remarkable gatherings were instituted consisting of the various nations and religions of the East. Every soul who entered these gatherings saw but one nation, one teaching, one pathway, one order, for the teachings of His Holiness Bahá'u'lláh were not limited to the establishment of Universal Peace. They embraced many teachings which supplemented and supported that of Universal Peace.

Among these teachings was the independent investigation of reality so that the world of humanity may be saved from the darkness of imitation and attain to the truth; may tear off and cast away this ragged and outgrown garment of 1,000 years ago and may put on the robe woven in the utmost purity and holiness in the loom of reality. As reality is one and cannot admit of multiplicity, therefore different opinions must ultimately become fused into one.

And among the teachings of His Holiness Bahá'u'lláh is the oneness of the world of humanity; that all human beings are the sheep of God and He is the kind Shepherd. This Shepherd is kind to all the sheep, because He created them all, trained them, provided for them and protected them. There is no doubt that the Shepherd is kind to all the sheep and should there be among these sheep ignorant ones, they must be educated; if there be children, they must be trained until they reach maturity; if there be sick ones, they must be cured. There must be no hatred and enmity, for as by a kind physician these ignorant, sick ones should be treated.

And among the teachings of His Holiness Bahá'u'lláh is, that religion must be the cause of fellowship and love. If it becomes the cause of estrangement then it is not needed, for religion is like a remedy; if it aggravates the disease then it becomes unnecessary.

And among the teachings of Bahá'u'lláh is, that religion must be in conformity with science and reason, so that it may influence the hearts of men. The foundation must be solid and must not consist of imitations.

And among the teachings of Bahá'u'lláh is, that religious, racial, political, economic and patriotic prejudices destroy the edifice of humanity. As long as these prejudices prevail, the world of humanity will not have rest. For a period of 6,000 years history informs us about the world of humanity. During these 6,000 years the world of humanity has not been free from war, strife, murder and bloodthirstiness. In every period war has been waged in one country or another and that war was due to either religious prejudice, racial prejudice, political prejudice or patriotic prejudice. It has therefore been ascertained and proved that all prejudices are destructive of the human edifice. As long as these prejudices persist, the struggle for existence must remain dominant, and blood-thirstiness and rapacity continue. Therefore, even as was the case in the past, the world of humanity cannot be saved from the darkness of nature and cannot attain illumination except through the abandonment of prejudices and the acquisition of the morals of the Kingdom.

If this prejudice and enmity are on account of religion (consider that) religion should be the cause of fellowship, otherwise it is fruitless. And if this prejudice be the prejudice of nationality (consider that) all mankind are of one nation; all have sprung from the tree of Adam, and Adam is the root of the tree. That tree is one and all these nations are like branches, while the individuals of humanity are like leaves, blossoms and fruits thereof. Then the establishment of various nations and the consequent shedding of blood and destruction of the edifice of humanity result from human ignorance and selfish motives.

As to the patriotic prejudice, this is also due to absolute ignorance, for the surface of the earth is one native land. Every one can live in any spot on the terrestrial globe. Therefore all the world is man's birthplace. These boundaries and outlets have been devised by man. In the creation, such boundaries and outlets were not assigned. Europe is one continent, Asia is one continent, Africa is one continent, Australia is one continent, but some of the souls, from personal motives and selfish interests, have divided each one of these continents and considered a certain part as their own country. God has set up no frontier between France and Germany; they are continuous. Yea, in the first centuries, selfish souls, for the promotion of their own interests, have assigned boundaries and outlets and have, day by day, attached more importance to these, until this led to intense enmity, bloodshed and rapacity in subsequent centuries. In the same way this will continue indefinitely, and if this conception of patriotism remains limited within a certain circle, it will be the primary cause of the world's destruction. No wise and just person will acknowledge these imaginary distinctions. Every limited area which we call our native country we regard as our mother-land, whereas the terrestrial globe is the mother-land of all, and not any restricted area. In short, for a few days we live on this earth and eventually we are buried in it, it is our eternal tomb. Is it worth while that we should engage in bloodshed and tear one another to pieces for this eternal tomb? Nay, far from it, neither is God pleased with such conduct nor would any sane man approve of it.

Consider! The blessed animals engage in no patriotic quarrels. They are in the utmost fellowship with one another and live together in harmony. For example, if a dove from the East and a dove from the West, a dove from the North and a dove from the South chance to arrive, at the same time, in one spot, they immediately associate in harmony. So is it with all the blessed animals and birds. But the ferocious animals, as soon as they meet, attack and fight with each other, tear each other to pieces and it is impossible for them to live peaceably together in one spot. They are all unsociable and fierce, savage and combative fighters.

Regarding the economic prejudice, it is apparent that whenever the ties between nations become strengthened and the exchange of commodities accelerated, and any economic principle is established in one country, it will ultimately affect the other countries and universal benefits will result. Then why this prejudice?

As to the political prejudice, the policy of God must be followed and it is indisputable that the policy of God is greater than human policy. We must follow the Divine policy that applies alike to all individuals. He treats all individuals alike: no distinction is made, and that is the foundation of the Divine Religions.

And among the teachings of His Holiness Bahá'u'lláh is the origination of one language that may be spread universally among the people. This teaching was revealed from the pen of His Holiness Bahá'u'lláh in order that this universal language may eliminate misunderstandings from among mankind.

And among the teachings of His Holiness Bahá'u'lláh is the equality of women and men. The world of humanity has two wings—one is women and the other men. Not until both wings are equally developed can the bird fly. Should one wing remain weak, flight is impossible. Not until the world of women becomes equal to the world of men in the acquisition of virtues and perfections, can success and prosperity be attained as they ought to be.

And among the teachings of Bahá'u'lláh is voluntary sharing of one's property with others among mankind. This voluntary sharing is greater than equality, and consists in this, that man should not prefer himself to others, but rather should sacrifice his life and property for others. But this should not be introduced by coercion so that it becomes a law and man is compelled to follow. Nay, rather, man should voluntarily and of his own choice sacrifice his property and life for others, and spend willingly for the poor, just as is done in Persia among the Bahá'ís.

And among the teachings of His Holiness Bahá'u'lláh is man's freedom, that through the ideal Power he should be free and emancipated from the captivity of the world of nature; for as long as man is captive to nature he is a ferocious animal, as the struggle for existence is one of the exigencies of the world of nature. This matter of the struggle for existence is the fountain-head of all calamities and is the supreme affliction.

And among the teachings of Bahá'u'lláh is that religion is a mighty bulwark. If the edifice of religion shakes and totters, commotion and chaos will ensue and the order of things will be utterly upset, for in the world of mankind there are two safeguards that protect man from wrong-doing. One is the law which punishes the criminal; but the law prevents only the manifest crime and not the concealed sin; whereas the ideal safeguard, namely, the religion of God, prevents both the manifest and the concealed crime, trains man, educates morals, compels the adoption of virtues and is the all-inclusive power which guarantees the felicity of the world of mankind. But by religion is meant that which is ascertained by investigation and not that which is based on mere imitation, the foundation of Divine Religions and not human imitations.

And among the teachings of Bahá'u'lláh is that although material civilization is one of the means for the progress of the world of mankind, yet until it becomes combined with Divine civilization, the desired result, which is the felicity of mankind, will not be attained. Consider! These battleships that reduce a city to ruins within the space of an hour are the result of material civilization; likewise the Krupp guns, the Mauser rifles, dynamite, submarines, torpedo boats, armed aircraft and bombing aeroplanes—all these weapons of war are the malignant fruits of material civilization. Had material civilization been combined with Divine civilization, these fiery weapons would never have been invented. Nay, rather, human energy would have been wholly devoted to useful inventions and would have been concentrated on praiseworthy discoveries. Material civilization is like a lamp-glass. Divine civilization is the lamp itself and the glass without the light is dark. Material civilization is like the body. No matter how infinitely graceful, elegant and beautiful it may be, it is dead. Divine civilization is like the spirit, and the body gets its life from the spirit, otherwise it becomes a corpse. It has thus been made evident that the world of mankind is in need of the breaths of the Holy Spirit. Without the spirit the world of mankind is lifeless, and without this light the world of mankind is in utter darkness. For the world of nature is an animal world. Until man is born again from the world of nature, that is to say, becomes detached from the world of nature, he is essentially an animal, and it is the teachings of God which convert this animal into a human soul.

And among the teachings of Bahá'u'lláh is the promotion of education. Every child must be instructed in sciences as much as is necessary. If the parents are able to provide the expenses of this education, it is all right, otherwise the community must provide the means for the teaching of that child.

And among the teachings of His Holiness Bahá'u'lláh is justice and right. Until these are realized on the plane of existence, all things shall be in disorder and remain imperfect. The world of mankind is a world of oppression and cruelty, and a realm of aggression and error.

In fine, such teachings are numerous. These manifold principles, which constitute the greatest basis for the felicity of mankind and are of the bounties of the Merciful, must be added to the matter of Universal Peace and combined with it, so that results may accrue. Otherwise the realization of Universal Peace (by itself) in the world of mankind is difficult. As the teachings of His Holiness Bahá'u'lláh are combined with Universal Peace, they are like a table provided with every kind of fresh and delicious food. Every soul can find, at that table of infinite bounty, that which he desires. If the question is restricted to Universal Peace alone, the remarkable results which are expected and desired will not be attained. The scope of Universal Peace must be such that all the communities and religions may find their highest wish realized in it. At present the teachings of His Holiness Bahá'u'lláh are such that all the communities of the world, whether religious, political or ethical, ancient or modern, find in the teachings of Bahá'u'lláh the expression of their highest wish.

For example, the people of religions find, in the teachings of His Holiness Bahá'u'lláh, the establishment of Universal Religion—a religion that perfectly conforms with present conditions, which in reality effects the immediate cure of the incurable disease, which relieves every pain, and bestows the infallible antidote for every deadly poison. For if we wish to arrange and organize the world of mankind in accordance with the present religious imitations and thereby to establish the felicity of the world of mankind, it is impossible and impracticable—for example, the enforcement of the laws of the Old Testament (Taurat) and also of the other religions in accordance with present imitations. But the essential basis of all the Divine Religions which pertains to the virtues of the world of mankind and is the foundation of the welfare of the world of man, is found in the teachings of His Holiness Bahá'u'lláh in the most perfect presentation.

Similarly, with regard to the peoples who clamour for freedom: the moderate freedom which guarantees the welfare of the world of mankind and maintains and preserves the universal relationships, is found in its fullest power and extension in the teachings of His Holiness Bahá'u'lláh.

So with regard to political parties: that which is the greatest policy directing the world of mankind, nay, rather, the Divine policy, is found in the teachings of His Holiness Bahá'u'lláh.

Likewise with regard to the party of "equality" which seeks the solution of the economic problems: until now all proposed solutions have proved impracticable except the economic proposals in the teachings of His Holiness Bahá'u'lláh which are practicable and cause no distress to society.

So with the other parties: when ye look deeply into this matter, ye will discover that the highest aims of those parties are found in the teachings of Bahá'u'lláh. These teachings constitute the all-inclusive power among all men and are practicable. But there are some teachings of the past, such as those of the Taurat, which cannot be carried out at the present day. It is the same with the other religions and the tenets of the various sects and the different parties.

For example, the question of Universal Peace, about which His Holiness Bahá'u'lláh says that the Supreme Tribunal must be established: although the League of Nations has been brought into existence, yet it is incapable of establishing Universal Peace. But the Supreme Tribunal which His Holiness Bahá'u'lláh has described will fulfil this sacred task with the utmost might and power. And His plan is this: that the national assemblies of each country and nation—that is to say parliaments—should elect two or three persons who are the choicest men of that nation, and are well informed concerning international laws and the relations between governments and aware of the essential needs of the world of humanity of this day. The number of these representatives should be in proportion to the number of inhabitants of that country. The election of these souls who are chosen by the national assembly, that is, the parliament, must be confirmed by the upper house, the congress and the cabinet and also by the president or monarch so these persons may be the elected ones of all the nation and the government. From among these people the members of the Supreme Tribunal will be elected, and all mankind will thus have a share therein, for every one of these delegates is fully representative of his nation. When the Supreme Tribunal gives a ruling on any international question, either unanimously or by majority-rule, there will no longer be any pretext for the plaintiff or ground of objection for the defendant. In case any of the governments or nations in the execution of the irrefutable decision of the Supreme Tribunal, be negligent or dilatory, the rest of the nations will rise up against it, because all the governments and nations of the world are the supporters of this Supreme Tribunal. Consider what a firm foundation this is! But by a limited and restricted *League* the purpose will not be realized as it ought and should. This is the truth about the situation, which has been stated.

Consider how powerful are the teachings of His Holiness Bahá'u'lláh. At a time when His Holiness was in the prison of 'Akká and was under the restrictions and threats of two blood-thirsty kings, notwithstanding this fact, His teachings spread with all power in Persia and other countries. Should any teaching, or any principle, or any community fall under the threat of a powerful and bloodthirsty monarch it will be annihilated within a short space of time. At present for fifty years the Bahá'ís in Persia and most regions have been under severe restrictions and the threat of sword and spear. Thousands of souls have given their lives in the arena of sacrifice and have fallen as victims under the swords of oppression and cruelty. Thousands of esteemed families have been uprooted and destroyed. Thousands of children have been made fatherless. Thousands of fathers have been bereft of their sons. Thousands of mothers have wept and lamented for their boys who have been beheaded. All this oppression and cruelty, rapacity and bloodthirstiness did not hinder or prevent the spread of the teachings of Bahá'u'lláh. They spread more and more every day, and their power and might became more evident.

It may be that some foolish person among the Persians will affix his name to the contents of the Tablets of His Holiness Bahá'u'lláh or to the explanations given in the letters (Tablets) of 'Abdu'l-Bahá and send it to that esteemed Assembly. Ye must be aware of this fact, for any Persian who seeks fame or has some other intention will take the entire contents of the Tablets of His Holiness Bahá'u'lláh and publish them in his own name or in that of his community, just as happened at the Universal Races Congress in London before the war. A Persian took the substance of the Epistles of His Holiness Bahá'u'lláh, entered that Congress, gave them forth in his own name and published them, whereas the wording was exactly that of His Holiness Bahá'u'lláh. Some such souls have gone to Europe and have caused confusion in the minds of the people of Europe and have disturbed the thoughts of some Orientalists. Ye must bear this fact in mind, for not a word of these teachings was heard in Persia before the appearance of Bahá'u'lláh. Investigate this matter so that it may become to you evident and manifest. Some souls are like parrots. They learn any note which they may hear, and sing it, but they themselves are unaware of what they utter. There is a sect in Persia at present made up of a few souls who are called Bábís, who claim to be the followers of His Holiness the Báb, whereas they are utterly unaware of His Holiness. They have some secret teachings which are entirely opposed to the teachings of Bahá'u'lláh and in Persia people know this. But when these souls come to Europe, they conceal their own teachings and utter those of His Holiness Bahá'u'lláh, for they know that the teachings of His Holiness Bahá'u'lláh are powerful and they therefore declare publicly those teachings of Bahá'u'lláh in their own name. As to their secret teachings, they say that they are taken from the Book of Bayán, and the Book of Bayán is from His Holiness the Báb. When ye get hold of the translation of the Book of Bayán, which has been translated in Persia, ye will discover the truth that the teachings of Bahá'u'lláh are utterly opposed to the teachings of this sect. Beware lest ye disregard this fact. Should ye desire to investigate the matter further, inquire from Persia.

In fine, when travelling and journeying throughout the world, wherever one finds construction, it is the result of fellowship and love, while everything that is in ruin shows the effect of enmity and hatred. Notwithstanding this, the world of humanity has not become aware and has not awakened from the sleep of heedlessness. Again it engages in differences, in disputes and wrangling, that it may set up ranks of war and may run to and fro in the arena of battle and strife.

So is it with regard to the universe and its corruption, existence and non-existence. Every contingent being is made up of different and numerous elements and the existence of everything is a result of composition. That is to say, when between simple elements a composition takes place a being arises; the creation of beings come about in this way. And when that composition is upset, it is followed by decomposition, the elements disintegrate, and that being becomes annihilated. That is to say, the annihilation of everything consists in the decomposition and the separation of elements. Therefore every union and colour of leaves, of flowers and of fruits, each will contribute to the beauty and charm of the others and will make an admirable garden, and will appear in the utmost loveliness, freshness and sweetness. Likewise, when difference and variety of thoughts, forms, opinions, characters and morals of the world of mankind come under the control of one Supreme Power, that influence of composition among the elements is the cause of life, while dissociation and separation is the cause of death. In short, attraction and harmony of things are the cause of the production of fruits and useful results, while repulsion and inharmony of things are the cause of disturbance and annihilation. From harmony and attraction, all living contingent beings, such as plant, animal and man, are realized, and from inharmony and repulsion decay sets in and annihilation becomes manifest. Therefore whatever is the cause of harmony, attraction and union among men is the life of the world of humanity, and whatever is the cause of difference, of repulsion and of separation is the cause of the death of mankind. And when you pass by a garden wherein vegetable beds and plants, flowers and fragrant herbs are all combined so as to form a harmonious whole, this is an evidence that this plantation and this rose garden have been cultivated and arranged by the care of a perfect gardener, while when you see a garden in disorder, lacking arrangement and confused, this indicates that it has been deprived of the care of a skilful gardener, nay, rather it is nothing but a mass of weeds. It has therefore been made evident that fellowship and harmony are indicative of the training by the real Educator, while separation and dispersion prove wildness and deprivation of Divine training.

Should any one object that, since the communities and nations and races and peoples of the world have different formalities, customs, tastes, temperaments, morals, varied thoughts, minds and opinions, it is therefore impossible for ideal unity to be made manifest and complete union among men to be realized, we say that differences are of two kinds: One leads to destruction, and that is like the difference between warring peoples and competing nations who destroy one another, uproot each other's families, do away with rest and comfort and engage in bloodshed and rapacity. That is blameworthy. But the other difference consists in variation. This is perfection itself and the cause of the appearance of Divine bounty. Consider the flowers of the rose garden. Although they are of different kinds, various colours and diverse forms and appearances, yet as they drink from one water, are swayed by one breeze and grow by the warmth and light of one sun, this variation and this difference cause each to enhance the beauty and splendour of the others. The differences in manners, in customs, in habits, in thoughts, opinions and in temperaments is the cause of the adornment of the world of mankind. This is praiseworthy. Likewise this difference and this variation, like the difference and variation of the parts and members of the human body, are the cause of the appearance of beauty and perfection. As these different parts and members are under the control of the dominant spirit, and the spirit permeates all the organs and members, and rules all the arteries and veins, this difference and this variation strengthen love and harmony and this multiplicity is the greatest aid to unity. If in a garden the flowers and fragrant herbs, the blossoms and fruits, the leaves, branches and trees are of one kind, of one form, of one colour and one arrange-ment, there is no beauty or sweetness, but when there is variety in the world of oneness, they will appear and be displayed in the most perfect glory, beauty, exaltation and perfection. Today nothing but the power of the Word of God which encompasses the realities of things can bring the thoughts, the minds, the hearts and the spirits under the shade of one Tree. He is the potent in all things, the vivifier of souls, the preserver and the controller of the world of mankind. Praise be to God, in this day the light of the Word of God has shone forth upon all regions, and from all sects, communities, nations, tribes, peoples, religions and denominations, souls have gathered under the shadow of the Word of Oneness and have in the most intimate fellowship united and harmonized !

XII. TABLET TO DR FOREL

A letter written to Dr Auguste Forel, Switzerland in 1921

¶ 187. O revered personage, lover of truth! Thy letter dated 28 July 1921, hath been received. The contents thereof were most pleasing and indicated that, praised be the Lord, thou art as yet young, and searchest after truth, that thy power of thought is strong and the discoveries of thy mind manifest.

Numerous copies of the epistle I had written to Dr Fisher are spread far and wide and every one knoweth that it hath been revealed in the year 1910. Apart from this, numerous epistles have been written before the war upon the same theme, and reference, too, hath been made to these questions in the Journal of the San Francisco University,[1] the date whereof is known beyond any doubt. In like manner have the philosophers of broad vision praised highly the discourse eloquently delivered in the above-named University. A copy of that paper is thus enclosed and forwarded. Thy works are no doubt of great benefit, and if published, send us a copy of each.

By materialists, whose belief with regard to Divinity hath been explained, is not meant philosophers in general, but rather that group of materialists of narrow vision that worship that which is sensed, that depend upon the five senses only, and whose criterion of knowledge is limited to that which can be perceived by the senses. All that can be sensed is to them real, whilst whatever falleth not under the power of the senses is either unreal or doubtful. The existence of the Deity they regard as wholly doubtful.

It is as thou hast written, not philosophers in general but narrow-minded materialists that are meant. As to deistic philosophers, such as Socrates, Plato and Aristotle, they are indeed worthy of esteem and of the highest praise, for they have rendered distinguished services to mankind. In like manner we regard the materialistic,

---

[1] Stanford University, Palo Alto, 1912.

accomplished, moderate philosophers, that have been of service (to mankind).

We regard knowledge and wisdom as the foundation of the progress of mankind, and extol philosophers that are endowed with broad vision. Peruse carefully the San Francisco University Journal that the truth may be revealed to thee.

Now concerning mental faculties, they are in truth of the inherent properties of the soul, even as the radiation of light is the essential property of the sun. The rays of the sun are renewed but the sun itself is ever the same and unchanged. Consider how the human intellect develops and weakens, and may at times come to naught, whereas the soul changeth not. For the mind to manifest itself, the human body must be whole; and a sound mind cannot be but in a sound body, whereas the soul dependeth not upon the body. It is through the power of the soul that the mind comprehendeth, imagineth and exerteth its influence, whilst the soul is a power that is free. The mind comprehendeth the abstract by the aid of the concrete, but the soul hath limitless manifestations of its own. The mind is circumscribed, the soul limitless. It is by the aid of such senses as those of sight, hearing, taste, smell and touch, that the mind comprehendeth, whereas, the soul is free from all agencies. The soul as thou observest, whether it be in sleep or waking, is in motion and ever active. Possibly it may, whilst in a dream, unravel an intricate problem, incapable of solution in the waking state. The mind, moreover, understandeth not whilst the senses have ceased to function, and in the embryonic stage and in early infancy the reasoning power is totally absent, whereas the soul is ever endowed with full strength. In short, the proofs are many that go to show that despite the loss of reason, the power of the soul would still continue to exist. The spirit however possesseth various grades and stations.

As to the existence of spirit in the mineral: it is indubitable that minerals are endowed with a spirit and life according to the requirements of that stage. This unknown secret, too, hath become known unto the materialists who now maintain that all beings are endowed with life, even as He saith in the Qur'án, "All things are living."

In the vegetable world, too, there is the power of growth, and that power of growth is the spirit. In the animal world there is the sense of feeling, but in the human world there is an all-embracing power. In all the preceding stages the power of reason is absent, but the soul existeth and revealeth itself. The sense of feeling understandeth not the soul, whereas the reasoning power of the mind proveth the existence thereof.

In like manner the mind proveth the existence of an unseen Reality that embraceth all beings, and that existeth and revealeth itself in all stages, the essence whereof is beyond the grasp of the mind. Thus the mineral world understandeth neither the nature nor the perfections of the vegetable world; the vegetable world understandeth not the nature of the animal world, neither the animal world the nature of the reality of man that discovereth and embraceth all things.

The animal is the captive of nature and cannot transgress the rules and laws thereof. In man, however, there is a discovering power that transcendeth the world of nature and controlleth and interfereth with the laws thereof. For instance, all minerals, plants and animals are captives of nature. The sun itself with all its majesty is so subservient to nature that it hath no will of its own and cannot deviate a hair's-breadth from the laws thereof. In like manner all other beings, whether of the mineral, the vegetable or the animal world, cannot deviate from the laws of nature, nay, all are the slaves thereof. Man, however, though in body the captive of nature is yet free in his mind and soul, and hath the mastery over nature.

Consider: according to the law of nature man liveth, moveth, and hath his being on earth, yet his soul and mind interfere with the laws thereof, and even as the bird he flieth in the air, saileth speedily upon the seas and as the fish soundeth the deep and discovereth the things therein. Verily this is a grievous defeat inflicted upon the laws of nature.

So is the power of electrical energy: this unruly violent force that cleaveth mountains is yet imprisoned by man within a globe! This is manifestly interfering with the laws of nature. Likewise man discovereth those hidden secrets of nature that in conformity with the laws thereof must remain concealed, and transfereth them from the invisible plane to the visible. This, too, is interfering with the law of nature. In the same manner he discovereth the inherent properties of things that are the secrets of nature. Also he bringeth to light the past events that have been lost to memory, and foreseeth by his power of induction future happenings that are as yet unknown. Furthermore, communication and discovery are limited by the laws of nature to short distances, whereas man, through that inner power of his that discovereth the reality of all things, connecteth the East with the West. This, too, is interfering with the laws of nature. Similarly, according to the law of nature all shadows are fleeting, whereas man fixeth them upon the plate and this, too, is interference with a law of nature. Ponder and reflect: all sciences, arts, crafts, inventions and discoveries, have been once the secrets of nature and in conformity with the laws thereof must remain hidden; yet man through his discovering power interfereth with the laws of nature and transfereth these hidden secrets from the invisible to the visible plane. This again is interfering with the laws of nature.

In fine, that inner faculty in man, unseen of the eye, wresteth the sword from the hands of nature, and giveth it a grievous blow. All other beings, however great, are bereft of such perfections. Man hath the powers of will and understanding, but nature hath them not. Nature is constrained, man is free. Nature is bereft of understanding, man understandeth. Nature is unaware of past events, but man is aware of them. Nature forecasteth not the future; man by his discerning power seeth that which is to come. Nature hath no consciousness of itself, man knoweth about all things.

Should any one suppose that man is but a part of the world of nature, and he being endowed with these perfections, these being but manifestations of the world of nature, and thus nature is the originator of these perfections and is not deprived therefrom, to him we make reply and say: the part dependeth upon the whole; the part cannot possess perfections whereof the whole is deprived.

By nature is meant those inherent properties and necessary relations derived from the realities of things. And these realities of things, though in the utmost diversity, are yet intimately connected one with the other. For these diverse realities an all-unifying agency is needed that shall link them all one to the other. For instance, the various organs and members, the parts and elements, that constitute the body of man, though at variance, are yet all connected one with the other by that all-unifying agency known as the human soul, that causeth them to function in perfect harmony and with absolute regularity, thus making the continuation of life possible. The human body, however, is utterly unconscious of that all-unifying agency, and yet acteth with regularity and dischargeth its functions according to its will.

Now concerning philosophers, they are of two schools. Thus Socrates the wise believed in the unity of God and the existence of the soul after death; as his opinion was contrary to that of the narrow-minded people of his time, that divine sage was poisoned by them. All divine philosophers and men of wisdom and understanding, when observing these endless beings, have considered that in this great and infinite universe all things end in the mineral kingdom, that the outcome of the mineral kingdom is the vegetable kingdom, the outcome of the vegetable kingdom is the animal kingdom and the outcome of the animal kingdom the world of man. The consummation of this limitless universe with all its grandeur and glory hath been man himself, who in this world of being toileth and suffereth for a time, with diverse ills and pains, and ultimately disintegrates, leaving no trace and no fruit after him. Were it so, there is no doubt that this infinite universe with all its perfections has ended in shame and delusion with no result, no fruit, no permanence and no effect. It would be utterly without meaning. They (the philosophers) were thus convinced that such is not the case, that this Great Workshop with all its power, its bewildering magnificence and endless perfections, cannot eventually come to naught. That still another life should exist is thus certain, and just as the vegetable kingdom is unaware of the world of man, so we, too, know not of the Great Life hereafter that followeth the life of man here below. Our non-comprehension of that life, however, is no proof of its non-existence. The mineral world, for instance, is utterly unaware of the world of man and cannot comprehend it, but the ignorance of a thing is no proof of its non-existence. Numerous and conclusive proofs exist that go to show that this infinite world cannot end with this human life.

Now concerning the essence of Divinity: in truth it is on no account determined by anything apart from its own nature, and can in nowise be comprehended. For whatsoever can be conceived by man is a reality that hath limitations and is not unlimited; it is circumscribed, not all-embracing. It can be comprehended by man, and is controlled by him. Similarly it is certain that all human conceptions are contingent, not absolute; that they have a mental existence, not a material one. Moreover, differentiation of stages in the contingent world is an obstacle to understanding. How then can the contingent conceive the Reality of the absolute? As previously mentioned, differentiation of stages in the contingent plane is an obstacle to understanding. Minerals, plants and animals are bereft of the mental faculties of man that discover the realities of all things, but man himself comprehendeth all the stages beneath him. Every superior stage comprehendeth that which is inferior and discovereth the reality thereof, but the inferior one is unaware of that which is superior and cannot comprehend it. Thus man cannot grasp the Essence of Divinity, but can, by his reasoning power, by observation, by his intuitive faculties and the revealing power of his faith, believe in God, discover the bounties of His Grace. He becometh certain that though the Divine Essence is unseen of the eye, and the existence of the Deity is intangible, yet conclusive (spiritual) proofs assert the existence of that unseen Reality. The Divine Essence as it is in itself is however beyond all description. For instance, the nature of ether is unknown, but that it existeth is certain by the effects it produceth, heat, light and electricity being the waves thereof. By these waves the existence of ether is thus proven. And as we consider the outpouring of Divine Grace we are assured of the existence of God. For instance, we observe that the existence of beings is conditioned upon the coming together of various elements and their non-existence upon the decomposition of their constituent elements. For decomposition causes the dissociation of the various elements. Thus, as we observe the coming together of elements giveth rise to the existence of beings, and knowing that beings are infinite, they being the effect, how can the Cause be finite?

Now, formation is of three kinds and of three kinds only: accidental, necessary, and voluntary. The coming together of the various constituent elements of beings cannot be accidental, for unto every effect there must be a cause. It cannot be compulsory, for then the formation must be an inherent property of the constituent parts and the inherent property of a thing can in nowise be dissociated from it, such as light that is the revealer of things, heat that causeth the expansion of elements and the (solar) rays which are the essential property of the sun. Thus under such circumstances the decomposition of any formation is impossible, for the inherent properties of a thing cannot be separated from it. The third formation remaineth and that is the voluntary one, that is, an unseen force described as the Ancient Power, causeth these elements to come together, every formation giving rise to a distinct being.

As to the attributes and perfections such as will, knowledge, power and other ancient attributes that we ascribe to that Divine Reality, these are the signs that reflect the existence of beings in the visible plane and not the absolute perfections of the Divine Essence that cannot be comprehended. For instance, as we consider created things we observe infinite perfections, and the created things being in the utmost regularity and perfection we infer that the Ancient Power on whom dependeth the existence of these beings, cannot be ignorant; thus we say He is All-Knowing. It is certain that it is not impotent, it must be the All-Powerful; it is not poor, it must be All-Possessing; it is not non-existent, it must be Ever-Living. The purpose is to show that these attributes and perfections that we recount for that Universal Reality are only in order to deny imperfections, rather than to assert the perfections that the human mind can conceive. Thus we say His attributes are unknowable.

In fine, that universal Reality with all its qualities and attributes that we recount is holy and exalted above all minds and understandings. As we, however, reflect with broad minds upon this infinite universe, we observe that motion without a motive force, and an effect without a cause are both impossible; that every being hath come to exist under numerous influences and continually undergoeth reaction. These influences, too, are formed under the action of still other influences. For instance, plants grow and flourish through the outpourings of vernal showers, whilst the cloud itself is formed under various other agencies and these agencies in their turn are reacted upon by still other agencies. For example, plants and animals grow and develop under the influence of what the philosophers of our day designate as hydrogen and oxygen and are reacted upon by the effects of these two elements; and these in turn are formed under still other influences. The same can be said of other beings whether they affect other things or be affected. Such process of causation goes on, and to maintain that this process goes on indefinitely is manifestly absurd. Thus such a chain of causation must of necessity lead eventually to Him who is the

Ever-Living, the All-Powerful, who is Self-Dependent and the Ultimate Cause. This Universal Reality cannot be sensed, it cannot be seen. It must be so of necessity, for it is All-Embracing, not circumscribed, and such attributes qualify the effect and not the cause.

And as we reflect, we observe that man is like unto a tiny organism contained within a fruit; this fruit hath developed out of the blossom, the blossom hath grown out of the tree, the tree is sustained by the sap, and the sap formed out of earth and water. How then can this tiny organism comprehend the nature of the garden, conceive of the gardener and comprehend his being? This is manifestly impossible. Should that organism understand and reflect, it would observe that this garden, this tree, this blossom, this fruit would in nowise have come to exist by themselves in such order and perfection. Similarly the wise and reflecting soul will know of a certainty that this infinite universe with all its grandeur and (perfect) order could not have come to exist by itself.

Similarly in the world of being there exist forces unseen of the eye, such as the force of ether previously mentioned, that cannot be sensed, that cannot be seen. However from the effects it produceth, that is from its waves and vibrations, light, heat, electricity appear and are made evident. In like manner is the power of growth, of feeling, of understanding, of thought, of memory, of imagination and of discernment; all these inner faculties are unseen of the eye and cannot be sensed, yet all are evident by the effects they produce.

Now as to the (infinite) Power that knoweth no limitations; limitation itself proveth the existence of the unlimited, for the limited is known through the unlimited, just as weakness itself proveth the existence of wealth. Without wealth there would be no poverty, without knowledge no ignorance, without light no darkness. Darkness itself is a proof of the existence of light for darkness is the absence of light.

Now concerning nature, it is but the essential properties and the necessary relations inherent in the realities of things. And though these infinite realities are diverse in their character yet they are in the utmost harmony and closely connected together. As one's vision is broadened and the matter observed carefully, it will be made certain that every reality is but an essential requisite of other realities.

Thus to connect and harmonize these diverse and infinite realities an all-unifying Power is necessary, that every part of existent being may, in perfect order, discharge its own function. Consider the body of man, and let the part (i.e. the human body) be an indication of the whole. Consider how these diverse parts and members of the human body are closely connected and harmoniously united one with the other. Every part is the essential requisite of all other parts and has a function by itself. It is the mind that is the all-unifying agency that so uniteth all the component parts one with the other that each dischargeth its specific function in perfect order, and thereby co-operation and reaction are made possible. All parts function under certain laws that are essential to existence. Should that all-unifying agency that directeth all these parts be harmed in any way there is no doubt that the constituent parts and members will cease functioning properly; and though that all-unifying agency in the temple of man be not sensed or seen and the reality thereof be unknown, yet by its effects it manifesteth itself with the greatest power.

Thus it hath been proven and made evident that these infinite beings in this wondrous universe will discharge their functions properly only when directed and controlled by that Universal Reality, so that order may be established in the world. For example, interaction and co-operation between the constituent parts of the human body are evident and indisputable, yet this does not suffice; an all-unifying agency is necessary that shall direct and control the component parts, so that these through interaction and co-operation may discharge in perfect order their necessary and respective functions.

You are well aware, praised be the Lord, that both interaction and co-operation are evident and proven amongst all beings, whether large or small. In the case of large bodies interaction is as manifest as the sun, whilst in the case of small bodies, though interaction be unknown, yet the part is an indication of the whole. All these interactions therefore are connected with that all-embracing power which is their pivot, their centre, their source and their motive power.

For instance, as we have observed, co-operation among the constituent parts of the human body is clearly established, and these parts and members render services unto all the component parts of the body. For instance, the hand, the foot, the eye, the ear, the mind, the imagination all help the various parts and members of the human body, but all these interactions are linked by an unseen, all-embracing power, that causeth these interactions to be produced with perfect regularity. This is the inner faculty of man, that is his spirit and his mind, both of which are invisible.

In like manner consider machinery and workshops and the interaction existing among the various component parts and sections, and how connected they are one with the other. All these relations and interactions, however, are connected with a central power which is their motive force, their pivot and their source. This central power is either the power of steam or the skill of the mastermind.

It hath therefore been made evident and proved that interaction, co-operation and interrelation amongst beings are under the direction and will of a motive Power which is the origin, the motive force and the pivot of all interactions in the universe.

Likewise every arrangement and formation that is not perfect in its order we designate as accidental, and that which is orderly, regular, perfect in its relations and every part of which is in its proper place and is the essential requisite of the other constituent parts, this we call a composition formed through will and knowledge. There is no doubt that these infinite beings and the association of these diverse elements arranged in countless forms must have proceeded from a Reality that could in no wise be bereft of will or understanding. This is clear and proven to the mind and no one can deny it. It is not meant, however, that that Universal Reality or the attributes thereof have been comprehended. Neither its Essence nor its true attributes hath any one comprehended. We maintain, however, that these infinite beings, these necessary relations, this perfect arrangement must of necessity have proceeded from a source that is not bereft of will and understanding, and this infinite composition cast into infinite forms must have been caused by an all-embracing Wisdom. This none can dispute save he that is obstinate and stubborn, and denieth the clear and unmistakable evidence, and becometh the object of the blessed Verse: "(They are) deaf, (they are) dumb, (they are) blind and shall return no more."

Now regarding the question whether the faculties of the mind and the human soul are one and the same. These faculties are but the inherent properties of the soul, such as the power of imagination, of thought, of understanding; powers that are the essential requisites of the reality of man, even as the solar ray is the inherent property of the sun. The temple of man is like unto a mirror, his soul is as the sun, and his mental faculties even as the rays that emanate from that source of light. The ray may cease to fall upon the mirror, but it can in no wise be dissociated from the sun.

In short, the point is this, that the world of man is supernatural in its relation to the vegetable kingdom, though in reality it is not so. Relatively to the plant, the reality of man, his power of hearing and sight, are all supernatural, and for the plant to comprehend that reality and the nature of the powers of man's mind is impossible. In like manner for man to comprehend the Divine Essence and the nature of the great Hereafter is in no wise possible. The merciful outpourings of that Divine Essence, however, are vouchsafed unto all beings and it is incumbent upon man to ponder in his heart upon the effusions of the Divine Grace, the soul (of man) being counted as one (sign of it), rather than upon the Divine Essence itself. This is the utmost limit for human understanding. As it hath previously been mentioned, these attributes and perfections that we recount of the Divine Essence, these we have derived from the existence and observation of beings, and it is not that we have comprehended the essence and perfection of God. When we say that the Divine Essence understandeth and is free, we do not mean that we have discovered the Divine Will and Purpose, but rather that we have acquired knowledge of them through the Divine Grace revealed and manifested in the realities of things.

Now concerning our social principles, namely the teachings of His Holiness Bahá'u'lláh spread far and wide fifty years ago, they verily comprehend all other teachings. It is clear and evident that without these teachings progress and advancement for mankind are in no wise possible. Every community in the world findeth in these Divine Teachings the realization of its highest aspirations. These teachings are even as the tree that beareth the best fruits of all trees. Philosophers, for instance, find in these heavenly teachings the most perfect solution of their social problems, and similarly a true and noble exposition of matters that pertain to philosophical questions. In like manner men of faith behold the reality of religion manifestly revealed in these heavenly teachings, and clearly and conclusively prove them to be the real and true remedy for the ills and infirmities of all mankind. Should these sublime teachings be diffused, mankind shall be freed from all perils, from all chronic ills and sicknesses. In like manner are the Bahá'í economic principles the embodiment of the highest aspirations of all wage-earning classes and of economists of various schools.

In short, all sections and parties have their aspirations realized in the teachings of Bahá'u'lláh. As these teachings are declared in churches, in mosques and in other places of worship, whether those of the followers of Buddha or of Confucius, in political circles or amongst materialists, all shall bear witness that these teachings bestow a fresh life upon mankind and constitute the immediate remedy for all the ills of social life. None can find fault with any of these teachings, nay rather, once declared they will all be acclaimed, and all will confess their vital necessity, exclaiming, "Verily this is the truth and naught is there beside the truth but manifest error."

In conclusion, these few words are written, and unto everyone they will be a clear and conclusive evidence of the truth. Ponder them in thine heart. The will of every sovereign prevaileth during his reign, the will of every philosopher findeth expression in a handful of disciples during his lifetime, but the Power of the Holy Spirit shineth radiantly in the realities of the Messengers of God, and strengtheneth their will in such wise as to influence a great nation for thousands of years and to regenerate the human soul and revive mankind. Consider how great is this power! It is an extra-ordinary Power, an all-sufficient proof of the truth of the mission of the Prophets of God, and a conclusive evidence of the power of a Divine Inspiration.

The Glory of Glories rest upon thee.

XIII. GOD AND HIS MANIFESTATIONS

1. GOD IS BEYOND HUMAN COMPREHENSION

¶ 188. In the Old Testament we read that God said "Let us make man in our Own Image." In the Gospel, Christ said, "I am in the Father, and the Father in Me."[1] In the Qur'án, God says, "Man is my Mystery and I am his." Bahá'u'lláh writes that God says, "Thy heart is My home, purify it for My descent. Thy spirit is My place of revelation, cleanse it for My manifestation."

All these sacred words show us that man is made in God's image: yet the Essence of God is incomprehensible to the human mind, for the finite understanding cannot be applied to this infinite Mystery. God contains all: He cannot be contained. That which contains is superior to that which is contained. The whole is greater than its parts.

Things which are understood by men cannot be outside their capacity for understanding, so that it is impossible for the heart of man to comprehend the nature of the Majesty of God. Our imagination can only picture that which it is able to create.

The power of the understanding differs in degree in the various kingdoms of creation. The mineral, vegetable, and animal realms are each incapable of understanding any creation beyond their own. The mineral cannot imagine the growing power of the plant. The tree cannot understand the power of movement in the animal, neither can it comprehend what it would mean to possess sight, hearing or the sense of smell. These all belong to the physical creation.

Man also shares in this creation; but it is not possible for either of the lower kingdoms to understand that which takes place in the mind of man. The animal cannot realize the intelligence of a human being, he only knows that which is perceived by his animal senses, he cannot imagine anything in the abstract. An animal could not learn that the world is round, that the earth revolves round the

[1] St John xiv, 2.

232

sun, or the construction of the electric telegraph. These things are only possible to man. Man is the highest work of creation, the nearest to God of all creatures.

All superior kingdoms are incomprehensible to the inferior; how therefore could it be possible that the creature, man, should understand the almighty Creator of all?

That which we imagine, is not the Reality of God; He, the Unknowable, the Unthinkable, is far beyond the highest conception of man.

All creatures that exist are dependent upon the Divine Bounty. Divine Mercy gives Life itself. As the light of the sun shines on the whole world, so the Mercy of the infinite God is shed on all creatures. As the sun ripens the fruits of the earth, and gives life and warmth to all living beings, so shines the Sun of Truth on all souls, filling them with the fire of Divine love and understanding.

The superiority of man over the rest of the created world is seen again in this, that Man has a soul in which dwells the divine spirit; the souls of the lower creatures are inferior in their essence.

There is no doubt then, that of all created beings man is the nearest to the nature of God, and therefore receives a greater gift of the Divine Bounty.

The mineral kingdom possesses the power of existing. The plant has the power of existing and growing. The animal, in addition to existence and growth, has the capacity of moving about, and the use of the faculties of the senses. In the human kingdom we find all the attributes of the lower worlds, with much more added thereto. Man is the sum of every previous creation, for he contains them all.

To man is given the special gift of the Intellect by which he is able to receive a larger share of the light Divine. The Perfect Man is as a polished mirror reflecting the Sun of Truth, manifesting the attributes of God.

The Lord Christ said, "He that hath seen Me hath seen the Father"—God manifested in Man.

The sun does not leave his place in the heavens and descend into the mirror, for the actions of ascent and descent, coming and going, do not belong to the Infinite, they are the methods of finite beings. In the Manifestation of God, the perfectly polished mirror, appear the qualities of the Divine in a form that man is capable of comprehending.

This is so simple that all can understand it, and that which we are able to understand we must perforce accept.

Our Father will not hold us responsible for the rejection of dogmas which we are unable either to believe or comprehend, for He is ever infinitely just to His children.

This example is however so logical, that it can easily be grasped by all minds willing to give it their consideration.

May each one of you become a shining lamp, of which the flame is the Love of God. May your hearts burn with the radiance of unity. May your eyes be illumined with the effulgence of the Sun of Truth!

2. THE SOURCE OF UNITY

¶ 189. What is real unity? When we observe the human world we find various collective expressions of unity therein. For instance, man is distinguished from the animal by his degree or kingdom. This comprehensive distinction includes all the posterity of Adam and constitutes one great household or human family which may be considered the fundamental or physical unity of mankind. Furthermore, a distinction exists between various groups of humankind according to lineage, each group forming a racial unity separate from the others. There is also the unity of tongue among those who use the same language as a means of communication; national unity where various peoples live under one form of government such as French, German, British, etc.; and political unity which conserves the civil rights of parties or factions of the same government. All these unities are imaginary and without real foundation, for no real result proceeds from them. The purpose of true unity is real and divine outcomes. From these limited unities mentioned only limited outcomes proceed whereas unlimited unity produces unlimited result. For instance, from the limited unity of race or nationality the results at most are limited. It is like a family living alone and solitary; there are no unlimited or universal outcomes from it.

The unity which is productive of unlimited results is first a unity of mankind which recognizes that all are sheltered beneath the overshadowing glory of the All-Glorious; that all are servants of one God; for all breathe the same atmosphere, live upon the same earth, move beneath the same heavens, receive effulgence from the same sun and are under the protection of one God. This is the most great unity, and its results are lasting if humanity adheres to it; but mankind has hitherto violated it, adhering to sectarian or other limited unities such as racial, patriotic or unity of self-interests; therefore no great results have been forthcoming. Nevertheless it is certain that the radiance and favours of God are encompassing, minds have developed, perceptions have become acute, sciences and arts are widespread and capacity exists for the proclamation and promulgation of the real and ultimate unity of mankind which will bring forth marvellous results. It will reconcile all religions, make warring nations loving, cause hostile kings to become friendly and bring peace and happiness to the human world. It will cement together the Orient and Occident, remove for ever the foundations of war and upraise the ensign of the Most Great Peace. These limited unities are therefore signs of that great unity which will make all the human family one by being productive of the attractions of conscience in mankind.

Another unity is the spiritual unity which emanates from the breaths of the Holy Spirit. This is greater than the unity of mankind. Human unity or solidarity may be likened to the body whereas unity from the breaths of the Holy Spirit is the spirit animating the body. This is a perfect unity. It creates such a condition in mankind that each one will make sacrifices for the other and the utmost desire will be to forfeit life and all that pertains to it in behalf of another's good. This is the unity which existed among the disciples of His Holiness Jesus Christ and bound together the prophets and holy souls of the past. It is the unity which through the influence of the divine spirit is permeating the Bahá'ís so that each offers his life for the other and strives with all sincerity to attain his good pleasure. This is the unity which caused twenty thousand people in Írán to give their lives in love and devotion to it. It made the Báb the target of a thousand arrows and caused Bahá'u'lláh to suffer exile and imprisonment forty years. This unity is the very spirit of the body of the world. It is impossible for the body of the world to become quickened with life without its vivification. His Holiness Jesus Christ—may my life be a sacrifice to Him!—promulgated this unity among mankind. Every soul who believed in Jesus Christ became revivified and resuscitated through this spirit, attained to the zenith of eternal glory, realized the life everlasting, experienced the second birth and rose to the acme of good fortune.

In the Word of God there is still another unity, the oneness of the Manifestations of God, His Holiness Abraham, Moses, Jesus Christ, Muḥammad, the Báb and Bahá'u'lláh. This is a unity divine, heavenly, radiant, merciful; the one reality appearing in its successive manifestations. For instance, the sun is one and the same but its points of dawning are various. During the summer season it rises from the northern point of the ecliptic; in winter it appears from the southern point of rising. Each month between it appears from a certain zodiacal position. Although these dawning-points are different, the sun is the same sun which has appeared from them all. The significance is the reality of prophethood which is symbolized by the sun, and the holy Manifestations are the dawning-places or zodiacal points.

There is also the divine unity or entity which is sanctified above all concept of humanity. It cannot be comprehended nor conceived because it is infinite reality and cannot become finite. Human minds are incapable of surrounding that reality because all thoughts and conceptions of it are finite, intellectual creations and not the reality of divine being which alone knows itself. For example, if we form a conception of divinity as a living, almighty, self-subsisting, eternal being, this is only a concept apprehended by a human intellectual reality. It would not be the outward, visible reality which is beyond the power of human mind to conceive or encompass. We ourselves have an external, visible entity but even our concept of it is the product of our own brain and limited comprehension. The reality of divinity is sanctified above this degree of knowing and realization. It has ever been hidden and secluded in its own holiness and sanctity above our comprehending. Although it transcends our realization, its lights, bestowals, traces and virtues have become manifest in the realities of the prophets, even as the sun becomes resplendent in various mirrors. These holy realities are as reflectors, and the reality of divinity is as the sun which although it is reflected from the mirrors, and its virtues and perfections become resplendent therein, does not stoop from its own station of majesty and glory and seek abode in the mirrors; it remains in its heaven of sanctity. At most it is this, that its lights become manifest and evident in its mirrors or manifestations. Therefore its bounty proceeding from them is one bounty but the recipients of that bounty are many. This is the unity of God; this is oneness;—unity of divinity, holy above ascent or descent, embodiment, comprehension or idealization;—divine unity. The prophets are its mirrors; its lights are revealed through them, its virtues become resplendent in them, but the Sun of Reality never descends from its own highest point and station. This is unity, oneness, sanctity; this is glorification whereby we praise and adore God.

3. RELIGION IS PROGRESSIVE

¶ 190. Religion is the outer expression of the divine reality. Therefore it must be living, vitalized, moving and progressive. If it be without motion and non-progressive it is without the divine life; it is dead. The divine institutes are continuously active and evolutionary; therefore the revelation of them must be progressive and continuous. All things are subject to re-formation. This is a century of life and renewal. Sciences and arts, industry and invention have been reformed. Law and ethics have been reconstituted, reorganized. The world of thought has been regenerated. Sciences of former ages and philosophies of the past are useless today. Present exigencies demand new methods of solution; world problems are without precedent. Old ideas and modes of thoughts are fast becoming obsolete. Ancient laws and archaic ethical systems will not meet the requirements of modern conditions, for this is clearly the century of a new life, the century of the revelation of the reality and therefore the greatest of all centuries. Consider how the scientific developments of fifty years have surpassed and eclipsed the knowledge and achievements of all the former ages combined. Would the announcements and theories of ancient astronomers explain our present knowledge of the sun-worlds and planetary systems? Would the mask of obscurity which beclouded mediaeval centuries meet the demand for clear-eyed vision and understanding which characterizes the world today? Will the despotism of former governments answer the call for freedom which has risen from the heart of humanity in this cycle of illumination? It is evident that no vital results are now forthcoming from the customs, institutions and standpoints of the past. In view of this, shall blind imitations of ancestral forms and theological interpretations continue to guide and control the religious life and spiritual development of humanity today? Shall man, gifted with the power of reason, unthinkingly follow and adhere to dogma, creeds and hereditary beliefs which will not bear the analysis of reason in this century of effulgent reality? Unquestionably this will not satisfy men of science, for when they find premise or conclusion contrary to present standards of proof and without real foundation, they reject that which has been formerly accepted as standard and correct and move forward from new foundations.

The divine prophets have revealed and founded religion. They have laid down certain laws and heavenly principles for the guidance of mankind. They have taught and promulgated the knowledge of God, established praiseworthy ethical ideals and inculcated the highest standards of virtues in the human world. Gradually these heavenly teachings and foundations of reality have been beclouded by human interpretations and dogmatic imitations of ancestral beliefs. The essential realities which the prophets laboured so hard to establish in human hearts and minds while undergoing ordeals and suffering tortures of persecution, have now well nigh vanished. Some of these heavenly messengers have been killed, some imprisoned; all of them despised and rejected while proclaiming the reality of divinity. Soon after their departure from this world, the essential truth of their teachings was lost sight of and dogmatic imitations adhered to.

Inasmuch as human interpretations and blind imitations differ widely, religious strife and disagreement have arisen among mankind, the light of true religion has been extinguished and the unity of the world of humanity destroyed. The prophets of God voiced the spirit of unity and agreement. They have been the founders of divine reality. Therefore if the nations of the world forsake imitations and investigate the reality underlying the revealed Word of God they will agree and become reconciled. For reality is one and not multiple.

The nations and religions are steeped in blind and bigoted imitations. A man is a Jew because his father was a Jew. The Muhammadan follows implicitly the footsteps of his ancestors in belief and observance. The Buddhist is true to his heredity as a Buddhist. That is to say they profess religious belief blindly and without investigation, making unity and agreement impossible. It is evident therefore that this condition will not be remedied without a reformation in the world of religion. In other words the fundamental reality of the divine religions must be renewed, reformed, revoiced to mankind.

From the seed of reality, religion has grown into a tree which has put forth leaves and branches, blossoms and fruit. After a time this tree has fallen into a condition of decay. The leaves and blossoms have withered and perished; the tree has become stricken and fruitless. It is not reasonable that man should hold to the old tree, claiming that its life forces are undiminished, its fruit unequalled, its existence eternal. The seed of reality must be sown again in human hearts in order that a new tree may grow therefrom and new divine fruits refresh the world. By this means the nations and peoples now divergent in religion will be brought into unity, imitations will be forsaken and a universal brotherhood in the reality itself will be established. Warfare and strife will cease among mankind; all will be reconciled as servants of God. For all are sheltered beneath the tree of His providence and mercy. God is kind to all; He is the giver of bounty to all alike, even as His Holiness Jesus Christ has declared that God "sendeth rain on the just and on the unjust"; that is to say, the mercy of God is universal. All humanity is under the protection of His love and favour, and unto all He has pointed the way of guidance and progress.

Progress is of two kinds, material and spiritual. The former is attained through observation of the surrounding existence and constitutes the foundation of civilization. Spiritual progress is through the breaths of the Holy Spirit and is the awakening of the conscious soul of man to perceive the reality of divinity. Material progress insures the happiness of the human world. Spiritual progress insures the happiness and eternal continuance of the soul. The prophets of God have founded the laws of divine civilization. They have been the root and fundamental source of all knowledge. They have established the principles of human brotherhood or fraternity which is of various kinds, such as the fraternity of family, of race, of nation and of ethical motives. These forms of fraternity, these bonds of brotherhood are merely temporal and transient in association. They do not insure harmony and are usually productive of disagreement. They do not prevent warfare and strife; on the contrary they are selfish, restricted and fruitful causes of enmity and hatred among mankind. The spiritual brotherhood which is enkindled and established through the breaths of the Holy Spirit unites nations and removes the cause of warfare and strife. It transforms mankind into one great family and establishes the foundation of the oneness of humanity. It promulgates the spirit of international agreement and insures Universal Peace. Therefore we must investigate the foundation reality of this heavenly fraternity. We must forsake all imitations and promote the reality of the divine teachings. In accordance with these principles and actions and by the assistance of the Holy Spirit, both material and spiritual happiness shall become realized. Until all nations and peoples become united by the bonds of the Holy Spirit in this real fraternity, until national and international prejudices are effaced in the reality of this spiritual brotherhood, true progress, prosperity and lasting happiness will not be attained by man. This is the century of new and universal nationhood. Sciences have advanced, industries have progressed, politics have been reformed, liberty has been proclaimed, justice is awakening. This is the century of motion, divine stimulus and accomplishment; the century of human solidarity and altruistic service; the century of Universal Peace and the reality of the divine kingdom.

4. RELIGIOUS CYCLES

¶ 191. In this material world time has cycles; places change through alternating seasons, and for souls there are progress, retrogression, and education.

Sometime it is the season of spring, at another time it is the season of autumn, and again it is the season of summer or the season of winter.

In the spring there are the clouds which send down the precious rain, the musk-scented breezes and life-giving zephyrs; the air is perfectly temperate, the rain falls, the sun shines, the fecundating wind wafts the clouds, the world is renewed, and the breath of life appears in plants, in animals, and in men. Earthly beings pass from one condition to another. All things are clothed in new garments, and the black earth is covered with herbage; mountains and plains are adorned with verdure, trees bear leaves and blossoms, gardens bring forth flowers and fragrant herbs. The world becomes another world, and it attains to a life-giving spirit. The earth was a lifeless body; it finds a new spirit, and produces endless beauty, grace, and freshness. Thus the spring is the cause of new life, and infuses a new spirit.

Afterwards comes the summer, when the heat increases, and growth and development attain their greatest power. The energy of life in the vegetable kingdom reaches to the degree of perfection, the fruit appears, and the time of harvest ripens; a seed has become a sheaf, and the food is stored for winter. Afterwards comes tumultuous autumn when unwholesome and sterile winds blow, it is the season of sickness, when all things are withered, and the balmy air is vitiated. The breezes of spring are changed to autumn winds, the fertile green trees have become withered and bare, flowers and fragrant herbs fade away, the beautiful garden becomes a dust-heap. Following this comes the season of winter, with cold and tempests. It snows, rains, hails, storms, thunders and lightens, freezes and congeals; all plants die, and animals languish and are wretched.

When this state is reached, again a new life-giving spring returns, and the cycle is renewed. The season of spring with its hosts of freshness and beauty, spreads its tent on the plains and mountains with great pomp and magnificence. A second time the form of the creatures is renewed, and the creation of beings begins afresh; bodies grow and develop, the plains and wildernesses become green and fertile, trees bring forth blossoms, and the spring of last year returns in the utmost fullness and glory. Such is, and such ought to be, the cycle and succession of existence; such is the cycle and revolution of the material world.

It is the same with the spiritual cycles of the Prophets. That is to say, the day of the appearance of the Holy Manifestations is the spiritual springtime, it is the divine splendour, it is the heavenly bounty, the breeze of life, the rising of the Sun of Reality. Spirits are quickened, hearts are refreshed and invigorated, souls become good, existence is set in motion, human realities are gladdened, and grow and develop in good qualities and perfections. Universal progress takes place, and there are resurrection and lamentation; for it is the day of judgment, the time of turmoil and distress, at the same time that it is the season of joy, of happiness, and of absolute attraction.

Afterwards the life-giving spring ends in fruitful summer. The word of God is exalted, the Law of God is promulgated; all things reach perfection. The heavenly table is spread, the holy breezes perfume the East and the West, the teachings of God conquer the world, men become educated, praiseworthy results are produced, universal progress appears in the world of humanity, and the divine bounties surround all things. The Sun of Reality rises from the horizon of the Kingdom with the greatest power and heat. When it reaches the meridian it will begin to decline and descend, and the spiritual summer will be followed by autumn, when growth and development are arrested. Breezes change into blighting winds, and the unwholesome season dissipates the beauty and freshness of the gardens, plains, and bowers. That is to say, attraction and goodwill do not remain, divine qualities are changed, the radiance of hearts is dimmed, the spirituality of souls is altered, virtues are replaced by vices, and holiness and purity disappear. Only the name of the Religion of God remains, and the exoteric forms of the divine teachings. The foundations of the Religion of God are destroyed and annihilated, and nothing but forms and customs exist. Divisions appear, firmness is changed into instability, and spirits become dead; hearts languish, souls become inert, and winter arrives; that is to say, the coldness of ignorance envelops the world and the darkness of human error prevails. After this come indifference, disobedience, inconsiderateness, indolence, baseness, animal instincts, and the coldness and insensibility of stones. It is like the season of winter when the terrestrial globe, deprived of the effect of the heat of the sun, becomes desolate and dreary. When the world of intelligence and thought has reached to this state, there remain only continual death and perpetual non-existence.

When the season of winter has had its effect, again the spiritual springtime returns and a new cycle appears. Spiritual breezes blow, the luminous dawn gleams, the divine clouds give rain, the rays of the Sun of Reality shine forth, the contingent world attains unto a new life, and is clad in a wonderful garment. All the signs and the gifts of the past springtime reappear, with perhaps even greater splendour in this new season.

The spiritual cycles of the Sun of Reality are like the cycles of the material sun; they are always revolving and being renewed. The Sun of Reality, like the material sun, has numerous rising and dawning places: one day it rises from the zodiacal sign of Cancer, another day from the sign of Libra or Aquarius, another time it is from the sign of Aries that it diffuses its rays. But the sun is one sun and one reality; the people of knowledge are lovers of the sun, and are not fascinated by the places of its rising and dawning. The people of perception are the seekers of the Truth, and not of the places of its appearance, nor of its dawning points; therefore they will adore the Sun from whatever point in the zodiac it may appear, and they will seek the Reality in every Sanctified Soul who manifests it. Such people always attain to the truth, and are not veiled from the Sun of the Divine World, So, the lover of the sun and the seeker of the light will always turn towards the sun, whether it shines from the sign of Aries or gives its bounty from the sign of Cancer, or radiates from Gemini; but the ignorant and uninstructed are lovers of the signs of the zodiac, and enamoured and fascinated by the rising-places, and not by the sun. When it was in the sign of Cancer they turned towards it, though afterwards the sun changed to the sign of Libra; as they were lovers of the sign they turned towards it and attached themselves to it, and were deprived of the influences of the sun merely because it had changed its place. For example, once the Sun of Reality poured forth its rays from the sign of Abraham, and then it dawned from the sign of Moses and illumin-ated the horizon; afterwards it rose with the greatest power and brilliancy from the sign of Christ: those who were the seekers of Reality, worshipped that Reality wherever they saw it, but those who were attached to Abraham were deprived of its influences, when it shone upon Sinai and illuminated the reality of Moses. Those who held fast to Moses when the Sun of Reality shone from Christ with the utmost radiance and lordly splendour, were also veiled; and so forth.

Therefore man must be the seeker after the Reality; and he will find that Reality in each of the Sanctified Souls. He must be fascin-ated and enraptured, and attracted to the divine bounty; he must be like the butterfly who is the lover of the light from whatever lamp it may shine, and like the nightingale who is the lover of the rose in whatever garden it may grow.

If the sun were to rise in the West, it would still be the sun; one must not withdraw from it on account of its rising-place, nor consider the West to be always the place of sunset. In the same way, one must look for the heavenly bounties, and seek for the Divine Aurora. In every place where it appears, one must become its distracted lover. Consider that if the Jews had not kept turning to the horizon of Moses, and had only regarded the Sun of Reality, without any doubt they would have recognized the Sun in the dawning-place of the reality of Christ, in the greatest divine splendour. But, alas! a thousand times alas! attaching themselves to the outward words of Moses, they were deprived of the divine bounties and the lordly splendours!

5. THE UNIVERSAL CYCLES

¶ 192. Each one of the luminous bodies in this limitless firmament has a cycle of revolution which is of a different duration, and every one revolves in its own orbit, and again begins a new cycle. So the earth, every three hundred and sixty-five days, five hours, forty-eight minutes and a fraction, completes a revolution; and then it begins a new cycle, that is to say, the first cycle is again renewed. In the same way, for the whole universe, whether for the heavens or for men, there are cycles of great events, of important facts and occurrences. When a cycle is ended, a new cycle begins, and the old one, on account of the great events which take place, is completely forgotten, and not a trace or record of it will remain. As you see, we have no records of twenty thousand years ago, although we have before proved by argument that life on this earth is very ancient. It is not one hundred thousand, or two hundred thousand, or one million or two million years old; it is very ancient, and the ancient records and traces are entirely obliterated.

Each of the Divine Manifestations has likewise a cycle, and during the cycle his laws and commandments prevail and are performed. When his cycle is completed by the appearance of a new Manifestation, a new cycle begins. In this way cycles begin, end, and are renewed, until a universal cycle is completed in the world, when important events and great occurrences will take place which entirely efface every trace and every record of the past; then a new universal cycle begins in the world, for this universe has no beginning. We have before stated proofs and evidences concerning this subject; there is no need of repetition.

Briefly, we say a universal cycle in the world of existence signifies a long duration of time, and innumerable and incalculable periods and epochs. In such a cycle the Manifestations appear with splendour in the realm of the visible, until a great and universal Manifestation makes the world the centre of his radiance. His appearance causes the world to attain to maturity, and the extension of his cycle is very great. Afterwards other Manifestations will arise under his shadow, who according to the needs of the time will renew certain commandments relating to material questions and affairs, while remaining under his shadow.

We are in the cycle which began with Adam, and its universal Manifestation is Bahá'u'lláh.

6. TWO CLASSES OF PROPHETS

¶ 193. Universally, the Prophets are of two kinds. One are the independent Prophets who are followed; the other kind are not independent, and are themselves followers.

The independent Prophets are the lawgivers and the founders of a new cycle. Through their appearance the world puts on a new garment, the foundations of religion are established, and a new book is revealed. Without an intermediary they receive bounty from the Reality of the Divinity, and their illumination is an essential illumination. They are like the sun which is luminous in itself: the light is its essential necessity; it does not receive light from any other star. These Dawning-places of the morn of Unity are the sources of Bounty, and the mirrors of the Essence of Reality.

The other Prophets are followers and promoters, for they are branches and not independent; they receive the Bounty of the independent Prophets, and they profit by the light of the Guidance of the universal Prophets. They are like the moon, which is not luminous and radiant in itself, but receives its light from the sun.

The Manifestations of universal Prophethood who appeared independently are, for example, Abraham, Moses, Christ, Muḥammad, the Báb, and Bahá'u'lláh. But the others who are followers and promoters are like Solomon, David, Isaiah, Jeremiah, and

Ezekiel. For the independent Prophets are founders; they establish a new religion and make new creatures of men; they change the general morals, promote new customs and rules, renew the cycle and the Law. Their appearance is like the season of spring, which arrays all earthly beings in a new garment, and gives them a new life.

With regard to the second sort of Prophets who are followers, these also promote the Law of God, make known the Religion of God, and proclaim His word. Of themselves they have no power and might, except what they receive from the independent Prophets.

7. COMMENTARY ON AN OLD TESTAMENT PROPHECY

¶ 194. In Isaiah, chapter 11 verses 1 to 10, it is said: "And there shall come forth a rod out of the stem of Jesse, and a Branch shall grow out of his roots: And the spirit of the Lord shall rest upon him, the spirit of wisdom and understanding, the spirit of counsel and might, the spirit of knowledge and of the fear of the Lord; And shall make him of quick understanding in the fear of the Lord: and he shall not judge after the sight of his eyes, neither reprove after the hearing of his ears: But with righteousness shall he judge the poor, and reprove with equity for the meek of the earth: and he shall smite the earth with the rod of his mouth, and with the breath of his lips shall he slay the wicked. And righteousness shall be the girdle of his loins and faithfulness the girdle of his reins. The wolf also shall dwell with the lamb, and the leopard shall lie down with the kid; and the calf and the young lion and the fatling together and a little child shall lead them. And the cow and the bear shall feed; their young ones shall lie down together: and the lion shall eat straw like the ox. And the sucking child shall play on the hole of the asp, and the weaned child shall put his hand on the cockatrice' den. They shall not hurt nor destroy in all My holy mountain: for the earth shall be full of the knowledge of the Lord, as the waters cover the sea."

This rod out of the stem of Jesse might be correctly applied to Christ, for Joseph was of the descendants of Jesse the father of David but as Christ found existence through the Spirit of God, he called himself the Son of God. If he had not done so, this description would refer to him. Besides this, the events which he indicated as coming to pass in the days of that rod, if interpreted symbolically, were in part fulfilled in the day of Christ, but not all; and if not interpreted, then decidedly none of these signs happened. For example, the leopard and the lamb, the lion and the calf, the child and the asp, are metaphors and symbols for various nations, peoples, antagonistic sects, and hostile races, who are as opposite and inimical as the wolf and lamb. We say that by the breath of the spirit of Christ they found concord and harmony, they were vivified, and they associated together.

But "they shall not hurt nor destroy in all My holy mountain: for the earth shall be full of the knowledge of the Lord, as the waters cover the sea." These conditions did not prevail in the time of the manifestation of Christ; for until today various and antagonistic nations exist in the world, very few acknowledge the God of Israel, and the greater number are without the knowledge of God. In the same way, universal peace did not come into existence in the time of Christ; that is to say, between the antagonistic and hostile nations there was neither peace nor concord, disputes and disagreements did not cease, and reconciliation and sincerity did not appear. So, even at this day, amongst the Christian sects and nations themselves, enmity, hatred, and the most violent hostility are met with.

But these verses apply word for word to Bahá'u'lláh: likewise in this marvellous cycle the earth will be transformed, and the world of humanity arrayed in tranquillity and beauty. Disputes, quarrels, and murders will be replaced by peace, truth, and concord; among the nations, peoples, races, and countries, love and amity will appear. Co-operation and union will be established, and finally war will be entirely suppressed. When the laws of the Most Holy Book are enforced, contentions and disputes will find a final sentence of absolute justice before a general tribunal of the nations and kingdoms, and the difficulties that appear will be solved. The five continents of the world will form but one, the numerous nations will become one, the surface of the earth will become one land, and mankind will be a single community. The relations between the countries, the mingling, union, and friendship of the peoples and communities, will reach to such a degree that the human race will be like one family and kindred. The light of heavenly love will shine, and the darkness of enmity and hatred will be dispelled from the world. Universal peace will raise its tent in the centre of the earth, and the Blessed Tree of Life will grow and spread to such an extent that it will overshadow the East and the West. Strong and weak, rich and poor, antagonistic sects and hostile nations—which are like the wolf and the lamb, the leopard and kid, the lion and the calf—will act towards each other with the most complete love, friendship, justice, and equity. The world will be filled with science, with the knowledge of the reality of the mysteries of beings, and with the knowledge of God.

Now consider, in this great century which is the cycle of Bahá'u'l-láh, what progress science and knowledge have made, how many secrets of existence have been discovered, how many great inventions have been brought to light, and are day by day multiplying in number. Before long, material science and learning, as well as the knowledge of God, will make such progress, and will show forth such wonders, that the beholders will be amazed. Then the mystery of this verse in Isaiah, "For the earth shall be full of the knowledge of the Lord," will be completely evident.

Reflect also that in the short time since Bahá'u'lláh has appeared, people from all countries, nations, and races have entered under the shadow of this Cause. Christians, Jews, Zoroastrians, Buddhists, Hindus, and Persians all associate together with the greatest friendship and love, as if indeed these people had been related and connected together, they and theirs, for a thousand years; for they are like father and child, mother and daughter, sister and brother. This is one of the meanings of the companionship of the wolf and the lamb, the leopard and the kid, and the lion and the calf.

One of the great events which is to occur in the Day of the manifestation of that Incomparable Branch[1] is the hoisting of the Standard of God among all nations. By this is meant that all nations and kindreds will be gathered together under the shadow of this Divine Banner, which is no other than the Lordly Branch itself, and will become a single nation. Religious and sectarian antagonism, the hostility of races and peoples, and differences among nations, will be eliminated. All men will adhere to one religion, will have one common faith, will be blended into one race, and become a single people. All will dwell in one common

[1] Bahá'u'lláh.

fatherland, which is the planet itself. Universal peace and concord will be realised between all the nations, and that incomparable Branch will gather together all Israel: signifying that in this cycle Israel will be gathered in the Holy Land, and that the Jewish people who are scattered to the East and West, South and North, will be assembled together.

Now see: these events did not take place in the Christian cycle, for the nations did not come under the One Standard which is the Divine Branch. But in this cycle of the Lord of Hosts all the nations and peoples will enter under the shadow of this Flag. In the same way, Israel, scattered all over the world, was not reassembled in the Holy Land in the Christian cycle; but in the beginning of the cycle of Bahá'u'lláh this divine promise, as is clearly stated in all the Books of the Prophets, has begun to be manifest. You can see that from all the parts of the world tribes of Jews are coming to the Holy Land; they live in villages and lands which they make their own, and day by day they are increasing to such an extent, that all Palestine will become their home.

XIV. CONCERNING CHRISTIANITY

1. PROPHECIES CONCERNING
THE COMING OF CHRIST

¶ 195. In the Bible there are prophecies of the Coming of Christ. The Jews still await the coming of the Messiah, and pray to God day and night to hasten His advent.

When Christ came they denounced and slew Him, saying: "This is not the One for whom we wait. Behold when the Messiah shall come, signs and wonders shall testify that He is in truth the Christ. We know the signs and conditions, and they have not appeared. The Messiah will arise out of an unknown city. He shall sit upon the throne of David, and behold, He shall come with a sword of steel, and with a sceptre of iron shall He rule! He shall fulfil the Law of the Prophets, He shall conquer the East and the West, and shall glorify His chosen people the Jews. He shall bring with Him a reign of peace, during which even the animals shall cease to be at enmity with man. For behold the wolf and the lamb shall drink from the same spring, and the lion and the doe shall lie down in the same pasture, the serpent and the mouse shall share the same nest, and all God's creatures shall be at rest."

According to the Jews, Jesus the Christ fulfilled none of these conditions, for their eyes were holden and they could not see.

He came from Nazareth, no unknown place. He carried no sword in His hand, nor even a stick. He did not sit upon the Throne of David, He was a poor man. He reformed the Law of Moses, and broke the Sabbath Day. He did not conquer the East and the West, but was Himself subject to the Roman Law. He did not exalt the Jews, but taught equality and brotherhood, and rebuked the Scribes and Pharisees. He brought in no reign of Peace, for during His lifetime injustice and cruelty reached such a height that even He Himself fell a victim to it, and died a shameful death upon the Cross.

Thus the Jews thought and spoke, for they did not understand the Scriptures nor the glorious truths that were contained in them.

The letter they knew by heart, but of the life-giving spirit they understood not a word.

Hearken, and I will show you the meaning thereof. Although He came from Nazareth, which was a known place, He also came from Heaven. His body was born of Mary, but his Spirit came from Heaven. The sword He carried was the sword of His tongue, with which He divided the good from the evil, the true from the false, the faithful from the unfaithful, and the light from the darkness. His Word was indeed a sharp sword! The Throne upon which He sat is the Eternal Throne from which Christ reigns for ever, a heavenly throne, not an earthly one, for the things of earth pass away but heavenly things pass not away. He reinterpreted and completed the Law of Moses and fulfilled the Law of the Prophets. His word conquered the East and the West. His Kingdom is Everlasting. He exalted those Jews who recognized Him. They were men and women of humble birth, but contact with Him made them great and gave them everlasting dignity. The animals who were to live with one another signified the different sects and races, who, once having been at war, were now to dwell in love and charity, drinking together the water of life from Christ the Eternal Spring.

Thus, all the spiritual prophecies concerning the coming of Christ were fulfilled, but the Jews shut their eyes that they should not see, and their ears that they should not hear, and the Divine Reality of Christ passed through their midst unheard, unloved and unrecognized.

It is easy to read the Holy Scriptures, but it is only with a clean heart and a pure mind that one may understand their true meaning. Let us ask God's help to enable us to understand the Holy Books. Let us pray for eyes to see and ears to hear, and for hearts that long for peace.

2. THE GREATNESS OF CHRIST IS DUE TO HIS PERFECTIONS

¶ 196. A great man is a great man, whether born of a human father or not. If being without a father is a virtue, Adam is greater and more excellent than all the Prophets and Messengers, for he had neither father nor mother. That which causes honour and greatness, is the splendour and bounty of the divine perfections. The sun is born from substance and form, which can be compared to father and mother, and it is absolute perfection; but the darkness has neither substance nor form, neither father nor mother, and it is absolute imperfection. The substance of Adam's physical life was earth, but the substance of Abraham was pure sperm; it is certain that the pure and chaste sperm is superior to earth.

Furthermore, in the first chapter of the Gospel of John, verses 12 and 13, it is said: "But as many as received him, to them gave he power to become the sons of God, even to them that believed on his name. Which were born, not of blood, nor of the will of the flesh, nor of the will of man, but of God."

From these verses it is obvious that the being of a disciple also is not created by physical power, but by the spiritual reality. The honour and greatness of Christ is not due to the fact that he did not have a human father, but to his perfections, bounties, and divine glory. If the greatness of Christ is his being fatherless, then Adam is greater than Christ, for he had neither father nor mother. It is said in the Old Testament, "And the Lord God formed man of the dust of the ground, and breathed into his nostrils the breath of life; and man became a living soul."[1] Observe that it is said that Adam came into existence from the Spirit of Life. Moreover, the expression which John uses in regard to the disciples, proves that they also are from the Heavenly Father. Hence it is evident that the holy reality, meaning the real existence of every great man, comes from God, and owes its being to the breath of the Holy Spirit.

The purport is that, if to be without a human father is the greatest human glory, then Adam is greater than all, for he had neither father nor mother. Is it better for a man to be created from a living substance or from earth? Certainly it is better if he be created from a living substance. But Christ was born and came into existence from the Holy Spirit.

To conclude: the splendour and honour of the holy souls and the Divine Manifestations come from their heavenly perfections, bounties, and glory, and from nothing else.

[1] Gen. ii. 7.

3. THE RESURRECTION OF CHRIST

¶ 197. The resurrections of the Divine Manifestations are not of the body. All their states, their conditions, their acts, the things they have established, their teachings, their expressions, their parables, and their instructions have a spiritual and divine signification, and have no connection with material things. For example, there is the subject of Christ's coming from heaven: it is clearly stated in many places in the Gospel that the Son of man came from heaven, he is in heaven, and he will go to heaven. So in chapter 6 verse 38 of the Gospel of John it is written: "For I came down from heaven"; and also in verse 42 we find: "And they said, Is not this Jesus, the son of Joseph, whose father and mother we know? How is it then that he saith, I came down from heaven?" Also in John, chapter 3 verse 13: "And no man hath ascended up to heaven, but he that came down from heaven, even the Son of man which is in heaven."

Observe that it is said "The Son of man is in heaven," while at that time Christ was on earth. Notice also that it is said that Christ came from heaven, though he came from the womb of Mary, and his body was born of Mary. It is clear, then, that when it is said that the Son of man is come from heaven, this has not an outward but an inward signification; it is a spiritual, not a material, fact. The meaning is that though, apparently, Christ was born from the womb of Mary, in reality he came from heaven, from the centre of the Sun of Reality, from the Divine World, and the Spiritual Kingdom. And as it has become evident that Christ came from the spiritual heaven of the Divine Kingdom, therefore his disappearance under the earth for three days has an inner signification, and is not an outward fact. In the same way, his resurrection from the interior of the earth is also symbolical; it is a spiritual and divine fact, and not material; and likewise his ascension to heaven is a spiritual and not material ascension.

Beside these explanations, it has been established and proved by science that the visible heaven is a limitless area, void and empty, where innumerable stars and planets revolve.

Therefore we say that the meaning of Christ's resurrection is as follows: the disciples were troubled and agitated after the martyrdom of Christ. The Reality of Christ, which signifies his teachings, his bounties, his perfections, and his spiritual power, was hidden and concealed for two or three days after his martyrdom, and was not resplendent and manifest. No, rather it was lost; for the believers were few in number and were troubled and agitated. The Cause of Christ was like a lifeless body; and, when after three days the disciples became assured and steadfast, and began to serve the Cause of Christ, and resolved to spread the divine teachings, putting his counsels into practice, and arising to serve him, the Reality of Christ became resplendent and his bounty appeared; his religion found life, his teachings and his admonitions became evident and visible. In other words, the Cause of Christ was like a lifeless body, until the life and the bounty of the Holy Spirit surrounded it.

Such is the meaning of the resurrection of Christ, and this was a true resurrection. But as the clergy have neither understood the meaning of the Gospels nor comprehended the symbols, therefore it has been said that religion is in contradiction to science, and science in opposition to religion; as, for example, this subject of the ascension of Christ with an elemental body to the visible heaven is contrary to the science of mathematics. But when the truth of this subject becomes clear, and the symbol is explained, science in no way contradicts it; but, on the contrary, science and the intelligence affirm it.

4. THE SYMBOLISM OF THE BREAD AND THE WINE

¶ 198. *Question:* The Christ said: "I am the living bread which came down from heaven, that a man may eat thereof and not die." What is the meaning of this utterance?

Answer: This bread signifies the heavenly food and divine perfections. So, "If any man eateth of this bread" means if any man acquires heavenly bounty, receives the divine light, or partakes of Christ's perfections, he thereby gains everlasting life. The blood also signifies the spirit of life and the divine perfections, the lordly splendour and eternal bounty. For all the members of the body gain vital substance from the circulation of the blood.

In the Gospel of St John, chapter 6 verse 26, it is written: "Ye seek me, not because ye saw the miracles, but because ye did eat of the loaves and were filled."

It is evident that the bread of which the disciples ate and were filled, was the heavenly bounty; for in verse 33 of the same chapter it is said: "For the bread of God is he which cometh down from heaven, and giveth life unto the world." It is clear that the body of Christ did not descend from heaven, but it came from the womb of Mary; and that which descended from the heaven of God was the spirit of Christ. As the Jews thought that Christ spoke of his body, they made objections, for it is said in the 42nd verse of the same chapter: "And they said, Is not this Jesus the son of Joseph, whose father and mother we know? how is it then that he saith, I came down from heaven?"

Reflect how clear it is that what Christ meant by the heavenly bread was his spirit, his bounties, his perfections, and his teachings; for it is said in the 63rd verse: "It is the spirit that quickeneth, the flesh profiteth nothing."

Therefore it is evident that the spirit of Christ is a heavenly grace which descends from heaven; whosoever receives light from that spirit in abundance, that is to say the heavenly teachings, finds everlasting life. That is why it is said in the 35th verse: "And Jesus said unto them, I am the bread of life: he that cometh to me shall never hunger; and he that believeth on me shall never thirst."

Notice that "coming to him" he expresses as eating, and "belief in him" as drinking. Then it is evident and established that the celestial food is the divine bounties, the spiritual splendours, the heavenly teachings, the universal meaning of Christ. To eat is to draw near to him, and to drink is to believe in him. For Christ had an elemental body and a celestial form. The elemental body was crucified, but the heavenly form is living and eternal, and the cause of everlasting life; the first was the human nature, and the second is the divine nature. It is thought by some that the Eucharist is the reality of Christ, and that the Divinity and the Holy Spirit descend into and exist in it. Now when once the Eucharist is taken, after a few moments it is simply disintegrated, and entirely transformed. Therefore how can such a thought be conceived? God forbid! certainly it is an absolute fantasy.

To conclude: through the manifestation of Christ, the divine teachings which are an eternal bounty, were spread abroad, the light of guidance shone forth, and the spirit of life was conferred on man. Whoever found guidance became living, whoever remained lost was seized by enduring death. This bread which came down from heaven was the divine body of Christ, his spiritual elements, which the disciples ate, and through which they gained eternal life.

The disciples had taken many meals from the hand of Christ; why was the last supper distinguished from the others? It is evident that the heavenly bread did not signify this material bread, but rather the divine nourishment of the spiritual body of Christ, the divine graces and heavenly perfections of which his disciples partook, and with which they became filled.

In the same way, reflect that when Christ blessed the bread and gave it to his disciples saying, "This is my body", and gave grace to them, he was with them in person, in presence, and form. He was not transformed into bread and wine: if he had been turned into bread and wine, he could not have remained with the disciples in body, in person, and in presence.

Then it is clear that the bread and wine were symbols which signified: I have given you my bounties and perfections, and when you have received this bounty, you have gained eternal life and have partaken of your share and your portion of the heavenly nourishment.

5. THE SECOND COMING OF CHRIST

¶ 199. It is said in the Holy Books that Christ will come again, and that his coming depends upon the fulfilment of certain signs: when he comes it will be with these signs. For example, "The sun will be darkened, and the moon shall not give her light, and the stars shall fall from heaven. . . And then shall appear the sign of the Son of man in heaven; and then shall all the tribes of the earth mourn, and they shall see the Son of man coming in the clouds of heaven with power and great glory." Bahá'u'lláh has explained these verses in the Kitáb-I-Íqán: there is no need of repetition; refer to it and you will understand these sayings.

But I have something further to say upon this subject. At his first coming also, Christ came from heaven, as it is explicitly stated in the Gospel. Christ himself says: "And no man hath ascended up to heaven, but he that came down from heaven, even the Son of man which is in heaven."

It is clear to all that Christ came from heaven, although apparently he came from the womb of Mary. At the first coming he came from heaven, though apparently from the womb; in the same way also, at his second coming, he will come from heaven, though apparently from the womb. The conditions that are indicated in the Gospel for the second coming of Christ are the same as those that were mentioned for the first coming, as we before said.

The Book of Isaiah announces that the Messiah will conquer the East and West, and all nations of the world will come under his shadow, that his Kingdom will be established, that he will come from an unknown place, that the sinners will be judged, and that justice will prevail to such a degree that the wolf and the lamb, the leopard and the kid, the sucking child and the asp, shall all gather at one spring, and in one meadow, and one dwelling. The first coming was also under these conditions, though outwardly none of them came to pass. Therefore the Jews rejected Christ, and, God forbid! called the Messiah masikh,[1] considered him to be the destroyer of the edifice of God, regarded him as the breaker of the Sabbath and the Law, and sentenced him to death. Nevertheless each one of these conditions had a signification that the Jews did not understand: therefore they were debarred from perceiving the truth of Christ.

The second coming of Christ also will be in like manner: the signs and conditions which have been spoken of all have meanings, and are not to be taken literally. Among other things it is said that the stars will fall upon the earth. The stars are endless and innumerable, and modern mathematicians have established and proved scientifically that the globe of the sun is estimated to be about one million and a half times greater than the earth, and each of the fixed stars to be a thousand times larger than the sun. If these stars were to fall upon the surface of the earth, how could they find place there? It would be as though a thousand million of Himalaya mountains were to fall upon a grain of mustard seed. According to reason and science this thing is quite impossible. What is even more strange is that Christ said: "Perhaps I shall come when you are yet asleep, for the coming of the Son of man is like the coming of a

---

[1] Masikh—i.e. the monster. In Arabic there is a play upon the words Masih, the Messiah, and masikh, the monster.

thief." Perhaps the thief will be in the house and the owner will not know it.

It is clear and evident that these signs have symbolic signification, and that they are not literal. They are fully explained in the Kitáb-i-Íqán: refer to it.

XV. MAN

1. THE ORIGIN OF MAN

¶ 200. Certain European philosophers agree that the species grows and develops, and that even change and alteration are also possible. One of the proofs that they give for this theory is that through the attentive study and verification of the science of geology it has become clear that the existence of the vegetable preceded that of the animal, and that of the animal preceded that of man. They admit that both the vegetable and the animal species have changed, for in some of the strata of the earth they have discovered plants which existed in the past and are now extinct; they have progressed, grown in strength, their form and appearance have changed, and so the species have altered. In the same way, in the strata of the earth there are some species of animals which have changed and are transformed. One of these animals is the serpent. There are indications that the serpent once had feet; but through the lapse of time those members have disappeared. In the same way, in the vertebral column of man there is an indication which amounts to a proof that, like other animals, he once had a tail. At one time that member was useful, but when man developed it was no longer of use, and therefore it gradually disappeared. As the serpent took refuge under the ground, and became a creeping animal, it was no longer in need of feet, so they disappeared; but their traces survive. The principal argument is this: that the existence of traces of members proves that they once existed; and as now they are no longer of service, they have gradually disappeared. Therefore while the perfect and necessary members have remained, those which are unnecessary have gradually disappeared by the modification of the species, but the traces of them continue.

The first answer to this argument is the fact that the animal having preceded man is not a proof of the evolution, change, and alteration of the species, nor that man was raised from the animal world to the human world. For while the individual appearance of these different beings is certain, it is possible that man came into exist-ence after the animal. So when we examine the vegetable kingdom, we see that the fruits of the different trees do not arrive at maturity at one time; on the contrary, some come first and others after-wards. This priority does not prove that the later fruit of one tree was produced from the earlier fruit of another tree.

Secondly, these slight signs and traces of members have per-haps a great reason of which the mind is not yet cognizant. How many things exist of which we do not yet know the reason! So the science of physiology, that is to say the knowledge of the compo-sition of the members, records that the reason and cause of the difference in the colours of animals, and of the hair of men, of the redness of the lips, and of the variety of the colours of birds, is still unknown; it is secret and hidden. But it is known that the pupil of the eye is black, so as to attract the rays of the sun; for if it were an-other colour, that is, uniformly white, it would not attract the rays of the sun. Therefore, as the reason of the things we have men-tioned is unknown, it is possible that the reason and the wisdom of these traces of members, whether they be in the animal or man, are equally unknown. Certainly there is a reason, even though it is not known.

Thirdly, let us suppose that there was a time when some animals, or even man, possessed some members which have now dis-appeared; this is not a sufficient proof of the change and evolution of the species. For man, from the beginning of the embryonic period till he reaches the degree of maturity, goes through differ-ent forms and appearances. His aspect, his form, his appearance, and colour change; he passes from one form to another, and from one appearance to another. Nevertheless, from the beginning of the embryonic period he is of the species of man; that is to say, an em-bryo of a man, and not of an animal; but this is not at first apparent, but later it becomes visible and evident. For example, let us sup-pose that man once resembled the animal, and that now he has pro-gressed and changed; supposing this to be true, it is still not a proof of the change of species; no, as before mentioned, it is merely like the change and alteration of the embryo of man until it reaches the degree of reason and perfection. We will state it more clearly: let us suppose that there was a time when man walked on his hands and feet, or had a tail; this change and alteration is like that of the foetus in the womb of the mother; although it changes in all ways, and grows and develops until it reaches the perfect form, from the beginning it is a special species. We also see in the vegetable kingdom that the original species of the genus do not change and alter, but the form, colour, and bulk will change and alter, or even progress.

To recapitulate: as man in the womb of the mother passes from form to form, from shape to shape, changes and develops, and is still the human species from the beginning of the embryonic period —in the same way man, from the beginning of his existence in the matrix of the world, is also a distinct species, that is, man, and has gradually evolved from one form to another. Therefore this change of appearance, this evolution of members, this development and growth, even though we admit the reality of growth and progress,[1] does not prevent the species from being original. Man from the beginning was in this perfect form and composition, and possessed capacity and aptitude for acquiring material and spiritual perfections, and was the manifestation of these words, "We will make man in Our image and likeness." He has only become more pleasing, more beautiful, and more graceful. Civilization has brought him out of his wild state, just as the wild fruits which are cultivated by a gardener become finer, sweeter, and acquire more freshness and delicacy.

The gardeners of the world of humanity are the Prophets of God.

2. THE SIGNIFICANCE OF HUMAN LIFE ON EARTH

¶ 201. The wisdom of the appearance of the spirit in the body is this: the human spirit is a Divine Trust, and it must traverse all conditions; for its passage and movement through the conditions of existence will be the means of its acquiring perfections. So, when a man travels and passes through different regions and numerous countries with system and method, it is certainly a means of his acquiring perfection; for he will see places, scenes, and countries, from which he will discover the conditions and states of other

---

[1] i.e. if we admit, for example, that man had formerly been a quadruped, or had had a tail.

nations. He will thus become acquainted with the geography of countries, and their wonders and arts; he will familiarize himself with the habits, customs, and usages of peoples; he will see the civilization and progress of the epoch; he will become aware of the policy of governments, and the power and capacity of each country. It is the same when the human spirit passes through the conditions of existence: it will become the possessor of each degree and station. Even in the condition of the body it will surely acquire perfections.

Besides this, it is necessary that the signs of the perfection of the spirit should be apparent in this world, so that the world of creation may bring forth endless results, and this body may receive life and manifest the divine bounties. So, for example, the rays of the sun must shine upon the earth, and the solar heat develop the earthly beings; if the rays and heat of the sun did not shine upon the earth, the earth would be uninhabited, without meaning, and its development would be retarded. In the same way, if the perfections of the spirit did not appear in this world, this world would be unenlightened and absolutely brutal. By the appearance of the spirit in the physical form, this world is enlightened. As the spirit of man is the cause of the life of the body, so the world is in the condition of the body, and man is in the condition of the spirit. If there were no man, the perfections of the spirit would not appear, and the light of the mind would not be resplendent in this world. This world would be like a body without a soul.

This world is also in the condition of a fruit-tree, and man is like the fruit; without fruit the tree would be useless.

Moreover, these members, these elements, this composition, which are found in the organism of man, are an attraction and magnet for the spirit; it is certain that the spirit will appear in it. So, a mirror which is clear will certainly attract the rays of the sun. It will become luminous, and wonderful images will appear in it. That is to say, when these existing elements are gathered together according to the natural order, and with perfect strength, they become a magnet, for the spirit, and the spirit will become manifest in them with all its perfections.

Under these conditions it cannot be said "what is the necessity for the rays of the sun to descend upon the mirror?"—for the connection which exists between the reality of things, whether they be spiritual or material, requires that when the mirror is clear and faces the sun, the light of the sun must become apparent in it. In the same way, when the elements are arranged and combined in the most glorious system, organization and manner, the human spirit will appear and be manifest in them. This is the decree of the Powerful, the Wise.

3. SOUL, SPIRIT, AND MIND

¶ 202. It has been before explained that spirit is universally divided into five categories: the vegetable spirit, the animal spirit, the human spirit, the spirit of faith, and the Holy Spirit.

The vegetable spirit is the power of growth which is brought about in the seed through the influence of other existences.

The animal spirit is the power of all the senses, which is realized from the composition and mingling of elements; when this composition decomposes, the power also perishes and becomes annihilated. It may be likened to this lamp: when the oil, wick, and fire are combined it is lighted, and when this combination is dissolved, that is to say when the combined parts are separated from one another, the lamp also is extinguished.

The human spirit which distinguishes man from the animal is the rational soul; and these two names—the human spirit and the rational soul—designate one thing. This spirit, which in the terminology of the philosophers is the rational soul, embraces all beings, and as far as human ability permits discovers the realities of things and becomes cognizant of their peculiarities and effects, and of the qualities and properties of beings. But the human spirit, unless assisted by the spirit of faith, does not become acquainted with the divine secrets and the heavenly realities. It is like a mirror which, although clear, polished, and brilliant, is still in need of light. Until a ray of the sun reflects upon it, it cannot discover the heavenly secrets.

But the mind is the power of the human spirit. Spirit is the lamp; mind is the light which shines from the lamp. Spirit is the tree, and the mind is the fruit. Mind is the perfection of the spirit, and is its essential quality, as the sun's rays are the essential necessity of the sun.

This explanation, though short, is complete; therefore reflect upon it, and if God wills, you may become acquainted with the details.

4. THE TWO NATURES IN MAN

¶ 203. In man there are two natures; his spiritual or higher nature and his material or lower nature. In one he approaches God, in the other he lives for the world alone. Signs of both these natures are to be found in men. In his material aspect he expresses untruth, cruelty and injustice; all these are the outcome of his lower nature. The attributes of his Divine nature are shown forth in love, mercy, kindness, truth and justice, one and all being expressions of his higher nature. Every good habit, every noble quality belongs to man's spiritual nature, whereas all his imperfections and sinful actions are born of his material nature. If a man's Divine nature dominates his human nature, we have a saint.

Man has the power both to do good and to do evil; if his power for good predominates and his inclinations to do wrong are conquered, then man in truth may be called a saint. But if, on the contrary, he rejects the things of God and allows his evil passions to conquer him, then he is no better than a mere animal.

Saints are men who have freed themselves from the world of matter and who have overcome sin. They live in the world but are not of it, their thoughts being continually in the world of the spirit. Their lives are spent in holiness, and their deeds show forth love, justice and godliness. They are illumined from on high; they are as bright and shining lamps in the dark places of the earth. These are the Saints of God. The apostles, who were the disciples of Jesus Christ, were just as other men are; they, like their fellows, were attracted by the things of the world, and each thought only of his own advantage. They knew little of justice, nor were the Divine perfections found in their midst. But when they followed Christ and believed in Him, their ignorance gave place to understanding, cruelty was changed to justice, falsehood to truth, darkness into light. They had been worldly, they became spiritual and divine. They had been children of darkness, they became sons of God, they became saints! Strive therefore to follow in their steps, leaving all worldly things behind, and striving to attain to the Spiritual Kingdom.

Pray to God that He may strengthen you in divine virtue, so that you may be as angels in the world, and beacons of light, to disclose the mysteries of the kingdom to those with understanding hearts. God sent His Prophets into the world to teach and enlighten man, to explain to him the mystery of the Power of the Holy Spirit, to enable him to reflect the light, and so, in his turn, to be the source of guidance to others. The Heavenly Books, the Bible, the Qur'án, and the other Holy Writings have been given by God as guides into the paths of Divine virtue, love, justice and peace.

Therefore I say unto you that ye should strive to follow the counsels of these Blessed Books, and so order your lives that ye may, following the examples set before you, become yourselves the saints of the Most High!

5. THE POWER OF THE HOLY SPIRIT

¶ 204. In the teaching of Bahá'u'lláh, it is written: "By the Power of the Holy Spirit alone is man able to progress, for the power of man is limited and the Divine Power is boundless." The reading of history brings us to the conclusion that all truly great men, the benefactors of the human race, those who have moved men to love the right and hate the wrong and who have caused real progress, all these have been inspired by the force of the Holy Spirit.

The Prophets of God have not all graduated in the schools of learned philosophy; indeed they were often men of humble birth, to all appearance ignorant, unknown men of no importance in the eyes of the world; sometimes even lacking the knowledge of reading and writing.

That which raised these great ones above men, and by which they were able to become Teachers of the truth, was the Power of the Holy Spirit. Their influence on Humanity, by virtue of this mighty inspiration, was great and penetrating.

The influence of the wisest philosophers, without this Spirit Divine, has been comparatively unimportant, however extensive their learning and deep their scholarship.

The unusual intellects, for instance, of Plato, Aristotle, Pliny and

Socrates, have not influenced men so greatly that they have been anxious to sacrifice their lives for their teachings; whilst some of those simple men so moved humanity that thousands of men have become willing martyrs to uphold their words; for these words were inspired by the Divine Spirit of God! The prophets of Judah and Israel, Elijah, Jeremiah, Isaiah and Ezekiel, were humble men, as were also the apostles of Jesus Christ.

Peter, the chief of the apostles, used to divide the proceeds of his fishing into seven parts, and when, having taken one part for each day's use, he arrived at the seventh portion, he knew it was the Sabbath day. Consider this! and then think of his future position; to what glory he attained because the Holy Spirit wrought great works through him.

We understand that the Holy Spirit is the energizing factor in the life of man. Whosoever receives this power is able to influence all with whom he comes into contact.

The greatest philosophers without this Spirit are powerless, their souls lifeless, their hearts dead! Unless the Holy Spirit breathes into their souls, they can do no good work. No system of philosophy has ever been able to change the manners and customs of a people for the better. Learned philosophers, unenlightened by the Divine Spirit, have often been men of inferior morality; they have not proclaimed in their actions the reality of their beautiful phrases.

The difference between spiritual philosophers and others is shown by their lives. The Spiritual Teacher shows His belief in His own teaching, by Himself being what He recommends to others.

An humble man without learning, but filled with the Holy Spirit, is more powerful than the most nobly-born profound scholar, without that inspiration. He who is educated by the Divine Spirit can, in his time, lead others to receive the same Spirit.

I pray for you that you may be informed by the life of the Divine Spirit, so that you may be the means of educating others. The life and morals of a spiritual man are, in themselves, an education to those who know him.

Think not of your own limitations, dwell only on the welfare of the Kingdom of Glory. Consider the influence of Jesus Christ on His apostles, then think of their effect upon the world. These simple men were enabled by the power of the Holy Spirit to spread the glad tidings!

So may you all receive Divine assistance! No capacity is limited when led by the Spirit of God!

The earth of itself has no properties of life, it is barren and dry, until fertilized by the sun and the rain; still the earth need not bewail its own limitations.

May you be given life! May the rain of the Divine Mercy and the warmth of the Sun of Truth make your gardens fruitful, so that many beautiful flowers of exquisite fragrance and love may blossom in abundance. Turn your faces away from the contemplation of your own finite selves and fix your eyes upon the Everlasting Radiance; then will your souls receive in full measure the Divine Power of the Spirit and the Blessings of the Infinite Bounty.

If you thus keep yourselves in readiness, you will become to the world of humanity a burning flame, a star of guidance, and a fruitful tree, changing all its darkness and woe into light and joy by the shining of the Sun of Mercy and the infinite blessings of the Glad Tidings.

This is the meaning of the Power of the Holy Spirit, which I pray may be bountifully showered upon you.

6. PAIN AND SORROW

¶ 205. In this world we are influenced by two sentiments, Joy and Pain.

Joy gives us wings! In times of joy our strength is more vital, our intellect keener, and our understanding less clouded. We seem better able to cope with the world and to find our sphere of usefulness. But when sadness visits us we become weak, our strength leaves us, our comprehension is dim and our intelligence veiled. The actualities of life seem to elude our grasp, the eyes of our spirits fail to discover the sacred mysteries, and we become even as dead beings.

There is no human being untouched by these two influences; but all the sorrow and the grief that exist come from the world of matter—the spiritual world bestows only the joy!

If we suffer it is the outcome of material things, and all the trials and troubles come from this world of illusion.

For instance, a merchant may lose his trade and depression ensues. A workman is dismissed and starvation stares him in the face. A farmer has a bad harvest, anxiety fills his mind. A man builds a house which is burnt to the ground and he is straightway homeless, ruined, and in despair.

All these examples are to show you that the trials which beset our every step, all our sorrow, pain, shame and grief, are born in the world of matter; whereas the spiritual Kingdom never causes sadness. A man living with his thoughts in this Kingdom knows perpetual joy. The ills all flesh is heir to do not pass him by, but they only touch the surface of his life, the depths are calm and serene.

Today, humanity is bowed down with trouble, sorrow and grief, no one escapes; the world is wet with tears; but, thank God, the remedy is at our doors. Let us turn our hearts away from the world of matter and live in the spiritual world! It alone can give us freedom! If we are hemmed in by difficulties we have only to call upon God, and by His great Mercy we shall be helped.

If sorrow and adversity visit us, let us turn our faces to the Kingdom and heavenly consolation will be outpoured.

If we are sick and in distress let us implore God's healing, and He will answer our prayer.

When our thoughts are filled with the bitterness of this world, let us turn our eyes to the sweetness of God's compassion and He will send us heavenly calm! If we are imprisoned in the material world, our spirit can soar into the Heavens and we shall be free indeed!

When our days are drawing to a close let us think of the eternal worlds, and we shall be full of joy!

You see all round you proofs of the inadequacy of material things—how joy, comfort, peace and consolation are not to be found in the transitory things of the world. Is it not then foolishness to refuse to seek these treasures where they may be found? The doors of the Spiritual Kingdom are open to all, and without is absolute darkness.

Thank God that you in this assembly have this knowledge, for in all the sorrows of life you can obtain supreme consolation. If your days on earth are numbered, you know that everlasting life awaits you. If material anxiety envelopes you in a dark cloud, spiritual radiance lightens your path. Verily, those whose minds are illumined by the Spirit of the Most High have supreme consolation.

I myself was in prison forty years—one year alone would have been impossible to bear—nobody survived that imprisonment more than a year! But, thank God, during all those forty years I was supremely happy! Every day, on waking, it was like hearing good tidings, and every night infinite joy was mine. Spirituality was my comfort, and turning to God was my greatest joy. If this had not been so, do you think it possible that I could have lived through those forty years in prison?

Thus, spirituality is the greatest of God's gifts, and "Life Everlasting" means "Turning to God". May you, one and all, increase daily in spirituality, may you be strengthened in all goodness, may you be helped more and more by the Divine consolation, be made free by the Holy Spirit of God, and may the power of the Heavenly Kingdom live and work among you.

This is my earnest desire, and I pray to God to grant you this favour.

7. HEALING BY SPIRITUAL MEANS

¶ 206. Know that there are four kinds of curing and healing without medicine. Two are due to material causes, and two to spiritual causes.

Of the two kinds of material healing, one is due to the fact that in man both health and sickness are contagious. The contagion of disease is violent and rapid, while that of health is extremely weak and slow. If two bodies are brought into contact with each other, it is certain that microbic particles will pass from one to the other. In the same way that disease is transferred from one body to another with rapid and strong contagion, it may be that the strong health of a healthy man will alleviate a very slight malady in a sick person. That is to say, the contagion of disease is violent and has a rapid effect, while that of health is very slow and has a small effect, and it is only in very slight diseases that it has even this small effect. The strong power of a healthy body can overcome a slight weakness of a sick body, and health results. This is one kind of healing.

The other kind of healing without medicine is through the magnetic force which acts from one body on another, and becomes the cause of cure. This force also has only a slight effect. Sometimes one can benefit a sick person by placing one's hand upon his head or upon his heart. Why? Because of the effect of the magnetism, and of the mental impression made upon the sick person which causes the disease to vanish. But this effect is also very slight and weak.

Of the two other kinds of healing which are spiritual—that is to say, where the means of cure is a spiritual power—one results from the entire concentration of the mind of a strong person upon a sick person, when the latter expects with all his concentrated faith that a cure will be effected from the spiritual power of the strong person, to such an extent that there will be a cordial connection between the strong person and the invalid. The strong person makes every effort to cure the sick patient, and the sick patient is then sure of receiving a cure. From the effect of these mental impressions an excitement of the nerves is produced, and this impression and this excitement of the nerves will become the cause of the recovery of the sick person. So when a sick person has a strong desire and intense hope for something, and hears suddenly the tidings of its realization, a nervous excitement is produced, which will make the malady entirely disappear. In the same way, if a cause of terror suddenly occurs, perhaps an excitement may be produced in the nerves of a strong person, which will immediately cause a malady. The cause of the sickness will be no material thing, for that person has not eaten anything, and nothing harmful has touched him; the excitement of the nerves is then the only cause of the illness. In the same way the sudden realization of a chief desire will give such joy that the nerves will be excited by it, and this excitement may produce health.

To conclude, the complete and perfect connection between the spiritual doctor and the sick person—that is, a connection of such a kind that the spiritual doctor entirely concentrates himself, and all the attention of the sick person is given to the spiritual doctor from whom he expects to realize health—causes an excitement of the nerves, and health is produced. But all this has effect only to a certain extent, and that not always. For if some one is afflicted with a very violent disease, or is wounded, these means will not remove the disease nor close and heal the wound. That is to say, these means have no power in severe maladies, unless the constitution helps, because a strong constitution often overcomes disease. This is the third kind of healing.

But the fourth kind of healing is produced through the power of the Holy Spirit. This does not depend on contact, nor on sight, nor upon presence; it is not dependent upon any condition. Whether the disease be light or severe, whether there be a contact of bodies or not, whether a personal connection be established between the sick person and the healer or not, this healing takes place through the power of the Holy Spirit.

8. REINCARNATION

¶ 207. The object of what we are about to say is to explain the reality—not to deride the beliefs of other people; it is only to explain the facts, that is all. We do not oppose any one's ideas, nor do we approve of criticism.

Know, then, that those who believe in reincarnation are of two classes: one class does not believe in the spiritual punishments and rewards of the other world, and they suppose that man by reincarnation, and return to this world, gains rewards and recompenses; they consider heaven and hell to be restricted to this world, and do not speak of the existence of the other world. Among these there are two further divisions: one division thinks that man sometimes returns to this world in the form of an animal, in order to undergo severe punishment, and that, after enduring this painful torment, he will be released from the animal world and will come again into the human world; this is called transmigration. The other division thinks that from the human world one again returns to the human world, and that by this return rewards and punishments for a former life are obtained; this is called reincarnation. Neither of these classes speak of any other world besides this one.

The second sort of believers in reincarnation affirm the existence of the other world, and they consider reincarnation the means of becoming perfect; that is, they think that man, by going from and coming again to this world, will gradually acquire perfections, until he reaches the inmost perfection. In other words, that men are composed of matter and force; matter in the beginning, that is to say in the first cycle, is imperfect, but on coming repeatedly to this world it progresses, and acquires refinement and delicacy, until it becomes like a polished mirror; and force, which is no other than spirit, is realized in it with all the perfections.

This is the presentation of the subject by those who believe in reincarnation and transmigration. We have condensed it; if we entered into the details it would take much time; this summary is sufficient. No logical arguments and proofs of this question are brought forward; they are only supposition and inferences from conjectures, and not conclusive arguments. Proofs must be asked for from the believers in reincarnation, and not conjectures, suppositions, and imaginations.

But you have asked for arguments of the impossibility of reincarnation; this is what we must now explain. The first argument for its impossibility, is that the outward is the expression of the inward; the earth is the mirror of the Kingdom; the material world corresponds to the spiritual world. Now observe that in the sensible world, appearances are not repeated, for no being in any respect is identical with, nor the same as, another being. The sign of singleness is visible and apparent in all things. If all the granaries of the world were full of grain, you would not find two grains absolutely alike, the same and identical without any distinction. It is certain that there will be differences and distinctions between them. As the proof of uniqueness exists in all things, and the Oneness and Unity of God is apparent in the reality of all things, the repetition of the same appearance is absolutely impossible. Therefore reincarnation, which is the repeated appearance of the same spirit with its former essence and condition in this same world of appearance, is impossible and unrealizable. As the repetition of the same appearance is impossible and interdicted for each of the material beings, so for spiritual beings also, a return to the same condition, whether in the arc of descent or in the arc of ascent, is interdicted and impossible for the material corresponds to the spiritual.

Nevertheless, the return of material beings with regard to species is evident; so, the trees which during former years brought forth leaves, blossoms, and fruits, in the coming years will bring forth exactly the same leaves, blossoms, and fruits. This is called the repetition of species. If any one makes an objection saying that the leaf, the blossom, and the fruit have been decomposed, and have descended from the vegetable world to the mineral world, and again have come back from the mineral world to the vegetable world, and therefore there has been a repetition—the answer is, that the blossom, the leaf, and the fruit of last year were decomposed, and these combined elements were disintegrated and were dispersed in space; and that the particles of the leaf and fruit of last year, after decomposition, have not again become combined, and have not returned. On the contrary, by the composition of new elements, the species has returned. It is the same with the human body, which after decomposition becomes disintegrated, and the elements which composed it are dispersed. If, in like manner, this body should again return from the mineral or vegetable world, it would not have exactly the same composition of elements as the former man; those elements have been decomposed and dispersed; they are dissipated in this vast space. Afterwards, other particles of elements have been combined, and a second body has been formed; it may be that one of the particles of the former individual has entered into the composition of the succeeding individual; but these particles have not been conserved and kept, exactly and completely, without addition or diminution, so that they may be combined again, and from that composition and mingling another individual may come into existence. So it cannot be proved that this body with all its particles has returned, that the former man has become the latter, and that consequently there has been repetition; that the spirit also, like the body, has returned, and that after death its essence has come back to this world.

If we say that this reincarnation is for acquiring perfections, so that matter may become refined and delicate, and that the light of the spirit may be manifest in it with the greatest perfection, this also is mere imagination. For, even supposing we believe in this argument, still change of nature is impossible through renewal and return: the essence of imperfection, by returning, does not become the reality of perfection; complete darkness, by returning, does not become the source of light; the essence of weakness is not transformed into power and might by returning, and an earthly nature does not become a heavenly reality. The tree of Zaqqum,[1] no matter how frequently it may come back, will not bring forth sweet fruit, and the good tree, no matter how often it may return, will not bear a bitter fruit. Therefore it is evident that returning and coming back to the material world does not become the cause of perfection. This theory has no proofs nor evidences, it is simply an idea. No, in reality the cause of acquiring perfections is the bounty of God.

[1] The infernal tree mentioned in the Qur'án.

The Theosophists believe that man on the arc of ascent[1] will return many times, until he reaches the supreme centre; in that condition matter becomes a clear mirror, the light of the spirit will shine upon it with its full power, and essential perfection will be acquired. Now, this is an established and deep theological proposition, that the material worlds are terminated at the end of the arc of descent, and that the condition of man is at the end of the arc of descent, and at the beginning of the arc of ascent, which is opposite to the Supreme Centre. Also from the beginning to the end of the arc of ascent, there are numerous spiritual degrees. The arc of descent is called beginning,[2] and that of ascent is called progress,[3] The arc of descent ends in materialities, and the arc of ascent ends in spiritualities. The point of the compass in describing a circle makes no retrograde motion, for this would be contrary to the natural movement and the divine order; otherwise the symmetry of the circle would be spoilt.

Moreover, this material world has not such value or such excellence that man, after having escaped from this cage, will desire a second time to fall into this snare. No, through the Eternal Bounty the worth and true ability of man becomes apparent and visible by traversing the degrees of existence, and not by returning. When the shell is once opened, it will be apparent, and evident whether it contains a pearl or worthless matter. When once the plant has grown it will bring forth either thorns or flowers; there is no need for it to grow up again. Besides, advancing and moving in the worlds in a direct order according to the natural law, is the cause of existence; and a movement contrary to the system and law of nature is the cause of non-existence. The return of the soul after death is contrary to the natural movement, and opposed to the divine system.

Therefore, by returning, it is absolutely impossible to obtain existence; it is as if man, after being freed from the womb, should return to it a second time. Consider what a puerile imagination this is which is implied by the belief in reincarnation and transmigration. Believers in it consider the body as a vessel, in which the spirit is contained, as water is contained in a cup; this water has been taken from one cup and poured into another. This is child's play. They do

---

[1] i.e. of the Circle of Existence.   [2] Lit. bringing forth.
[3] Lit. producing something new.

not realize that the spirit is an incorporeal being, and does not enter and come forth, but is only connected with the body, as the sun is with the mirror. If it were thus, and the spirit by returning to this material world could pass through the degrees, and attain to essential perfection, it would be better if God prolonged the life of the spirit in the material world, until it had acquired perfections and graces; it then would not be necessary for it to taste of the cup of death, or to acquire a second life.

The idea that existence is restricted to this perishable world, and the denial of the existence of divine worlds, originally proceeded from the imaginations of certain believers in reincarnation; but the divine worlds are infinite. If the divine worlds culminated in this material world, creation would be futile: nay, existence would be pure child's play. The result of these endless beings, which is the noble existence of man, would come and go for a few days in this perishable dwelling, and after receiving punishments and rewards, at last all would become perfect. The divine creation of the infinite existing beings would be perfected and completed, and then the Divinity of the Lord, and the names and qualities of God, on behalf of these spiritual beings, would, as regards their effect, result in laziness and inaction! "Glory to thy Lord, the Lord who is sanctified from all their descriptions."

Such were the limited minds of the former philosophers, like Ptolemy and the others who believed and imagined that the world, life, and existence, were restricted to this terrestrial globe, and that this boundless space was confined within the nine spheres of heaven, and that all were empty and void. Consider how greatly their thoughts were limited and how weak their minds. Those who believe in reincarnation think that the spiritual worlds are restricted to the worlds of human imagination. Moreover, some of them, like the Druses and Nusairis, think that existence is restricted to this physical world. What an ignorant supposition! For, in this universe of God, which appears in the most complete perfection, beauty, and grandeur, the luminous stars of the material universe are innumerable. Then we must reflect how limitless and infinite are the spiritual worlds, which are the essential foundation. "Be attentive, O people of insight."

But let us return to our subject. In the Divine Scriptures and Holy Books "return" is spoken of, but the ignorant have not understood the meaning, and those who believed in reincarnation have made conjectures on the subject. For what the divine Prophets meant by "return" is not the return of the essence, but that of the qualities; it is not the return of the Manifestation, but that of the perfections. In the Gospel it says that John the son of Zacharias is Elias. These words do not mean the return of the rational soul and personality of Elias in the body of John, but rather that the perfections and qualities of Elias were manifested and appeared in John.

A lamp shone in this room last night, and when tonight another lamp shines, we say the light of last night is again shining. Water flows from a fountain, then it ceases, and when it begins to flow a second time, we say, this water is the same water flowing again; or we say, this light is identical with the former light. It is the same with the spring of last year, when blossoms, flowers, and sweet-scented herbs bloomed, and delicious fruits were brought forth; next year we say that those delicious fruits have come back, and those blossoms, flowers, and blooms have returned and come again. This does not mean that exactly the same particles composing the flowers of last year have, after decomposition, been again combined, and have then come back and returned. On the contrary, the meaning is that the delicacy, freshness, delicious perfume, and wonderful colour of the flowers of last year are visible and apparent in exactly the same manner in the flowers of this year. Briefly, this expression refers only to the resemblance and likeness which exist between the former and latter flowers. The "return" which is mentioned in the Divine Scriptures is this: it is fully explained by the Supreme Pen[1] in the Kitáb-i-Íqán; refer to it, so that you may be informed of the truth of the divine mysteries.

Upon you be greetings and praise.

9. IMMORTALITY OF CHILDREN

¶ 208. *Question:* What is the condition of children who die before attaining the age of discretion, or before the appointed time of birth?

Answer: These infants are under the shadow of the favour of God; and as they have not committed any sin, and are not soiled with the

[1] Bahá'u'lláh.

impurities of the world of nature, they are the centres of the manifestation of bounty, and the Eye of Compassion will be turned upon them.

10. PSYCHIC FORCES

¶ 209. To tamper with psychic forces while in this world interferes with the condition of the soul in the world to come. These forces are real, but, normally, are not active on this plane. The child in the womb has its eyes, ears, hands, feet, etc., but they are not in activity. The whole purpose of life in the material world is the coming forth into the world of Reality, where those forces will become active. They belong to that world.

11. PERFECTIONS ARE WITHOUT LIMIT

¶ 210. Know that the conditions of existence are limited to the conditions of servitude, of prophethood, and of Deity, but the divine and the contingent perfections are unlimited. When you reflect deeply, you discover that also outwardly the perfections of existence are also unlimited, for you cannot find a being so perfect that you cannot imagine a superior one. For example, you cannot see a ruby in the mineral kingdom, a rose in the vegetable kingdom, or a nightingale in the animal kingdom, without imagining that there might be better specimens. As the divine bounties are endless, so human perfections are endless. If it were possible to reach a limit of perfection, then one of the realities of the beings might reach the condition of being independent of God, and the contingent might attain to the condition of the absolute. But for every being there is a point which it cannot overpass; that is to say, he who is in the condition of servitude, however far he may progress in gaining limitless perfections, will never reach the condition of Deity. It is the same with the other beings: a mineral, however far it may progress in the mineral kingdom, cannot gain the vegetable power; also in a flower, however far it may progress in the vegetable kingdom, no power of the senses will appear. So this silver mineral cannot gain hearing or sight; it can only improve in its own condition, and become a perfect mineral, but it cannot acquire the power of growth, or the power of sensation, or attain to life; it can only progress in its own condition.

For example, Peter cannot become Christ. All that he can do is, in the condition of servitude, to attain endless perfections; for every existing reality is capable of making progress. As the spirit of man after putting off this material form has an everlasting life, certainly any existing being is capable of making progress; therefore it is permitted to ask for advancement, forgiveness, mercy, beneficence, and blessings for a man after his death, because existence is capable of progression. That is why in the prayers of Bahá'u'lláh forgiveness and remission of sins are asked for those who have died. Moreover, as people in this world are in need of God, they will also need Him in the other world. The creatures are always in need, and God is absolutely independent, whether in this world or in the world to come.

The wealth of the other world is nearness to God. Consequently it is certain that those who are near the Divine Court are allowed to intercede, and this intercession is approved by God. But intercession in the other world is not like intercession in this world: it is another thing, another reality, which cannot be expressed in words.

If a wealthy man at the time of his death bequeaths a gift to the poor and miserable, and gives a part of his wealth to be spent for them, perhaps this action may be the cause of his pardon and forgiveness, and of his progress in the Divine Kingdom.

Also a father and mother endure the greatest troubles and hardships for their children; and often when the children have reached the age of maturity, the parents pass on to the other world. Rarely does it happen that a father and mother in this world see the reward of the care and trouble they have undergone for their children. Therefore children, in return for this care and trouble, must show forth charity and beneficence, and must implore pardon and forgiveness for their parents. So you ought, in return for the love and kindness shown you by your father, to give to the poor for his sake, with greatest submission and humility implore pardon and remission of sins, and ask for the supreme mercy.

It is even possible that the condition of those who have died in sin and unbelief may become changed; that is to say, they may become the object of pardon through the bounty of God, not through His justice; for bounty is giving without desert, and justice is giving what is deserved. As we have power to pray for these souls here, so likewise we shall possess the same power in the other world, which is the Kingdom of God. Are not all the people in that world the creatures of God? Therefore in that world also they can make progress. As here they can receive light by their supplications, there also they can plead for forgiveness, and receive light through entreaties and supplications. Thus as souls in this world, through the help of the supplications, the entreaties, and the prayers of the holy ones, can acquire development, so is it the same after death. Through their own prayers and supplications they can also progress; more especially when they are the object of the intercession of the Holy Manifestations.

XVI. SOME ETHICAL AND SOCIAL
TEACHINGS

1. 'ABDU'L-BAHÁ'S FIRST PUBLIC ADDRESS IN THE WEST

❡ 211. O noble friends; seekers after God!

Praise be to God! Today the light of Truth is shining upon the world in its abundance; the breezes of the heavenly garden are blowing throughout all regions; the call of the Kingdom is heard in all lands, and the breath of the Holy Spirit is felt in all hearts that are faithful. The Spirit of God is giving eternal life. In this wonderful age the East is enlightened, the West is fragrant, and everywhere the soul inhales the holy perfume. The sea of the unity of mankind is lifting up its waves with joy, for there is real communication between the hearts and minds of men. The banner of the Holy Spirit is uplifted, and men see it, and are assured with the knowledge that this is a new day.

This is a new cycle of human power. All the horizons of the world are luminous, and the world will become indeed as a garden and a paradise. It is the hour of unity of the sons of men and of the drawing together of all races and all classes. You are loosed from ancient superstitions which have kept men ignorant, destroying the foundations of true humanity.

The gift of God to this enlightened age is the knowledge of the oneness of mankind and of the fundamental oneness of religion. War shall cease between nations, and by the will of God the Most Great Peace shall come; the world will be seen as a new world, and all men will live as brothers.

In the days of old an instinct for warfare was developed in the struggle with wild animals; this is no longer necessary; nay, rather, co-operation and mutual understanding are seen to produce the greatest welfare of mankind. Enmity is now the result of prejudice only.

In the "Hidden Words" Bahá'u'lláh says "Justice is to be loved above all." Praise be to God, in this country the standard of justice has been raised; a great effort is being made to give all souls an equal and a true place. This is the desire of all noble natures; this is today the teaching for the East and for the West; therefore the East and the West ᵛill understand each other and reverence each other, and embrace like long-parted lovers who have found each other.

There is one God; mankind is one; the foundations of religion are one. Let us worship Him, and give praise for all His great Prophets and Messengers who have manifested His brightness and glory.

The blessings of the Eternal One be with you in all richness, that each soul according to his measure may take freely of Him. Amen.

2. THE WORLD IS INFIRM

¶ 212. O ye friends of God! The world is like the body of man— it hath become sick, feeble and infirm. Its eye is devoid of sight, its ear hath become destitute of hearing and its faculties of sense are entirely dissolved. The friends of God must become as wise physicians and care for and heal this sick person, in accord with the divine teachings, in order that—God willing—it may perchance gain health, find eternal healing and that its lost powers may be restored; and that the person of the world may find such health, freshness and purity that it will appear in the utmost beauty and charm.

The first remedy is to guide the people, so that they may turn unto God, hearken unto the divine commandments and go forth with a hearing ear and seeing eye. After this swift and certain remedy hath been applied, then according to the divine teachings, they ought to be trained in the conduct, morals and deeds of the Supreme Concourse, encouraged and inspired with the gifts of the Kingdom of Abhá. The hearts should be purified and cleansed from every trace of hatred and rancour and enabled to engage in truthfulness, conciliation, uprightness and love toward the world of humanity; so that the East and the West may embrace each other like unto two lovers, enmity and animosity may vanish from the human world and the universal peace be established!

O ye friends of God! Be kind to all peoples and nations, have love for all of them, exert yourselves to purify the hearts as much as you can, and bestow abundant effort in rejoicing the souls. Be ye a sprinkling of rain to every meadow and a water of life to every tree. Be ye as fragrant musk to every nostril and a soul-refreshing breeze to every invalid. Be ye salutary water to every thirsty one, a wise guide to every one led astray, an affectionate father or mother to every orphan, and, in the utmost joy and fragrance, a son or daughter to every one bent with age. Be ye a rich treasure to every indigent one; consider love and union as a delectable paradise, and count annoyance and hostility as the torment of hell-fire. Exert with your soul; seek no rest in body; supplicate and beseech with your heart and search for divine assistance and favour, in order that ye may make this world the Paradise of Abhá and this terrestrial globe the arena of the Supreme Kingdom. If ye make an effort, it is certain that these lights will shine, this cloud of mercy shall rain, this soul-nourishing breeze shall waft, and the scent of this most fragrant musk be diffused.

3. DISPEL THIS DARKNESS

¶ 213. O people of the world!

The dawn of the Sun of Reality is assuredly for the illumination of the world and for the manifestation of mercy. In the assemblage of the family of Adam results and fruits are praiseworthy, and the holy bestowals of every bounty are abundant. It is an absolute mercy and a complete bounty, the illumination of the world, fellowship and harmony, love and union; nay, rather, mercifulness and oneness, the elimination of discord and the unity of whosoever are on the earth in the utmost of freedom and dignity. The Blessed Beauty[1] said: "All are the fruits of one tree and the leaves of one branch." He likened the world of existence to one tree and all the souls to leaves, blossoms and fruits. Therefore all the branches, leaves, blossoms and fruits must be in the utmost of freshness, and the bringing about of this delicacy and sweetness depends upon union and fellowship. Therefore they must assist each other with all their power and seek everlasting life. Thus the friends of God must manifest the mercy of the Compassionate Lord in the world of existence and must show forth the bounty of the visible and invisible King. They must purify their sight, and look upon

[1] Bahá'u'lláh.

mankind as the leaves, blossoms and fruits of the tree of creation, and must always be thinking of doing good to someone, of love, consideration, affection and assistance to somebody. They must see no enemy and count no one as an ill wisher. They must consider every one on the earth as a friend; regard the stranger as an intimate, and the alien as a companion. They must not be bound by any tie, nay, rather, they should be free from every bond. In this day the one who is favoured in the threshhold of grandeur is the one who offers the cup of faithfulness and bestows the pearl of gift to the enemies, even to the fallen oppressor, lends a helping hand, and considers every bitter foe as an affectionate friend.

These are the commands of the Blessed Beauty, these are the counsels of the Greatest Name. O ye dear friends! The world is engaged in war and struggle, and mankind is in the utmost conflict and danger. The darkness of unfaithfulness has enshrouded the earth and the illumination of faithfulness has become concealed. All nations and tribes of the world have sharpened their claws and are warring and fighting with each other. The edifice of man is shattered. Thousands of families are wandering disconsolate. Thousands of souls are besmeared with dust and blood in the arena of battle and struggle every year, and the tent of happiness and life is overthrown. The prominent men become commanders and boast of bloodshed, and glory in destruction. One says: .'I have severed with my sword the necks of a nation," and one: "I have levelled a kingdom to the dust"; and another: "I have overthrown the foundation of a government." This is the pivot around which the pride and glory of mankind are revolving. In all regions friendship and uprightness are denounced and reconciliation and regard for truth are despised. The herald of peace, reformation, love and reconciliation is the Religion of the Blessed Beauty which has pitched its tent on the apex of the world and proclaimed its summons to the people.

Then, O ye friends of God! Appreciate the value of this precious Revelation, move and act in accordance with it and walk in the straight path and the right way. Show it to the people. Raise the melody of the Kingdom and spread abroad the teachings and ordinances of the loving Lord so that the world may become another world, the darkened earth may become illumined and the dead body of the people may obtain new life. Every soul may seek everlasting life through the breath of the Merciful. Life in this mortal world will quickly come to an end, and this earthly glory, wealth, comfort and happiness will soon vanish and be no more. Summon ye the people to God and call the souls to the manners and conduct of the Supreme Concourse. To the orphans be ye kind fathers, and to the unfortunate a refuge and shelter. To the poor be a treasure of wealth, and to the sick a remedy and healing. Be a helper of every oppressed one, the protector of every destitute one, be ye ever mindful to serve any soul of mankind. Attach no importance to self-seeking, rejection, arrogance, oppression and enmity. Heed them not. Deal in the contrary way. Be kind in truth, not only in appearance and outwardly. Every soul of the friends of God must concentrate his mind on this, that he may manifest the mercy of God and the bounty of the Forgiving One. He must do good to every soul whom he encounters, and render benefit to him, becoming the cause of improving the morals and correcting the thoughts so that the light of guidance may shine forth and the bounty of His Holiness the Merciful One may encompass. Love is light in whatsoever house it may shine and enmity is darkness in whatsoever abode it dwell.

O friends of God! Strive ye so that this darkness may be utterly dispelled and the Hidden Mystery may be revealed and the realities of things made evident and manifest.

4. O ARMY OF LIFE

¶ 214. O Army of Life! East and West have joined to worship stars of faded splendour, and have turned in prayer unto darkened horizons. Both have utterly neglected the broad foundation of God's sacred laws, and have grown unmindful of the merits and virtues of His religion. They have regarded certain customs and conventions as the basis of the Divine faith, and have firmly established themselves therein. They have imagined themselves as having attained a glorious pinnacle of achievement and prosperity, when in reality they have touched the innermost depths of heedlessness and deprived themselves wholly of God's bounteous gifts.

The cornerstone of the religion of God is the acquisition of divine perfections and the sharing in His manifold bestowals. The essential purpose of faith and belief is to ennoble the inner being of man with the outpourings of grace from on high. If this be not attained, it is, indeed, deprivation. It is the realization of this deprivation that is the true eternal fire.

Therefore, it is incumbent upon all Bahá'ís to ponder this delicate and vital matter in their hearts, that, unlike other religions, they may not content themselves with the noise, the clamour, the hollowness of religious doctrine. Nay, rather, they should exemplify in every aspect of their lives the attributes and virtues that are born of God, and should arise to distinguish themselves by their goodly behaviour. They should justify their claim to be Bahá'ís by deeds, not by name.

He is a true Bahá'í who strives by day and by night to progress and advance along the path of human endeavour, whose cherished desire is so to live and act as to enrich and illumine the world; whose source of inspiration is the Essence of Divine perfection; whose aim in life is to conduct himself so as to be the cause of infinite progress. Only when he attains unto such perfect gifts can it be said of him that he is a Bahá'í.

In this holy dispensation, the crowning glory of bygone ages and cycles, faith is no mere acknowledgement of the unity of God, but rather the living of a life that manifests the virtues and perfections implied in such belief.

His Holiness the exalted One, may my life be a sacrifice to Him, has shown us the way of behaviour, has guided us to the path of self-sacrifice, has taught us how to despise earthly rest and comfort, and how to lay down our lives for each other. That sanctioned Being, despite the loftiness of His position and the exaltation of His spirit, chose to be chained and fettered that we might obtain the light of divine guidance. All the days of His life He rested not for a moment. He sought no repose nor laid His head upon the couch of ease and security. His days were passed amid afflictions and suffering. How can we follow Him and yet remain idle and at ease?

O my friends, arise to tend the pure and widely-scattered seed planted in the hearts of men. Dedicate yourselves wholly to the service of humanity. Then will the world be turned into a paradise; then will the surface of the earth mirror forth the glory of the Abhá Kingdom. Should you fail in this, great will be your deprivation and grievous your loss.

O servant of truth, wouldst thou obtain the sovereignty of earth and heaven? Seek nought but true servitude upon the threshhold of the Abhá Beauty. Wouldst thou win the joy of liberty in this world and the next? Desire but submission unto His holy will. Wouldst thou discover the true way to God? Follow the path of His covenant. Wouldst thou behold the light of eternal splendour? Fix thy gaze upon His bountiful grace vouchsafed from the Abhá Kingdom.

5. HARMONY IN DIVERSITY

¶ 215. The Creator of all is One God.

From this same God all creation sprang into existence, and He is the one goal, towards which everything in Nature yearns. This conception was embodied in the words of Christ, when He said, "I am the Alpha and the Omega, the beginning and the end." Man is the sum of Creation, and the Perfect Man is the expression of the complete thought of the Creator—the Word of God.

Consider the world of created beings, how varied and diverse they are in species, yet with one sole origin. All the differences that appear are those of outward form and colour. This diversity of type is apparent throughout the whole of Nature.

Behold a beautiful garden full of flowers, shrubs and trees. Each flower has a different charm, a peculiar beauty, its own delicious perfume and beautiful colour. The trees too, how varied are they in size, in growth, in foliage—and what different fruits they bear! Yet all these flowers, shrubs and trees spring from the self-same earth, the same sun shines upon them and the same clouds give them rain.

So is it with humanity. It is made up of many races, and its peoples are of different colour, white, black, yellow, brown and red—but they all come from the same God, and all are servants to Him. This diversity among the children of men has unhappily not the same effect as it has among the vegetable creation, where the spirit shown is more harmonious. Among men exists the diversity of animosity, and it is this that causes war and hatred among the different nations of the world.

Differences which are only those of blood also cause them to destroy and kill one another. Alas! that this should still be so. Let us look rather at the beauty in diversity, the beauty of harmony, and learn a lesson from the vegetable creation. If you beheld a garden in which all the plants were the same as to form, colour and perfume, it would not seem beautiful to you at all, but, rather monotonous and dull. The garden which is pleasing to the eye and which makes the heart glad, is the garden in which are growing side by side flowers of every hue, form and perfume, and the joyous contrast of colour is what makes for charm and beauty. So is it with trees. An orchard full of fruit trees is a delight; so is a plantation planted with many species of shrubs. It is just the diversity and variety that constitutes its charm; each flower, each tree, each fruit, besides being beautiful in itself, brings out by contrast the qualities of the others, and shows to advantage the special loveliness of each and all.

Thus should it be among the children of men! The diversity in the human family should be the cause of love and harmony, as it is in music where many different notes blend together in the making of a perfect chord. If you meet those of different race and colour to yourself, do not mistrust them and withdraw yourself into your shell of conventionality, but rather be glad and show them kindness. Think of them as different coloured roses growing in the beautiful garden of humanity, and rejoice to be among them.

Likewise, when you meet those whose opinions differ from your own, do not turn away your face from them. All are seeking truth, and there are many roads leading thereto. Truth has many aspects, but it remains always and for ever one.

Do not allow difference of opinion, or diversity of thought to separate you from your fellow-men, or to be the cause of dispute, hatred and strife in your hearts.

Rather, search diligently for the Truth and make all men your friends.

Every edifice is made of many different stones, yet each depends on the other to such an extent that if one were displaced the whole building would suffer; if one is faulty the structure is imperfect.

Bahá'u'lláh has drawn the circle of unity, he has made a design for the uniting of all the peoples, and for the gathering of them all under the shelter of the tent of universal unity. This is the work of the Divine Bounty, and we must all strive with heart and soul until we have the reality of unity in our midst, and as we work, so will strength be given unto us. Leave all thought of self, and strive only to be obedient and submissive to the Will of God. In this way only shall we become citizens of the Kingdom of God, and attain into life everlasting.

6. SOME BAHÁ'Í PRINCIPLES

¶ 216. Truth may be likened to the sun! The sun is the luminous body that disperses all shadows; in the same way does truth scatter the shadows of our imagination. As the Sun gives life to the body of humanity so does truth give life to their souls. Truth is a sun that rises from different points on the horizon.

Sometimes the sun rises from the centre of the horizon, then in summer it rises further north, in winter further south—but it is always the self-same sun, however different are the points of its rising.

In like manner truth is one, although its manifestations may be very different. Some men have eyes and see. These worship the sun, no matter from which point on the horizon it may dawn; and when the sun has left the winter sky to appear in the summer one, they know how to find it again. Others there are who worship only the spot from which the sun arose, and when it arises in its glory from another place they remain in contemplation before the spot of its former rising. Alas! these men are deprived of the blessings of the sun. Those who in truth adore the sun itself will recognize it from whatsoever dawning-place it may appear, and will straightway turn their faces towards its radiance.

We must adore the sun itself and not merely the place of its appearance. In the same way men of enlightened heart worship truth on whatever horizon it appears. They are not bound by personality, but they follow the truth, and are able to recognize it no matter from whence it may come. It is this same truth which helps humanity to progress, which gives life to all created beings, for it is the Tree of Life!

In his teaching Bahá'u'lláh gives us the explanation of truth, and I wish to speak to you briefly about this, for I see that you are capable of understanding.

i. The first principle of Bahá'u'lláh is:

THE SEARCH FOR TRUTH

Man must cut himself free from all prejudice and from the result of his own imagination, so that he may be able to search for truth unhindered. Truth is one in all religions, and by means of it the unity of the world can be realized.

All the peoples have a fundamental belief in common. Being one, truth cannot be divided, and the differences that appear to exist among the nations only result from their attachment to prejudice. If only men would search out truth, they would find themselves united.

ii. The second principle of Bahá'u'lláh is:

THE UNITY OF MANKIND

The one all-loving God bestows His divine Grace and Favour on all mankind; one and all are servants of the Most High, and His Goodness, Mercy and Loving Kindness are showered upon all His creatures. The Glory of Humanity is the heritage of each one.

All men are the leaves and fruit of one same tree, they are all branches of the tree of Adam, they all have the same origin. The same rain has fallen upon them all, the same warm sun makes them grow, they are all refreshed by the same breeze. The only differences that exist and that keep them apart are these: there are the children who need guidance, the ignorant to be instructed, the sick to be tended and healed; thus, I say that the whole of humanity is enveloped by the Mercy and Grace of God. As the Holy Writings tell us: All men are equal before God. He is no respecter of persons.

iii. The third principle of Bahá'u'lláh is:

RELIGION SHOULD BE THE CAUSE OF LOVE AND AFFECTION

Religion should unite all hearts and cause wars and disputes to vanish from the face of the earth, give birth to spirituality, and bring life and light to each heart. If religion becomes a cause of dislike, hatred and division, it were better to be without it, and to withdraw from such a religion would be a truly religious act. For it is clear that the purpose of a remedy is to cure; but if the remedy should only aggravate the complaint it had better be left alone. Any religion which is not a cause of love and unity is no religion. All the holy prophets were as doctors to the soul; they gave prescriptions for the healing of mankind; thus any remedy that causes disease does not come from the great and supreme Physician.

IV. The fourth principle of Bahá'u'lláh is:

THE UNITY OF RELIGION AND SCIENCE

We may think of Science as one wing and religion as the other; a bird needs two wings for flight, one alone would be useless. Any religion that contradicts science or that is opposed to it, is only ignorance—for ignorance is the opposite of knowledge.

Religion which consists only of rites and ceremonies of prejudice is not the truth. Let us earnestly endeavour to be the means of uniting religion and science.

'Alí, the son-in-law of Muḥammad, said: "That which is in conformity with science is also in conformity with religion." Whatever the intelligence of man cannot understand, religion ought not to accept. Religion and science walk hand in hand, and any religion contrary to science is not the truth.

V. The fifth principle of Bahá'u'lláh is:

PREJUDICES OF RELIGION, RACE OR SECT DESTROY THE FOUNDATION OF HUMANITY

All the divisions in the world, hatred, war and bloodshed, are caused by one or other of these prejudices.

The whole world must be looked upon as one single country, all the nations as one nation, all men as belonging to one race. Religions, races, and nations are all divisions of man's making only, and are necessary only in his thought; before God there are neither Persians, Arabs, French nor English; God is God for all, and to Him all creation is one. We must obey God, and strive to follow Him by leaving all our prejudices and bringing about peace on earth.

VI. The sixth principle of Bahá'u'lláh is:

EQUAL OPPORTUNITY OF THE MEANS OF EXISTENCE

Every human being has the right to live; they have a right to rest, and to a certain amount of well-being. As a rich man is able to live in his palace surrounded by luxury and the greatest comfort, so should a poor man be able to have the necessaries of life. Nobody should die of hunger; everybody should have sufficient clothing; one man should not live in excess while another has no possible means of existence.

Let us try with all the strength we have to bring about happier conditions, so that no single soul may be destitute.

vii. The seventh principle of Bahá'u'lláh is:

THE EQUALITY OF MEN—EQUALITY BEFORE THE LAW

The law must reign, and not the individual; thus will the world become a place of beauty and true brotherhood will be realized. Having attained solidarity, men will have found Truth.

viii. The eighth principle of Bahá'u'lláh is:

UNIVERSAL PEACE

A Supreme Tribunal shall be elected by the peoples and governments of every nation, where members from each country and government shall assemble in unity. All disputes shall be brought before this Court, its mission being to prevent war.

ix. The ninth principle of Bahá'u'lláh is:

THAT RELIGION SHOULD NOT CONCERN ITSELF WITH POLITICAL QUESTIONS

Religion is concerned with things of the spirit, politics with things of the world. Religion has to work with the world of thought, whilst the field of politics lies with the world of external conditions.

It is the work of the clergy to educate the people, to instruct them, to give them good advice and teaching so that they may progress spiritually. With political questions they have nothing to do.

x. The tenth principle of Bahá'u'lláh is:

EDUCATION AND INSTRUCTION OF WOMEN

Women have equal rights with men upon earth; in religion and in society they are a very important element. As long as women are prevented from attaining their highest possibilities, so long will men be unable to achieve the greatness which might be theirs.

XI. The eleventh principle of Bahá'u'lláh is:

THE POWER OF THE HOLY SPIRIT, BY WHICH ALONE SPIRITUAL DEVELOPMENT IS ACHIEVED

It is only by the breath of the Holy Spirit that spiritual development can come about. No matter how the material world may progress, no matter how splendidly it may adorn itself, it can never be anything but a lifeless body unless the soul is within, for it is the soul that animates the body; the body alone has no real significance. Deprived of the blessings of the Holy Spirit the material body would be inert.

Here are, very briefly explained, some of the principles of Bahá'u'lláh.

In short, it behoves us all to be lovers of truth. Let us seek her in every season and in every country, being careful never to attach ourselves to personalities. Let us see the Light wherever it shines, and may we be enabled to recognize the light of truth no matter where it may arise. Let us inhale the perfume of the rose from the midst of thorns which surround it; let us drink the running water from every pure Spring.

7. COLLECTIVE SECURITY

¶ 217. True civilization will unfurl it's banner in the midmost heart of the world whenever a certain number of its distinguished and high-minded sovereigns—the shining exemplars of devotion and determination—shall, for the good and happiness of all mankind, arise, with firm resolve and clear vision, to establish the Cause of Universal Peace. They must make the Cause of Peace the object of general consultation, and seek by every means in their power to establish a Union of the nations of the world. They must conclude a binding treaty and establish a covenant, the provisions of which shall be sound, inviolable and definite. They must proclaim it to all the world and obtain for it the sanction of all the human race. This supreme and noble undertaking—the real source of the peace and well-being of all the world—should be regarded as sacred by all that dwell on earth. All the forces of humanity must be mobilized to ensure the stability and permanence of this Most Great Covenant. In this all-embracing Pact the limits and frontiers of each and every nation should be clearly fixed, the principles underlying the relations of governments towards one another definitely laid down, and all international agreements and obligations ascertained. In like manner, the size of the armaments of every government should be strictly limited, for if the military forces of any nation should be allowed to increase, they will arouse the suspicion of others. The fundamental principle underlying this solemn Pact should be so fixed that if any government later violate any one of its provisions, all the governments on earth should arise to reduce it to utter submission, nay the human race as a whole should resolve, with every power at its disposal, to destroy that government. Should this greatest of all remedies be applied to the sick body of the world, it will assuredly recover from its ills and will remain eternally safe and secure.

A few, unaware of the power latent in human endeavour, consider this matter as highly impracticable, nay even beyond the scope of man's utmost efforts. Such is not the case, however. On the contrary, thanks to the unfailing grace of God, the loving kindness of His favoured ones, the unrivalled endeavours of wise and capable souls, and the thoughts and ideas of the peerless leaders of this age, nothing whatsoever can be regarded as unattainable. Endeavour, ceaseless endeavour, is required. Nothing short of an indomitable determination can possibly achieve it. Many a cause which past ages have regarded as purely visionary, yet in this day have become most easy and practicable. Why should this most great and lofty Cause—the day star of the firmament of true civilization and the cause of the glory, the advancement, the well-being and the success of all humanity—be regarded as impossible of achievement? Surely the day will come when it's beauteous light shall shed illumination upon the assemblage of man.

8. INDUSTRIAL JUSTICE

¶ 218. You have questioned me about strikes. This question is and will be for a long time the subject of great difficulties. Strikes are due to two causes. One is the extreme sharpness and rapacity of the capitalists and manufacturers; the other, the excesses, the avidity and ill-will of the workmen and artisans. It is therefore necessary to remedy these two causes.

But the principal cause of these difficulties lies in the laws of the present civilization; for they lead to a small number of individuals accumulating incomparable fortunes, beyond their needs, whilst the greater number remains destitute, stripped and in the greatest misery. This is contrary to justice, to humanity, to equity; it is the height of iniquity, the opposite to what causes divine satisfaction.

This contrast is peculiar to the world of man: with other creatures that is to say with nearly all animals, there is a kind of justice and equality. Thus in a shepherd's flock of sheep, in a troop of deer in the country, among the birds of the prairie, of the plain, of the hill or of the orchard, almost every animal receives a just share based on equality. With them such a difference in the means of existence is not to be found: so they live in the most complete peace and joy.

It is quite otherwise with the human species, which persists in the greatest error, and in absolute iniquity. Consider an individual who has amassed treasures by colonizing a country for his profit: he has obtained an incomparable fortune, and has secured profits and incomes which flow like a river, whilst a hundred thousand unfortunate people, weak and powerless, are in need of a mouthful of bread. There is neither equality nor brotherhood. So you see that general peace and joy are destroyed, the welfare of humanity is partially annihilated, and that collective life is fruitless. Indeed, fortune, honours, commerce, industry are in the hands of some industrials, whilst other people are submitted to quite a series of difficulties and to limitless troubles: they have neither advantages nor profits, nor comforts, nor peace.

Then rules and laws should be established to regulate the excessive fortunes of certain private individuals, and limit the misery of millions of the poor masses; thus a certain moderation would be obtained. However, absolute equality is just as impossible, for absolute equality in fortunes, honours, commerce, agriculture, industry would end in a want of comfort, in discouragement, in disorganization of the means of existence, and in universal disappointment: the order of the community would be quite destroyed. Thus, there is a great wisdom in the fact that equality is not imposed by law: it is, therefore, preferable for moderation to do its work. The main point is, by means of laws and regulations to hinder the constitution of the excessive fortunes of certain individuals, and to protect the essential needs of the masses. For instance, the manufacturers and the industrials heap up a treasure each day, and the poor artisans do not gain their daily sustenance: that is the height of iniquity, and no just man can accept it. Therefore, laws and regulations should be established which would permit the workmen to receive from the factory owner their wages and a share in the fourth or the fifth part of the profits, according to the capacity of the factory; or in some other way the body of workmen and the manufacturers should share equitably the profits and advantages. Indeed, the direction and administration of affairs come from the owner of the factory, and the work and labour, from the body of the workmen. In other words, the workmen should receive wages which assure them an adequate support, and when they cease work, becoming feeble or helpless, they should receive from the owner of the factory a sufficient pension. The wages should be high enough to satisfy the workmen with the amount they receive, so that they may be able to put a little aside for days of want and helplessness.

When matters will be thus fixed, the owner of the factory will no longer put aside daily a treasure which he has absolutely no need of (without taking into consideration that if the fortune is disproportionate, the capitalist succumbs under a formidable burden, and gets into the greatest difficulties and troubles; the administration of an excessive fortune is very difficult, and exhausts man's natural strength). And, the workmen and artisans will no longer be in the greatest misery and want, they will no longer be submitted to the worst privations at the end of their life.

It is, then, clear and evident that the reparation of excessive fortunes amongst a small number of individuals, while the masses are in misery is an iniquity and an injustice. In the same way, absolute equality would be an obstacle to life, to welfare, to order and to the peace of humanity. In such a question a just medium is preferable. It lies in the capitalists being moderate in the acquisition of their profits, and in their having a consideration for the welfare of the poor and needy; that is to say, that the workmen and artisans receive a fixed and established daily wage, and have a share in the general profits of the factory.

It would be well, with regard to the social rights of manufacturers, workmen and artisans, that laws be established, giving moderate profits to manufacturers, and to workmen the necessary means of existence and security for the future. Thus, when they become feeble and cease working, get old and helpless, and die leaving children under age, these children will not be annihilated by excess of poverty. And it is from the income of the factory itself, to which they have a right, that they will derive a little of the means of existence.

In the same way, the workmen should no longer rebel and revolt, nor demand beyond their rights; they should no longer go out on strike, they should be obedient and submissive, and not ask for impudent wages. But the mutual rights of both associated parties will be fixed and established according to custom by just and impartial laws. In case one of the two parties should transgress, the courts of justice would have to give judgment, and by an efficacious fine put an end to the transgression; thus order will be re-established, and the difficulties settled. The interference of courts of justice and of the Government in difficulties pending between manufacturers and workmen is legal, for the reason that current affairs between workmen and manufacturers cannot be compared with ordinary affairs between private persons, which do not concern the public, and with which the Government should not occupy itself. In reality, although they appear to be matters between private persons, these difficulties between patrons and workmen produce a general detriment; for commerce, industry, agriculture and the general affairs of the country are all intimately linked together. If one of these suffers an abuse, the detriment affects the mass. Thus the difficulties between workmen and manufacturers become a cause of general detriment.

The court of justice and the Government have therefore the right of interference. When a difficulty occurs between two individuals with reference to private rights, it is necessary for a third to settle the question: this is the part of the Government: then the question of strikes—which causes troubles in the country and are often connected with the excessive vexations of the workmen, as well as with the rapacity of manufacturers—how could it remain neglected?

Good God! is it possible that, seeing one of his fellow-creatures starving, destitute of everything, a man can rest and live comfortably in his luxurious mansion? He who meets another in the greatest misery, can he enjoy his fortune? That is why, in the Religion of God, it is prescribed and established that wealthy men each year give over a certain part of their fortune for the maintenance of the poor and unfortunate. That is the foundation of the Religion of God, and the most essential of the Commandments.

As now man is not forced nor obliged by the Government, if by the natural tendency of his good heart, with the greatest spirituality, he goes to this expense for the poor, this will be a thing very much praised, approved and pleasing.

Such is the meaning of the good works in the Divine Books and Tablets.

9. JUSTICE, CRIME, AND FORGIVENESS

¶ 219. There are two sorts of retributory punishments. One is vengeance, the other chastisement. Man has not the right to take vengeance, but the community has the right to punish the criminal; and this punishment is intended to warn and to prevent, so that no other person will dare to commit a like crime. This punishment is for the protection of man's rights, but it is not vengeance; vengeance appeases the anger of the heart by opposing one evil to another. This is not allowable; for man has not the right to take vengeance. But if criminals were entirely forgiven, the order of the world would be upset. So punishment is one of the essential necessities for the safety of communities, but he who is oppressed by a transgressor has not the right to take vengeance: on the contrary, he should forgive and pardon, for this is worthy of the world of man.

The communities must punish the oppressor, the murderer, the malefactor, so as to warn and restrain others from committing like crimes. But the most essential thing is that the people must be educated in such a way that no crimes will be committed; for it is possible to educate the masses so effectively that they will avoid and shrink from perpetrating crimes, so that the crime itself will appear to them as the greatest chastisement, the utmost condemnation and torment. Therefore no crimes which require punishment will be committed.

We must speak of things that are possible of performance in this world. There are many theories and high ideas on this subject, but they are not practicable; consequently we must speak of things that are feasible.

For example, if some one oppresses, injures, and wrongs another, and the wronged man retaliates, this is vengeance, and is censurable. If the son of 'Amru kills the son of Zaid, Zaid has not the right to kill the son of 'Amru; if he does so, this is vengeance. If 'Amru dishonours Zaid, the latter has not the right to dishonour 'Amru; if he does so, this is vengeance, and it is very reprehensible. No, rather he must return good for evil, and not only forgive, but also, if possible, be of service to his oppressor. This conduct is worthy of man: for what advantage does he gain by vengeance? The two actions are equivalent; if one action is reprehensible, both are reprehensible. The only difference is that one was committed first, the other later.

But the community has the right of defence and of self-protection; moreover, the community has no hatred nor animosity for the murderer: it imprisons or punishes him merely for the protection and security of others. It is not for the purpose of taking vengeance upon the murderer, but for the purpose of inflicting a punishment by which the community will be protected. If the community and the inheritors of the murdered one were to forgive and return good for evil, the cruel would be continually ill-treating others, and assassinations would continually occur. Vicious people, like wolves, would destroy the sheep of God. The community has no ill-will and rancour in the infliction of punishment, and it does not desire to appease the anger of the heart; its purpose is by punishment to protect others, so that no atrocious actions may be committed.

Thus when Christ said: "Whosoever shall smite thee on the right cheek, turn to him the left one also," it was for the purpose of teaching men not to take personal revenge. He did not mean that if a wolf should fall upon a flock of sheep and wish to destroy it, that the wolf should be encouraged to do so. No, if Christ had known that a wolf had entered the fold and was about to destroy the sheep, most certainly he would have prevented it.

As forgiveness is one of the attributes of the Merciful One, so also justice is one of the attributes of the Lord. The tent of existence is upheld upon the pillar of justice, and not upon forgiveness. The continuance of mankind depends upon justice and not upon forgiveness. So if, at present, the law of pardon were practised in all countries, in a short time the world would be disordered, and the foundations of human life would crumble. For example, if the governments of Europe had not withstood the notorious Attila, he would not have left a single living man.

Some people are like bloodthirsty wolves: if they see no punishment forthcoming, they will kill men merely for pleasure and diversion. One of the tyrants of Persia killed his tutor merely for the sake of making merry, for mere fun and sport. The famous Mutawakkil, ·the 'Abbasid, having summoned his ministers, councillors, and functionaries to his presence, let loose a box full of scorpions in the assembly, and forbade any one to move. When the scorpions stung those present, he burst forth into boisterous laughter.

To recapitulate: the constitution of the communities depends upon justice, not upon forgiveness. Then what Christ meant by forgiveness and pardon is not that, when nations attack you, burn your homes, plunder your goods, assault your wives, children, and relatives, and violate your honour, you should be submissive in the presence of these tyrannical foes, and allow them to perform all their cruelties and oppressions. No, the words of Christ refer to the conduct of two individuals towards each other: if one person assaults another, the injured one should forgive him. But the communities must protect the rights of man. So, if some one assaults, injures, oppresses, and wounds me, I will offer no resistance, and I will forgive him. But if a person wishes to assault Siyyid Manshádí[1] certainly I will prevent him. Although for the malefactor non-interference is apparently a kindness, it would be an oppression to Manshádí. If at this moment a wild Arab were to enter this place with a drawn sword, wishing to assault, wound, and kill you, most assuredly I would prevent him. If I abandoned you to the Arab,

[1] A Bahá'í sitting at the table.

that would not be justice but injustice. But, if he injure me person-ally, I would forgive him.

One thing remains to be said: it is that the communities are day and night occupied in making penal laws, and in preparing and organizing instruments and means of punishment. They build prisons, make chains and fetters, arrange places of exile and banish-ment, and different kinds of hardships and tortures, and think by these means to discipline criminals; whereas, in reality, they are causing destruction of morals and perversion of characters. The community, on the contrary, ought day and night to strive and endeavour with the utmost zeal and effort to accomplish the educa-tion of men, to cause them day by day to progress and to increase in science and knowledge, to acquire virtues, to gain good morals and to avoid vices, so that crimes may not occur. At the present time the contrary prevails; the community is always thinking of enforcing the penal laws, and of preparing means of punishment, instruments of death and chastisement, places for imprisonment and banishment; and they expect crimes to be committed. This has a demoralizing effect.

But if the community would endeavour to educate the masses, day by day knowledge and sciences would increase, the understand-ing would be broadened, the sensibilities developed, customs would become good, and morals normal; in one word, in all these classes of perfections there would be progress, and there would be fewer crimes.

It has been ascertained that among civilized peoples crime is less frequent than among uncivilized, that is to say, among those who have acquired the true civilization, which is divine civilization—the civilization of those who unite all the spiritual and material per-fections. As ignorance is the cause of crimes, the more knowledge and science increases, the more crimes will diminish. Consider how often murder occurs among the barbarians of Africa; they will even kill one another in order to eat each other's flesh and blood! Why do not such savageries occur in Switzerland? The reason is evident: it is because education and virtues prevent them.

Therefore the communities must think of preventing crimes, rather than of rigorously punishing them.

10. PRACTISE KINDNESS TO STRANGERS

¶ 220. When a man turns his face to God he finds sunshine everywhere. All men are his brothers. Let not conventionality cause you to seem cold and unsympathetic when you meet strange people from other countries. Do not look at them as though you suspected them of being evil-doers, thieves and boors. You think it necessary to be very careful, not to expose yourselves to the risk of making acquaintance with such, possibly, undesirable people.

I ask you not to think only of yourselves. Be kind to the strangers, whether come they from Turkey, Japan, Persia, Russia, China or any other country in the world.

Help to make them feel at home; find out where they are staying, ask if you may render them any service; try to make their lives a little happier.

In this way, even if, sometimes, what you at first suspected should be true, still go out of your way to be kind to them—this kindness will help them to become better.

After all, why should any foreign people be treated as strangers?

Let those who meet you know, without your proclaiming the fact, that you are indeed a Bahá'í.

Put into practice the Teaching of Bahá'u'lláh, that of kindness to all nations. Do not be content with showing friendship in words alone, let your heart burn with loving kindness for all who may cross your path.

Oh, you of the Western nations, be kind to those who come from the Eastern world to sojourn among you. Forget your conventionality when you speak with them; they are not accustomed to it. To Eastern peoples this demeanour seems cold, unfriendly. Rather let your manner be sympathetic. Let it be seen that you are filled with universal love. When you meet a Persian or any other stranger, speak to him as to a friend; if he seems to be lonely try to help him, give him of your willing service; if he be sad console him, if poor succour him, if oppressed rescue him, if in misery comfort him. In so doing you will manifest that not in words only, but in deed and in truth, you think of all men as your brothers.

What profit is there in agreeing that universal friendship is good, and talking of the solidarity of the human race as a grand ideal? Unless these thoughts are translated into the world of action, they are useless.

The wrong in the world continues to exist just because people talk only of their ideals, and do not strive to put them into practice. If actions took the place of words, the world's misery would very soon be changed into comfort.

A man who does great good, and talks not of it, is on the way to perfection.

The man who has accomplished a small good and magnifies it in his speech is worth very little.

If I love you, I need not continually speak of my love—you will know without any words. On the other hand if I love you not, that also will you know—and you would not believe me, were I to tell you in a thousand words, that I loved you.

People make much profession of goodness, multiplying fine words because they wish to be thought greater and better than their fellows, seeking fame in the eyes of the world. Those who do most good use fewest words concerning their actions.

The children of God do the works without boasting, obeying His laws.

My hope for you is that you will ever avoid tyranny and oppression; that you will work without ceasing till justice reigns in every land, that you will keep your hearts pure and your hands free from unrighteousness.

This is what the near approach to God requires from you, and this is what I expect of you.

11. KINDNESS TO ANIMALS

¶ 221. O ye friends of God! Ye must not only have kind and merciful feelings for mankind, but ye should also exercise the utmost kindness towards every living creature. The physical sensibilities and instincts are common to animal and man. Man is, however, negligent of this reality and imagines that sensibility is peculiar to mankind, therefore he practices cruelty to the animal. In reality what difference is there in physical sensations! Sensibility is the same whether you harm man or animal: there is no difference. Nay, rather, cruelty to the animal is more painful because man has a tongue and he sighs, complains and groans when he receives an injury and complains to the government and the government protects him from cruelty; but the poor animal cannot speak, it can neither show its suffering nor is it able to appeal to the government. If it is harmed a thousand times by man it is not able to defend itself in words nor can it seek justice or retaliate. Therefore one must be very considerate towards animals and show greater kindness to them than to man. Educate the children in their infancy in such a way that they may become exceedingly kind and merciful to the animals. If an animal is sick they should endeavour to cure it; if it is hungry, they should feed it; if it is thirsty, they should satisfy its thirst; if it is tired, they should give it rest.

Man is generally sinful and the animal is innocent; unquestionably one must be more kind and merciful to the innocent. The harmful animals, such as the bloodthirsty wolf, the poisonous snake and other injurious animals are excepted, because mercy towards these is cruelty to man, and other animals. For instance, if you show kindness to a wolf this becomes a tyranny to the sheep, for it may destroy an entire flock of sheep. If you give the opportunity to a mad dog it may be the cause of the destruction of a thousand animals and men. Therefore, sympathy to the ferocious animal is cruelty to the peaceful animal, so they should be done away with. To the blessed animals, however, the utmost kindness should be exercised: the more the better it will be.

This sympathy and kindness is one of the fundamental principles of the divine kingdom. Ye should pay great attention to this question.

12. BAHÁ'Í MARRIAGE

¶ 222. Among the majority of the people marriage consists of physical relationship and this union and relationship is temporary for at the end physical separation is destined and ordained. But the marriage of the people of Bahá must consist of both physical and spiritual relationship for both of them are intoxicated with the wine of one cup, are attracted by one Peerless Countenance, are quickened with one Life and are illumined with one Light. This is the spiritual relationship and everlasting union. Likewise in the physical world they are bound together with strong and unbreakable ties.

When relationship, union, and concord exist between the two from a physical and spiritual standpoint, that is the real union, therefore everlasting. But if the union is merely from the physical point of view, unquestionably it is temporal and at the end separation is inevitable.

Consequently when the people of Bahá desire to enter the sacred union of marriage, eternal connection and ideal relationship, spiritual and physical association of thoughts and conceptions of life must exist between them, so that in all the grades of existence, all the worlds of God, this union may continue for ever and ever, for this real union is a splendour of the light and love of God.

Likewise if the souls become real believers they will find themselves ushered into this exalted state of relationship, becoming the manifestors of the love of the Merciful and exhilarated with the cup of the love of God. Undoubtedly that union and relationship is eternal.

The souls who sacrifice self become detached from the perfections of the realm of man and free from the shackles of this ephemeral world, assuredly the splendours of the rays of divine union shall shine in their hearts and in the eternal paradise they shall find ideal relationship, union and happiness.

13. PRAYER

¶ 223. O thou spiritual friend! Thou hast asked the wisdom of prayer. Know thou that prayer is indispensable and obligatory, and man under no pretext whatsoever is excused from performing the prayer unless he be mentally unsound, or an insurmountable obstacle prevent him. The wisdom of prayer is this: That it causeth a connection between the servant and the True One, because in that state man with all heart and soul turneth his face towards His Highness the Almighty, seeking His association and desiring His love and compassion. The greatest happiness for a lover is to converse with his beloved, and the greatest gift for a seeker is to become familiar with the object of his longing; that is why with every soul who is attracted to the Kingdom of God, his greatest hope is to find an opportunity to entreat and supplicate before his Beloved, appeal for His mercy and grace and be immersed in the ocean of His utterance, goodness and generosity.

Besides all this, prayer and fasting is the cause of awakening and mindfulness and conducive to protection and preservation from tests.

14. OBLIGATION TO DELIVER THE MESSAGE

¶ 224. It is known and clear that today the unseen divine assistance encompasseth those who deliver the Message. And if the work of delivering the Message be neglected, the assistance shall be entirely cut off, for it is impossible that the friends of God could receive assistance unless they be engaged in delivering the Message.

15. CONSULTATION

¶ 225. The prime requisites for them that take counsel together are purity of motive, radiance of spirit, detachment from all else save God, attraction to His Divine Fragrances, humility and lowliness amongst His loved ones, patience and long-suffering in difficulties and servitude to His exalted Threshold. Should they be graciously aided to acquire these attributes, victory from the unseen Kingdom of Bahá shall be vouchsafed to them. In this day, Assemblies of consultation are of the greatest importance and a vital necessity. Obedience unto them is essential and obligatory. The members thereof must take counsel together in such wise that no occasion for ill-feeling or discord may arise. This can be attained when every member expresseth with absolute freedom his own opinion and setteth forth his argument. Should any one oppose, he must on no account feel hurt for not until matters are fully discussed can the right way be revealed. The shining spark of truth cometh forth only after the clash of differing opinions. If, after discussion, a decision be carried unanimously, well and good; but if, the Lord forbid, differences of opinion should arise, a majority of voices must prevail.

The first condition is absolute love and harmony amongst the members of the Assembly. They must be wholly free from estrangement and must manifest in themselves the Unity of God, for they are the waves of one sea, the drops of one river, the stars of one heaven, the rays of one sun, the trees of one orchard, the flowers of one garden. Should harmony of thought and absolute unity be non-existent, that gathering shall be dispersed and that Assembly be brought to naught. The second condition: They must, when coming together, turn their faces to the Kingdom on High and ask aid from the Realm of Glory. They must then proceed with the utmost devotion, courtesy, dignity, care and moderation to express their views. They must in every matter search out the truth and not insist upon their own opinion, for stubbornness and persistence in one's views will lead ultimately to discord and wrangling and the truth will remain hidden. The honoured members must with all freedom express their own thoughts and it is in no wise permissible for one to belittle the thought of another, nay, he must with moderation set forth the truth, and should differences of opinion arise a majority of voices must prevail, and all must obey and submit to the majority. It is again not permitted that any one of the honoured members object to or censure, whether in or out of the meeting, any decision arrived at previously, though that decision be not right for such criticism would prevent any decision from being enforced. In short, whatsoever thing is arranged in harmony and with love and purity of motive, its result is light, and should the least trace of estrangement prevail the result shall be darkness upon darkness. . .

If this be so regarded, that Assembly shall be of God, but otherwise it shall lead to coolness and alienation that proceed from the Evil One. Discussions must all be confined to spiritual matters that pertain to the training of souls, the instruction of children, the relief of the poor, the help of the feeble throughout all classes in the world, kindness to all peoples, the diffusion of the fragrances of God and the exaltation of His Holy Word. Should they endeavour to fulfil these conditions the Grace of the Holy Spirit shall be vouchsafed unto them, and that Assembly shall become the centre of the Divine blessings, the hosts of Divine confirmation shall come to their aid, and they shall day by day receive a new effusion of Spirit.

XVII. EXCERPTS FROM THE WILL AND TESTAMENT OF 'ABDU'L-BAHÁ

¶ 226. All praise to Him Who, by the Shield of His Covenant, hath guarded the Temple of His Cause from the darts of doubtfulness, Who by the Hosts of His Testament hath preserved the Sanctuary of His Most Beneficent Law and protected His Straight and Luminous Path, staying thereby the onslaught of the company of Covenant-breakers, that have threatened to subvert His Divine Edifice; Who hath watched over His Mighty Stronghold and All-glorious Faith, through the aid of men whom the slander of the slanderer affects not, whom no earthly calling, glory and power can turn aside from the Covenant of God and His Testament, established firmly by His clear and manifest words, writ and revealed by His All-glorious Pen and recorded in the Preserved Tablet.

Salutation and praise, blessing and glory rest upon that primal branch of the Divine and Sacred Lote-Tree, grown out, blest, tender, verdant and flourishing from the Twin Holy Trees; the most wondrous, unique and priceless pearl that doth gleam from out the twin surging seas; upon the offshoots of the Tree of Holiness, the twigs of the Celestial Tree, they that in the Day of the Great Dividing have stood fast and firm in the Covenant; upon the Hands (pillars) of the Cause of God that have diffused widely the Divine Fragrances, declared His Proofs, proclaimed His Faith, published abroad His Law, detached themselves from all things but Him, stood for righteousness in this world, and kindled the Fire of the Love of God in the very hearts and souls of His servants; upon them that have believed, rested assured, stood steadfast in His Covenant and followed the Light that after my passing shineth from the Dayspring of Divine Guidance—for behold! he is the blest and sacred bough that hath branched out from the Twin Holy Trees. Well is it with him that seeketh the shelter of his shade that shadoweth all mankind.

O ye beloved of the Lord! The greatest of all things is the protection of the True Faith of God, the preservation of His Law, safeguarding of His Cause and service unto His Word. Ten thousand souls have shed streams of their sacred blood in this path, their precious lives they offered in sacrifice unto Him, hastened wrapt in holy ecstasy unto the glorious field of martyrdom, upraised the Standard of God's Faith and writ with their life-blood upon the Tablet of the world the verses of His Divine Unity. The sacred breast of His Holiness, the Exalted One (may my life be a sacrifice unto Him) was made a target to many a dart of woe, and in Mázindarán, the Blessed feet of the Abhá Beauty (may my life be offered up for His loved ones) were so grievously scourged as to bleed and be sore wounded. His neck also was put into captive chains and His feet made fast in the stocks. In every hour, for a period of fifty years, a new trial and calamity befell Him and fresh afflictions and cares beset Him. One of them: after having suffered intense vicissitudes, He was made homeless and a wanderer and fell a victim to still new vexations and troubles. In 'Iráq, the Day-Star of the world was so exposed to the wiles of the people of malice as to be eclipsed in splendour. Later on He was sent an exile to the Great City (Constantinople) and thence to the Land of Mystery (Adrianople), whence, grievously wronged, He was eventually transferred to the Most Great Prison ('Akká). He Whom the world hath wronged (may my life be offered up for His loved ones) was four times banished from city to city, till at last condemned to perpetual confinement, He was incarcerated in this Prison, the prison of highway robbers, of brigands and of manslayers. All this is but one of the trials that have afflicted the Blessed Beauty, the rest being even as grievous as this.

According to the direct and sacred command of God we are forbidden to utter slander, are commanded to show forth peace and amity, are exhorted to rectitude of conduct, straightforwardness and harmony with all the kindreds and peoples of the world. We must obey and be the well-wishers of the governments of the land, regard disloyalty unto a just king as disloyalty to God Himself and wishing evil to the government a transgression of the Cause of God.

O God, my God! Thou seest this wronged servant of Thine, held fast in the talons of ferocious lions, of ravening wolves, of bloodthirsty beasts. Graciously assist me, through my love for Thee, that I may drink deep of the chalice that brimmeth over with faithfulness to Thee and is filled with Thy bountiful Grace; so that, fallen upon the dust, I may sink prostrate and senseless whilst my vesture is dyed crimson with my blood. This is my wish, my heart's desire, my hope, my pride, my glory. Grant, O Lord my God, and my Refuge, that in my last hour, my end, may even as musk shed its fragrance of glory! Is there a bounty greater than this? Nay, by Thy Glory! I call Thee to witness that no day passeth but that I quaff my fill from this cup, so grievous are the misdeeds wrought by them that have broken the Covenant, kindled discord, showed their malice, stirred sedition in the land and dishonoured Thee amidst Thy servants. Lord! Shield Thou from these Covenant-breakers the mighty Stronghold of Thy Faith and protect Thy secret Sanctuary from the onslaught of the ungodly. Thou art in truth the Mighty, the Powerful, the Gracious, the Strong.

O God, my God! Shield Thy trusted servants from the evils of self and passion, protect them with the watchful eye of Thy loving kindness from all rancour, hate and envy, shelter them in the impregnable stronghold of Thy Cause and, safe from the darts of doubtfulness, make them the manifestations of Thy glorious Signs. Illumine their faces with the effulgent rays shed from the Day-spring of Thy Divine Unity, gladden their hearts with the verses revealed from Thy Holy Kingdom, strengthen their loins by Thy all-swaying power that cometh from Thy Realm of Glory. Thou art the All-Bountiful, the Protector, the Almighty, the Gracious!

O ye that stand fast in the Covenant! When the hour cometh that this wronged and broken-winged bird will have taken its flight unto the celestial concourse, when it will have hastened to the Realm of the Unseen and its mortal frame will have been either lost or hidden neath the dust, it is incumbent upon the Afnán, that are steadfast in the Covenant of God, and have branched from the Tree of Holiness; the Hands (pillars) of the Cause of God (the glory of the Lord rest upon them), and all the friends and loved ones, one and all to bestir themselves and arise with heart and soul and in one accord,

to diffuse the sweet savours of God, to teach His Cause and to promote His Faith. It behoveth them not to rest for a moment, neither
to seek repose. They must disperse themselves in every land, pass
by every clime and travel throughout all regions. Bestirred, without rest and steadfast to the end they must raise in every land the
triumphal cry "O Thou the Glory of Glories!" (Yá-Bahá'u'l-
Abhá), must achieve renown in the world wherever they go, must
burn brightly even as a candle in every meeting and must kindle the
flame of Divine Love in every assembly; that the light of truth may
rise resplendent in the midmost heart of the world, that throughout
the East and throughout the West a vast concourse may gather
under the shadow of the Word of God, that the sweet savours of
holiness may be diffused, that faces may shine radiantly, hearts be
filled with the Divine spirit and souls be made heavenly.

In these days, the most important of all things is the guidance of
the nations and peoples of the world. Teaching the Cause is of utmost importance for it is the head cornerstone of the foundation
itself. This wronged servant has spent his days and nights in pro-
moting the Cause and urging the peoples to service. He rested not a
moment, till the fame of the Cause of God was noised abroad in the
world and the celestial strains from the Abhá Kingdom roused the
East and the West. The beloved of God must also follow the same
example. This is the secret of faithfulness, this is the requirement of
servitude to the Threshold of Bahá.

The disciples of Christ forgot themselves and all earthly things,
forsook all their cares and belongings, purged themselves of self
and passion and with absolute detachment scattered far and wide
and engaged in calling the peoples of the world to the Divine
Guidance, till at last they made the world another world, illumined
the surface of the earth and even to their last hour proved self-
sacrificing in the pathway of that Beloved One of God. Finally in
various lands they suffered glorious martyrdom. Let them that are
men of action follow in their footsteps!

O my loving friends! After the passing away of this wronged one
it is incumbent upon the Aghsán (Branches), the Afnán (Twigs) of
the Sacred Lote-Tree, the Hands (pillars) of the Cause of God and
the loved ones of the Abhá Beauty to turn unto Shoghi Effendi—
the youthful branch branched from the two hallowed and sacred
Lote-Trees and the fruit grown from the union of the two offshoots

of the Tree of Holiness—as he is the sign of God, the chosen branch, the guardian of the Cause of God, he unto whom all the Aghsán, the Afnán, the Hands of the Cause of God and His loved ones must turn. He is the interpreter of the Word of God and after him will succeed the first-born of his lineal descendants.

The sacred and Youthful Branch, the Guardian of the Cause of God, as well as the Universal House of Justice to be universally elected and established, are both under the care and protection of the Abhá Beauty, under the shelter and unerring guidance of the Exalted One (may my life be offered up for them both). Whatsoever they decide is of God. Whoso obeyeth him not, neither obeyeth them, hath not obeyed God; whoso rebelleth against him and against them hath rebelled against God; whoso opposeth him hath opposed God; whoso contendeth with them hath contended with God; whoso disputeth with him hath disputed with God; whoso denieth him hath denied God; Whoso disbelieveth in him hath disbelieved in God; whoso deviateth, separateth himself and turneth aside from him hath in truth deviated, separated himself and turned aside from God. May the wrath, the fierce indignation, the vengeance of God rest upon him! The mighty stronghold shall remain impregnable and safe through obedience to him who is the Guardian of the Cause of God. It is incumbent upon the members of the House of Justice, upon all the Aghsán, the Afnán, the Hands of the Cause of God to show their obedience, submissiveness and subordination unto the guardian of the Cause of God, to turn unto him and be lowly before him. He that opposeth him hath opposed the True One, will make a breach in the Cause of God, will subvert His word and will become a manifestation of the Centre of Sedition. Beware, beware, lest the days after the ascension (of Bahá'u'lláh) be repeated when the Centre of Sedition waxed haughty and rebellious and with Divine Unity for his excuse deprived himself and perturbed and poisoned others. No doubt every vainglorious one that purposeth dissension and discord will not openly declare his evil purposes, nay rather, even as impure gold, would he seize upon divers measures and various pretexts that he may separate the gathering of the people of Bahá. My object is to show that the Hands of the Cause of God must be ever watchful and so soon as they find anyone beginning to oppose and protest against the guardian of the Cause of God cast him out from the congregation of the people of Bahá and in no wise accept any excuse from him. How often hath grievous error been disguised in the garb of truth, that it might sow the seeds of doubt in the hearts of men!

O ye beloved of the Lord! It is incumbent upon the guardian of the Cause of God to appoint in his own life-time him that shall become his successor, that differences may not arise after his passing. He that is appointed must manifest in himself detachment from all worldly things, must be the essence of purity, must show in himself the fear of God, knowledge, wisdom and learning. Thus, should the first-born of the guardian of the Cause of God not manifest in himself the truth of the words: "The child is the secret essence of its sire," that is, should he not inherit of the spiritual within him (the guardian of the Cause of God) and his glorious lineage not be matched with a goodly character, then must he (the guardian of the Cause of God), choose another branch to succeed him.

The Hands of the Cause of God must elect from their own number, nine persons that shall at all times be occupied in the important services in the work of the guardian of the Cause of God. The election of these nine must be carried either unanimously or by majority from the company of the Hands of the Cause of God and these whether unanimously or by a majority vote, must give their assent to the choice of the one whom the guardian of the Cause of God hath chosen as his successor. This assent must be given in such wise as the assenting and dissenting voices may not be distinguished (secret ballot).

O friends! The Hands of the Cause of God must be nominated and appointed by the guardian of the Cause of God. All must be under his shadow and obey his command. Should any within or without the company of the Hands of the Cause of God disobey, and seek division, the wrath of God and His vengeance will be upon him, for he will have caused a breach in the true Faith of God.

The obligations of the Hands of the Cause of God are to diffuse the Divine Fragrances, to edify the souls of men, to promote learning, to improve the character of all men and to be, at all times and under all conditions, sanctified and detached from earthly things. They must manifest the fear of God by their conduct, their manners, their deeds and their words.

This body of the Hands of the Cause of God is under the direction of the guardian of the Cause of God. He must continually urge them to strive and endeavour to the utmost of their ability to diffuse the sweet savours of God, and to guide all the peoples of the world, for it is the light of the Divine Guidance that causeth all the universe to be illumined. To disregard, though it be for a moment, this absolute command which is binding upon everyone, is in no wise permitted, that the existent world may become even as the Abhá Paradise, that the surface of the earth may become heavenly, that contention and conflict amidst peoples, kindreds, nations and governments may disappear, that all the dwellers on earth may become one people and one race, that the world may become even as one home. Should differences arise they shall be amicably and conclusively settled by the Supreme Tribunal, that shall include members from all the governments and peoples of the world.

O ye beloved of the Lord! In this sacred Dispensation, conflict and contention are in no wise permitted. Every aggressor deprives himself of God's grace. It is incumbent upon everyone to show the utmost love, rectitude of conduct, straightforwardness and sincere kindliness unto all the peoples and kindreds of the world, be they friend or strangers. So intense must be the spirit of love and lovingkindness, that the stranger may find himself a friend, the enemy a true brother, no difference whatsoever existing between them. For universality is of God and all limitations earthly. Thus man must strive that his reality may manifest virtues and perfections, the light whereof may shine upon everyone. The light of the sun shineth upon all the world and the merciful showers of Divine Providence fall upon all peoples. The vivifying breeze reviveth every living creature and all beings endued with life obtain their share and portion at His heavenly board. In like manner, the affections and loving kindness of the servants of the One True God must be bountifully and universally extended to all mankind. Regarding this, restrictions and limitations are in no wise permitted.

Wherefore, O my loving friends! Consort with all the peoples, kindreds and religions of the world with the utmost truthfulness, uprightness, faithfulness, kindliness, goodwill and friendliness; that all the world of being may be filled with the holy ecstasy of the grace of Bahá, that ignorance, enmity, hate and rancour may vanish from the world and the darkness of estrangement amidst the peoples and kindreds of the world may give way to the Light of Unity. Should other peoples and nations be unfaithful to you show your fidelity unto them, should they be unjust toward you show justice towards them, should they keep aloof from you attract them to yourself, should they show their enmity be friendly towards them, should they poison your lives sweeten their souls, should they inflict a wound upon you be a salve to their sores. Such are the attributes of the sincere! Such are the attributes of the truthful.

And now, concerning the House of Justice which God hath ordained as the source of all good and freed from all error, it must be elected by universal suffrage, that is, by the believers. Its members must be manifestations of the fear of God and daysprings of knowledge and understanding, must be steadfast in God's faith and the well-wishers of all mankind. By this House is meant the Universal House of Justice, that is, in all countries, a secondary House of Justice must be instituted, and these secondary Houses of Justice must elect the members of the Universal one. Unto this body all things must be referred. It enacteth all ordinances and regulations that are not to be found in the explicit Holy Text. By this body all the difficult problems are to be resolved and the guardian of the Cause of God is its sacred head and the distinguished member for life of that body. Should he not attend in person its deliberations, he must appoint one to represent him. Should any of the members commit a sin, injurious to the common weal, the guardian of the Cause of God hath at his own discretion the right to expel him, whereupon the people must elect another one in his stead. This House of Justice enacteth the laws and the government enforceth them. The legislative body must reinforce the executive, the executive must aid and assist the legislative body so that through the close union and harmony of these two forces, the foundation of fairness and justice may become firm and strong, that all the regions of the world may become even as Paradise itself.

O ye beloved of the Lord! It is incumbent upon you to be submissive to all monarchs that are just and show your fidelity to every righteous king. Serve ye the sovereigns of the world with utmost truthfulness and loyalty. Show obedience unto them and be their well-wishers. Without their leave and permission do not meddle with political affairs, for disloyalty to the just sovereign is disloyalty to God himself.

This is my counsel and the commandment of God unto you. Well is it with them that act accordingly.

O dearly beloved friends! I am now in very great danger and the hope of even an hour's life is lost to me. I am thus constrained to write these lines for the protection of the Cause of God, the preservation of His Law, the safeguarding of His Word, and the safety of His Teachings. By the Ancient Beauty! This wronged one hath in no wise borne nor doth he bear a grudge against any one; towards none doth he entertain any ill-feeling and uttereth no word save for the good of the world. My supreme obligation, however, of necessity, prompteth me to guard and preserve the Cause of God. Thus, with the greatest regret, I counsel you saying: "Guard ye the Cause of God, protect His law and have the utmost fear of discord. This is the foundation of the belief of the people of Bahá (may my life be offered up for them). His Holiness, the Exalted One (the Báb), is the Manifestation of the Unity and Oneness of God and the Forerunner of the Ancient Beauty. His Holiness the Abhá Beauty, (may my life be a sacrifice for His steadfast friends) is the Supreme Manifestation of God and the Dayspring of His Most Divine Essence. All others are servants unto Him and do his bidding." Unto the most Holy Book every one must turn and all that is not expressly recorded therein must be referred to the Universal House of Justice. That which this body, whether unanimously or by a majority doth carry, that is verily the Truth and the Purpose of God Himself. Whoso doth deviate therefrom is verily of them that love discord, hath shown forth malice and turned away from the Lord of the Covenant. By this House is meant that Universal House of Justice which is to be elected from all countries, that is, from those parts in the East and West where the loved ones are to be found, after the manner of the customary elections in Western countries such as those of England.

It is incumbent upon these members (of the Universal House of Justice) to gather in a certain place and deliberate upon all problems which have caused difference, questions that are obscure and matters that are not expressly recorded in the Book. Whatsoever they decide has the same effect as the Text itself. And inasmuch as this House of Justice hath power to enact laws that are not expressly recorded in the Book and bear upon daily transactions, so also it hath power to repeal the same. Thus for example, the House of Justice enacteth today a certain law and enforceth it, and a hundred years hence, circumstances having profoundly changed and the conditions having altered, another House of Justice will then have power, according to the exigencies of the time, to alter that law. This it can do because that law formeth no part of the Divine Explicit Text. The House of Justice is both the Initiator and the Abrogator of its own laws.

And now, one of the greatest and most fundamental principles of the Cause of God is to shun and avoid entirely the Covenant-breakers, for they will utterly destroy the Cause of God, exterminate His Law and render of no account all efforts exerted in the past. O friends! It behoveth you to call to mind with tenderness the trials of His Holiness, the Exalted One and show your fidelity to the Ever-Blest Beauty. The utmost endeavour must be exerted lest all these woes, trials and afflictions, all this pure and sacred blood that hath been shed so profusely in the Path of God, may prove to be in vain.

O ye beloved of the Lord! Strive with all your heart to shield the Cause of God from the onslaught of the insincere, for souls such as these cause the straight to become crooked and all benevolent efforts to produce contrary results.

O God, my God! I call Thee, Thy Prophets and Thy Messengers, Thy Saints and Thy Holy Ones, to witness that I have declared conclusively Thy Proofs unto Thy loved ones and set forth clearly all things unto them, that they may watch over Thy Faith, guard Thy Straight Path and protect Thy Resplendent Law. Thou art, verily, the All-Knowing, the All-Wise!

Whosoever and whatsoever meeting becometh a hindrance to the diffusion of the Light of Faith, let the loved ones give them counsel and say: "Of all the gifts of God the greatest is the gift of Teaching. It draweth unto us the Grace of God and is our first obligation. Of such a gift how can we deprive ourselves? Nay, our lives, our goods, our comforts, our rest, we offer them all as a sacrifice for the Abhá Beauty and teach the Cause of God." Caution and prudence, however, must be observed even as recorded in the Book. The veil must in no wise be suddenly rent asunder. The Glory of Glories rest upon you.

O ye the faithful, loved ones of 'Abdu'l-Bahá! It is incumbent upon you to take the greatest care of Shoghi Effendi, the twig that hath branched from and the fruit given forth by the two hallowed and Divine Lote-Trees, that no dust of despondency and sorrow may stain his radiant nature, that day by day he may wax greater in happiness, in joy and spirituality, and may grow to become even as a fruitful tree.

For he is, after 'Abdu'l-Bahá, the guardian of the Cause of God; the Afnán, the Hands (pillars) of the Cause and the beloved of the Lord must obey him and turn unto him. He that obeyeth him not, hath not obeyed God; he that turneth away from him, hath turned away from God, and he that denieth him, hath denied the True One. Beware lest anyone falsely interpret these words, and like unto them that have broken the Covenant after the Day of Ascension (of Bahá'u'lláh) advance a pretext, raise the standard of revolt, wax stubborn and open wide the door of false interpretation. To none is given the right to put forth his own opinion or express his particular convictions. All must seek guidance and turn unto the Centre of the Cause and the House of Justice. And he that turneth unto whatsoever else is indeed in grievous error.

The Glory of Glories rest upon you!

LIST OF REFERENCES

KEY

Abbreviation	Title of book
A.S.M.	America's Spiritual Mission (1936)
B.P.P.	Bahá'í Peace Programme (1930)
B.W.F.	Bahá'í World Faith (1943)
D.B.	Dispensation of Bahá'u'lláh (British Edition 1947)
E.T.C.	Teaching Manual used at the 1948 European Teaching Conference
G.	Gleanings from the Writings of Bahá'u'lláh
H.W.A.	Hidden Words (Arabic)
H.W.P.	Hidden Words (Persian)
P.M.	Prayers and Meditations
P.D.C.	Promised Day is Come (1941)
P.T.	Paris Talks (British Edition 1951)
P.U.P.	Promulgation of Universal Peace (1922)
S.A.Q.	Some Answered Questions (1930)
S.W.	Star of the West (various volumes specified)
T.A.B.	Tablets of 'Abdu'l-Bahá (1909)
T.B.	Tablets of Bahá'u'lláh (1917)

The dates are those of the first impressions of the editions consulted. Where no date is given, references are to section numbers, which remain invariant; otherwise references are to page numbers. American editions were used if no British edition existed.

BAHÁ'U'LLÁH

1. Proclamation to the Kings and Leaders of Religion

1. G.CV
2. P.D.C.20, G.CXVI, G.CXVIII
3. P.D.C.34, G.CXX, G.CXIX, P.D.C. 35
4. Epistle to the Son of the Wolf, 46
5. P.D.C. 32
6. P.D.C. 36
7. P.D.C. 37
8. G.CXIV
9. P.D.C. 40
10. P.D.C. 30
11. G.XCVIII
12. P.D.C. 81
13. P.D.C. 115

II. *Selection from "Gleanings from the Writings of Bahá'u'lláh"*

III. *Selection from the Hidden Words*

IV. *The Seven Valleys*

V. *Some Important Tablets*

VI. *The Covenant*

vii. *Meditations*

'ABDU'L-BAHÁ

viii. *The Covenant*

ix. *The Master's Last Tablet to America*

x. *From the Tablets of the Divine Plan*

xi. *Tablet to the Hague*

xii. *Tablet to Dr Forel*

xiii. *God and His Manifestations*

xiv. *Concerning Christianity*

INDEX